Grammar

Grammar

A student's guide

JAMES R. HURFORD

Professor of General Linguistics, University of Edinburgh

CAMBRIDGE
UNIVERSITY PRESS

PUBLISHED BY THE PRESS SYNDICATE OF THE UNIVERSITY OF CAMBRIDGE
The Pitt Building, Trumpington Street, Cambridge, United Kingdom

CAMBRIDGE UNIVERSITY PRESS
The Edinburgh Building, Cambridge CB2 2RU, UK
40 West 20th Street, New York, NY 10011–4211, USA
477 Williamstown Road, Port Melbourne, VIC 3207, Australia
Ruiz de Alarcón 13, 28014 Madrid, Spain
Dock House, The Waterfront, Cape Town 8001, South Africa

http://www.cambridge.org

First published 1994
Tenth printing 2004

Printed in the United Kingdom at the University Press, Cambridge

A catalogue record for this book is available from the British Library

Library of Congress Cataloguing in Publication data
Hurford, James R.
  Grammar: a student's guide / James R. Hurford.
    p.   cm.
  Includes index.
  ISBN 0 521 45409 3. (hardback). ISBN 0 521 45627 4 (paperback)
  1. English language – Grammar – Handbooks, manuals, etc. I. Title
PE1112.H857   1994
428.2–dc20   93–48228 CIP

ISBN 0 521 45409 3 hardback
ISBN 0 521 45627 4 paperback

TS

For Sue N. Davis,
superlative, perfect, proper,
active, positive, agreeable relative.

Contents

CONTENTS

Introduction

Who and what this book is for

This book is for people who want to know, or need to revise, the meanings of words like *adverb, clause, conjunction, passive, subject*, and so on. Imagine trying to begin learning chemistry without knowing the meanings of words such as *liquid, solid, gas, air, water* and *heat*. Or trying to begin to learn biology without knowing what *bird, fish, backbone, plant, animal, reproduce, parent* and *offspring* mean. If you did not have this basic vocabulary, you'd have to do a bit of elementary homework before starting on these subjects. The study of language also has its own basic terminology, which any student needs to know from the outset. This terminology is useful whether you are just studying one or two languages, say French and German (or even English!), or whether you are interested in human languages in a more general, far-reaching way, in which case you may be drawn into linguistics. This book provides explanations of the basic vocabulary it is useful to know before starting to study any language, or before starting to study the theory of them all, that is, linguistics.

This book is intended to be useful to:

- College (and perhaps high school) students of languages who find clear statements about grammar helpful to their language-learning efforts.
- Students of English making systematic studies of texts and language in use.
- English and foreign-language teachers.
- Beginning students of linguistics.

Dictionary or textbook?

This book is organized alpabetically like a dictionary, for quick access to any term, with no assumption that the reader will have read any other entries first. On the other hand, there are fewer entries than in a typical dictionary, and the entries are fuller and more instructive, and can be read like passages in a textbook. This stems from a conviction that the study of grammar is open-ended, and that learning and discussing the meanings and interrelationships of basic terms is an integral part of exploring language. This is why the book gives **explanations** and **examples**, rather than brief cut-and-dried, or open-and-shut, definitions.

Traditional grammar and modern linguistics

The meanings of the terms explained in this book are not dogmatically set in concrete, or immune from revision. It is made clear in a few entries that some of the traditional terms are in fact based on misconceptions, and could well, indeed should, have their assumed definitions revised, or should even be abandoned altogether. But overall, the way in which all these grammatical terms interlock is impressively cohesive. The traditional terminology reflects the consensus of centuries of intelligent thinking and talking about the structure of language. It would be surprising if it were just a house of cards that collapsed when the brisk wind of modern analysis swept over it. None the less, human thinking is fallible, and traditions of thought are apt to get stuck in ruts. Although modern linguistics has made use of these solid traditional foundations, it has also proposed new technical terms (mostly not discussed in this book), and revised some of the old definitions. In principle, all the terminology is revisable, but not, obviously, all at once! Over the last thirty years, modern linguistics has made inroads into the consciousness of English teachers and language teachers, so that some relatively modern terms and concepts are common currency alongside very ancient ones. In this book, a sensible and useful blend of ancient and modern systems of terms and concepts is attempted.

Linguistics, including syntax, the part of linguistics that uses these terms, is not about merely labelling bits of language, but about asking questions such as 'WHY do languages have such bits as these? WHAT are they used FOR? DO ALL languages have them? If not, HOW do they manage without them? DO SOME languages organize their grammars in ways different from English?' The answers obviously have something to do with semantics (meaning), communication, human psychology and (to a lesser extent) the history of the human cultures that languages are embedded in.

Form and function

Languages have shape (form) and they are used for many purposes (functions). Neither form nor function alone constitutes the essence of a language. A literally formless system (if that is not a contradiction in terms!) can have no possible function; and a system with complicated form but no function is literally useless, and unlikely to have arisen. Grammar is the field of a constant tug-of-war between form and function, between organization and usefulness, like any working or living space. This book attempts to do justice to both the formal and the functional aspects of grammar.

A useful exercise in connection with all the terms explained in this book is to ask the question 'What if English did not use such things?' For instance, it is relatively easy to imagine doing without adverbs, as in fact many languages do. Instead of saying *He ran quickly*, you could say *The way he ran was quick*, managing without the adverb, and using an adjective instead. But can you imagine a language whose speakers managed to do without nouns and verbs? How about doing without prepositions (perhaps not easy to imagine, unless the language has some equivalent to substitute – some languages have POST positions instead of prepositions)? Or doing without the passive voice (manageable, I reckon)? Or doing without the distinction between subject and object? Could there be a language which never used prefixes and suffixes? (Yes, in fact Chinese and many other languages are like this – they just don't have words made up out of bits, like English.)

Other languages, other dialects

The traditional terminology is also biased toward European languages. There are many other languages across the world, in which patterns and rules exist for which there are no traditional grammatical labels. This book does not go into this new territory, but it does occasionally try to whet the reader's appetite for discovering new and strange facts about languages.

Other languages have rules which are different from the rules of English, obviously. It is their different rules and their different vocabulary that actually make them different languages. And there isn't just one English language, with one set of rules, and a universal vocabulary. There are many varieties of English – in short, different dialects. For the most part, the examples in this guide are from standard English, a 'dialect' which is something of a convenient fiction, but which includes all the grammatical constructions that most educated speakers use, most of the time. Occasionally, for comparison, an example from a non-standard dialect of English is used. It is important to realize that this is not done to encourage the use of the standard language, or to discourage the non-standard forms, but simply to show the possibility of different dialects, like different languages, having different rules. In discussing the double negative, for instance, or an unusual use of *without*, a passage such as the following, alleged to be representative of the dialect of Pike County, Missouri, might be cited.

> *You don't know about me, without you have read a book by the name of* The Adventures of Tom Sawyer, *but that ain't no matter.*

A few of the examples used have a distinctly American or distinctly British flavour. Rather than aiming for a bland mid-Atlantic lowest common denominator of examples, I have included such examples for their vitality, and to quietly celebrate the sheer value of diversity, in language as in other aspects of life.

Style

The first version of this book was called *The User-Friendly Dictionary of Grammar* (acronym *TUFDOG*). One person's friendliness is another's over-familiarity. I have tried to keep the style both attractive to the young and inoffensive to the old, probably an impossible goal.

Organization of the guide

Main entries

There are one hundred main entries, all organized along the same lines, beginning with a brief **Explanation** and some **Examples**. At the end of most entries, there is a simple **Exercise** section. The purpose of these exercises is quite limited. Use them just to check that you understand the basic use of the terms concerned. If you are only doing a quick look-up of some term, to get its rough sense, it should be enough just to read the brief **Explanation** and the **Examples**, and perhaps to check your understanding by doing the **Exercise**. **Answers** to the **Exercises** are at the back of the book.

Grammatical terms are interrelated, and so an explanation of one term often uses other terms. This is a problem with any dictionary; words are defined in terms of other words. If one starts with no prior understanding at all, it is impossible to break into the system. But starting with just ordinary non-technical knowledge of language, it is possible to penetrate the system. The examples help. And the more you read, the quicker you'll understand what you read, and begin to feel fully at ease with grammatical terms.

For fuller understanding, each entry also contains a section called **Contrasts** and almost all entries continue with a section called **Relationships**; these show how the term being explained fits into the whole conceptual framework of terms in grammar. For the more inquisitive, many entries contain a section called **For interest**. If you find these sections interesting and want to know more, you will probably be interested in linguistics and in trying to understand the general principles of how human languages work.

Bold type, *italics* and *asterisks

In each entry, terms which are also explained in this guide, and which would be worth looking up, to see how terms interrelate, are given **in bold typeface, like this** (except in the **For interest** and **Exercise** sections). A point to note here is that several words in succession may appear in bold print. This could mean that each of these words has its own separate entry, as with **noun phrase**, for example, where there is an entry for **noun** and another entry for **phrase** (but no separate entry for **noun phrase**) – you can find out about noun phrases by reading under both **noun** and **phrase**. In other cases, a sequence of words in boldface indicates that there is an entry for the whole expression, as with **indirect object** or **subordinate clause**, for example.

Sentences, phrases and words used as examples, mainly drawn from English, but sometimes from other languages, are given in italics, as in *This is an example of an example sentence.*

Sometimes, examples are given of what is not grammatical, to illustrate restrictions that can be stated using the terms defined. Such hypothetical examples are always prefixed by an asterisk, as in *This be example of bad example.*

Index and crossreferences

If you don't find a term explained in a main entry, look it up in the Index at the back. This lists a large number of topics related to grammar, referring the reader to the main entries where those topics are mentioned. The Index can also be used to locate important crossreferences between concepts for which there are main entries. Terms for which there are main entries are in capital letters in the Index.

Spot the quote competition

In order to give examples from real use, and to add interest to the guide, a number of the examples used are the opening words of well-known literary works. Most of these, but not all, are novels, including some translations into English, but there are also quotations from the openings of poems, short stories and at least one work of history. Overall, there are ninety-four such quotations in the book, all from the very beginning words of well-known works. The author will give a modest prize to the first person in each calendar year to write to him with a list of at least ninety of these quotations. (Send your list to him at: Linguistics Department, University of Edinburgh.)

I wish you good use of this book.

Acknowledgements

Helpful comments on earlier drafts of this book have been made by many people, including academic linguists, students and school English teachers. My thanks to Larry Trask, above all, and also to Judith Ayling, Lizzie Barnes, Friedrich Braun, Deborah Cameron, Ronnie Cann, Philip Carpenter, Grev Corbett, David Crystal, Ben Hambidge, Martin Haspelmath, Rosie and Sue Hurford, Catriona McPherson, Edith Moravcsik, Jonathan Price, Suzanne Romaine, Scott Russell, Mick Short, John Stewart, Rudolph Troike, Ivan Uemlianin, several anonymous referees, and students at a Hauptseminar on grammatical terminology at the Technical University of Berlin. Participation in a European Science Foundation research project on the typology of European languages has also added a dimension, for which I am grateful.

Abbreviations

ABS	absolutive
ACC	accusative
DAT	dative
DEF	definitive
ERG	ergative
EXCL	exclusive
FEM	feminine
FUT	future
GEN	genitive
HABIT	habitual
INCL	inclusive
MASC	masculine
NOM	nominative
OBJ	object
PART	partitive
PASS	passive
PERF	perfect
PLUR	plural
PRES	present
QUES	question
RECIP	reciprocal
REFL	reflexive
SING	singular
SUBJ	subject
VOC	vocative

The guide

Abstract noun

Explanation Abstract nouns are **nouns** that typically refer to abstractions, such as activities, emotions, virtues, vices, forces, ideologies, religions, attitudes, times, distances and professions. Generally, the things referred to by abstract nouns are ones that we can sensibly talk about, so they do exist in some sense, but we cannot experience them directly with our senses.

Examples *Courage, envy, intelligence, bigotry, war, tennis, love, fear, gravity, communism, emotion, force, optimism, inertia, philanthropy, month, mile* and *accountancy* are all abstract nouns.

Contrasts The **common nouns** which are not abstract are called 'concrete'.
Abstract nouns are a type of **common noun**, and thus also contrast with **proper name**.

Relationships Abstract nouns, like other **common nouns**, divide into two subtypes, **count nouns** and **mass nouns**. The abstract **count nouns**, which are in a minority, have **plural** forms, and can be freely used with an **article**. Examples are *idea, problem, religion, difficulty, worry* and *personality*. So we can say *the ideas, a problem, great religions* and *two difficulties*.

Although they are mentioned by traditional grammarians and in schools, recognizing abstract nouns is relatively unimportant, as far as **grammar** is concerned. This is because there are few, if any, particular grammatical processes that affect just the set of abstract nouns. The difference between **mass nouns** and **count nouns**, for instance, is more important grammatically, because this difference goes with differences in the positions in which these two types of **noun** can occur. One suspects that the reason for the recurrent mention of abstract nouns is the clash between their (abstract) meanings and the traditional definition of a **noun** as the 'name of a person, place, or thing'. The existence of obvious **nouns** such *liberty, action, sin* and *time* is a sore embarrassment to such a definition, and the pragmatic response has been to apply a distinctive label to the problematic **words**.

Abstract nouns, like other **common nouns**, can be modified by **adjectives, possessives, demonstratives, prepositional phrases** and **relative clauses**, as the following parallel examples show.

ABSTRACT	CONCRETE
admirable courage	*hot water*
Dave's grumpiness	*Bill's car*
that religion	*these apples*
democracy in the twentieth century	*wine in bottles*
optimism which is typical of youth	*mud which sticks to your boots*

Many abstract nouns are formed from other **words** by adding **suffixes**. For example *sadness* is formed from *sad*, *tendency* from *tend*, *government* from *govern*, and so on. The addition of the **suffix** often makes the meaning of the **word** a degree or so more abstract.

For interest There is some disagreement about exactly which nouns should count as abstract, especially given the usual definition (as above) in terms of perceptibility by the five senses. One kind of problematic example is illustrated by the noun *whiteness*. We would presumably agree that we can see things which are white, so in a clear sense the adjective *white* is not abstract. The noun *whiteness* seems to be an abstraction from this adjective *white*, and so in some sense the noun *whiteness* is more abstract than *white*. But we tend to want to say, nevertheless, that we can actually see whiteness, which should lead us to decide that *whiteness* is not an abstract noun after all.

In fact, when we come to think carefully about just what is perceptible to the senses and what requires some element of extra judgement on our part, it becomes clear that many things that at first appear entirely concrete involve some degree of abstraction, however slight. Despite this kind of problem, the traditional term 'abstract noun' retains some usefulness as a first-approximation, common-sense descriptive term.

Exercise Identify the abstract nouns in the following sentences. You may be uncertain about some of them, in which case count them as 'possibles', or borderline cases between abstract and concrete. Including such doubtful cases, there are eight abstract nouns below in total.

1 *Murder didn't mean much to Raven.*
2 *Under certain circumstances there are few hours in life more agreeable than the hour dedicated to the ceremony known as afternoon tea.*

Accusative case

Explanation A **noun** which can be identified as the **direct object** of a **verb** by its shape (e.g. by a **suffix**) is said to be in the accusative case. In familiar European languages with **case**-marking systems (e.g. Latin, German, Russian), there are specific accusative forms for **direct objects**. For English, this term is not actually of much use, except for the **personal pronouns**, many of which have a special accusative form.

Examples *Me* is the accusative case form of *I*, because *I* doesn't occur right after a **verb**; *me* is used instead. **Mary hit I* is ungrammatical in standard English (though it is fine in some dialects); *Mary hit me*, with the accusative **pronoun**, is the standard way of saying this. The only other distinctly **accusative** forms in English are the **pronouns** *him, her, us, them* and (in some **dialects**) *whom*. In earlier English, *thee* existed as the accusative coresponding to *thou*.

Contrasts   In English, accusative only usefully contrasts with **nominative**. If a form in a given sentence is in the accusative, it can't be in the **nominative**, or any other **case**. In languages with more extensive **case** systems, **accusative** contrasts with other **case** terms not relevant to English, such as **dative** and **genitive**.

The English **word** *her* is ambiguous; it is an accusative pronoun in *We all admired her*, but it is a **possessive** in *Her fiancé is Welsh*.

Relationships   Accusative and **nominative** are **cases**. Accusative case is the **case** of the **direct object** of a **verb**. In English, exactly the same forms are also used for the **indirect objects** of **verbs**, as in *Mary wrote me a letter* and *Henk sent me a note*. In other languages, such **indirect objects** might be distinguished from **direct objects** by a different **case**. But to the extent that English uses **case** at all, it uses the same **case** for both. This **case**, usually called 'accusative' (though 'objective' might be a better term) is also, in English, the case of the **object** of a **preposition**, as shown by **phrases** such as *to me, by us, with them, for him* and *at her*.

In languages with extended **agreement** systems in addition to **case** systems, accusative (and other **cases**) can appear on such **word**-classes as **adjectives**, **articles** and **demonstratives**, by **agreement** with a **noun** in **direct object** position.

In most colloquial speaking styles of English, the accusative **pronouns** are used after the **verb** *be*, as in *It's us, That's him*, and *If you were me*, . . . Such forms are sometimes felt to be non-standard and are replaced by rather stilted-sounding forms like *It is I, This is she*, and *Those are they*.

Accusative forms are also sometimes felt to be non-standard after certain **prepositions**, in particular the *than* of the **comparative**. Thus the normal colloquial *She is taller than me* might be replaced by the over-correct sounding *She is taller than I*. The reason might be offered that this is in fact a shortening of *She is taller than I am*. But note that a similar logic should dictate the definitely stilted (at best) *★He arrived after I* as a shortening of *He arrived after I did*. Marilyn Monroe used a comic example of such overcorrection in the movie *Some Like it Hot*, when she said *A girl like I*.

Many non-standard English **dialects** prefer the accusative forms before or after a **conjunction**, even in **subject** position, as in *Me and him was going down there*. This area is fraught with confusion. Knowing that *John and me went* is non-standard and that *John and I went* is standard, some people extend the replacement to **object** position, and say things like the over-correct *They invited John and I* rather than the standard *They invited John and me*.

For interest   In languages with extensive case systems, such as German, there can be quite complicated rules for the use of such cases as accusative and dative, and often there doesn't seem to be any great naturalness to these rules – they are grammatical facts which just have to be learnt.

German distinguishes between accusative and dative (and other) cases. Here are the various forms of the definite article:

	MASCULINE	FEMININE	NEUTER
ACCUSATIVE	*den*	*die*	*das*
DATIVE	*dem*	*der*	*dem*

Some German prepositions, such as *durch – through*, always take an accusative noun phrase after them. So, illustrating with a neuter example, we have:

durch   das   Haus
*through the+*ACC *house*   (= *through the house*)

Other German prepositions, such as *nach – toward* or *after*, always take a dative noun phrase after them. So we have:

nach   dem   Haus
*toward the+*DAT *house*   (= *toward the house*)

Still other German prepositions, such as *in – in/into* and *auf – on/onto*, sometimes take an accusative, and sometimes a dative, depending on whether they are used to express motion or position. For expressing motion toward something (as with English *into* and *onto*), German uses the accusative with these prepositions. And for expressing location (as often with English *in* and *on*), German uses the dative with these same prepositions. So we have:

Er ging in das   Haus
*He went into the+*ACC *house*   (= *He went into the house.*)

Er stand in dem   Haus
*He stood in the+*DAT *house*   (= *He is in the house.*)

The same verb can be followed by either accusative or dative case, depending on whether motion toward the thing referred to is involved. Thus *Er tanzte in das Haus*, with an accusative, means *He danced into the house*, while *Er tanzte in dem Haus* means *He danced in the house.*

Exercise   Identify the specifically accusative pronouns in the following. There are eight altogether.

1 *When her mother told me she was leaving, I sent them a card.*
2 *Send not to know for whom the bell tolls; it tolls for thee.*
3 *You should be paying us, not him.*
4 *'It's me', he called out to her.*

Active voice

Explanation   In a typical **clause** in the active voice, the doer of the action (or the person or thing mainly responsible for it) is expressed as the **subject** of the **clause**, and the thing most affected by this action is typically expressed as the **(direct) object**. In less typical cases, where there is no clear action, as with **verbs** like *remember* or *know*, you can tell an active clause by its basic shape (especially by the shape of its **verb**), which is like the basic shape in the more typical active **clauses**.

Examples All the following **sentences** consist of simple active **clauses**:

- *Mary kissed John.*
- *In 1906 an earthquake destroyed San Francisco.*
- *Many people remember that movie.*
- *The horse knows the way.*

Contrasts Active contrasts, in English, mainly with **passive**. For most active **clauses**, there is a corresponding **passive clause**, which has almost exactly the same meaning, but a different emphasis. **Passive clauses (sentences)** corresponding to the active **clauses (sentences)** given above are:

- *John was kissed by Mary.*
- *In 1906 San Francisco was destroyed by an earthquake.*
- *That movie is remembered by many people.*
- *The way is known by the horse.*

As you can see, some **passive sentences**, like the last one above, are at least a little awkward.

Relationships Active **clauses** generally have **transitive verbs**. It is not usual to call **clauses** with **intransitive verbs** active, although some grammarians occasionally do so.

Both **main clauses** and **subordinate clauses** can be active, as in *Mary told me that someone had pinched her* or *Mary persuaded someone to pinch her*.

Active (and **passive**) voice combine almost freely with **declarative, interrogative** and **imperative moods**. Five of the six possible combinations occur. For example:

	VOICE	MOOD
The burglar stole the silver.	active	**declarative**
Did the burglar steal the silver?	active	**interrogative**
Steal the silver!	active	**imperative**
The silver was stolen by the burglar.	**passive**	**declarative**
Was the silver stolen by the burglar?	**passive**	**interrogative**

Although the **imperative** *Steal the silver!* doesn't have a **subject**, it is still said to be active, because we understand *You* to be the **subject**, referring to the person who is to do the action, and there is still an **object** (here *the silver*), the main thing affected by the action, as in other active **sentences**.

Only a hypothetical **passive imperative** such as *★Be stolen by the burglar!* is distinctly odd. This is because, when you want to command something to be done, you naturally address the person who is to carry it out, and not the recipient of the action.

The regular correspondence between actives and **passives** can be stated in terms of **subjects** and **direct objects**. The **noun phrase** which is the **subject** of a **passive sentence** is the **direct object** of the corresponding active **sentence**. Thus, the **subject** of *The bride was kissed by Dracula*, namely *the bride*, turns up as the **direct object** of *Dracula kissed the bride*. Because **subject** and direct object are equated, for languages with **case** systems, with **nominative** and **accusative case**, respectively, the correspondence between actives and **passives** can also be stated in terms of **case**.

The active form of a **clause** is the normal form, and the **passive** form typically depicts its meaning from the slightly less usual perspective of the recipient of an action.

For interest　There is a kind of English clause which is half-way between actives and passives. Such clauses are said to be in the 'middle voice'. Examples are *These clothes wash well* and *Bramley apples cook well*. Their grammar is similar to that of active clauses, having no passive auxiliary *be*, but their subjects are nevertheless understood to refer to the recipient, rather than the doer, of the action concerned. Can you think of other examples, besides *wash* and *cook*, of English verbs which allow this 'middle voice'?

Exercise　Just five of the following eight sentences are active. Which ones are they?

1　*Madonna often wears a wig.*
2　*Steven Spielberg is middle-aged.*
3　*The government repaired the Statue of Liberty.*
4　*The war was lost by the politicians.*
5　*I love my computer.*
6　*Has anyone seen my white umbrella?*
7　*Dustin fell down the stairs.*
8　*Take your time!*

Adjective

Explanation　An adjective is a **word** typically used to **modify** a **noun**, and describes some property of the thing referred to by the **noun**, such as its shape, colour, age, value, size, origin or the impression it gives. Some rough tests for being an adjective in English are:

- You can put an adjective in place of the *X* in *the X thing* or *some X stuff*.
- You can put an adjective in place of the *X* in *The thing was X* or *The stuff was X*.
- You can **modify** many, but not all, adjectives with the word *very*.

Examples　*Circular, purple, old, nasty, big, French, grizzly* and *tasteless* are all adjectives.

Contrasts　Adjective is a **part of speech**, and so contrasts with other **parts of speech**, such as **noun**, **verb**, **preposition** and **adverb**. In a given **sentence**, if a particular **word** is an adjective, it is not any other **part of speech**, such as a **noun**, **verb**, **preposition** or **adverb**. Note that we have to talk of **words** being adjectives in specific contexts, because many **words** can be used as more than one **part of speech**. Thus, for example, *square* is an adjective in *The garden is square*, and *Pass me the square tray*, but not in *Put the circle inside the square* (where *square* is a **noun**).

Other **parts of speech**, such as **demonstratives** (e.g. *those*), **numerals** (e.g. *seven*) and even **possessives** (e.g. *my*) are sometimes called adjectives, but it is actually better to keep all these terms separate, as the kinds of words they refer to occur in rather different positions.

Relationships Most English adjectives can go before, and **modify**, **nouns**, as in *big houses*, *an expensive car* and *an original idea*. Adjectives which can go in this position are called **attributive** adjectives. Some English adjectives, such as *awake* and *ajar*, are not **attributive**, as you can't say, for instance, **the awake janitor* or **an ajar door*.

The other position in which English adjectives can occur is as **predicate** adjectives or in **predicate** adjective **phrases**. This is the position following **copular verbs**, of which the main example is the **verb** *be*. Adjectives that can go in this position are called 'predicative adjectives'. *Big*, *expensive*, *original*, *awake* and *ajar* are **predicative** adjectives. So we can have, for example, *Joan's car was expensive*, *The janitor was awake* and *The door was slightly ajar*. Some English adjectives, such as *mere* and *latter*, are **attributive**, but not **predicative**, as we can't have, for instance, **The typos were mere* or **The example was latter*.

Most English adjectives, however, are both **attributive** and **predicative**; that is, they can go in both the typical adjective positions.

There can be adjective **phrases**, built around adjectives, with the adjective as the **head** or central item. Examples of adjective **phrases**, with the adjective **head words** underlined, are: *very <u>polite</u>*, *too <u>expensive</u> for me*, *<u>taller</u> than John*, *not <u>expensive</u> enough*. In English, such **phrases** can generally occur either as **attributives** or **predicatives**, depending on the adjective.

Attributive adjective **phrases** in English often go after, rather than before, the **nouns** they modify. So we have *a big diamond*, with the adjective before the **noun**, but *a diamond as big as the Ritz*, with the adjective **phrase**, *as big as the Ritz*, after the **noun**.

Some **words** such as *very*, *quite*, *rather* and *somewhat*, which **modify** adjectives and **adverbs**, are sometimes called **adverbs**, but that is not a very good name for these, because all sorts of other **words** are also called **adverbs**, and the term begins to get vague and unspecific. (Actually, linguists use the terms 'intensifier' or 'degree **modifier**' for *very*, *quite*, *rather* and *somewhat*.) Some **words**, such as *awfully* and *fantastically*, which serve elsewhere as **adverbs** of manner, lose their literal meanings when **modifying** adjectives and serve only to intensify the adjective. For example, *This sauce is awfully tasty* does not mean the same thing as *This sauce is tasty in an awful way*.

Adjectives (but not all of them), along with some **adverbs**, are the only **parts of speech** which have **comparative** and **superlative** forms, such as *bigger*, *nastier*, *biggest*, *nastiest*. (These **comparatives** and **superlatives** are themselves still adjectives.)

Participles can often be used as adjectives. Thus *a man who is running* can be paraphrased as *a running man*, with the **present participle** *running* put before the **noun** to appear as an adjective. Likewise, *a picture-frame which has been lacquered* can be paraphrased as *a lacquered picture-frame* with the **past participle** *lacquered* used as an adjective.

For interest Most languages have adjectives, though some have very few. There are even some languages that have no adjectives at all. Acehnese, a language spoken by about a million and a half people in northern Sumatra, Indonesia, is one such language without adjectives.

How do languages without adjectives manage to express ideas like *The box is square* or *The big house*? Some such languages do it with verbs, so there would be a verb meaning *to be square*, giving sentences which to us would seem like **The box squares. The big house* would come out in these languages as something like **The being-big house* or **The bigging house*. Other languages convey adjectival meanings with nouns, so that there would be single nouns equivalent to *red thing* and *high thing*. In such a language, you would have to translate *The mountain is high* into something not so distinguishable from *The mountain is a high-thing* as it is in English. And the phrase *the high mountain* could be expressed in such a language as *the mountain, the high-thing*.

You can string lots of adjectives together, as in *The big white fluffy Persian cat*, but the order in which they occur is usually quite strict, so you wouldn't say, for instance, **The Persian fluffy white big cat*. Try to work out which kinds of adjectives typically go early in such a string, and which ones go late.

Exercise Pick out the adjectives in the following sentences. There are nineteen of them in total.

1 *Ten solemn elders sat round an oval table.*
2 *An ancient tractor was blocking the narrow road.*
3 *He fell into the great grey-green greasy Limpopo river.*
4 *The sky was overcast and dark.*
5 *Mr. Utterson the lawyer was a man of rugged countenance, that was never lighted by a smile; cold, scanty and embarrassed in discourse; backward in sentiment; lean, long, dusty, dreary, and yet somehow lovable.*

Adverb

Explanation Adverb is a **part of speech**. The most typical adverbs add specific information about time, manner or place to the meanings of **verbs** or whole **clauses**; thus there are adverbs of time, adverbs of manner and adverbs of place. (These three do not actually cover everything that has been called an adverb, however.) Many, but not all, adverbs of manner are formed by adding the **suffix** *-ly* to an **adjective**. In English adverbs can often be placed at the beginning, middle or end of a **clause**, with only a difference of emphasis, although sometimes there is also a subtle difference in meaning (see **For Interest** below). Adverbs are always optional elements of **clauses**; if you omit an adverb, you just get less information, but the **clause** still makes sense without it.

Examples *Today, tomorrow, yesterday, then, now, sometimes, frequently, rarely, soon, recently, occasionally* and *always* are adverbs of time, because they add information about the time at which (i.e. when) something happens.

Slowly, quickly, fast, reluctantly, unwillingly, frankly, early, badly and *well* are adverbs of manner, because they add information about the manner in which (i.e. how) something is done. There are many more adverbs of manner in English.

Here, there, somewhere, everywhere, downstairs, upstairs and *underground* are adverbs of place, because they add information about the place at which (i.e. where) something happens.

Contrasts Adverb contrasts with other **parts of speech**, such as **noun**, **verb**, **adjective** and **preposition**. If a **word** is an adverb in a given **sentence**, it isn't any other **part of speech**.

Adverb should also be regarded as contrasting with a class of **words** called 'intensifiers' or 'degree **modifiers**'. See **Relationships** below.

Relationships Adverbs mostly **modify clauses** and **verbs**.

A few adverbs can also **modify** other **parts of speech**. Thus, *absolutely, perfectly* and *relatively* can **modify adjectives**, as in *absolutely ideal, perfectly round* and *relatively new*. It is reasonable to call these **words** 'adverbs' because they can, without shifting their meaning, also **modify verbs** and **clauses**, as in *I condemn this absolutely, She writes perfectly* and *It expanded relatively*. Some similar **words**, however, should probably not be counted as adverbs when **modifying** an **adjective**, because they shift in meaning. Thus, for example, *awfully* is synonymous with *badly* in *She writes awfully*; but *awfully good* does not mean *badly good*! *Awfully* **modifying** an **adjective** is best counted as an 'intensifier' or 'degree **modifier**'.

Words such as *exactly, approximately* and *roughly* can modify **numerals**, as in *exactly seven, approximately three hundred* and *roughly thirty*; these **words** can also modify **verbs** and **clauses**, as in *We measured it exactly, We matched it approximately* and *We copied it roughly*, so it is reasonable to count these as adverbs as well.

The **words** that can modify adverbs themselves, **words** such as *very, quite, rather, too, enough*, can also modify **adjectives**. These **words** are themselves sometimes called adverbs, but this stretches the meaning of the term too far; linguists prefer to call **words** like *very, quite, rather, too* and *enough* 'intensifiers'.

Some **words** can be used, in different **sentences**, either as an adverb or as another **part of speech**. An example of a **word** which can be used both as an adverb and as an **adjective** is *fast*. In *He ran fast* it is an adverb; but in *This is a fast car* it is an **adjective**.

The same **word** can also act sometimes as an adverb, sometimes as a **noun**. For instance, in these two **sentences**,

- *It rained yesterday.*
- *Yesterday it rained.*

yesterday is used as an adverb (of time), specifying when it rained; here the variety of position (back of **sentence**, front of **sentence**), and the fact that you can drop the *yesterday* and still have a good **sentence** (*It rained*), shows that *yesterday* is being used as an adverb. But in

- *Yesterday was wet.*

we have to say that *yesterday* is being used as a **noun** (in fact the **subject** of the **sentence**), because you can't move it to the other end of the **sentence** (giving *★Was wet yesterday*) or leave it out (giving *★Was wet*).

Often the work done by an adverb can be done by a whole **phrase** (called an 'adverbial **phrase**' by linguists). Thus the **phrase** *the next day* makes the same sort of contribution to meaning, and has the same positional mobility (back of **sentence**, front of **sentence**), as the single-**word** adverb *tomorrow*.

Adverbial **phrases** are so called because they can occur in the same range of positions as single adverbs; but many such adverbial **phrases**, paradoxically, do not contain an adverb. Such adverb-less adverbial **phrases** are typically **prepositional phrases**, as underlined in the examples below:

- *On Friday night, I'm playing squash.*
- *Their marriage broke up in the most painful way.*
- *May I, on behalf of the shareholders, congratulate you?*

But there are also many adverb **phrases** containing an adverb as their central element or **head**. For example:

- *Quite coincidentally, he was playing squash.*
- *Their marriage broke up most painfully.*
- *May I, very sincerely, congratulate you?*

In addition to adverbial **phrases**, there are also whole adverbial **clauses** which can occur in the same range of positions as single adverbs. Such adverbial **clauses** (which are **subordinate clauses**) are introduced by such subordinating **conjunctions** as *when*, *while* and *where*. Examples are:

- *When he came back, he was feeling better.*
- *Hit him where it hurts!*
- *Did you remember, while I was out, to phone the school?*

For interest Quite a few languages don't have adverbs as a separate part of speech. German, for example, mainly uses its adjectives for adverbs, allowing them to modify verbs and sentences as well as nouns. Thus German uses one word (*schnell*) for both *quick* and *quickly*, and one word (*gut*) for both *good* and *well*. Some dialects of English also do this to some extent. In such dialects, *She did it real good* (which uses no adverbs) is a way of saying *She did it really well.*

The following two sentences mean different things, due to the adverb being in a different position.

- *It is better to talk frankly to her sister.*
- *Frankly, it is better to talk to her sister.*

Try to work out just what the difference in meanings is. Are both instances of *frankly* manner adverbs, describing the manner in which something was to happen?

Here's another interesting comparison. Try to state clearly the difference in meaning between the following two sentences. Do it by describing, in words of your own, the slightly different situations these two sentences would be true of.

- *We lit all the candles slowly.*
- *Slowly, we lit all the candles.*

Exercise   1 In the following sentences, there are five adverbs; identify them.

- *Slowly but surely, the recession is coming to an end.*
- *We had a lovely time at the beach yesterday.*
- *Unfortunately, we have here a case of criminal incompetence.*

2 For each of the following phrases, give a single-word adverb which paraphrases it.

- *at this particular moment in time*
- *in a suspicious manner*
- *at that particular place*

Affix

Explanation   An affix is a meaningful part of a **word** which can be broken off but can't stand on its own. That is, an affix is never a **word** in its own right, and always needs a stem (which can be a **word**) to attach to. Affixes are either **prefixes**, attaching to the front of **words**, or **suffixes**, attaching to the back of **words**.

Examples   *un-, pre-, dis-, anti-* are all affixes (**prefixes**).
-ed, -s, -ment, -al, -ness, -ful are all affixes (**suffixes**).

Contrasts   Affix contrasts mainly with **word**. If something is an affix, it cannot also be a **word**.

Relationships   Affixes do not belong to **parts of speech**, such as **noun, verb** and **preposition**. Only whole **words** belong to **parts of speech**.

Affixes often express quite particular sorts of meanings or grammatical relationships, typical of which are

- **tense**, e.g. English -*ed*;
- **number**, i.e. **singular** or **plural**, e.g. English -*s*;
- **gender**, e.g. Italian -*a*, marking feminine **nouns** and **adjectives**;
- **case**, e.g. German -*es*, marking (some) **genitive nouns**.

Some affixes change the **part of speech** of the **word** they are attached to. Thus

- -*ness* as in *shyness* makes an **adjective** into a **noun**.
- -*ful* as in *careful* makes a **noun** into an **adjective**.
- -*er* as in *preacher* makes a **verb** into a **noun**.

Affixes can get piled up on other affixes, as in *polarization*, which ends with three affixes, -*ar*, -*ize* and -*ation*, and *organizers* which ends in -*ize*, -*er* and -*s*.

Quite often, affixes undergo slightly modified spelling and/or pronunciation, influenced by the adjacent part of the **word** they attach to. Thus the **prefix** *ex*- sounds a bit different in the **words** *exotic* and *export*. It seems reasonable to treat *con*- and *com*-, as in *conduct*, *converse*, *compatible* and *compartment* as variants of the same **prefix**, influenced by the following consonant.

Generally, **suffixes** are more common than **prefixes**.

For interest   The only kinds of affix in English are prefixes and suffixes, but other languages have more exotic devices, such as 'circumfixes' (which attach around words), and 'infixes' (which attach inside words). An example of a circumfix is Colloquial Arabic *ma – š*, which fixes around a verb to make it negative. Thus *darab* means 'hit'; and *madarabš* means 'didn't hit'. (This is like French *ne . . . pas*, except that French *ne* and *pas* are not affixes.)

Some languages get even more complicated, with complex '-fixes' which combine prefixing, infixing and suffixing.

Some languages use affixes, especially on verbs, much more than English, so that in such languages a sentence can often be a single word, made up of a verb with a lot of affixes attached to it. Turkish is a language which works like this. For example, the single Turkish word *istemedim* translates the English four-word sequence *I did not want*. The Turkish word is in fact made up of a stem plus three suffixes, like this:

iste -me- -di- -m
want not PAST I   (= *I did not want*)

The various Eskimo languages also work like this.

Other languages don't use any affixes at all. Chinese is such a language (although some linguists claim that some affixes are creeping into modern Chinese).

Exercise   How many prefixes and how many suffixes are there in the word *antidisestablishmentarianism*?

Agreement

Explanation Agreement is the relationship between one **word** in a **sentence** or **phrase** and some other **word**, whereby the form of one **word** is dictated by the other **word**. The **word** whose form is determined by the other is said to agree with it. Agreement can operate over short or long distances in a sentence.

Examples

- *The arrows over this sentence show which words agree with which.*

- *So do the arrows over this sentence and the one below.*

- *I am merry, you are tired and emotional, but he is disgustingly drunk.*

Contrasts There is not much that could potentially be confused with agreement. Other instances, not involving agreement, where one part of a **sentence** has a relationship with another, more or less distant, part, are:

- the selection of **case** on a **pronoun** by a preceding **verb** or **preposition**, e.g. *loves me, to them*;
- the relation of a **pronoun** to another **noun phrase** potentially referring to the same person or thing, e.g. *John was tired when he arrived*, where *he* can refer to the same person as *John*. Here, linguists would call *John* the 'antecedent' of the **pronoun** *he*.

Neither of these is agreement.

Relationships In English, agreement is relatively limited. It occurs between the **subject** of a **clause** and a **present tense verb**, so that, for example, with a 3rd **person singular subject** (e.g. *John*), the **verb** must have the *-s* **suffix** ending. That is, the **verb** agrees with its **subject** by having the appropriate ending. Thus *John drinks a lot* is grammatical, but **John drink a lot* isn't grammatical as a **sentence** on its own, because the **verb** doesn't agree.

Agreement also occurs in English between **demonstratives** and **nouns**. A **demonstrative** has to agree in **number** with its **noun**. So with a **plural noun** such as *books*, you have to use a **plural** *these* or *those*, giving *these books* or *those books*. With a **singular noun**, such as *book*, you use a **singular** *this* or *that*, giving *this book* or *that book*. **This books* or **those book* would be ungrammatical, because the **demonstrative** doesn't agree with the **noun**.

In English, the **verb** *be* has a richer involvement with agreement than other **verbs**. *Am* is required with the 1st **person singular subject** *I*, so in standard English **I is here* is ungrammatical; you have to say *I am here*, making the **verb** agree with its **subject**. The **verb** *be* is also the only English **verb** where

15

singular/plural agreement applies in the **past tense**. So in standard English, *was* goes with **singular subjects**, and *were* goes with **plural subjects**.

The **part of speech** that other **words** agree with is usually a **noun** or a **pronoun**. In agreement, **nouns** and **pronouns** typically 'call the shots'.

Agreement can involve factors such as

- **number** (e.g. **singular/plural**);
- **gender** (e.g. masculine/feminine/neuter);
- **person** (e.g. 1st/2nd/3rd);
- **case** (e.g. **nominative/accusative/dative/** and so on).

Agreement does not necessarily involve all of these factors at once.

Agreement on **verbs** involves only **finite verbs**, by the normally assumed definition of **finite**, which includes 'showing agreement'.

The term 'concord' is also used, meaning the same thing as 'agreement'.

For interest   Many languages use agreement much more than English. In French, for example, adjectives and articles have to agree in number and gender with nouns. French definite articles are *le*, *la* and *les*; French words for *beautiful* are *beau*, *belle*, *beaux*, and *belles*. In French you have to choose the right article and adjective, to agree with the noun involved. So *la belle femme* is the French for *the beautiful woman*; **le beau femme*, **la beau femme*, **le belle femme* and **les beaux femme* would all be wrong, because in them the article and the adjective don't agree with the noun. This is something that English speakers needn't bother about, and which they find difficult and perplexing when starting to learn French.

Among European languages that use agreement much more than English are German, Italian, Spanish, Dutch, Russian, Polish and Swedish.

Many languages allow words to be moved around in sentences for stylistic purposes, and such movements may cross over the lines linking other pairs of words in the sentence which agree with each other. Here is an example from Russian. First, a basic, unemphatic sentence, with the agreement relationships shown by arrows.

ja videl   takogo   xorošego   čeloveka
I saw+MASC+SING *such*+ACC *good*+ACC *man*+ACC (= *I saw such a good man.*)

But for stylistic effect, especially in spoken Russian, one could say:

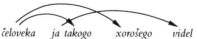

čeloveka   ja takogo   xorošego   videl
man+ACC *I such*+ACC *good*+ACC *saw*+MASC+SING (= *I saw such a good man.*)

Exercise   Draw arrows over the following sentences, as in the example above, to indicate which words agree with which. Some of these sentences have more than one case of agreement in them. You should find nine cases altogether (so draw nine arrows). Some of these arrows will arch over other arrows; but note that they never actually cut across each other.

- *Those kids at the shop were swearing at us.* (2 arrows)

- *The shop those kids were at is on Broadway.* (3 arrows)

- *Broadway is the street that the shop those kids were at is on.* (4 arrows)

(The last sentence is quite complicated and perhaps awkward, and it might help to say it aloud in a fluent colloquial way.)

Apposition

Explanation When two **noun phrases** occur immediately next to each other, both referring to the same thing, but giving different information about it, the second one is said to be in apposition to the first. In writing, there is often a comma between the two **phrases**; and in speech, there may be a slight pause.

Examples In each of these **sentences**, the underlined **word** or **phrase** is in apposition to the one just before it.

- *My son Benjamin is a doctor.*
- *My son the doctor lives in Belair.*
- *We soon came to Middlebury, the next town along the road.*
- *The next town along the road, a rather sleepy place, was Middlebury.*
- *This is Joanna, an old friend of mine.*

Contrasts Appositive constructions are not the same as **relative clauses**, though they often carry a similar meaning. Appositive constructions are also not the same as the adjacent pairs of **phrases** which can occur in lists, as in *Tom, his mother, Harry, and the vicar were all at the morning work-out.*

Relationships Only **noun phrases** occur in apposition. Often, one of the **nouns** involved is a **proper name**, as in some of the examples above. **Personal pronouns** can never be in apposition, though other **phrases** can be in apposition to them. Thus *We, the people, demand a voice* is fine, but *★The people, we, demand a voice* is not.

Appositive **phrases** can occur in any relation to a **verb**, i.e. as **subjects**, **direct objects**, **indirect objects**, and in the whole range of other positions where **noun phrases** can occur, as the examples given above begin to show.

17

Appositive constructions can often be paraphrased by **relative clauses**. So the following are paraphrases of the relevant parts of some of the examples given above:

- *Middlebury, which was the next town along the road*
- *the next town along the road, which was a rather sleepy place*
- *Joanna, who is an old friend of mine*

But this doesn't always work, as, for example, **My son, who is Benjamin* is odd. Presumably, this has something to do with the occurrence of **proper names**. But it isn't quite that simple, because *The next town along the road, which was Middlebury* is acceptable. What is the rule?

Appositive **phrases** feel parenthetical.

Exercise   In the passages below, there are six appositive phrases (including one inside another). Identify them.

1 *The* Nellie, *a cruising yawl, swung to her anchor without a flutter of the sails and was at rest.*
2 *Mr Baker, chief mate of the ship* Narcissus, *stepped in one stride out of his lighted cabin into the darkness of the quarter-deck.*
3 *There, far below, is the knobbly backbone of England, the Pennine Range.*
4 *One summer afternoon Mrs Oedipa Maas came home from a Tupperware party whose hostess had put perhaps too much kirsch in the fondue to find that she, Oedipa, had been named executor, or she supposed executrix, of the estate of one Pierce Inverarity, a California real estate mogul who had once lost two million dollars in his spare time but still had assets numerous and tangled enough to make the job of sorting it all out more than honorary.*

Article

Explanation   Article is one of the traditional **parts of speech**. It is a very small **part of speech**, with just two members in English, the **words** *the* and *a* (or its variant *an*). *The* is called the **definite** article; and *a* is called the **indefinite** article. That's all – there are no more articles.

Examples   We've just given all the (English) examples there are – *the* and *a*!

Contrasts   As article is a **part of speech**, it contrasts with all other **parts of speech**, such as **noun**, **verb** and **preposition**. Articles are similar to, but still contrast with, **demonstratives, possessives** and **numerals** – see **Relationships** below.

Relationships   In fact, the traditional idea that just these two **words**, *the* and *a*, belong together in their own **word**-class, or **part of speech**, called 'article', seems to be wrong.

On the one hand, *the* behaves very much like the **demonstratives** *this*, *that*, *these* and *those*, and the **possessives** such as *my*, *your*, *his* and *our*; and on the other hand, *a* behaves quite like an unstressed version of the **numeral** *one*. The following examples demonstrate this. (Remember that an asterisk indicates an example that is actually not grammatical.)

- *the three houses*
- *those three houses*
- *our three houses*
- *⋆a three houses*
- *a house*
- *one house*

Article, then, is a case where traditional grammatical terms embody a traditional misconception, namely that the pair of **words** *the* and *a* have enough in common to warrant giving them a separate grammatical label of their own. Despite this traditional misanalysis, the terms '**definite** article' and '**indefinite** article' can still be used (if you want to sound a bit formal) to refer to the **words** *the* and *a*.

The term 'determiner' is used in linguistics to refer to a larger class of **words**, including articles, **demonstratives** and **possessives** (but not **numerals**). So all of the following would be classed as determiners: *a*, *the*, *this*, *those*, *my*, *your*. All such determiners **modify nouns** and they all go before any **adjectives** that may happen also to **modify** the **noun**.

For interest Many languages don't have any articles at all, i.e. nothing corresponding to either English *the* or *a*. Russian and Polish are like this, which accounts for some of the mistakes Russians and Poles make when speaking English. Some languages have only one article. Here are the possibilities, with examples of some of the languages exhibiting them.

No articles at all:	Russian, Polish
Definite, but no indefinite, article:	Welsh, Arabic
Indefinite, but no definite, article:	Turkish
Both definite and indefinite articles:	English, Swedish, Romanian

Interestingly, in both Swedish and Romanian, the indefinite article is a word which goes before the noun, but the definite article is a suffix placed on the end of the noun itself. Here are some simple examples.

SWEDISH
en park   *parken*
a park (= a park)   *park*+DEF   (= the park)
ROMANIAN
un om   *omul*
a man (= a man)   *man*+DEF   (= the man)

The fact that articles may be affixes illustrates that they are typically 'lightweight' elements. Even in English, the indefinite article *an* sometimes appears in writing prefixed to the following word, as in *another*.

Attributive

Explanation　An **adjective** is used attributively when it **modifies** a **noun** in a **noun phrase**. (This is not the only possible use for **adjectives** – see **Contrasts** below.)

Examples　In the following examples, the **adjectives** which are used attributively are underlined.

- *Amy has made <u>remarkable</u> progress this term.*
- *A <u>great fat</u> slug was eating my lettuces.*
- *A <u>wise</u> mother is patient and frank with her child.*
- *<u>Mental</u> development and <u>linguistic</u> development are in <u>reciprocal</u> <u>positive</u> interaction.*

Contrasts　The attributive use of **adjectives** contrasts with their **predicative** use. An **adjective** is used **predicatively** when it follows a **copular verb**, as in *Johnny is <u>impatient</u>* or *The weather will remain <u>sunny</u>*.

Relationships　Most English **adjectives** can be used both attributively and predicatively. For instance, *fat* and *thin* can both **modify** *man* as in *the fat man* or *the thin man*; and both can follow a **copula**, as in *He's fat* or *He's thin*.

But a tiny handful of **adjectives** can occur only in attributive position. Examples are *mere* and *former*. You can say, for instance, *a mere whippersnapper* or *my former boss*, but you cannot say *★He is mere* or *★My boss is former*.

Correspondingly, there are a few English **adjectives** which cannot occur in attributive position. *Asleep, alive* and *ajar* are examples. You can say *He is asleep* or *She is alive*, or *It is ajar*, but you cannot (in most **dialects**) say *★an asleep dog* or *★an alive fish* or *★an ajar door*.

Auxiliary verb

Explanation　An auxiliary (or 'helping') verb in English is one of the following:

- a form of *have* or *be*, which is used to 'help' another **verb** to express details about the timing of the events described;
- a **modal verb**, such as *can, may, will, might, should* or *must*;
- a form of *be* used with the **passive**;
- one of a small and varied set of other little 'helping' **verbs**, including *do, need* and *ought* (these are less central cases).

Examples　In the sentences below, the auxiliary verbs are underlined.

- *The Minister of Information <u>has</u> died in an accident.*
- *The flags <u>are</u> flying at half mast.*
- *I <u>had</u> not heard about the accident.*

- *Everybody was talking about it.*
- *He might have committed suicide.*
- *He has been looking ill for some time.*
- *Someone could have been trying to get rid of him.*

Contrasts Auxiliary verbs contrast with **main verbs**. An auxiliary verb usually occurs with a **main verb**; if a **main verb** is not actually present, because of **ellipsis**, the **sentence** is always understood as if one were present, as in *I will* or *It is*. A **main verb** can be the only **verb** in a **sentence**, but an auxiliary verb cannot (except where the **main verb** is understood as omitted by **ellipsis**).

Relationships The auxiliaries *have* and *be* always require specific **participle** forms of the **main verbs** they occur with. Auxiliary *be* requires a **present participle**, with an *-ing* ending, as in *Mary is flying her kite*. This combination of *be* and a **present participle** expresses the **progressive** aspect. Auxiliary *have* requires a **past participle**, which usually has either an *-ed* or an *-en* ending, as in *Someone has walked off with my Walkman*, or *Someone has taken my bike*. This combination of *have* and a **past participle** expresses the **perfect** aspect.

Note that forms of both *have* and *be* can also occur as **main verbs**, rather than as auxiliaries, as in the following **sentences**.

- *Inigo is very naughty.*
- *We have guests for dinner.*
- *Miss Marples has the measles.*

The forms of *have* and *be* in these **sentences** are not auxiliaries, but **main verbs**. But since *have* and *be* can be **main verbs**, they can also be 'helped' by (other instances of) *have* and *be* as auxiliaries, in the same **sentence**. This is shown below, where the auxiliaries are underlined.

- *Inigo is being very naughty.*
- *Inigo has been very naughty.*
- *We are having guests for dinner.*
- *We have had guests for dinner.*

Some **sentences** have no auxiliaries at all, but you can get up to three auxiliaries in one simple **sentence** (or even four, if you count the forms of *be* that occur with the **passive**). Here are some examples of such piled-up auxiliaries, with all the auxiliaries underlined, and the number of auxiliaries shown in parentheses.

- *Fred had been taking the dog for a walk.* (2)
- *I may be flying to London tomorrow.* (2)
- *I should have been catching up on some paperwork.* (3)
- *My expenses were being paid by the BBC.* (2)
- *Or at least, they should have been being paid by the BBC.* (4)

Whenever English auxiliaries pile up like this, they always go in a fixed order: a **modal verb** always goes before any other auxiliary; a *have* form always goes before any *be* form; and if there is a **passive** *be* form, it always goes after any other auxiliary. Whichever auxiliary happens to occur first, it is the one which is involved with **agreement**, **tense**, **interrogative**-formation and **negation**.

The first auxiliary in a **sentence**, if there is one, is what **agrees** with the **subject** of the **sentence** and what shows **present** or **past tense**; otherwise it is the **main verb** that **agrees** and shows **tense**. In the examples below, the forms which show **agreement** and **tense** (not always auxiliaries) are underlined.

- *Myron talks incessantly.*
- *Myra was still talking.*
- *They have been talking for ages.*

(Actually, **modal verbs** are partial exceptions to this, as they do not take **agreement** and their **present** and **past tense** forms (e.g. *may, might, can, could, shall, should*) have rather specialized meanings.)

In **interrogative sentences** (questions), it is just the first auxiliary, if there is one, that gets switched around the **subject** to the front of the **sentence** (or near it), as in:

- *Had Fred been taking the dog for a walk?*
- *Might she have made a mistake?*
- *Were my expenses being paid by the BBC?*

If there isn't an auxiliary (or a **main verb** *have* or *be*), the **interrogative** is formed by putting a form of the special auxiliary *do* before the **subject**, as in:

- *Do bears live in the woods?*
- *Why does Rosie always interrupt me?*

In **negative sentences**, the *not* or *-n't* gets put after (or attached to) the first auxiliary, if there is one; otherwise, a form of the auxiliary *do* is introduced to take the *not* or *-n't*. Examples are:

- *Fred had not been taking the dog for a walk.*
- *She mightn't have made a mistake.*
- *I may not be flying to London tomorrow.*
- *She doesn't always interrupt you.*

For interest   Many other languages have systems of auxiliary verbs, resembling English in varying degrees, but the details can be very different. French, German and Italian all have something corresponding to the English perfect with *have*, but they don't have anything closely corresponding to the English progressive with *be*. Other languages, such as Russian and Arabic, express these kinds of meanings in rather different ways, for example by putting affixes onto the main verbs.

Historically, many present-day auxiliary verbs are derived from what were once main verbs. So the English auxiliary *have* was once used only in its main-verb sense, indicating possession.

The meanings expressed by auxiliary verbs are typically more general, and applicable to more situations, than the meanings expressed by main verbs. That is presumably why, in any language, there is only a small number of auxiliary verbs, and a very large number of other (main) verbs. Some brief indications of the meanings expressed by auxiliaries in English are shown below.

MEANING	AUXILIARY	EXAMPLE
Completed action	*have* + past participle	*It has rained.*
Ongoing action	*be* + present participle	*It is raining.*
Future time	Modal verb *will*	*It will rain.*
Possibility	Modal verb *may*	*It may rain.*
Necessity	Modal verb *must*	*It must rain.*

The idea common to all of these examples is the idea of 'it raining', and the meanings of the various auxiliaries are applied to this basic meaning, expressed by the main verb *rain*. Take another main verb, *kiss*, involving two people, say Lesley and Sandy, so that the basic idea is of Lesley kissing Sandy. This basic meaning can be modified by all the English auxiliaries mentioned above, to give

- *Lesley has kissed Sandy.*
- *Lesley is kissing Sandy.*
- *Lesley will kiss Sandy.*
- *Lesley may kiss Sandy.*
- *Lesley must kiss Sandy.*

The typical auxiliary meanings can be applied to any situation that can be imagined. The meanings of main verbs, on the other hand, are not so versatile, each one being typically restricted to particular types of participants, like *kiss*, just mentioned, whose subject must normally be human, and whose object must normally be concrete.

Exercise How many auxiliary verbs are there in each of the following sentences, and which words are they?

1 *Term had just begun.*
2 *The Liberals will win the election.*
3 *The Minister of Culture is having an affair with an actress.*
4 *Justice must be done.*
5 *Justice must be seen to be done.*
6 *I have never begun a novel with more misgiving.*

Cardinal numeral

Explanation **Numeral** is a **word**-class (see PART OF SPEECH), and cardinal is a subdivision of the **numerals**. Cardinal numerals are the **words** and longer expressions we count by, and express how many items there are in some collection of things.

23

Examples   *One, two, three, . . . , ten, eleven, twelve, thirteen, . . . , twenty, thirty, forty, . . . , hundred, thousand, million, . . .* are all cardinal numeral **words**. There are also longer cardinal numeral expressions, composed of such **words**, such as:

- *three hundred and forty-two*
- *twenty-five thousand*

Contrasts   Cardinal contrasts primarily with **ordinal**, the other kind of **numeral**. Cardinal numeral, as a **word**-class, contrasts with all other **word**-classes or **parts of speech**, such as **noun, verb, adjective** and **preposition**. If a **word** in a given **sentence** is a (cardinal) numeral, it can't be any other **part of speech**.

Some grammarians have included cardinal numerals among the **adjectives**, but there are differences between cardinal numerals and typical **adjectives**, which make them at best a quite special kind of **adjective**. Some of these differences are given below.

(Cardinal) numerals always occur before any **adjectives** in a string of **words** modifying a **noun**. Thus, *seven big white houses* is grammatical, but both **big seven white houses* and **big white seven houses* are ungrammatical. There are, however, some (less typical) cases where an **adjective** may (but not must) precede a cardinal numeral, as in *the previous three matches*.

Whereas you can make very complex **numeral** expressions, using addition and multiplication, out of basic **numeral words**, you can't build up complex **adjective phrases** in the same systematic way. And in English, at least, you can't put a cardinal numeral after the **verb** *be*, as you can with an **adjective**. Thus, *Those houses are expensive* is fine, but **Those houses are twenty* is not.

One must be careful to distinguish between the cardinal numeral *one* and the **impersonal pronoun** *one* (as used at the beginning of this **sentence**).

Words like *many*, *several* and *few* have meanings quite like the cardinal numerals. The main difference is that the meanings of the cardinal numerals are exact numbers, whereas the meanings of *many*, *several* and *few* are vague. These **words** can go in many of the same grammatical positions as the cardinal numerals, e.g. *twenty of my friends, many of my friends, several of my friends, few of my friends*. But these **words** are nevertheless not traditionally called '**numerals**'; linguists call them, and some other **words**, 'quantifiers'.

Relationships   All cardinal numerals except *one*, the first in the sequence, are **plural** in meaning, and trigger **plural agreement**, as in *those twenty new houses*. One, of course, is **singular**.

There are relatively few **words** which can **modify** cardinal numerals. They include such **adverbs** as *approximately, roughly, exactly, nearly* and *almost*.

By **ellipsis** of a **noun**, a cardinal numeral can be left looking as if it were a **noun**, as in *I invited all the students, but only three came*. Clearly it is reasonable to understand an omitted *students* after *three* here.

In English, cardinals are used **attributively**, as in *Judith's five assistants*, but cannot be used **predicatively**. For example, **They are five* is not grammatical;

one has to say *There are five of them*, instead. In French, however, cardinal numerals can be used **predicatively** as in *Elles sont cinq*.

English cardinal numerals almost always precede all the **adjectives** in their **noun phrase**: *The three beautiful tall trees* is grammatical, but **the beautiful three tall trees* is not (except perhaps in rather unusual circumstances).

For interest Some languages don't have any numerals at all, surprising as this may seem. Many Australian aboriginal languages are like this, having no sequence of words for their users to count things with. The aborigines survived without numerals for millennia. When Australian aborigines are introduced to a numeral system, such as that of English, they have no trouble in mastering it.

Most languages' numeral systems are decimal, using 10 as a base, but there are quite a few which make extensive use of 5 and 20 as bases as well. You may be familiar with *quatre vingts* (4 20s), the French expression for *eighty*, which is an isolated use of 20 as a base. Other 20-based languages are more thorough in their use of 20. For example, Mixtec, an Indian language of Mexico, expresses 250 in words most directly translated as *ten two twenty ten* – in mathematical notation, $(((10 + 2) \times 20) + 10)$.

The Nigerian language Yoruba has a very complicated numeral system, using various bases, including 20, and making liberal use of subtraction. Thus a Yoruba expression for 46 would be translated most directly as something like *four from ten from twenty three*. To resolve this puzzle, see it with the understood arithmetical relationships explicitly written in $- 4$ from $(10$ from $(20 \times 3))$.

Many such rather exotic numeral systems are now being replaced, more or less gradually, by simple decimal systems imported from European languages.

Exercise Identify the cardinal numerals in the following sentences:

1 *Four days later, on March the ninth, two detectives called at my house.*
2 *When purchasing caviar, one normally expects to pay at least twenty pounds for two or three ounces.*
3 *But I was astonished to have to pay fifty for just one.*

Case

Explanation Many languages (but English hardly) use a different form of a **noun** or **pronoun** to indicate the relationship it bears to its **verb**, where this relationship may be such as **subject, direct object** or **indirect object**. The case of such a **noun** or **pronoun** in a given **clause** corresponds in most instances to this relationship with the **verb**. The most commonly talked about cases are those below, paired up with their corresponding **noun–verb** relations.

CASE	RELATION of NOUN to VERB
nominative	subject
accusative	direct object
dative	indirect object

In addition, there is **genitive** case, which typically corresponds to the 'possessor' relation between two **nouns**.

The terminology of case (**nominative, accusative, dative**, etc.) is generally only applied to languages in which **words** vary in form according to their case. Hence for English, the term 'case' is not actually of much use, except for the **personal pronouns**, many of which have a special **accusative** forms.

Examples   The English **pronouns** which have different case forms are given below.

NOMINATIVE	ACCUSATIVE
I	*me*
he	*him*
she	*her*
we	*us*
they	*them*
who	*whom*

Contrasts   Case marks a relationship between a **noun** (or **pronoun**) and something else in the **clause** (e.g. a **verb**). Thus case contrasts with factors such as **gender** (masculine/feminine), **person** (1st/2nd/3rd) and **number (singular/plural)** which are properties inherent in the **noun** (or **pronoun**) itself, regardless of how it is used in a **clause**.

Relationships   In a basic sense, **nouns** and **pronouns** are the primary **parts of speech** that can take cases; and as we have seen, in English it is in fact only the **pronouns**. But in other languages with fuller **case** systems, such as Latin, Russian and German, other **parts of speech**, such as **adjectives, articles** and **demonstratives**, can get cases marked on them by **agreement**.

Nouns and **pronouns** 'receive' (or 'are in') cases, and **verbs** 'assign' cases to them, according to their relationships in a **clause**. **Nouns** and **pronouns** may also 'receive' cases assigned to them by **prepositions**, as shown in English by **phrases** such as *to me, by us, with them, for him* and *at her*.

The **genitive** case, in particular, is assigned to a **noun** or **pronoun** by another **noun**. There is no good example of this in English, unless we say (as some grammarians do) that the **possessives**, such as *my, your, his, her* and *its* are the **genitive** case forms of *I, you, he, she* and *it*. Taking this point of view, *her* in *her book* would be **genitive** due to its relation to the **noun** *book*. Similarly, the **suffix** *-'s* on **nouns** would also be a marker of **genitive** case in English. Looked at this way, *John's* in *John's book* would be said to be assigned **genitive** case by the **noun** *book*.

As cases indicate basic relationships between the parts of a **clause**, all case markings can occur in both **main** and **subordinate clauses**.

The English **accusative** forms listed above can be used for both **direct** and **indirect objects** and also for the objects of **prepositions**. In view of this wide range of use, it has been suggested that 'objective', being more general, might be a better term for the English forms than '**accusative**'. But '**accusative**' is commonly used. Other English **pronouns** *you* and *it* do not have distinct case forms.

For interest   Many other languages have much richer case systems than English. This means that they have more different cases, and that more different parts of speech show these cases. A well-known example is Latin, which is said to have the following cases, with roughly the uses given:

LATIN CASE	TYPICAL USE or MEANING
Nominative	subject of clause
Vocative	the case used to address the person being spoken to
Accusative	direct object of clause, and of certain prepositions
Genitive	possessor of thing referred to by noun
Dative	indirect object of clause
Ablative	object of certain prepositions

Here are some examples. Look at the different endings on the stem *Brut-* (for Brutus, a man's name).

> *Brutus   necavit Caesarem*
> *Brutus*+NOM killed *Caesar*+ACC   (= *Brutus killed Caesar.*)

Here, *Brutus* is in the nominative, marked by *-us*, because *Brutus* is the subject of the verb *necavit*.

> *Et   tu   Brute ?*
> *And you Brutus*+VOC ?   (= *You too, Brutus?*)

Here, *Brute* is in the vocative, marked by *-e*, because Brutus is being addressed by Caesar (with his dying words).

> *Quis   necavit Brutum ?*
> *Who*+ACC killed *Brutum*+ACC ?   (= *Who killed Brutus?*)

Here, *Brutum* is in the accusative, marked by *-um*, because *Brutus* is the direct object of the verb *necavit*.

German and Russian also have well-developed case systems.

Some languages, such as Lezghian, a language spoken in the Caucasus mountains, have very complex case systems, with well over twenty different cases. There is a whole terminology of rarer case terms, whose use is restricted to such lesser-known languages.

The basic nominative/accusative organization of a case system is not the only way in which the basic cases in a language can be organized. (See under NOMINATIVE CASE.)

Adopting the nominative/accusative terminology of case for English, what cases are the underlined words in the following sentences?

1 *She hit him with a handbag.*
2 *I asked her to give me the book.*

Clause

Explanation A clause is a part of a **sentence**, which itself has all or many of the basic ingredients of a whole **sentence**, including a **verb** (always in English) and a **subject**, and perhaps **direct** and/or **indirect objects**. It is important to note that clauses may contain other clauses wholly inside them. Some clauses look exactly like whole **sentences**, just inserted into another **sentence**, but other clauses may appear somewhat different from whole **sentences**, for example, by having a different form of the **verb**, or by omitting a **subject** or an **object**. Technically speaking, any simple **sentence** is also a clause, but there is seldom any usefulness in referring to simple **sentences** as clauses.

Examples In the **sentences** below, the clauses are underlined. Note that there may be more than one underline, and that one underline may wholly include another, indicating how one clause may wholly contain another.

- *John gave Mary a book.*
- *Did Nick tell you that his mother had died?*
- *It is a pity that you arrived so late.*
- *I want Mary to come here this minute.*
- *I can't stand the kids making so much noise.*
- *Greta wanted to be left alone.*
- *Tell Nick that Greta wants to be left alone.*
- *When I die, please bury me where my mother is buried.*
- *I'm the man who broke the bank at Monte Carlo.*
- *I came, I saw, I conquered.*

Contrasts Clause contrasts with **sentence**. Except in the case of a whole **sentence**, which is technically said to be also a clause, a clause is always smaller than the **sentence** that contains it.

Clause also contrasts with **phrase**. Clauses contain **phrases**. Clauses are bigger than the simple **phrases** they contain. The crucial characteristic of a clause, which is lacking from a **phrase**, is that a clause normally has its own **verb** and all or many of the other basic ingredients of a whole **sentence**. So

Billy's brand new bicycle and *on Sunday morning at ten o'clock* are both **phrases** but not clauses, because neither includes a **verb**.

Clauses can themselves be contained in complex **phrases**; such clauses are always, by definition, **subordinate** clauses.

Relationships The whole **sentence** that contains other smaller clauses is the **main** clause. Contained clauses are all **subordinate** clauses, except for those joined together by *and*, *or* or *but*, which are coordinate clauses.

In English, a **verb** is essential to a clause. Any part of a **sentence** without some kind of **verb** in it cannot be a clause. Note that all the clauses underlined in the examples above have their own **verbs**. Further, a clause never (with one exception) has more than one **main** (i.e. non-**auxiliary**) **verb**. So there is a generally very useful rule: 'one clause – one **main verb**'. The single exception to this rule is the case of conjoined, or coordinated, **main verbs**, as in *Lisa buys and sells securities*, which is one clause, despite having two **main verbs**.

The **verb** of a **main** clause is always **finite**, showing **tense** and/or **agreement** (or else has a **finite auxiliary**, which shows **tense** and/or **agreement** for it). The **verb** of a **subordinate** clause may or may not be **finite**; if it is not **finite**, it may be an **infinitive** or a **gerund**, or possibly a **participle**.

Traditionally, the basic division of any clause is into its **subject** and its **predicate**. Every clause has a **subject**, normally explicitly present, but if not, at least understood. For example, *her son* is the **subject** of the **subordinate** clause in *Rita wanted her son to be left alone*. In *Rita wanted to be left alone*, we understand *Rita* to be the **subject** of *to be left alone*.

Clauses often have other ingredients of **sentences**, too, such as **objects** and **adverbs**.

Subordinate clauses are often, but not always, introduced by a special **pronoun** or **conjunction**, such as *that*, *which*, *who*, *whom* or *when*.

In English, there are three main kinds of **subordinate** clauses, namely **relative** clauses, **complement** clauses and **adverbial** clauses.

Main clauses can be in any **mood** (**declarative, interrogative** or **imperative**), but clear **mood** distinctions are less obvious in **subordinate** clauses.

A clause, having all the basic ingredients of a **sentence** carries the same kind of meaning as a whole **sentence**, describing some event, situation or state of affairs. Having **subordinate** clauses provides a way of expressing these meanings as the **subjects, objects**, etc., in other **sentences**. Thus whole **(subordinate)** clauses can themselves be **subjects, objects**, etc. For example, the clause *that John arrived late* is the **subject** of the **verb** *embarrassed* in *That John arrived late embarrassed his sponsors*. And in *We all regret that John arrived late*, the same clause is the **object** of the **verb** *regret*. A **subordinate** clause used in this way, as the **subject** or **object** in another clause is called a '**complement clause**'.

For interest Every language has clauses, but some languages use subordinate clauses much less than English, preferring to string out coordinate clauses. In such a language, a sentence such as *When I went into town, I met a man that I had met before* would be more likely to be expressed as something like *I went into town, and I met a man; I had met him before.*

In any language with subordination, the only limit to how many clauses you can pack inside each other is an approximate practical limit on how much a hearer can take in at once, or on how much a speaker can keep in his head while producing a long complicated sentence. There are no precise grammatical rules in any language placing a definite limit on how many subordinate clauses you can use at once. 'As many as you can manage', or 'No more than you can get away with' seems to be the practical guideline.

Exercise In each of the following sentences, underline all the clauses (including the main clause), as in the examples given above. Remember you may get multiple underlining because of one clause being inside another.

1 *Give me a break!*

2 *Where is the book that I lent you?*

3 *Wesley didn't turn up until after the others had left.*

4 *The fact that Wesley didn't turn up on time bothered me.*

5 *Bill told me that Jill wanted him to marry her.*

6 *I tried putting it in upside-down but it didn't work.*

7 *I heard Jay tell Sue that Al wanted me to see him before he died.*

Common noun

Explanation A common noun is a type of **noun** which can be used, as occasion demands, to refer to members of classes of people, things or masses of stuff. The same common noun, used in different contexts, can pick out different individual people or things. As the name suggests, common nouns are the most common type of **noun**. Typically, English common nouns are not spelt with an initial capital letter.

Examples *Apple, desks, elephant, girls, hatred, intertextuality, phenomenon, sky, soil, town, weather, zoo* are all common nouns.

Contrasts Common noun contrasts primarily with **proper name**, the other main type of **noun**. In meaning, typical common nouns apply to whole classes of things. Thus *cow* can be used in connection with any of the millions of cows in the world (and indeed even fictitious cows). By contrast, **proper names** refer to specific individual things (such as people and places). Thus *London* picks out a single particular place.

As common nouns are a subclass of **nouns**, common noun contrasts with all other **parts of speech**, such as **verb, adjective** and **preposition**. If a **word** in a given **sentence** is a common noun, it can't be any other **part of speech**.

/ **Relationships**   There are two subtypes of common noun, which differ grammatically, namely **count** and **mass nouns**. These differ in the positions they can occur in, and in their typical meanings. See COUNT NOUN and MASS NOUN.

There is another distinction that can be drawn among common nouns: they can be either **abstract** or concrete. **Abstract nouns** typically refer to abstract notions, such as activities (e.g. *war, tennis*), emotions (e.g. *love, fear*) and forces (e.g. *gravity, inertia*). Concrete common nouns are the ones that are not **abstract**. Given the two dimensions, **count** versus **mass**, and **abstract** versus concrete, all four possibilities occur, as shown in this table.

	COUNT	MASS
CONCRETE	*pebble, dog*	*acid, rice*
ABSTRACT	*idea, problem*	*generosity, linguistics*

Common nouns can be **modified** by a variety of other **parts of speech** and types of **phrase**, including **articles, demonstratives, possessives, adjectives, prepositional phrases** and **relative clauses**. The examples below show some of the possibilities.

- *these two short planks*
- *Frank's tubby red-haired wife*
- *a bath with Rosie*
- *a tune that anyone can whistle*

In each of these examples, the underlined common noun acts as the **head** of a **noun phrase**. In this role as the **head** of a **noun phrase**, a common noun can function as the **subject** or (**direct** or **indirect**) **object** of a **clause**.

Sometimes **words** of other **parts of speech** can be adapted to use as common nouns. For example, *red*, which is basically an **adjective**, can be used as a common noun, as in *the red of my blouse* or *a rather darker red*. Similarly *yesterday*, which is basically an **adverb** of time is adapted for use as a common noun in the poetic *all our yesterdays*. It can happen to **verbs**, too, as with *scream* in *I heard two loud screams*.

For interest   All languages have common nouns.

Like many distinctions in grammar, the boundary between common nouns and proper names is permeable in both directions. Common nouns can become used as proper names (*Smith, Baker, Farmer, Cook, Slater*), and can become incorporated in longer expressions which effectively function as proper names (*the United States, Tower Hill, Pearl Harbor*). This is a historical process, sometimes taking several generations for the transition from common noun to proper name to establish itself in the language of the community.

The reverse process, from proper name to common noun, is often more a matter of the inventiveness of individual speakers. The typical use of a proper name is to identify a particular unique single person, place or thing. There is only one New York, as far as a speaker knows. But a speaker can, in some sense, conversationally divide this unique place into several different entities, and say, for example, *I'll show you MY New York, not the New York of the travel brochures or Hollywood's New York!*

Another frequent version of the transition from proper names to common nouns involves commercial brand names or the names of inventors. All of the following started life as proper names, but are now more often used as common nouns: *Hoover* (or *hoover*), *Xerox, Tippex, stetson, Kleenex, cardigan, wellingtons, Levis*. Note that the longer-established of these (*stetson, cardigan, wellingtons*) have now lost their initial capitals; *Hoover* (or *hoover*) seems to be just on the brink of settling into the written language as an ordinary common noun, by losing its capital letter.

Exercise Identify the common nouns in the following sentences. There are eleven of them in total. And look out – there's a trick.

1 *Einstein had the greatest mind for physics of this century.*
2 *Dualism is the theory that the soul and the body are different things.*
3 *Floyd was born somewhere between Tallahassee and St Louis.*
4 *Arsenic is not a poison, if taken in small quantities.*

Comparative

Explanation A comparative is used to express a difference along some implicitly one-dimensional scale. Many English **adjectives** and **adverbs** have comparative forms, ending in the **suffix** *-er*. Comparatives can also be formed by putting the **word** *more* in front of the **adjective** or **adverb** concerned.

Less frequently, forms expressing a similarity along some implicitly one-dimensional scale are also called 'comparatives'.

Examples *Bigger, better, larger, worse, cleaner, lovelier, uglier, harder* and *easier* are all comparatives of **adjectives**. *Better* and *harder* are also comparatives of **adverbs** (*well* and *hard*). Examples of comparatives with *more* are *more beautiful, more generous, more devastating, more diligently, more exquisitely* and *more fundamentally*.

Sometimes, expressions such as *as big as* and *as long as* are also called 'comparatives'.

Contrasts Comparative contrasts primarily with the basic, uncompared form of the **adjective** or **adverb**, and with **superlative**. Comparatives are the middle elements in three-element contrastive series, such as *good – better – best, dark – darker – darkest*, and *rude – ruder – rudest*.

Relationships Only **adjectives** and **adverbs** (and not all of those) have single-word comparatives formed with *-er*. **Adjectives** with no natural comparative include *asleep, male, and unique*. You can't use *-er* to form the comparative of a **noun** or a **verb**. But you can express the comparative idea with **nouns** and **verbs**, using *more*, as in *This is more of a mansion than a house*, or *She loves you more than I do*.

The rules for when to form a comparative with *-er* and when to use *more* are quite complex, but have something to do with the length of the **adjective** or **adverb** concerned. Only shorter **adjectives** and **adverbs** can take *-er*. You can't say **beautifuller, *calamitouser* or **disagreeabler*. (Lewis Carroll was being playful when he had Alice say **curiouser and curiouser*.)

The irregular comparatives of *good* and *bad* don't look anything like them – *better* and *worse*.

English comparatives have a special **preposition** of their own, *than*, for linking them to a following **phrase**, as in *He is taller than his brother*. *Than* only occurs in connection with comparatives (except in some American dialects which also use *than* with *different*).

For interest Many languages don't make a distinction between comparative and superlative, just using the same form for both.

It is tempting to treat English *more* as the comparative of *many*, with *most* as its superlative, but this idea hasn't found support among grammarians or logicians, perhaps because *many, more* and *most* are not adjectives or adverbs. (Linguists call them 'quantifiers'.) But there seems to be a clear parallelism between *many/much – more – most, few – fewer – fewest*, and acknowledged trios with comparatives such as *big – bigger – biggest*. What are the similarities and differences?

Exercise Identify the comparatives in the following sentences. There are seven in all.

1 *The lion tamer asked for a tamer lion.*
2 *You can't get fitter than a Kwik-Fit fitter.*
3 *Please lower the higher shelf and raise the lower one.*
4 *The taller stranger was stranger than the shorter one.*

Complement clause

Explanation Recently, linguists working in the influential theory known as 'generative grammar' have used the term 'complement' to refer to various closely related kinds of **subordinate clause**, namely:

1 **Subordinate clauses** which on their own serve as the **direct object of verbs** such as *believe, tell, say, know* and *understand*; the **subordinate clauses** are the complements of these **verbs**.

2 **Subordinate clauses** which **modify** various **nouns** such as *story, rumour* and *fact*, and **adjectives** such as *proud, happy* and *sad*; the **subordinate clauses** are the complements of these **nouns** and **adjectives**.

3 **Subordinate clauses** which on their own act as the **subject** of sentences with such **predicates** as *be a pity, be a nuisance, be unfortunate, seem* and *happen*. These **clauses** are called '**subject** complements' or '**subject** complement clauses'.

Complements in this sense are distinguished by being called 'complement clauses' in this guide. Sometimes the term 'complement clause' is extended to the adverbial type of **subordinate clause**, as well.

Examples
1 In the following examples, the underlined **subordinate clauses** are complements of the **verbs** before them (*believe, tell, say, know*).

- *I don't believe that it will work.*
- *Tell John not to wake me.*
- *Irma said she was going home early.*
- *We all know why she went.*

(As the example with *tell* shows, the complement of a **verb** does not have to come immediately after it, but can be separated from the **verb** by another **word** or **phrase**.)

2 In the next examples, the underlined **subordinate clauses** are the complements of the various **nouns** (*story, rumour, fact*) and **adjectives** (*proud, happy, sad*) immediately before them.

- *The story that Christ visited England is just wishful thinking.*
- *The staff were worried by the rumour that a takeover was imminent.*
- *The fact that you're safe is all that I care about.*
- *We are proud that the President came to visit us.*
- *He was very happy to oblige us.*
- *But we were sad that he could not stay.*

3 Finally, the underlined **subordinate clauses** below are the **subject** complements of the **predicates** (*be a pity, be a nuisance, be unfortunate, seem wrong, happen*) immediately following them.

- *For Helen not to see her father was a great pity.*
- *That the bees swarmed in your apple tree was a nuisance.*
- *That you arrived just at that moment was most unfortunate.*
- *To do it on my own seems wrong.*
- *That humans evolved in this particular way just happened.*

Contrasts
Complement clauses contrast with other kinds of **subordinate clauses**, such as **relative clauses** and adverbial **clauses**.

The contrast with **relative clauses** is perhaps subtle, but important to note, as the two kinds of **clauses** convey different kinds of meaning. Here are some contrastive examples, in which the two kinds of **clauses** are underlined.

COMPLEMENT CLAUSE	RELATIVE CLAUSE
the rumour <u>that Elvis is alive</u>	the rumour <u>that Elvis denied</u>
the belief <u>that he is Napoleon</u>	the belief <u>that haunts him</u>
the allegation <u>that we planned this disaster</u>	the allegation <u>that hurts us most</u>

What makes the grammatical difference in such examples is that the complement clause (minus its introducing *that*) could stand as a full **sentence**, e.g. *Elvis is alive*, whereas the **relative clauses** are all in a sense incomplete and could not stand on their own as full **sentences** (e.g. **Elvis denied* and **Haunts him*). The difference in meaning between the two types of **clause** can be illustrated by taking the examples following *rumour* above. The complement clause *that Elvis is alive* tells us what the rumour IS, whereas the **relative clause** *that Elvis denied* tells us about some event or action that the rumour was involved in, namely Elvis denying it.

Here are some examples in which complement clauses are contrasted with adverbial **clauses**.

COMPLEMENT CLAUSE	ADVERBIAL CLAUSE
Jan asked <u>if I was going</u>.	<u>If I was going</u>, I would take my umbrella.
Mary wondered <u>where she was</u>.	Mary stayed <u>where she was</u>.

In the second example here, the relationship between *wondered* and the following **clause** is quite different from the relationship between *stayed* and that same **clause**. The adverbial **clause**, *where she was*, tells us about Mary's position. But the same **clause** used as a complement clause with *wondered* does not similarly tell us where Mary wondered (but, rather, WHAT she wondered).

Relationships   Complement clauses, being **clauses**, contain all the usual ingredients of **clauses**, namely a **verb** (always), a **subject** (normally) and **direct** and **indirect objects** (sometimes).

Complement clauses in English are usually introduced by subordinating **conjunctions** (or 'complementizers' in modern linguistic terminology), such as *that*, *what*, *why* and *when*.

Complement clauses can be **finite** or non-**finite**. Here are some examples with **finite** and non-**finite** complement clauses (underlined).

WITH FINITE COMPLEMENT CLAUSE	WITH NON-FINITE COMPLEMENT CLAUSE
Juliet expected <u>that Dierdre would be home</u>.	Juliet expected <u>Dierdre to be home</u>.
<u>That John coughed then</u> was rude.	<u>For John to cough then</u> was rude.
	<u>John's coughing then</u> was rude.
Morag is proud <u>that she is Scottish</u>.	Morag is proud <u>to be Scottish</u>.
The fact <u>that he can win grants</u> is clear.	His ability <u>to win grants</u> is clear.
We advise <u>that you leave early</u>.	We advise <u>you to leave early</u>.

Complement clauses after **verbs** act as their **direct objects**. So in the following example the underlined expressions (one a complement clause, the other a **noun phrase**) are both in the same relationship (namely **direct object**) to the **verb** *believe*.

Nobody believed <u>that he was dead</u>.   *Nobody believed* <u>the story</u>.

Besides acting as **direct objects**, complement clauses can act as **subjects**, as in *That she played her drums at midnight annoyed me* (and as also illustrated several times above). But complement clauses never act as **indirect objects**, at least in English. This is because **indirect objects** typically refer to humans (or at least animate beings), whereas complement clauses typically describe facts, events or situations.

Within each **part of speech** that can take a complement clause, that is **verbs, nouns** and **adjectives**, only a relatively small number of **words** can in fact take complement clauses. So for each of these **parts of speech**, there is a small subset of complement-clause-taking **words**. Most **verbs** (e.g. *drink, drive, walk*), **nouns** (e.g. *chair, house, cat*) and **adjectives** (e.g. *red, large, noisy*) cannot in fact take complement clauses. So, for example, *★I drank that he was coming*, *★The chair that the earth is flat is wrong* and *★The children were noisy that they had won* are all ungrammatical.

Subjunctives occur in complement clauses after a small set of specific **verbs** in English, including *recommend, suggest, request, require* and *advise*. Examples are *My client requests that he <u>be</u> allowed to phone home* and *I recommend that she <u>take</u> these pills*.

As complement clauses are **subordinate clauses** it is possible to have one complement clause inside another (inside another), as in:

- *I bet you all thought I would be angry <u>that <u>you had done that</u></u>.*

For interest   Clauses express what philosophers call 'propositions'. The philosopher's idea of a proposition is something like the traditional grammarian's idea of a 'single complete thought expressed by a sentence'. A proposition is a neatly encapsulated fact about the world (either the real world or some fictitious world). People can believe propositions, regret them, assert them, deny them, recall them, know them, desire them to be true, and so on. That is, people can have what philosophers call 'propositional attitudes', in relation to particular propositions. If, for example, I believe that there are brick houses on Elm Street, I have a particular 'attitude' to the proposition that there are brick houses on Elm Street, namely the attitude of belief.

The ability of complement clauses to go with specific verbs, nouns and adjectives is what allows us to describe people's propositional attitudes. That is, language enables us not only to describe real situations, but also, through complement clauses, to describe possibly fictitious or unreal situations that other people have some psychological attitude (such as belief or desire or knowledge) toward. It is interesting that some of the verbs that can take complement clauses only show these propositions 'opaquely'. That is, after some verbs, there is an unresolvable ambiguity as to whether the proposition involved holds in the real world of the speaker or in the (perhaps imaginary) world of the person said to have the attitude.

To make this more concrete with an example, consider a context in which a person called Ethel is the departmental secretary. The office phone rings, and I answer it, and the caller says to me '*Can I speak to the departmental secretary?*' I report to the other people in the room by saying: '*Somebody wants to speak to Ethel.*' Now, even though Ethel is indeed the departmental secretary, and the caller said she wanted to speak to the departmental secretary, it may be false to claim that the caller wanted to speak to Ethel, because the caller may not have known that Ethel is the departmental secretary. My report of what was in the caller's mind assumed the equations and identities (e.g. Ethel = departmental secretary) that are in my own mind, and I have no guarantee that these are shared by the person (the caller) whose wishes I am reporting. The exact references made by the complement clause *to speak to Ethel* get muddied, or made inaccessible, by the very fact that this is a complement clause of the verb *want*.

Philosophers describe this phenomenon by saying that complement clauses[1] of this type have two different readings, or interpretations, which they call (in Latin) *de re* (meaning *of the thing*) and *de dicto* (meaning *of what was said*).

This kind of discussion is not just a game for philosophers. It can have very real consequences. For instance, in a recent trial, a jury had to decide whether an accused policeman '*intended to kill Stephen Waldorf*'. Here, *to kill Stephen Waldorf* is a complement clause of the verb *intend*, which creates the kind of opacity, or ambiguity, that we are discussing. Now even though Stephen Waldorf and the person shot were the same person, it would have been possible to intend to kill the person shot without intending to kill Stephen Waldorf, if you didn't know that 'they' are the same person. With an accusation expressed in such terms, as indeed they sometimes are, one would hope that a jury would have a very clear understanding of these linguistic and philosophical intricacies. If they did not, exactly what would they be deciding?

Exercise Identify the complement clauses in the following examples.

1 *That you lied to me disturbs me deeply.*
2 *For it to snow now would be very improbable.*
3 *The ancient Greeks knew that the earth was round.*
4 *Nobody expected Perrot to win.*
5 *The fact that he is Chinese is irrelevant.*
6 *Nobody now believes the theory that the earth is flat.*
7 *They were determined that no-one would pass them.*

---

1 Actually the philosophers don't use this grammatical terminology.

Complement of a copular verb

Explanation In older, more traditional works, a **phrase** following the **verb** *be* (or any other **copular verb**) is said to be its 'complement'. A complement is thus a part of the **predicate** of a certain kind of **clause**; in fact, in this sense 'complement' is often used synonymously with ' **predicate phrase**'. To distinguish this sense of the term, the longer expression 'complement of a copular verb' is used where necessary in this guide. There are also cases of complements in the sense of this entry where the **verb** *be* is not actually present, but is understood.

Examples In the following examples, the underlined parts are complements of copular verbs.

- *The chairman is <u>a former cabinet minister</u>.*
- *The dog is <u>man's best friend</u>.*
- *The kids were <u>as happy as larks</u>.*
- *Only one little problem remained <u>on the horizon</u>.*
- *Everyone seemed <u>delighted to see us</u>.*

Here are some examples in which the underlined **phrases** are complements in the same sense as above, where the **verb** *be* is omitted, but can be understood to be implied. The examples without *be* are paired with implied **sentences** including *be*, for comparison.

That makes me <u>really mad</u>.	(*I am really mad.*)
They elected Bill <u>president</u>.	(*Bill is president.*)
We consider these truths <u>self-evident</u>.	(*These truths are self-evident.*)
They drove the cat <u>under the sideboard</u>.	(*The cat is under the sideboard.*)
They baked their clay <u>incredibly hard</u>.	(*Their clay is incredibly hard.*)

Contrasts Complement of a copular verb contrasts with **direct object**. **Copular verbs**, such as *be*, *remain* and *seem*, do not have **objects**, but have complements instead. Even though they can be directly followed by a **noun phrase**, as in *That lady is my aunt* or *Algernon remained his closest ally*, these **verbs** are not **transitive**, because there is no kind of 'carrying over' of an action or effective relationship from the **subject** to this **noun phrase**. Indeed, in most cases the **subject** and the **noun phrase** following the **copular verb** actually refer to, or describe, the same person or thing, as in the two examples just mentioned. So, rather than being called the '**objects**' of their **verbs**, such **noun phrases** are called something else, namely 'complements'.

The complements occurring without an explicit **copular verb** (where *be* is only implied) also contrast with other roles in a **clause** such as **direct** or **indirect object**. Compare the following (in their most plausible interpretations) and look for the subtle differences in meaning. In each pair, the same **noun phrase** (underlined) occurs once as a complement and once as a **direct object**.

WITH **NOUN PHRASE** AS **COMPLEMENT**	WITH **NOUN PHRASE** AS **DIRECT OBJECT**
The event made Bobby a martyr.	*The event gave the movement a martyr.*
He painted his nails a shade of pink.	*He showed his subjects a shade of pink.*

Sometimes a **sentence** can be ambiguous, with the possibility of either a reading understood to involve a complement or a reading involving some other role, such as **direct object** or adverbial. An example would be *I found Myra a genius*, which could be paraphrased either as *I found Myra to be a genius* (complement reading), or as *I found a genius for Myra* (**direct object** interpretation). Another example would be *Goya painted the Maja fully clothed*. The most natural interpretation of this has the Maja fully clothed (and says nothing about Goya's state of dress); this is the complement interpretation. But another possible interpretation has Goya fully clothed (and says nothing about the Maja's state of dress); in this *fully clothed* is probably best taken as an adverbial **phrase**.

Complement also contrasts with other kinds of expression that happen to follow the **verb** *be* in English, such as:

- the **present participle** (and what may follow it) in the **progressive**, as in *Phil is tearing his hair out;*
- the **past participle** (and what may follow it) in the **passive**, as in *Phil is admired by his class*.

The underlined expressions here are not complements.

Relationships Naturally, as the name suggests, complements of copular verbs only occur with **copular verbs** (or where the **verb** *be* is understood). Examples of **copular verbs** are *be, appear, seem, feel, remain, stay, look, smell* and *turn* in some, but not all, senses of these **verbs**. For instance, the **verb** *feel* in *Mary felt a fool* is a **copular verb**, and *a fool* is its complement; but in *Mary felt the wall*, the same **verb** is used as a **transitive verb** and *the wall* is its **(direct) object**. In the same way, the **verb** *smell* as in *This soup smells foul* is a **copular verb** and *foul* is its complement; but in *The dog smelt the bone*, the **verb** *smell* is a **transitive verb** and *the bone* is its **direct object**.

Complements of copular verbs can be **noun phrases, adjective phrases** or **prepositional phrases** – in fact all the same kinds of **phrases** as can be **predicate phrases**. There are examples of each kind in the '**Examples**' above.

A **noun phrase** which is the complement of a copular verb is most often **indefinite**, as in *My sister is a primary school teacher*, or *Her husband seems a nice guy*.

But **definite noun phrases** can occur as complements of the **verbs** *be*, as in *The man on the left is my husband* or *Rangers are the new Scottish champions*. When the complement of the **verb** *be* is a **definite noun phrase** like this, the **sentence** involved is called an 'equative **sentence**'. Such equative **sentences** can usually be reversed, so that the complement and the **subject** are interchanged, with only a change of emphasis, as in *The new Scottish champions are Rangers*.

It is possible for a given **clause** to be a complement both in the sense of complement of a copular verb and in the sense of **complement clause**, as in *The bad news is <u>that your uncle has remarried</u>*.

For interest   A classic pair of examples in modern syntactic theory is:

- *John is eager to please.*
- *John is easy to please.*

Traditional grammatical descriptions would label both the adjective phrases *eager to please* and *easy to please* as 'complements' of the verb *be*, and perhaps not make any further distinction between the two. But there is a crucial difference in meaning, which the superficial similarity in grammatical structure obscures. In *John is eager to please*, it is understood that the person who is to do the pleasing is John, whereas in *John is easy to please*, it understood that John is the person whom other people please easily. The second sentence can be paraphrased as *It is easy to please John*, but the first one cannot be paraphrased as **It is eager to please John*.

This example is just the tip of an iceberg, illustrating that superficially similar grammatical patterns can often carry quite different kinds of meanings, depending on the particular nouns, verbs and adjectives that fill their slots. This intriguing mismatch between grammar and meaning is not a peculiarity of English, but is found across languages generally.

It was just this kind of example that led a generation of linguists, in a scholarly movement called 'transformational grammar', to make a distinction between two different levels of grammatical structure, which they called 'deep structure' and 'surface structure'. The surface structure is (very roughly) how we see or hear a sentence; the deep structure is a related structure in which the elements might be re-arranged to give a more transparent representation of how we understand the sentence. In the example we have been discussing, the deep structure of *John is easy to please* would have been shown as something more like:

For someone to please John is easy.

And the deep structure of *John is eager to please* would have been shown as something more like.

John is eager (for John) to please people.

The theory of transformational grammar, inspired and led for over thirty years now by Noam Chomsky, has kept changing its details. But the fundamental insight, that there is more to the structure of sentences than meets the eye, has led to a very wide interest in the psychological nature of language, and has had some indirect practical spin-offs, in such fields as machine translation by computers.

Exercise Identify the words or phrases acting as complements of copular verbs in the following. There are six altogether.

1 *Gary is the champion and Nigel is desperate to beat him.*
2 *When he appeared to Mary, Gabriel appeared dazzling.*
3 *The weather turned cold and Seth turned the log on the fire.*
4 *When Zuleika came, his dreams came true.*
5 *Murray looked pale as he looked over the wintry scene.*

Compound sentence

Explanation A compound sentence is a **sentence** with two or more **main clauses** conjoined (or 'coordinated') by a **conjunction**.

Examples These are compound sentences:

- *I came, I saw, I conquered.*
- *Snowy died and he was buried in the garden.*
- *Either that child goes or I resign!*

Contrasts Compound sentences contrast with **sentences** which have only one **main clause**. These may be simple **sentences**, with no **subordinate clauses** or they may contain **subordinate clauses**. So the following are not compound sentences.

- *I came.*
- *When Snowy died, he was buried in the garden.*
- *If that child doesn't go, I resign!*

The definition of compound sentences involves the coordination of whole **sentences**, complete with all their normal parts. So cases in which just **verb phrases** or **predicate phrases** are **conjoined** do not produce compound sentences. Thus the following are not compound sentences.

- *I came, saw, and conquered.*
- *Snowy died and was buried in the garden.*

Relationships The **conjunctions** that can be used to form English compound sentences are *and, but* and *or*.

The **main clauses** conjoined in a compound sentence are usually in the same **mood (declarative/interrogative/imperative)**, but other combinations do occur, as in:

I keep telling him, but does he listen?	DECLARATIVE with INTERROGATIVE
Go now, and I'll catch you up.	IMPERATIVE with DECLARATIVE
Have some sherry, or would you prefer juice?	IMPERATIVE with INTERROGATIVE

41

Exercise Three of the following examples are compound sentences, consisting of two conjoined main clauses. Which are they? Identify the conjoined main clauses.

1 *Nineteen people were killed and twenty-two injured in a gun attack on black commuters.*
2 *The handwriting did not match that on Mr Maybrick's will, nor the Victorian style.*
3 *I had thought that I was a valued employee, but this action made me feel I was not really wanted.*
4 *I am happy with the compensation and think it is fair.*
5 *The man is believed to be a waiter from Radcliffe, but police said he would not be named until his parents had been informed.*
6 *They have been very short of grey mares on Dartmoor this year, and a grey gelding was the nearest to the real thing the organizing committee could produce.*

Compound tense

Explanation A construction traditionally called a 'compound tense' is one which uses more than one **word** to express some meaning related to time. Such compound tenses are formed using **auxiliary verbs**. In English, the **perfect, pluperfect** and **progressive** (and for some, also the **future**) are forms generally referred to as 'compound tenses'.

Examples The underlined forms in these **sentences** are compound tense forms.

- *Sue is weeding the front path.*
- *She has already done the back garden.*
- *She has been working at it all day.*

Contrasts Compound tenses contrast with simple **tenses**, which are formed by using just a single **word**, usually with some **affix**, such as the **present** and **past tenses** in English.

Although English **passives** use an **auxiliary verb** *be*, they are not necessarily examples of compound tenses, because the **passive** construction does not express a meaning related to time. Thus:

Murphy was accused.   PASSIVE in SIMPLE (PAST) TENSE
Murphy has been accused.   PASSIVE in COMPOUND TENSE (PERFECT)
Murphy had been accused.   PASSIVE in COMPOUND TENSE (PLUPERFECT)

Exercise Three of the following sentences use compound tenses. Which are they?

1 *The confessions are a hoax.*
2 *The will was written by someone else.*
3 *This would have been the publisher's best-selling book this year.*
4 *Lack of cash is threatening the party's future.*

5 *Both the central office and the research department have been told to accept cuts in their budgets.*

6 *Labour wants a ceiling on national expenditure during election campaigns.*

Compound word

Explanation   A compound word is a **word** or short sequence of **words**, composed of shorter **words**, but acting more or less as a single **word**. Compound words are longer than simple **words** but do not usually make whole **phrases** on their own. There can be compound words of various **parts of speech**, such as compound **nouns**, compound **verbs**, compound **adjectives** and even compound **conjunctions**. In English, the spelling rules for compound words are quite haphazard; sometimes they are spelt as single words, with no space between the parts, and sometimes as several **words**, with spaces, and sometimes with hyphens.

Examples   • *Bellboy, tractor driver, bus stop, airport, door key* and *lamppost* are English compound **nouns**.
• *spin-dry, hand wash, house-hunt, pistol-whip* and *earmark* are English compound **verbs**.
• *Red hot, medium-sized, blue-green, brick-hard* and *god-awful* are English compound **adjectives**.
• *Into* and *onto* can be seen as compound **prepositions**.
• *And/or* is a compound **conjunction**.

Contrasts   A compound word, though composed of several **words**, is not a **phrase**, as it cannot by itself serve as one of the major parts of a **sentence**, such as its **subject** or **predicate**. For example, *bellboy* needs an **article** to make it into a grammatically usable **subject** or **object** of a **sentence**, as in *The bellboy brought it* or *I gave it to a bellboy.*

A compound **noun** is different from a sequence of an **adjective** and a **noun**, because of the way the meanings of the parts combine to make the meaning of the whole. Compare, for example, *tractor driver* (compound **noun**) with *careless driver* (**adjective**-plus-**noun**). A careless driver is both careless and a driver, while a tractor driver is a driver but is certainly not a tractor! Note that the two sequences differ in the way they are normally stressed in pronunciation; *TRACTOR driver*, with stress on the first **word**, versus *careless DRIVER*, with stress on the second **word**. Note also that a **modifying adjective** must generally go before the first **word** of a compound **noun**, as in *careless tractor driver*, **tractor careless driver* is not grammatical.

Compound words contrast with **words** built up by the use of **affixes**. Thus, for example, *re-use, substandard, hyperventilate, prehistoric* and *pro-communist* would not usually be counted as compound words, because their first elements (*re-*,

43

sub-, hyper-, pre- and *pro-*) are **affixes** and cannot stand on their own as single **words**.

Relationships

One part of a compound word is usually clearly its **head**, in a general way able to represent the meaning of the whole compound. The **heads** of the various types of compound word are underlined in this list: *bellboy, spin-dry, red hot, into, and/or*. It can be seen that in English, the **head** of a compound word is always the last element, on the right-hand end. (This is not true of compound words in all languages, however.)

The ways in which the meanings of compound words are arrived at from the meanings of their parts are rather erratic and unpredictable. Some well-known examples are:

alligator shoes	shoes of alligator skin,	NOT shoes for alligators.
horseshoes	shoes for horses,	NOT shoes of horse skin.
bus shelter	shelter used waiting for a bus,	NOT shelter against buses.
bomb shelter	shelter against bombs,	NOT shelter used waiting for a bomb.

Many compound words are somewhat restricted in the forms in which they can occur. This is especially true of English compound **verbs**. For example, the **gerund** forms *hillwalking* and *rockclimbing* are acceptable, but these compound **verbs** do not occur in **finite** forms, such as **He hillwalked* or **She rockclimbs*.

Compound words can often be embedded inside other compound words, to form quite complex compound words. This is especially true of English compound **nouns**. Some examples follow, with underlining used to indicate the way in which the successive expressions nest inside one another.

- *mahogany coffee table*
- *malt whisky distillery*
- *felt-tip pen*
- *Parker fountain pen*
- *motor industry trouble-shooter*
- *compound word formation rules*
- *world champion freestyle relay swimming team*

For interest

As we have seen, the internal structure of compound words is in some ways erratic and unpredictable. This is also true to some extent of their pronunciation. Sometimes the stress (or normal emphasis in pronunciation) goes on the head of the compound, and sometimes on the modifying element. Some well-known English contrasting pairs are given below, with phonetic stress shown by capital letters.

OXFORD Street	Oxford CIRCUS	Oxford ROAD
CHRISTMAS cake	CHRISTMAS present	Christmas PUDDING
ORANGE juice	ORANGE peel	orange SQUASH

Say these examples out loud, to be sure you understand what the capital letters correspond to. It has so far proved impossible to formulate any general principle describing where the stress falls in such compounds.

The notoriously long words found in German are usually compound words. German simply doesn't put spaces inside its compound words. Examples are: *Jugendgemeinschaftdienst* (= *youth community service*), *Kleinkinderbewahranstalt* (= *little children care establishment (day nursery)*) and *Landesangehörigkeit* (= *country belongness (nationality)*).

Exercise   Identify the compound words in the following. There are eight altogether, including some more than two words long.

1 *In the village community centre, where there's a country music band on the loose, things are getting frenetic.*
2 *We cut hours off the journey time and benefit from the ideal spring weather conditions.*
3 *Joel wanted me to teach him to body-surf, but all I wanted to do was sun-bathe.*
4 *Dirk plunged into the pitch black ice-cold waters of the lake.*

Conditional

Explanation   A conditional clause is a **subordinate clause** introduced in English by *if* or *unless*, stating some condition under which an adjacent **clause** applies. In some languages, such as French, but not in English, there is a separate conditional **tense** for **verbs** which typically occur with conditional **clauses**. The closest English equivalents to a conditional **tense** involve *would* or, less frequently, *were to*. English **sentences** with *would*, if understood in a conditional way, even if there is no *if* present are sometimes also called conditional **sentences**.

Examples   The underlined **clauses** in the **sentences** below are conditional **clauses**.

- *If he takes my pawn, I'll win his knight.*
- *I'll win his knight if he takes my pawn.*
- *If he were to take my pawn, I would win his knight.*
- *I would win his knight if he were to take my pawn.*

Here is a French translation of the third of these examples, with the conditional **verb** underlined.

- *S'il prenait mon pion, je gagnerais son cavalier.*

Contrasts   Conditional **clauses**, introduced by *if*, are a type of adverbial **clause** (see SUBORDINATE CLAUSE). Other adverbial **clauses**, which are not

45

conditionals, are introduced by different **conjunctions**, such as *when, as, after, before* and *since* for temporal (or time) **clauses**, *where* for place **clauses** and *because* for reason **clauses**.

Clauses introduced by *if* in the sense of *whether*, as in *She asked if I was coming*, are not conditional **clauses**; they are **indirect** questions, and do not express any condition.

Relationships As the examples above show, a conditional **clause** can either precede or follow the **clause** on which it states a condition. This is true of adverbial **clauses** generally. The difference in ordering of the **clauses** is mainly a matter of emphasis.

Conditional **clauses** which express 'counterfactual' conditions, or conditions known not to be true, often contain a **subjunctive** form of the **verb** *be*, as in *If he were really my friend, he would bail me out*.

Reduced forms of conditional **clauses** can occur, such as *if so, if not* and *if the latter*. These should be called conditional **phrases**, as they contain no **verb**.

For interest You can get conditions inside conditions inside conditions, and so on without limit (as chess players know!). But these get hard to follow in the sentences of a human language. Using a variety of *ifs* and *unlesses*, and *then* can help to make some complicated examples clearer. For example:

- *If we're playing by the new rules, then if you haven't yet moved one of your pawns, then if you want to, you can move it two squares at once.*

Try to make up a more complex example than this, but keeping it as natural-sounding as possible.

Does *unless* mean *if... not*? Think carefully whether the next two sentences describe exactly the same conditions on John's taking the car.

- *John always takes the car, unless the weather is nice.*
- *John always takes the car, if the weather isn't nice.*

Exercise Underline the conditional clauses or phrases in the sentences below.

1 *If you come on Monday, we'll meet at 10.00; if on Tuesday, make it 11.00.*
2 *If it rains, you can stay here, if you like.*
3 *I hope to see you tomorrow, but if not, good luck!*
4 *Unless I hear to the contrary, I'll assume you want to go.*

Conjunction

Explanation A conjunction is a little **word** used to join together ('conjoin') two or more **clauses, phrases** or single **words**. For the most common type of conjunction, the **clauses, phrases** or **words** joined together are of the same type as each other. Linguists call such **words** which conjoin items of the same type 'coordinating conjunctions'

'Conjunction' is also applied, in the term 'subordinating conjunction' to certain **words** used to introduce **subordinate clauses**.

Examples   *And, or* and *but* are the most common English coordinating conjunctions, used to conjoin **clauses, phrases** and **words** of the same type.

English examples of subordinating conjunctions, used to introduce **subordinate clauses**, are *as, if, since, because, when, while, that.*

Contrasts   Conjunction is a **part of speech**, and so contrasts with all other **parts of speech**, such as **noun, verb, adjective** and **preposition**. In practice, the only other **part of speech** which is perhaps in danger of being confused with conjunction is **preposition**, because both conjunctions and **prepositions** are little **words** that can occur before **noun phrases**.

Some, but not all, subordinating conjunctions can also occur as **prepositions**, e.g. *as, since, before, after.* Thus *as* occurs as a subordinating conjunction in *I heard a loud bang as I was coming down the stairs.* But *as* occurs as a **preposition** in *As your father, I advise against it.*

Again, some, but not all, subordinating conjunctions can also occur as **interrogative words**, e.g. *when* and *where.* Thus *when* is a subordinating conjunction in *I was here when you came*; but it is an **interrogative word** in *When did you come?*

Relationships   Coordinating conjunctions can conjoin **clauses**, as in:

- *George played guitar and Ringo played the drums.*
- *George played guitar but Ringo played the fool.*
- *Did John write the lyrics or was it Paul?*

The **clauses** thus conjoined are usually of the same **mood**, i.e. both **declaratives**, or both **imperatives**, or both **interrogatives**. It is occasionally possible to conjoin a **declarative** and an **interrogative** with *but*, as in *The Democrats are ahead in the polls, but can they stay there?* (All of these examples are of coordinated **main clauses**, and so are **compound sentences**.)

Below are some examples where *and* and *or* conjoin single **words** (underlined). Note that the **words** conjoined always belong to the same **part of speech** (**common noun, verb, adjective, preposition**, etc.).

- *Antony and Cleopatra died tragically.*
- *Remember to get bread, milk, cheese and cereals.*
- *We jived and boogied till dawn.*
- *A French or Italian kid was looking for you.*
- *Can you reach under or behind the sideboard?*

Finally, some examples of **phrases** conjoined by coordinating conjunctions, with the conjoined **phrases** underlined.

- *Heaven is <u>two punnets of raspberries</u>, <u>some double cream</u>, and <u>a bottle of Cabernet Sauvignon</u>.*
- *The boy with fair hair <u>lowered himself down the last few feet of rock</u> and <u>began to pick his way towards the lagoon</u>.*
- *Mr. Jones, of the Manor Farm, <u>had locked the hen-houses for the night</u>, but <u>was too drunk to remember to shut the pop-holes</u>.*
- *He's either <u>desperate for attention</u> or <u>high on magic mushrooms</u>.*
- *It went <u>under the settee</u> or <u>behind the sideboard</u>.*
- *In my <u>younger</u> and <u>more vulnerable</u> years my father gave me some advice that I've been turning over in my mind ever since.*

Again, the conjoined items usually have to be of the same type. For example, you can't use a coordinating conjunction to link a **verb phrase** with an adverbial **phrase**, as in **Janet smokes Turkish cigarettes and too much.*

Some coordinating conjunctions have an optional companion **word** that goes before the whole set of conjoined items, and can often make the meaning a bit clearer. Thus with *or*, we get *either*, as in *Either apologize or leave now!* And the **word** *both* similarly can go with *and*, as in *Both John and Paul wrote lyrics.*

Noun phrases conjoined with *and*, even if they are all individually **singular**, produce a single 'coordinate' **plural noun phrase**. Thus, even though *the world* is **singular**, and so is *his wife*, the **phrase** made by conjoining the two is **plural**, as can be seen by the **agreement** in *The world and his wife were at Scunthorpe market today.* Conversely, when **singular** items are conjoined with *or*, the resulting **phrase** is still **singular**, as in *Either Father Blaney or the Monsignor is going to perform the ceremony.*

When more than two items are conjoined, it is usual to use only one coordinating conjunction, between the last two items in the list (e.g. *John, Paul, George and Ringo*). But sometimes the conjunction is also inserted earlier, for a kind of emphasis.

For interest Sentences with conjoined clauses can often be roughly paraphrased by less long-winded sentences with conjoined phrases, so the following pairs describe similar situations:

- *We saw penguins, we saw gibbons and we saw a gorilla.*
  We saw penguins, gibbons, and a gorilla.
- *Mum will meet you from school or I will meet you from school.*
  Mum or I will meet you from school.

It is possible to formulate an exact rule which produces the shorter versions from the longer versions by a process of deleting repeated elements (and adjusting agreement, where necessary). Here's a first stab at the rule:

RULE

When conjoined clauses contain identical material in the same positions, delete all copies of this material except for any copy at the outer edge (left or right) of the whole sentence.

Thus in the first example above, the second and third instances of the repeated *we saw* can get deleted, and if you delete them, you are left with the appropriate shorter sentence. Try it, with a pencil. In the second example, the repeated material is *will meet you from school*; here we have to delete the first copy of this, as the second is at an outer edge of the sentence. Do it, and you get the appropriate shorter sentence.

Is life always so rewardingly neat and simple for grammarians who want to make exact statements about the languages they describe? Would the rule just given work for cases like the following? Using a pencil, try doing the deletions allowed by the rule, to see if you get an appropriate result.

- *We meet on Sunday mornings and we meet on Wednesday evenings.*
  We meet on Sunday mornings and Wednesday evenings.

- *Bill gave Helen a book, and Bill gave Mary a book.*
  Bill gave Helen and Mary a book.

- *Jane read 'War and Peace' and Julia read 'Ulysses'.*
  Jane read 'War and Peace' and Julia 'Ulysses'.

Well, the rule works fine for the first two pairs of examples. The second pair is particularly impressive, because it involves two different sets of repeated material, namely *Bill gave* at the front of each clause, and *a book* at the back of each clause. Deleting the innermost examples of each, you get the desired shorter sentence. But, dammit, the rule won't work for the last pair, will it? According to the rule, you should be able to delete both instances of *read*, because neither is on the outside edge of the whole sentence. But if you do that, you lose the word *read*, and the information it conveys, altogether, with the garbled **Jane 'War and Peace' and Julia 'Ulysses'*. Back to the drawing board – see if you can modify the rule to give the right results.

Exercise In the following sentences, there are many instances of conjoined structures, some inside others. Underline the conjoined items in each case. You will get double underlining in some places, due to conjoined structures being inside each other. The first example is done for you, to give you the idea.

- *Once upon a time there were four little rabbits, and*

  their names were Flopsy, Mopsy, Cotton-tail and Peter.

(This is two clauses conjoined to make a sentence; inside the second clause, four words (all proper names) are conjoined.)

Now you do these below:

1 *You may go into the fields or down the lane, but don't go into Mr. McGregor's garden.*
2 *Now run along and don't get into mischief.*
3 *Then old Mrs. Rabbit took a basket and her umbrella, and went through the wood to the baker's.*

4 *Flopsy, Mopsy, and Cotton-tail, who were good little bunnies, went down the lane to gather blackberries:*
but Peter, who was very naughty, ran straight away to Mr. McGregor's garden, and squeezed under the gate!

Contraction

Explanation An **affix** or a **word** which has been produced by simply leaving out a few sounds or letters from a longer **word** or sequence of several **words** is a contraction. In English, the missing letters are often signalled by an apostrophe.

Examples English *I'm, you'll, we'd, she's, they've, wouldn't, won't, 'em* and *o'* are **contractions** of *I am, you will, we would* (or *we had*), *she is* (or *she has*), *they have, would not, will not, them* and *of*, respectively.

Contrasts Not all English forms with an apostrophe are contractions. So **possessive** forms such as *John's, Mary's* and *those people's* are not contractions, because they have not been shortened from anything else. On the other hand, the instances of *-'s* in forms spelt identically, as in *John's here at last* or *Mary's got the measles* are contractions, of *is* and *has*, respectively.

The leaving out of whole **words** or sequences of **words**, because they can be understood from the context, as in *Amanda did* (did what?) is not contraction, but, usually, **ellipsis**.

Relationships Contractions almost invariably involve the minor **parts of speech** (or 'function words'), such as **auxiliaries** and **pronouns**. They hardly ever involve the major **parts of speech** (or 'content words'), such as **nouns, main verbs** and **adjectives**. So, for example, forms of the **verb** *have* used as **auxiliaries**, as in *Jean has gone* and *We have won* can be contracted, as in *Jean's gone* and *We've won*. But the same forms used as **main verbs**, as in *Jean has the measles* and *We have three children* cannot (in most **dialects**) be contracted, as in the hypothetical **Jean's the measles* and **We've three children*. (This last example is more acceptable than the former, however.)

When a **word** from a major **part of speech**, such as a **noun, main verb** or **adjective** is involved in a contraction, this is usually a sign that the **word** concerned is changing its status, and becoming more like a **word** from a minor **part of speech**. So, for example, in some (mainly American) dialects, the contraction of *want to* to *wanna* and *going to* to *gonna* is a sign that *want (to)* and *going (to)* are becoming more like **auxiliaries**.

English follows many quite intricate rules in its possibilities for contraction. For example, only the first *is* can be contracted in *Judy is here, and Penny is too*. And only the first *has* in *Phil has taken more than Bill has* can be contracted. The rule here seems to be that a contraction is not allowed immediately before a missing but 'understood' **word** or **phrase**, like the understood final *here* in the first example, or the understood final *taken* in the second. Somehow the full weight of the uncontracted form seems to be needed to fill the space left by the omitted **words**.

In English, at least, contractions typically don't pile up on each other. So *she is not* can be contracted to either *she isn't* or *she's not*, but not to *she'sn't. And *of them* can be contracted to either *o'them* or *of 'em*, but not to *o'em. The reason may often be the relative unpronounceability of a double contraction, in which unusual sequences of vowels or consonants are brought together.

Sometimes a contraction is accompanied by a slight change in the rest of the resulting **word**. This happens, for example, when English *will not* is contracted to *won't*, where the *-ill* is replaced by *-o-*.

There is nothing inherently ungrammatical about contractions. Most languages have them as part of their system of **grammar**, and, as we have seen from the English examples, the possibilities for contraction are often closely bound up with other grammatical factors.

Contractions occur more frequently in speech than in writing.

For interest   The short form *'em* is now naturally thought of as a contraction of *them*. But in fact dropping an initial *th-* like this is not general. Can you think of any other English words beginning with a *th-* sound that can be dropped in this way? Even the closely related *their* and *they* cannot be contracted in this way. You can't reduce *of their* to *of 'eir or *have they* to *have'ey (in standard spoken English). Actually the short form *'em* is historically not related to *them*, but comes from a competing Middle English pronoun *hem*, which survives in the short form *'em*.

Exercise   In the following sentence, five separate contractions are possible. Write the sentence down with all the contractions carried out.

   • *Jessica is aware that we have taken her car, but I am afraid we did not tell her that it has got a dent in its side.*

Copula, Copular verb

Explanation   In English, the copula is any form of the **verb** *be* used as a 'link' or 'coupling' between its **subject** and a following **phrase**. The link either expresses identity or describes some property or attribute of the **subject**. (*Copula* is Latin for *link*.)

Copular verbs are a small set of **verbs** which are understood in a very similar way to *be*, in identifying a **subject** or linking it with some property or attribute.

Examples   For English, the **verb** *be* (but not in all its uses – see **Contrasts** below) is often referred to as 'the copula'. That is, *be* is often taken as the only copula, just as *the* is the only **definite article**. But sometimes other copular verbs are, for simplicity, also called 'copulas'.

Applied to some other languages, *être* is the French copula, and *sein* is the German copula.

English copular verbs include *seem, appear, remain, become, look, sound, taste, feel* and *smell*. The last five **verbs** in this list are only copular in one of their uses (see **Contrasts** below).

In the **sentences** below, the copular verbs, including forms of *be*, are underlined:

- *It was love at first sight.*
- *Washington is the capital of the USA.*
- *George Washington became the first president.*
- *The wine tasted bitter.*

Contrasts   Forms of the **verb** *be* which occur as **auxiliaries** in the **progressive** (e.g. *Jutta is finishing her thesis*) or the **passive** (e.g. *Barry was sued by his landlord*) are not normally regarded as instances of the copula, as their main job in such **sentences** is indicating something about the meaning of the **main verb**.

Some **verbs**, including *look, sound, taste, feel* and *smell*, have both a copular use and a non-copular use. Here are some examples.

USE AS COPULAR VERB	USE AS NON-COPULAR (TRANSITIVE) VERB
Rosie sounds very cheerful.	*Rosie sounded the alarm.*
The roses smelt past their best.	*Jody smelt the roses.*
Helen looked foolish.	*Helen looked down the road.*
The wine tasted oily.	*Sue tasted the wine.*

The key to counting as a copular verb is the possibility of an obvious implication involving the **verb** *be*. Thus, with *The wine tasted oily*, an obvious implication is that the wine really IS oily.

Relationships   The **phrase** after a copular verb, which the copular verb links to its **subject**, is always its **predicate**, or **predicate phrase**; such a **phrase** is also known, due to the forest of terminology in this particular area, as the **complement** of the copular verb.

A copular verb is always a **main verb**, and never an **auxiliary**, although it can combine with **auxiliaries** (including *be*), as in *Joanne had not felt well* or *Nicola is being a pest* or *I will be remaining here*. In their ability to combine with the range of **auxiliaries**, English copular verbs are just like other **main verbs**.

Copular verbs fall into two broad groups:

1 Describing some kind of state that the thing or person referred to by the **subject** is in; **verbs** of this sort include *be, remain, seem* and *appear*.
2 Describing the result of some change affecting the thing or person referred to by the **subject**; **verbs** of this sort include *become, turn, grow* and *get*.

Copular verbs can occur in both **main** and **subordinate clauses**.

For interest   Some languages have no copula, or equivalent of the English verb *be*. Other languages have no copula in the present tense, though they do have a copula in other tenses. Russian and Arabic are such languages. In such languages, there can be sentences with no verbs at all. Here are some examples:

RUSSIAN
On amerikanyets
He American   (= *He is an American.*)
ARABIC
Huuwa il   mudarris
He   the teacher   (= *He is the teacher.*)

But if these sentences are converted into the past tense, then a past tense form of a copula appears, as in:

RUSSIAN
On byl amerikanyets
He was American   (= *He was an American.*)
ARABIC
Huuwa kaan il   mudarris
He   was the teacher   (= *He was the teacher.*)

The fact that languages can do without a copula, or only use one for certain tenses, shows that the English copula in fact carries very little meaning. It is often said that the copula is merely a carrier of tense and possibly agreement, and has no proper verb-like meaning of its own.

There once was a movement known as 'General Semantics', founded by Alfred Korzybski and taken further by S. I. Hayakawa. Many of the writings of this movement were inspired by the worthy intention of making people aware of how language can be abused, and they were concerned with making practical suggestions for improving the use of words for clear and honest communication. But some of their suggestions were not so practical; one idea put forward (it is difficult to tell how seriously) was to replace the English language by a new and modified version of English, called 'E-prime', from which the verb *be* had been eliminated entirely[2]. Whatever advantages this might conceivably have had, it is a fact that it has never been possible to enforce revision on such a sweeping scale on a whole language community.

Exercise   Identify the copular verbs in these examples:

1 *On top of it all, the cancer wing was 'number thirteen'.*
2 *That winter was the coldest in living memory.*
3 *Gayle appears more isolated than she used to.*
4 *She is becoming less dependent on her neighbours.*
5 *I hope she won't grow too eccentric.*

---

2 See *To Be or Not: an E-Prime Anthology*, edited by D. D. Bourland and P. D. Johnston, (ISGS, San Francisco, 1991).

Count noun

Explanation A count noun is a type of **common noun** which can be used to refer to an individual object or to the objects in a countable collection, rather than to a mass of indivisible stuff.

Examples *Apple, barn, desks, envelope, elephant, girls, idea, month, mountain, ravine, phenomenon, principle, towns* and *yacht* are all count nouns.

Contrasts Count nouns contrast primarily with **mass nouns** (such as *water, nonsense, hydrogen* and *impoliteness*).

A count noun is a type of **common noun**, and therefore contrasts also with **proper name** and, further afield, with other **parts of speech**, such as **verb** and **adjective**.

Relationships **Count nouns** have both **singular** and **plural** forms. So *lamp* is a count noun, as it has a **plural** *lamps*.

As the name implies, count nouns occur comfortably with **cardinal numerals**, as in *five hundred envelopes* or *twenty months*.

In English, the 'quantifiers' *many* and *fewer* occur **modifying** count nouns, but not **mass nouns**; compare *many rivers* with **many water*, and *fewer bottles* with **fewer wine*.

Some **nouns** can serve as both **count** and **mass nouns**. The **noun** *war* is an example. In *War is ghastly*, *war* is a mass **noun**, whereas in *The wars between Rome and Carthage were ruinous*, *war* is used as a count noun. Other examples are *love* and *difficulty*. In *Love is a many-splendoured thing*, *love* is a **mass noun**, but in *The three greatest loves of my life are Wagner, Wagner and Wagner*, *love* is used as a count noun, in the **plural** form and with an **article**. In *She did it without difficulty*, *difficulty* is a **mass noun**, but in *There are three difficulties with your suggestion*, it is a count noun. When such **nouns** (which need not be **abstract**) are used as **mass nouns**, they typically have a **generic** sense.

Count nouns can be used with all the usual kinds of **modifiers** of **common nouns**, such as **articles, demonstratives, possessives, adjectives, relative clauses** and **prepositional phrases**.

Count nouns can be either **abstract** or concrete, as the examples above show.

For interest Some English common nouns, like *sheep* and *deer*, have an 'uninflected plural'; the singular and plural forms are identical. Other examples are *fish, trout, salmon* and *greenfly*. What these cases seem to have in common is that the creatures concerned can be treated as a mass – the individual animals aren't important. So these nouns are in a sense halfway between count nouns and mass nouns. They can still be used with numerals, but they have no distinct plural. The names of a number of wild animals are like this for some speakers, but not for others, so a big-game hunter might say *I shot three lion*, or *There are elephant in those trees*. A historian of the American West might well write *The buffalo were all killed by the railroad companies.*

In English, some plants are named by count nouns, like *rose, azalea, daffodil* and *tulip,* while other plants are named by mass nouns, like *grass, seaweed* and *moss.* You can say *I bought a rose and three tulips,* but *I bought a grass and three mosses* is odd (although it would be less odd to a fanatical gardener!). Try to fill out these lists of count and mass plant names with another twenty or so examples of each. Do you find borderline cases?

Exercise Identify the count nouns in the following sentences. There are thirteen of them in total, including a repetition.

1 *Oxford is the city of dreaming spires, but Cambridge is the city of aspiring dreams.*
2 *Once there were more winners of Nobel prizes from one Cambridge college than from Japan.*
3 *The editor will send manuscripts to specialists in biology and linguistics.*
4 *I have now discussed the design of your book with a designer.*

Dative case

Explanation In a language with a **case** system, if the **indirect object** in a **clause** can be recognized as such from its form, it is typically said to be in the dative case. The term is not useful for English, which has no distinctively dative forms (as there are in languages with extensive **case** systems, such as Latin, German and Russian).

Examples Here are some German forms where datives are distinct (the **singular personal pronouns**):

ENGLISH	GERMAN		
	NOMINATIVE	ACCUSATIVE	DATIVE
I/me	*ich*	*mich*	*mir*
you	*Du*	*Dich*	*Dir*
he/him	*er*	*ihn*	*ihm*
she/her	*sie*	*sie*	*ihr*
it	*es*	*es*	*ihm*

French has a very few forms where **accusative** and dative are distinguished. *Lui* (= *to him, to her, to it*) and *leur* (= *to them*) are specifically dative pronouns.

Contrasts In languages which have it, dative case contrasts with other **cases**, such as **nominative** and **accusative**. But whereas these last two have different forms in English for at least a few **personal pronouns** (*I/me, he/him, she/her, we/us, they/them*), there is no distinctive dative form of any **word** in English.

Relationships   Dative case, in languages where it occurs, is always closely identified with **indirect objects**, which occur with 'ditransitive' **verbs**, such as (the translations of) *give*, *send* and *return*.

The items which receive dative, or any other **case**, are always **nouns**, **pronouns** or **noun phrases**. In languages with **case** systems and **agreement** systems, dative case, like other **cases**, may be marked on other **parts of speech** which **modify nouns**, such as **demonstratives**, **articles** and **adjectives**.

Declarative

Explanation   A declarative **clause**, used on its own, is the typical way of making a statement, or assertion, as opposed to asking a question or giving an order. In English, the grammatical shape of a normal declarative **clause** involves a **subject** occurring before all the **verbs** in the **clause**. A declarative **clause** standing on its own is a declarative **sentence**.

Examples   The following are declarative **sentences**:
- *My father had a small estate in Nottinghamshire.*
- *Someone must have been telling lies about Joseph K.*
- *Well, Prince, so Genoa and Lucca are now just family estates of the Buonapartes.*
- *At about nine o'clock in the morning at the end of November, during a thaw, the Warsaw train was approaching Petersburg at full speed.*

Contrasts   Declarative contrasts with two other types of **clause**, namely **interrogative** and **imperative**. An **interrogative** is typically used to ask a question, and its **finite verb** (or **auxiliary**) precedes its **subject**. An **imperative** is typically used to give a command, and has no **subject** at all.

Relationships   In a few declaratives, the **subject** switches initial position with another **phrase**, often an adverbial **phrase**, to achieve a particular stylistic or rhetorical effect, as in *In the beginning was the Word*, or *Naked came the stranger*.

Where they do not stand on their own, as whole declarative **sentences**, several declarative **clauses** can be joined by **conjunctions**, such as *and*, *or* and *but*, to other declarative **clauses**, to make **compound sentences**. For example:
- *It was a bright cold day in April, and the clocks were striking thirteen.*
- *The schoolmaster was leaving the village and everybody seemed sorry.*
- *To the red country and part of the gray country of Oklahoma, the last rains came gently, and they did not cut the scarred earth.*

Declarative **clauses** (but rarely **imperative** or **interrogative clauses**) can occur as **subordinate clauses**, or provide the basis from which **subordinate**

clauses are formed, as below, where the declarative (or declarative-based) **subordinate clauses** are underlined:

- *It is a truth universally acknowledged, <u>that a single man in possession of a good fortune, must be in want of a wife</u>.*
- *Miss Brooke had that kind of beauty <u>which seems to be thrown into relief by poor dress</u>.*
- *Stately, plump Buck Mulligan came from the stairhead, <u>bearing a bowl of lather on which a mirror and a razor lay crossed</u>.*

A declarative **clause** is sometimes said to be 'in the declarative **mood**'. The term '**mood**' similarly applies to **interrogative** and **imperative**. (But '**mood**' is, unfortunately, also used for the contrast between **indicative** and **subjunctive** forms of a **verb**, which is in fact a different matter.)

For interest In general, the typical uses of declaratives, interrogatives and imperatives are as follows:

Declarative	making a statement
Interrogative	asking a question
Imperative	giving a command

But this pattern is often broken to achieve indirect effects, for such reasons as politeness. For example, *Note that this office is closed between 1.00 and 2.00* is imperative in form, starting with a verb and lacking an explicit subject, but is essentially used to make a statement, rather than to give a command. Similarly, *Could you pass the salt?*, which has the form of an interrogative, is essentially a disguised, polite way of expressing a command.

Exercise Identify the declarative clauses in the following. There are eighteen in all.

1 *Except for the Marabar Caves – and they are twenty miles off – the city of Chandrapore represents nothing extraordinary.*

2 *Ours is essentially a tragic age, so we refuse to take it tragically.*

3 *It was the best of times, it was the worst of times, it was the age of wisdom, it was the age of foolishness, it was the epoch of belief, it was the epoch of incredulity, it was the season of Light, it was the season of Darkness, it was the spring of hope, it was the winter of despair, we had everything before us, we had nothing before us, we were all going direct to Heaven, we were all going direct the other way.*

Definite

Explanation The term 'definite' is traditionally used almost exclusively in connection with the definite **article**, *the*, to distinguish it from the **indefinite article**, *a*.

It is in fact very useful to extend the use of 'definite' (and '**indefinite**') to whole **noun phrases**, so that we can talk, for example, about 'definite **noun** phrases'. The typical use of 'definite **noun phrases**' is to refer to some specific object (person, thing, idea, and so on) that the hearer is already aware of, either from general knowledge, or from the specific context of the conversation.

Examples *The* is the definite **article**.

The prototypical English definite **noun phrase** begins with *the*, as in *the winner of the 1994 London Marathon*. Other English **noun phrases** classified as definite by linguists include:

- **phrases** beginning with a **demonstrative**, such as *this* or *those*, e.g. *that woman*;
- **phrases** beginning with a **possessive**, such as *my*, *your*, *his*, *their*, e.g. *my former house*;
- **proper names**, e.g. *Dan Quayle*, *New York*, *Philip*,
- most **personal pronouns**, e.g. *I*, *me*, *you*, *him*, *us*.

Contrasts The definite **article**, *the*, contrasts with *a*, the **indefinite article**.

Definite **noun phrases** contrast with **indefinite noun phrases**, which begin with the **indefinite article** or have no **article** at all, **phrases** such as *an ostrich*, *some water* and *unripe bananas*.

Most **personal pronouns**, such as *I*, *he*, *she* and *it* are definite, but the word *one* can be used as an **indefinite pronoun**, as in *I was looking for a tie, but couldn't find one*. Compare this with *I was looking for a tie, but couldn't find it*, where the final **pronoun** *it* is definite.

Relationships Only **noun phrases** (i.e. not other kinds of **phrase**, such as **verb phrases** or **adjective phrases**) can be definite or **indefinite**.

'Definite' can be thought of as basically meaning 'already known to the hearer'. So we say *the sun*, because there is only one sun (in our usual day-to-day world view), and everyone knows about it. Similarly, if I say to you *Put it on the compost heap*, I seem, by using *the*, to presuppose that you know the particular compost heap I am talking about. Likewise the use of **possessive** *her* in *I put it in her pigeonhole* presupposes that the hearer will be able to identify the particular pigeonhole in question. Again, one doesn't use a **personal pronoun**, such as *she* 'out of the blue', or one's hearer will not know who one is talking about.

In addition to this typical use of definite expressions, there are others. One clearly different use is in **generic** expressions, like *The blue whale migrates to its breeding grounds every spring*. Obviously this is not referring to any specific individual animal that the hearer already knows about, but to a whole species.

For interest Not all languages have a definite article, and they have to indicate definiteness by other means, perhaps by demonstratives.

In some languages, there is a stricter connection between definiteness and the structure of the whole sentence than in English. For example, in some languages (Arabic is one), the subject of a sentence must be definite. So you can't translate, for example, *A man was looking for you just now* directly into such a language. You have to get around the restriction by a paraphrase – perhaps an 'existential' construction, something like *There was a man looking for you just now*.

Russian has no definite article. How, then, does Russian manage to express the difference between *the book* and *a book*? It does it by ordering the words in a sentence differently. Here are some relevant examples.

> *na stole kniga*
> on table book (= *There is a book on the table.*)
>
> *kniga na stole*
> book on table (= *The book is on the table.*)

Hungarian, unusually and interestingly, reflects the definiteness of an object noun phrase in the form of the verb. Here are some examples – note the different endings on *làt* (= *saw*).

> *a pék làt egy lànyt*
> the baker saw a girl (= *The baker saw a girl.*)
>
> *a pék làtjà a lànyt*
> the baker saw the girl (= *The baker saw the girl.*)
>
> *làtsz egy lànyt*
> (you) saw a girl (= *You saw a girl.*)
>
> *làtod a lànyt*
> (you) saw the girl (= *You saw the girl.*)

The whole system of Hungarian verb endings in fact reflects, not just the definiteness or indefiniteness of the object, but also information concerning the person and number of the subject and the person (1st, 2nd, 3rd) of the object.

Exercise   Identify the definite noun phrases in the following sentences. There are eleven of them in all, including one inside another. (Remember all the different kinds mentioned in **Relationships** above.)

1 *When she was home from her boarding school I used to see her almost every day sometimes, because their house was right opposite the Town Hall Annexe.*
2 *Wilson sat on the balcony of the Bedford Hotel with his bald pink knees thrust against the ironwork.*

Demonstrative

Explanation   A demonstrative is a **word** that typically **modifies** a **noun**, and is used to indicate the position of something in relation to the speaker. In speech, demonstratives are often accompanied by a pointing gesture.

Examples   There are just four demonstratives in English, the **words** *this, that, these* and *those.*

Contrasts   Demonstrative is a **word**-class and thus contrasts with all other **word**-classes and **parts of speech**, such as **noun, article, adjective** and **pronoun**. If a **word** in a given **sentence** is a demonstrative, it cannot be any other **part of speech** in that **sentence**.

Some grammarians have called the **words** *this, that, these,* and *those* 'demonstrative **adjectives**', which is understandable because both demonstratives and **adjectives modify nouns**. But there are differences between them. Demonstratives always precede any **numerals** and **adjectives modifying** a **noun**, as in *these five elegant old houses.* **Adjectives** cannot precede **numerals** like this. Also, while most **adjectives** can be used predicatively after the **verb** *be,* as in *The policemen was angry,* demonstratives cannot normally be used in this position, as **The policeman was that* is odd.

The demonstrative *that,* which is always pronounced with a full, unreduced [a] vowel (rhyming with *hat*), should not be confused with the other **word** spelt the same way, but usually pronounced with a reduced 'schwa', or neutral, vowel (rhyming with the last syllable in *delicate*). The latter **word** occurs in **sentences** such as *The man that I'm looking for isn't here* or *Please say that I'm not at home,* where it is either a **relative pronoun** or a subordinating **conjunction**.

Relationships   Demonstratives in English are very much like the **definite article** and the **possessives**, occurring with almost exactly the same combinations of other **words** as them. As noted above, demonstratives, like *the* and the **possessives**, always precede any other **words**, such as **numerals** and **adjectives**, **modifying nouns**. So we can get <u>the</u> *three old red blouses,* <u>those</u> *three old red blouses,* <u>these</u> *three old red blouses,* and <u>her</u> *three old red blouses.*

Linguistics identifies a **word**-class called 'determiner', to which demonstratives, **possessives** and **articles** belong.

The main difference between English demonstratives and *the* is that, by **ellipsis**, the **noun** implicitly modified by a demonstrative may be omitted, leaving the demonstrative standing alone, although the omitted **noun** is generally understood by the hearer from the context in which this happens. Examples are seen in *Those are old but <u>these</u> are new.* In such cases, it might be preferable to say that the demonstratives actually occur as **pronouns**, as they do occupy the place of a whole **noun phrase**. In any case, you can't leave *the* standing on its own like this, as in **The are old.*

Demonstratives are always **definite**, again like the **definite article** and the **possessives**, introducing (or standing for, as above) **phrases** which identify specific things presupposed to be known to the hearer. I can't sensibly use the expression *that woman* to you, unless you know which woman I am talking about. I might simultaneously make this clear by a pointing gesture, or I might have mentioned the woman in question before.

The English demonstratives make a neat two-by-two system, combining **number (singular/plural)** with relative nearness to, or relative distance from, the speaker, as shown in the table below.

	SINGULAR	PLURAL
NEAR TO SPEAKER	*this*	*these*
FAR FROM SPEAKER	*that*	*those*

Words, like demonstratives especially, which anchor the reference of an expression to the actual situation of speaking, are known as 'deictic' **words** (from the Greek **word** for *pointing*).

In some non-standard **dialects** of English, *they* and *them* are used as demonstratives, as in *They hippies is at it again* or *Give me two of them green ones*. It would be interesting to know whether any such **dialect** uses both *they* and *them* as demonstratives, systematically keeping *they* for **nominative (subject) noun phrases** and *them* for **accusative (object) noun phrases**.

For interest In some other languages, demonstratives are less likely to be conflated with adjectives, because they more clearly occur in different positions. In French and Italian, for example, demonstratives precede nouns, but adjectives typically follow nouns. Examples, both meaning *this* (or *that*) *white house* are:

FRENCH
cette   maison blanche
this/that house   white

ITALIAN
questa   casa   bianca
this   house   white

And in other languages, demonstratives do not behave like the definite article. In Arabic, for example, a noun phrase can have both the definite article before and a demonstrative after the modified noun, as in:

il   walad da
the boy   this   (= *this boy*)

The English demonstratives, as noted above, make a two-way distinction between 'near to speaker' and 'far from speaker'. Some other languages make a three-way distinction, and not necessarily in the same way. For example, Spanish demonstratives make the following distinctions:

NEAR TO SPEAKER	*este*
IN BETWEEN FAR FROM AND NEAR TO SPEAKER	*ese*
FAR FROM SPEAKER	*aquel*

And Japanese has a rather different three-way system:

NEAR TO SPEAKER	*kono*
NEAR TO HEARER	*sono*
FAR FROM BOTH SPEAKER AND HEARER	*ano*

Finally, we show the extremely rich and complex system of demonstratives from the Alaskan Yup'ik Eskimo language[3]. In this system, there are three classes of demonstratives, for referring to three different types of things. The three different demonstrative classes are called 'extended', 'restricted' and 'obscured'. The main uses of these three kinds of demonstratives are as follows.

DEMONSTRATIVE TYPE	USED FOR REFERRING TO
Extended	large expanses of land or water, or lengthy or moving objects
Restricted	fairly small, close and visible objects that are stationary or not moving very much
Obscured	objects farther away and not clearly in sight.

Now, this is by no means the end of the complexity in this system. These three different classes of demonstratives are applied in combination with a refined classification of relationships to the speaker or hearer, as follows.

EXTENDED	RESTRICTED	OBSCURED	
man'a	*una*		*this* (near speaker)
tamana	*tauna*		*that* (near listener)
		imna	*the aforementioned one*
ukna			*the one approaching speaker*
augna	*ingna*	*amna*	*the one going away from the speaker*
agna	*ikna*	*akemna*	*the one across there*
qaugna	*kiugna*	*qamna*	*the one inland, inside, upriver*
qagna	*keggna*	*qakemna*	*the one outside*
un'a	*kan'a*	*camna*	*the one below, toward river*
unegna	*ugna*	*cakemna*	*the one downriver, by the exit*
paugna	*pingna*	*pamna*	*the one up there, away from river*
pagna	*pikna*	*pakemna*	*the one up above*

Exercise Identify the demonstratives in the following sentences. There are five in all.

1 *We know that that man was seen at the scene later that day.*
2 *That Molly never had children herself is one of those tragic ironies.*
3 *Moses chose those roses to decorate these theses.*

3 The data here comes from Stephen Anderson and Ed Keenan's article 'Deixis' in *Language Typology and Syntactic Description, volume III: Grammatical Categories and the Lexicon*, edited by Timothy Shopen (Cambridge University Press, 1985). Anderson and Keenan originally got this data from a report, *Yup'ik Eskimo Grammar*, by Irene Reed, Osahito Miyaoka, Steven Jacobson, Paschel Afcan and Michael Krauss, published by the Alaska Native Language Center, University of Alaska, Fairbanks, Alaska, 1977.

Dialect

Explanation   A dialect is any distinct form of a language, identifiable by its **grammar** and vocabulary, associated with a group of people. Normally, a group of people has to be widely noticeable, as a group, before it becomes associated in the minds of the general public with a particular named dialect. Everybody speaks a dialect, since everybody can be associated with some social group, even if the dialect (or the group) does not have a well-known name.

Examples   In Britain, well-known dialects of English (and the places associated with them) include: Cockney (London), Scouse (Liverpool), Geordie (Newcastle), Brummie (Birmingham). For the United States, some people identify 'Black English' as a dialect, and various states or regions, such as Texas or the Deep South, are associated with their own characteristic dialects.

Not everyone living in a city speaks its dialect, just as not every person belonging to some identifiable group speaks a dialect associated with it. In Britain, at least, there can be some social stigma in speaking a regional dialect, and some people adopt features of the standard dialect, not strongly identified with any geographical locality. But inevitably such a move tends to identify such speakers with more upper-class, or more upwardly mobile, sections of society. In areas where there is much immigration (e.g. Alaska, New York City, London) there are usually speakers of many dialects (or even languages), associated with the origins of the incomers, rather than with their newly adopted groups.

Contrasts   In careful usage, the term 'dialect' is contrasted with 'accent', which is a matter of pronunciation, rather than of vocabulary and **grammar**. But dialect and accent typically go together; if you speak with the accent of one group, you normally speak with its dialect as well. Bernard Shaw highlighted this amusingly when he had his heroine Eliza Doolittle speak with the **grammar** and vocabulary of her Cockney dialect, but in the accent of upper-class British English. For the following extract from *Pygmalion*, try reading Eliza's part aloud in your best upper-class British accent, and note the incongruity.

> LIZA [darkly] *My aunt died of influenza: so they said. But it's my belief they done the old woman in.*
>
> MRS HIGGINS [puzzled] *Done her in?*
>
> LIZA *Y-e-e-es, Lord love you! Why should she die of influenza? She come through diphtheria right enough the year before. I saw her with my own eyes. Fairly blue with it, she was. They all thought she was dead; but my father kept ladling gin down her throat till she came to so sudden that she bit the bowl off the spoon.*
>
> MRS EYNSFORD HILL [startled] *Dear me!*
>
> LIZA [piling up the indictment] *What call would a woman with that strength in her have to die of influenza? What become of her straw hat that should have come to me? Somebody pinched it; and what I say is, them as pinched it done her in.*

MRS EYNSFORD HILL [to Eliza, horrified] *You surely don't believe that your aunt was killed.*

LIZA *Do I not! Them she lived with would have killed her for a hat-pin, let alone a hat.*

MRS EYNSFORD HILL *But it can't have been right for your father to pour spirits down her throat like that. It might have killed her.*

LIZA *Not her. Gin was mother's milk to her. Besides, he'd poured so much down his own throat that he knew the good of it.*

MRS EYNSFORD HILL *Do you mean that he drank?*

LIZA *Drank! My word! Something chronic.*

In practice, grammarians and linguists do not always carefully separate dialect from accent. One might hear a linguist, for example, state that a particular dialect uses a glottal stop, clearly a reference to its pronunciation, rather than to its **grammar**. But the distinction is maintained in so far as one would never talk of a foreigner 'speaking English with a foreign dialect'.

Dialect also contrasts with language; but this contrast is more a matter of degree than marked by a clear division. Most people would say that American English is a distinct dialect of English (spoken with a variety of distinctive accents), but there are some who speak about 'the American language'. A rough definition uses the test of mutual intelligibility. If two speakers, speaking their own dialects, can understand each other, then, so this proposed definition states, these must be dialects of the same language. But this rough demarcation between dialect and language is often overridden by political considerations. If Sweden and Norway were not separate nations, probably Swedish and Norwegian would be counted as distinct dialects of one language, rather than as separate languages. By contrast, it is customary to speak of the various 'dialects' of Chinese, such as Mandarin and Cantonese, but in fact a mono-dialectal speaker of Mandarin cannot hold a successful conversation with a monodialectal speaker of Cantonese. (Interestingly, though, they could write to each other successfully, as the writing system is not based on the spoken language.)

Dialect contrasts with jargon, in the main sense of the term 'jargon'. A jargon is typically a vocabulary devoted to a specialized topic, such as drag-car racing, surfing, nuclear physics, neurosurgery or linguistics. A jargon does not usually have its own **grammar**, so, for example, you can talk with the vocabulary of neurosurgery, in any dialect (though, for social reasons, this might be odd). Jargons are usually thought of as belonging to specific topics that people might want to talk about, whereas dialects are associated with specific groups of speakers.

Relationships Every dialect has its own **grammar**, with characteristic rules which distinguish it from other dialects. Dialect is emphatically NOT a matter of lack of **grammar**, just of different **grammar**. Here are some examples illustrating the different grammatical rules of various English dialects.

DIALECT	EXAMPLE	GRAMMATICAL FEATURE
Northern England	*She were a great worker.*	*were* with **singular subject**
Cockney	*We was just talkin' about that.*	*was* with **plural subject**
Northern England	*He needs his head examining.*	**present participle** in certain **participial object clauses**.
Some Scottish, Irish and American dialects	*The car needs washed.*	**past participle** in certain (other) **participial object clauses**.
Southern U.S.A.	*Y'all are welcome.*	Specifically **plural** 2nd **person pronoun**
Northern England	*Don't walk on 't grass.*	Use of *'t* as **definite article**

Grammatical correctness is relative to particular dialects. The systematic, conventional rules of one dialect may or may not also be rules in another dialect. Nobody speaks without a dialect (unless they suffer from a form of aphasia, a medical condition in which people lose control of their everyday spoken **grammar**). To say that someone 'speaks without any dialect' is as contradictory as saying that some physical object 'has no shape'. A physical object cannot be a physical object without having some (more or less complex) shape or other. And likewise, a variety of language cannot be a variety of language without having some characteristic organization or rules.

One may hear the expression 'neutral dialect'; the term 'neutral' in this context expresses a social judgement about the speakers of this dialect, and does not describe any kind of 'neutrality' in the **grammar** of that dialect.

A speaker who uses one grammatical pattern characteristic of a particular dialect may not use other patterns characteristic of that dialect. Dialects are fuzzy at the edges and blend into one another; neighbouring dialects usually differ in only a few grammatical features, while more distantly related dialects differ in relatively many features.

Dialects differ in their vocabulary. Here are some examples of **words** which are characteristic of certain dialects: Scots: *wee, bairn, outwith, lass, cowp*; Australian: *daggy, bludger, dunny, jeep* (for a shopping trolley).

If people speak different dialects, communication may occasionally fail, due to the different rules in the two dialects. In the English-speaking world, at least, this is actually quite rare. Most people have a working knowledge of the dialects with which they come into daily contact, and communicate easily with people who speak other dialects.

For interest   Some pairs of languages which are clearly distinct from each other, such as German and Dutch, or French and Italian, have (or used to have) dialects at their boundaries which it is hard to identify as belonging to one language or the other. For example, there could be a patois spoken in a village high in the Alps which it is hard to identify as either Italian or French, being something between the French spoken in Lyon and the Italian spoken in Turin.

Here is a rare example of the potential for disastrous failure of communication, due to a dialect difference. The dialect of parts of Lancashire, in the north of England, uses the word *while* with a meaning associated in other dialects with the word *until*. Thus, in this area, you can hear such sentences as *Wait while Christmas* and *The grass'll keep on growing while the colder weather comes* (meaning, in the standard dialect, *Wait until Christmas* and *The grass will keep growing until the colder weather comes*). In Lancashire, a story circulated, which may have been an urban myth, that there was a sign at a road/railway level crossing, evidently composed by non-locals, warning drivers and pedestrians DO NOT CROSS WHILE LIGHTS FLASH. In the standard dialect, this would imply that if the lights are flashing, a person should not cross, but may do so when the lights stop flashing. But in the Lancashire dialect, the same warning would, disastrously, imply just the reverse, that if the lights are not flashing, a person should not cross, but may do so when the lights start to flash.

One may draw various morals from this tale, according to one's social/political persuasion, about appropriate measures for avoiding such potential misunderstandings. A 'centralist' view would advise teaching the locals to abandon their use and understanding of the word *while* in favour of the standard usage. A 'regionalist' view would advocate that the people composing public signs should know the dialect of the people who are to read them. In fact, both views are fraught with practical difficulties; dialects are well rooted in their communities and cannot be easily changed; and road signs are read by speakers of different dialects. Cultivating a general awareness about differences between dialects would certainly be a step in the right direction.

Exercise According to the explanation given above, two of the following example statements use the term 'dialect' appropriately and two use it inappropriately. Identify the appropriate usages.

1 *My French uncle speaks English with a thick Parisian dialect.*
2 *The mountain dialects of this language have no grammar.*
3 *The English dialect of the western suburbs of Philadelphia uses a double negative.*
4 *In this creole dialect, verbs do not agree with their subjects.*

Direct object

Explanation The direct object of a **verb** expressing an action is typically the **noun phrase** which expresses the recipient, or patient, or 'undergoer' of that action, the person or thing most clearly affected by this action.

With other **verbs**, not expressing any action, such as *know*, *remember*, *see* and *believe*, the direct object of these **verbs** is the **noun phrase** that occupies the position in relation to the **verb** occupied by the direct object of 'action' **verbs**. In English, the direct object of a **verb** is often, but not always, the **noun phrase** immediately following it.

It is also convenient to apply the term 'direct object' to the **nouns** and **pronouns** which are the **heads** of direct object **noun phrases**.

Examples   In the following **sentences**, the direct object **noun phrases** are underlined.

- *A Turk called Mehmet shot <u>the Pope</u>.*
- *The Italian authorities imposed <u>a long prison sentence</u>.*
- *The Holy Father visited <u>Mehmet</u> in prison.*
- *He forgave <u>him</u> and gave <u>his blessing</u> to him.*

Contrasts   Direct object contrasts with **indirect object**. If a **verb** has two **objects**, one of them is the direct object and the other is the **indirect object**; but, in English at least, if a **verb** only has one **object**, it is always the direct object. That is, **indirect objects** never occur without direct objects also being present. Typically, **indirect objects** refer to humans or animals, and not to inanimate things, but direct objects can refer to a very wide range of 'things'.

Both direct object and **indirect object** contrast with **subject**. If in a given **sentence** a **noun phrase** is the direct object of a **verb**, it cannot simultaneously be the **subject** or **indirect object** of that **verb**.

Direct object contrasts with **complement** (in one sense of that term) or, equivalently, with **predicate noun phrase**. These are **phrases** after the **verb** *be* (and some other **verbs**), as in, for example, *Tatiana is <u>a reluctant Californian</u>.*

Relationships   Only **transitive verbs** have (direct) objects. So **auxiliaries**, **intransitive verbs** and the **verb** *be* and others like it (**copular verbs**) do not take (direct) objects.

Direct object is closely associated with **accusative case**. In English, this is only relevant to the **personal pronouns**, which have distinctive **accusative case** forms, such as *me*, *him*, *her* and *us*. These **accusative** forms are the forms of the **pronouns** which occur as direct objects, as in *John saw them* and *Mary heard him*.

In English **clauses** with both a direct and an **indirect object**, there are two common orders of these **phrases**. If the **indirect object** is marked by a **preposition** (usually *to*), the direct object comes immediately after the **verb**, and the **phrase** with the **indirect object** comes after that, as in *I sent a letter to my love*, where *a letter* is the direct object of *sent*. In the alternative order, there is no **preposition**, and the direct object is the second of the two **noun phrases**, as in *I sent my love a letter* (where *a letter* is still the direct object of *sent*).

Verbs in all kinds of **clauses**, both **main** and **subordinate**, can have direct objects. The examples given earlier all involved simple (**main**) **clauses**. Here are some examples with **subordinate clauses**, with the direct objects of the **verbs** in the **subordinate clauses** underlined.

- *Most people believe that Columbus discovered <u>America</u>.*
- *Columbus' discovering <u>America</u> was a fluke.*
- *He had hoped to find <u>a new route to the Indies</u>.*
- *By sailing <u>his ship</u> westward, he hoped to reach <u>the Far East</u>.*

These examples also show that the whole range of different forms of **verbs**, namely **finite** forms, **infinitives**, **gerunds** and **participial** forms, freely take direct objects. (Of course, they must be forms of **transitive verbs**.)

The term '**object**' is sometimes used for the **noun phrase** immediately following a **preposition** as in *for <u>him</u>, to <u>them</u>* and *in <u>the Old Town</u>*. When using '**object**' in this way, in relation to **prepositions**, no distinction is made between direct and **indirect objects**.

Linguists find it useful to say that not only **noun phrases**, but also whole **clauses**, can be direct objects of certain **verbs**, such as *say, believe, report* and *understand*. In the following **sentences** it seems reasonable to regard the whole **subordinate clause** *that you have been looking for me* as the direct object of these **verbs**.

- *John said <u>that you have been looking for me</u>.*
- *I don't believe <u>that you have been looking for me</u>.*
- *My secretary reported <u>that you have been looking for me</u>.*

These direct object **clauses** are a kind of **complement clause**.

For interest   The direct object of an English verb typically expresses the recipient, or patient, or 'undergoer' of the action expressed by the verb, the person or thing most clearly affected by this action. For example, in the event described by *The senators killed Julius Caesar*, the party most affected by these violent happenings was Julius Caesar.

This is not always the case, however. With verbs of perception, such as *see, hear, smell* and *taste*, it could well be argued that the person or thing most affected is expressed by the subject of the verb, rather than by its object. For example, in the sentences *John smelt the coffee*, or *John saw the knife*, what is being pointed out is an effect on John, not on the coffee or the knife.

Exercise   In the following sentences, the verbs *sell, buy, borrow* and *lend* occur in various forms, and in both main and subordinate clauses. For each sentence, identify the direct object of the verb from this list that it contains.

1 *I'm going to have to sell my house.*
2 *But I can't think who would want to buy it.*
3 *Nobody can borrow money from banks these days.*
4 *Lending such large sums of money is a risky business.*

Direct speech

Explanation   A part of a **sentence** is in direct speech when it represents verbatim something uttered or written by someone (that is, in the reported speaker's very own **words**). Usually, parts of a **sentence** in direct speech are enclosed between single or double quotation marks (inverted commas). In less typical cases, the **words** reported may not have been uttered (spoken, whispered, shouted, etc.), but merely thought.

Examples   The sequences of **words** between single quotation marks in the **sentences** below are in direct speech.

- *He shouted 'God save the King!' and leaped off the scaffold.*
- *'Why, you doublecrossing son of a bitch', he spluttered.*
- *All I said was 'How much will it cost me?'*
- *'Cui bono?' were the words that came to my mind.*

Contrasts   Direct speech contrasts with **indirect speech**, which is the reporting of someone else's **words**, but not verbatim. The following pairs illustrate the contrast.

DIRECT SPEECH	INDIRECT SPEECH
He said, 'I will come.'	*He said that he would come.*
She shouted 'Help!'	*She shouted for help.*
They asked, 'Are you busy?'	*They asked if she was busy.*

In fact the contrast between direct and **indirect speech** is not absolute. There can be intermediate cases, as we shall see below.

Relationships   Passages in direct speech are typically used with a limited set of **verbs**, which express vocal acts, verbs such as *say, mutter, whisper, scream, shout, call, snap* and *growl*. But other **verbs**, expressing acts which are not necessarily vocal, such as *explain, comment, think, wonder, enquire, reply, repeat, write* and *scribble* can also take direct speech. And direct speech can also be used with **nouns** expressing vocal or linguistic acts, such as *words, reply* and *answer*. The only restriction is a common-sense one on what can reasonably be thought of as having actual speech (or written language) as its **subject** or **(direct) object**. Here are examples of some of the possibilities.

- *I thought, 'Wait a minute, that's odd.'*
- *The words 'Mene, mene, tekel upharsin' appeared on the wall.*
- *Someone had scribbled 'Fuck the IRA' on the door.*
- *'Shut up', he explained.* (Used ironically)

As the second example above shows, a passage in direct speech is not necessarily in the same language as the rest of the **sentence**. In fact a passage in direct speech does not have to be in any language at all, so long as it can be thought of as the object of a vocal act. So we can have *We heard something that sounded like 'Pffuuuaaghssss' coming from inside the cupboard.* Where the reported

69

noises or **words** are not in the language of the rest of the **sentence**, then in fact direct speech must be used, as there is no possibility of **indirect speech**.

Passages in direct speech enjoy more variety of position in relation to the rest of their **sentence** than normal **phrases**. They can go before, after or even around the rest of the **sentence**, as these examples show.

- *I thought to myself, 'What's going on here?'*
- *'What', I thought to myself, 'is going on here?'*
- *'What's going on here?', I thought to myself.*

The essential characteristic of direct speech is that it quotes the exact **words** used. Now a few **words** change their reference according to who is speaking them. The **pronouns** *I* and *you*, for example, do this. Thus if Thomas Jefferson had said *'I love Monticello'*, the **pronoun** *I* here obviously referred to Thomas Jefferson. If another speaker reports Jefferson's words, it can be done directly or indirectly. If his words are reported in **indirect speech**, the original *I* must be changed to a *he*, to preserve the correct reference to Thomas Jefferson, as in *Thomas Jefferson said that he loved Monticello*. Notice also the change from the **present tense** *love* in Jefferson's original words to the **past tense** *loved* in the indirectly reported speech. There are a number of other such systematic changes that relate direct to **indirect speech** (see further under INDIRECT SPEECH).

Writers sometimes find it advantageous to blur the distinction between direct and **indirect speech**. Steps in this direction include

- leaving out the quotation marks;
- leaving out punctuation marks distinctive of a free-standing **sentence** (e.g. beginning capital letter, final full stop, period, question mark or exclamation mark);
- making some, but not all, of the systematic changes associated with **indirect speech** (e.g. from *I* to *he* or *she* and from **present** to **past tense**).

Here is an example containing a passage which has some, but not all, of the characteristics of direct speech.

- *In the latter days of July in the year 185–, a most important question was for ten days hourly asked in the cathedral city of Barchester, and answered every hour in various ways – Who was to be the new Bishop?*

The literal question which was on everybody's lips in Barchester was *'Who is to be the new Bishop?'* The author of the above passage has kept the beginning capital letter and final question mark identifying this as a free-standing **sentence**, but has chosen not to set it inside quotation marks, and has, further, made the switch from **present tense** *is* to **past tense** *was*.

For interest Direct speech is not easy to express in spoken, as opposed to written, language. This may seem paradoxical, as speech is spoken language, but therein lies the problem. The problem in reporting someone else's words verbatim, while speaking, is somehow to mark where one's own words stop and the other person's begin. In written language, quotation marks can be placed explicitly around the quoted passage, but there is no very convenient counterpart to quotation marks in speech. A rather clumsy way to do it is to say '*quote*' at the beginning of the quoted passage, and '*unquote*' at the end, but this is often awkward and not easy to follow. Some speakers try to get over this awkwardness by saying '*quote unquote*' at the beginning of the quotation, but the obvious problem with this is that it doesn't mark where the quoted passage ends, and the speaker's own words resume.

An interesting new way of signalling direct speech has recently developed among younger English speakers, and is spreading from the United States to Britain. This occurs entirely in spoken conversation, rather than in writing, and so printing it here for the sake of giving examples in some ways misrepresents its nature, but here are some examples, anyway. (It may help to imagine an American teenager speaking these examples.)

- *When I saw it, I was like* [PAUSE] *'This is amazing!'*
- *... so all of sudden, he was like* [PAUSE] *'What are you doin' here?'*
- *From the first day she arrived, she was like* [PAUSE] *'This is my house, not yours.'*
- *So I'm like 'Well, sure', and she's like 'I'm not so sure . . .'.*

This is a very recent development, and so you may not yet have noticed it. Be on the lookout for it when listening to young (under twenty-five) speakers in colloquial conversation. Though the construction is new and not yet standard, its meaning is very clear. It seems to be used more often to report thoughts rather than actual speech.

Exercise Identify the passages in direct speech in the following sentences.

1 *'I regret exceedingly —' said M. Hercule Poirot.*
2 *'It can't hurt now', was Mr Sherlock Holmes's comment when for the tenth time in as many years, I asked his leave to reveal the following narrative.*
3 *'Days of wine and roses', said Wilt to himself.*
4 *'The Signora had no business to do it', said Miss Bartlett, 'no business at all. She promised us south rooms with a view close together, instead of which here are north rooms, looking into a courtyard, and a long way apart. Oh Lucy!'*

Ellipsis

Explanation Ellipsis means 'leaving out' or 'omitting'. **Words**, **phrases** and whole **clauses** can be omitted by ellipsis. That is, they can be left out of a **sentence** with a reasonably good expectation that a hearer will be able to fill them in, or understand what was intended, from knowledge of the context in which the **sentence** was used. The clearest cases of ellipsis leave **sentences** that are obviously incomplete in some way.

Examples In the conversation below, the places where ellipsis seems to have taken place are indicated by dots. The **word** or **phrase** most reasonably understood in place of the dots is given afterwards in square brackets.

ROSIE: *Can you go swimming today?*
MATTY: *No, I can't...*   [*go swimming today*]
ROSIE: *Why can't you...?*   [*go swimming today*]
MATTY: *My Mum said I have to tidy my room.*
ROSIE: *Ooh, do you really have to...?*   [*tidy your room*]
        When do you think you'll be able to...? [*go swimming*]
MATTY: *Maybe...on Monday.*   [*I'll be able to go swimming*]

Contrasts Ellipsis differs from the **contraction**, or shortening, seen in forms such as *can't, won't, wouldn't, I'm, we'll, she's*. Unlike such **contractions**, ellipsis involves the omission of whole **words** or **phrases**.

Grammarians vary in how far they are prepared to apply the term 'ellipsis', but most would apply it only to understood elements which rely on the context in a specific conversation or text for their 'filling in'. So, for example, the regularly understood, but absent, *you* in **imperative sentences**, like *Go jump in a lake!*, would not normally be called a case of ellipsis.

The omission of **articles** and some other little **words** in newspaper headlines and telegrams, as *MOB ATTACKS POLICE AT STADIUM* or *ARRIVING AIRPORT WEDNESDAY PLEASE MEET*, would not be counted as a central case of ellipsis, because it is the reader's knowledge of English **grammar**, rather than the specific context of the headline or telegram, that allows him or her to reconstruct what was meant. Nevertheless, such omissions might be called 'ellipsis' by some grammarians.

Ellipsis differs from the use of what linguists call a 'pro-form' to replace an element which would otherwise be repeated. *One* is a pro-form replacing some **noun** in *I saw a big one*. *Do so* is a pro-form replacing some **verb phrase** in *They refused to do so*. With pro-forms, replacement, not omission, is involved.

Relationships Elliptical **sentences**, that is **sentences** in which something is omitted by ellipsis, are common as answers to questions with question words such as *what, which, when* and *where*. In answers to such questions, often a whole part of the question **sentence** (which would otherwise just be repeated) is omitted. For example:

Q: *Where are my glasses?*   A: *On the bookshelf.*
                                  (Ellipsis of *Your glasses are*)
Q: *When did Seamus arrive?*   A: *Late last night.*
                                  (Ellipsis of *Seamus arrived*)
Q: *What would you like for breakfast?* A: *A kipper.*
                                  (Ellipsis of *I would like...for breakfast*)

Not just any part of a **sentence** can be omitted by ellipsis – far from it. Ellipsis affects quite specific kinds of **words** and **phrases**, in quite specific positions. In English, it is the major or central **parts of speech**, namely **nouns, verbs, adjectives,** and **adverbs,** and the **phrases** built around these, that are mainly prone to ellipsis, specifically when they are modified by some more marginal **part of speech,** such as a **demonstrative, numeral, auxiliary,** or an 'intensifier' (a word like *very* or *somewhat*). Here are some examples, in imaginary question–answer dialogues:

Q: *Which bananas do you want?* A: *I want those.*
(Ellipsis of a **noun** (*bananas*) after a **demonstrative**)

Q: *How many hotels do you want?* A: *I want three.*
(Ellipsis of a **noun** (*hotels*) after a **numeral**)

Q: *Will you marry me?*   A: *Yes, I will.*
(Ellipsis of a **verb phrase** (*marry you*) after an **auxiliary**)

Q: *Hot, isn't it?*   A: *Very.*
(Ellipsis of an **adjective** (*hot*) after *very*, an intensifier)

For interest   To show that ellipsis may work for one part of speech, but not for another, consider a situation such as the following. I say to you: *Four men came.* Imagine you wish to deny this, because you know that in fact three men came. Then you can say, elliptically, *No, three came.* Here you have left out the noun *men*. But now imagine you have a different reason for denying my statement, because (in this new case) you know that four women came. Now, you cannot similarly apply ellipsis to the numeral *four*, and say **No, women came.* At the very least, this is much less natural.

People who know each other very well often have very elliptical conversations, because they share a lot of background knowledge which doesn't need to be mentioned. Even people who don't know each other can sometimes have quite elliptical conversations, if the context makes it clear what is meant. When one is writing a book or article, one cannot guarantee that one has much in common with one's readers, and the traditional recommendation to 'use whole sentences' may, on the whole, be useful. But for spoken conversation between people who know each other, or even people who don't, ellipsis, leading to the use of incomplete sentences, is both economical and communicatively effective.

Exercise   In the following imaginary dialogues, supply the word(s) omitted by ellipsis.

1 FRED: *Did he react angrily?* DORIS: *Well, somewhat.*
2 FRED: *I'm taking the car.*   DORIS: *Oh no, you're not.*
3 FRED: *Why did you hit him?* DORIS: *Because he was lying to me.*
4 FRED: *Linford ran a great race.* DORIS: *His best ever.*

Finite

Explanation   A finite **verb** in English is a form of a **verb** that shows **agreement** with a **subject** and is marked for **tense**. All kinds of **verbs**, including **main verbs**, **auxiliaries**, **transitive** and **intransitive verbs** can be in either finite or non-finite form.

A finite **clause** is simply a **clause** whose **verb** is finite.

Examples   In the following **sentences**, the finite **verbs** are underlined.
  • *The buck stops here.*
  • *I am afraid to have to tell you that you have failed your exams.*
  • *The hamster has escaped and we are worried about the cat catching it.*
  • *It is an ill wind that blows nobody any good.*

Contrasts   Finite **verb** forms contrast with non-finite forms, which include **infinitives**, **gerunds** and **participles**.

Relationships   Only **verbs** can have finite or non-finite forms. The finite/non-finite distinction does not apply to any other **part of speech**.

In English, one **verb** in a **main clause** is always finite. The **verb** in a **main clause** that is finite is the **auxiliary verb**, if there is one; otherwise it is the **main verb**.

Grammarians vary somewhat in whether they choose to call **modal verbs** (which don't show **agreement**) and **verbs** in **imperatives** 'finite' or not. We will say that **modals** and the **verbs** in **imperatives** are indeed finite, as this preserves the simple generalization that one **verb** in a **main clause** is always finite.

Subordinate clauses may or may not contain a finite **verb**. **Verbs** in **clauses** introduced by *that* are typically finite, as for example in the **clause** after *that* in *Sarah told us that Dave was remarrying shortly*. But many **subordinate clauses** contain **verbs** in the **infinitive** form, as in *Sarah advised Dave to remarry quickly*; these are not finite.

Other **subordinate clauses** have **verbs** in a **participial** form, such as *walking* in *Walking past Jenner's the other day, I saw Alex*, or *forced* in *Forced to give up, he collapsed in a heap*. These participial forms of **verbs** are not finite.

Subordinate clauses with **gerunds** are not finite. Thus the first **clause** in *Going to the pictures used to be a pleasure* is not finite.

For interest   'Finite' is also a mathematical term, contrasting with 'infinite'. Scientists talk about finite and infinite distances. Finite distances are ones which have an end, or limit, and can be measured, like 3,000 miles, or 6 metres; infinite distances go on for ever without limit, and cannot be measured in units such as miles or metres. Is there a connection with the grammatical terminology? Yes, there is a vague link. The meanings of finite verbs are in a sense limited in time by the tense marking that they carry, and limited in application by the agreement that associates them with a particular subject. The meanings of some non-finites, on the other hand, are less tied down to a particular time and subject. This parallel with the mathematical terminology is quite tenuous, however.

What is the point of singling out a particular form of verbs and giving it the special label 'finite'? Do so-called finite verbs behave any differently from non-finite verbs? Yes, in some languages, verb forms which show agreement and mark tense (i.e. just the finite forms of verbs) do behave in special ways. We will illustrate from English and German.

English makes interrogative (question) sentences in a somewhat exotic way (compared to most other languages), by switching the positions of the subject and the finite verb of the sentence. Thus *Michael has gone to Yale* becomes *Has Michael gone to Yale?*, with subject *Michael* and finite auxiliary *has* reversed in position. If a sentence has no auxiliary, the corresponding interrogative nevertheless introduces a finite form of the 'dummy' verb *do*. So *Michael finished his PhD thesis* becomes *Did Michael finish his PhD thesis?* This shows how one process of English grammar, making questions, uses just the finite verbs, and no others.

In German, too, just the finite verb forms are used for making interrogatives (in a slightly different way from English, not always involving auxiliaries). But German has another construction in which just the finite verb forms are singled out for special treatment. German has quite special rules about where in a sentence it puts its finite verbs. In declarative main clauses, the finite verb always begins the second phrase in the sentence; and in subordinate clauses introduced by a subordinating conjunction, such as *dass* (= *that*), or *wenn* (= *if*), the finite verb always comes at the end of the clause. Here are some examples. Watch how, in each type of clause, the finite verbs *liebt* and *liebst* are positioned.

DECLARATIVE	INTERROGATIVE	SUBORDINATE
Hans liebt mich	*Liebt Hans mich*	*Ich weiss, dass Hans mich liebt*
Jack loves me	*Loves Jack me*	*I know that Jack me loves*
(= *Jack loves me*)	(= *Does Jack love me?*)	(= *I know that Jack loves me*)
Du liebst Hans	*Liebst Du Hans*	*Ich weiss, dass Du Hans liebst*
You love Jack	*Love you Jack*	*I know that you Jack love*
(= *You love Jack*)	(= *Do you love Jack?*)	(= *I know that you love Jack*)

Finiteness in verbs was explained above as involving both tense and agreement with a subject. The contrasting non-finite verb forms in English and German, such as infinitives and participles, show neither tense nor agreement. So the distinction between finite and non-finite verbs for these languages is particularly clear-cut. But some languages have intermediate cases, for example verb forms which show agreement with a subject but are not marked for tense. Arabic, for instance, has this kind of 'semi-finite' (or 'semi-infinitive') form of verbs. Here are some examples:

inta mumkin tiktib
you can   write+2ND+SING+MASC (= *You can write.*)

huwwa mumkin yiktib
he   can   write+3RD+SING+MASC (= *He can write.*)

ihna mumkin niktib
we   can   write+1ST+PLUR (= *We can write.*)

Note that the different Arabic forms for *write* here, with prefixes indicating agreement with the subject of the sentence, are all translated into English by the non-agreeing form *write*. We don't say, in English *★He can writes*, even though *He writes* is grammatical.

Exercise   Identify the finite verbs in the following two passages. There are seven in all.

- *The education bestowed on Flora Poste by her parents had been too expensive, athletic and prolonged; and when they died within a few weeks of one another during the annual epidemic of the influenza or Spanish Plague which occurred in her twentieth year, she was discovered to possess every art and grace save that of earning her own living.*
- *When the east wind blows up Helford river the shining waters become troubled and disturbed, and the little waves beat angrily upon the sandy shores.*

Future

Explanation   The future, in any language, is whatever form of a **verb** is most commonly used to express events happening after the time of speaking or writing. The common future in English is expressed by the **modal auxiliary** *will* followed by the bare form of the **verb** concerned. *Be going to* is also commonly used to express future time. Some dialects of English also use *shall*. Other languages express the future in a variety of ways, including **suffixes** and **prefixes**.

Examples   The following English sentences express the future.

- *We will fight them on the beaches.*
- *We shall never surrender.*
- *Joanna is going to have a baby.*
- *Will you be home in time for tea?*
- *Tomorrow, he will have lived here for thirty years.*

In French, the future is expressed by a special of set of **affixes**, which **agree** in **person** and **number** with the **subject** of the **clause**.

Je boirai   cinq bouteilles
I drink+FUT five bottles   (= *I will drink five bottles.*)

Tu boiras   quatre verres
You drink+FUT four   glasses   (= *You will drink four glasses.*)

> Il boira   trois gouttes
> He drink+FUT three drops   (= He will drink three drops.)

Contrasts   It is conventional to talk of three main 'tenses', namely **present**, **past** and future, corresponding to the division of time into the stretches and points most significant for our daily lives, namely NOW, BEFORE NOW and AFTER NOW. In this sense, future contrasts with **present** and **past**. This is a contrast on the basis of meaning.

Relationships   When one looks in detail at the ways in which languages express **past**, **present** and future, one sees that very often the **grammar** of a language does not work according to this simple three-way division of time. English is an example. It expresses **past** and **present** by **affixes** (-ed and -s) after the **verb**; but it expresses future by a **modal auxiliary** before the **verb**.

> talks
> talked
> will talk

In English and other languages, future can combine with other **tenses** and aspects, making complex forms expressing more subtle shades of meaning.

FUTURE PERFECT   *He will have gone.*
FUTURE PERFECT PROGRESSIVE   *He will have been going.*

These are examples of **compound tenses**.

Although English *will* is commonly used to express future time, it is by no means the only way of expressing it. Both the simple **present tense** and the **present progressive** and a form of the **verb** *go* are also commonly used to express time after the present, as these examples show.

SIMPLE PRESENT	*Tomorrow we die.*	(= ... *will die*)
	Tonight, I dine at the Ritz.	(= ... *will dine* ...)
PRESENT PROGRESSIVE	*She is arriving at 3.00.*	(= ... *will arrive* ...)
	John is following later.	(= ... *will follow* ...)
PRESENT PROGRESSIVE with *go*	*We are going to die.*	(= ... *will die*)
	John is going to follow.	(= ... *will follow* ...)

Exercise   Pick out the sentences from those below which clearly express future time. Half of them do, and half of them don't.

1 *Sarajevo will surrender.*
2 *If you will it, this whole estate is yours.*
3 *The President commands the armed forces.*
4 *The President addresses the nation on TV at noon tomorrow.*
5 *Eve is studying architecture.*
6 *Eve is spending next year in Paris.*
7 *Slow down! We're going too fast!*
8 *We are going to fast tomorrow.*

Gender

Explanation In many languages, but not in English, **nouns** are divided into separate groups with different characteristic effects on other elements in the **sentence**. Such groups of **nouns** are genders. Sometimes, but not always, there is a correspondence between the gender of a **noun** and some aspect of its shape, such as its ending (or other kind of marking).

Again, sometimes, but not always, there is a correspondence between the gender of a **noun** and part of its meaning, such as the sex (or lack of it) of the person or thing the **noun** refers to. Thus 'gender', as a strictly grammatical term, has no necessary connection with biological sex or social gender roles. (See **For interest** below for some discussion.)

Examples In Italian, you can often tell the gender of a **noun** by the vowel it ends in. **Nouns** which end in -*o* almost all belong to the so-called 'masculine' gender. If a **definite article** is used with any **singular** 'masculine' **noun**, it must be *il* (or *lo* for **nouns** beginning with *s*- and another letter). Examples are:

il treno	*the train*
il vino	*the wine*
il formaggio	*the cheese*
lo sbaglio	*the mistake*

(*La mano* – *the hand* is a notorious exception, feminine despite ending in -*o*.)

On the other hand, **nouns** which end in -*a* almost all belong to the so-called 'feminine' gender. If a **definite article** is used with any **singular** feminine **noun**, it must be *la*. Examples are:

la casa	*the house*
la chiesa	*the church*
la ragazza	*the girl*
la sforza	*the force*

The letters *o* and *a* are not the only ones that Italian **nouns** can end in. For many other **nouns**, you cannot tell from the final vowel what gender a **noun** belongs to; you just have to know whether it is masculine or feminine. But every **noun** in Italian belongs to one of these two genders; and the gender it belongs to dictates which **definite article**, *il* or *la*, must be used with it, along with a range of other similar effects on other parts of the **sentence**.

Contrasts Gender contrasts with other properties which **nouns** can have, such as (depending on the language) **number (singular/plural)** and **case (nominative/accusative/ . . .)**. The gender of a **noun** never changes; whatever **sentence** it is used in, the gender of a **noun** is always the same. But the **number** and **case** of a **noun** may vary from use in one **sentence** to use in the next.

In some languages (e.g. Latin) gender must be distinguished from what grammarians call the 'declension' of a **noun**. A declension is a pattern of marking on **nouns** for such factors as **case** and **number**, independent (or partially independent) of gender.

Relationships   If a language uses gender at all, it has at least two different genders. There would be no point in saying a language used gender, if all its **nouns** belonged to a single gender.

As indicated above, **nouns** are the basic carriers of gender.

In languages which have it, gender is usually heavily involved with **agreement. Parts of speech** such as **verbs, adjectives, articles, possessives** and **demonstratives** in these languages often must, or may, **agree** with **nouns** in gender.

Gender terms are sometimes applied to the English **pronouns**, with *he* being labelled 'masculine', *she* 'feminine' and *it* 'neuter', but the implied classification has limited effect on other parts of the **sentence**. The only possible instance of gender **agreement** in English affects the choice of **reflexives**, which must be of the same 'gender' as the **subject** of their **clause**. So, for instance, you can't say *The man shot herself*. (Cases like this involve complex interactions between English **grammar** and the possible meanings of **sentences**, because, similarly, you can't say *The man shot her own husband*.)

The connection between gender and such aspects of the meanings of **nouns** as sex varies from one language to another. In Italian and French, there is an almost exceptionless tendency for **nouns** referring to male creatures to be masculine, and for **nouns** referring to female creatures to be feminine, as in Italian *l'uomo* – *the man, il ragazzo* – *the boy, la donna* – *the lady* and *la ragazza* – *the girl*. Of course, this leaves **nouns** referring to most of the things in the world, which are essentially sexless, to be assigned to one gender or the other in more or less random fashion.

In German, the connection between sex and grammatical gender barely exists in any systematic way. Notoriously, *Weib*, a German word for *woman*, is 'neuter', and *Sache*, a word meaning *thing*, is 'feminine'!

For interest   Avoiding sexist language is important, and might seem to have a lot to do with gender. In fact, 'gender' as linguists and grammarians use the term, is often not central to the issue of sexism in language, although there are some areas in the grammars of languages where sexism does arise. First, to be clear about what is involved, let's look at a fact about grammatical gender which does not relate to sexism in any way. In French, every noun for any inanimate object is either masculine or feminine. No implicit insult or compliment to women can be gleaned from the fact that *maison* (*house*) is a feminine noun; and the fact that *toit* (*roof*) is masculine does not reveal any niche of male privilege.

But when it comes to nouns referring to professions, French grammar does seem to reflect certain sexist assumptions, which are only now being challenged. The words *médecin* (*doctor*), *architecte* (*architect*), *ingenieur* (*engineer*) and *philosophe* (*philosopher*) are all masculine, which contributes to an expectation that doctors, architects, engineers and philosophers will be male. It is not clear how closely

French speakers' habits of thought about professional people are affected by the grammatical gender of nouns referring to them, but almost certainly at least some sexist assumptions are reinforced.

What can French speakers do about this? Although it is a bold step for any individual to take, one solution might be to start using both feminine and masculine agreement forms, as appropriate to the situation. One might sometimes say *la médecin, for instance.

The same kind of problem does not arise in English, which has no grammatical gender on nouns. A sexist assumption is present in an example like *When a taxpayer has completed this form, he should sign it and return it to the office.* This presupposes that the taxpayer will be male. But the use of *he* here is not obligatory in English; the use of *she* or *he or she* would be quite grammatical. (*She or he* is grammatical, too, but its oddness might also reveal a sexist presupposition.)

English and Japanese are languages with no genders (in the grammatical sense, of course). Italian, French and Arabic have two genders, called 'masculine' and feminine'. German and Russian have three genders, called 'masculine', 'feminine' and 'neuter'.

In fact, languages can have as many as ten genders, though, when there are so many, the term 'noun-class' tends to be used instead of 'gender'. In Sesotho, a language of the Bantu family, from southern Africa, one can distinguish eight different genders or noun-classes. These differ according to the prefixes they use in the singular and plural forms. Some examples follow:[4]

NAME OF GENDER	EXAMPLE NOUN	
	SINGULAR	PLURAL
mǫ/ba	*mǫ-thǫ* (*person*)	*ba-thǫ* (*persons*)
zero/bo	*rakháli* (*aunt*)	*bo-rakháli* (*aunts*)
mǫ/mę	*mǫ-sę* (*dress*)	*mę-sę* (*dresses*)
lę/ma	*lę-tsatsí* (*day*)	*ma-tsatsí* (*days*)
şe/li	*şe-liba* (*well*)	*li-liba* (*wells*)
Ø/li	*Ø-ntjá* (*dog*)	*li-ntjá* (*dogs*)
bǫ/ma	*bǫ-hɔbe* (*bread*)	*ma-hɔbe* (*loaves*)
hǫ	*ho-phɛha* (*to cook, cooking*)	[no plural form]

Do you see how it works? For each noun in the Sesotho language, you have to learn which of the eight classes it belongs to, and form the singular and plural with the appropriate prefix. For instance, if a noun belongs to the '*mǫ/ba*' class, or gender, its singular always has the *mǫ-* prefix, and its plural has the *ba-* prefix. And so on. But that's not all. Each separate noun-class dictates particular different agreement prefixes elsewhere in the sentence, for example on verbs and adjectives.

4 Data adapted from 'Niger-Congo noun class and agreement systems in language acquisition and historical change', by K. Demuth, N. Faraclas and L. Marchese, in *Noun Classes and Categorization*, edited by C. Craig (John Benjamins, Amsterdam, 1986).

Exercise What gender are the following Italian nouns, and how can you tell?

1 *il libro* – *the book*
2 *il monte* – *the mountain*
3 *la mente* – *the mind*
4 *la piazza* – *the square*
5 *il problema* – *the problem*
6 *il camion* – *the lorry*
7 *lo sport* – *the sport*

Generic

Explanation An expression is used generically, or in a generic sense, when it refers to a whole kind of thing, rather than just one or several specific individuals. With generic expressions, a **word** such as *all* or *any* or *typically* (or their equivalents in other languages), is either present or implicitly understood.

Examples The underlined parts of the left-hand **sentences** below are used generically; explicitly generic paraphrases are given on the right.

The whale is a mammal.	*All whales are mammals.*
Women live longer than men.	*Women typically live longer than men typically do.*
A mature oak tree weighs 50 tons.	*A typical mature oak tree weighs 50 tons.*
I adore smoked salmon.	*I adore all smoked salmon.*
Sleeping in a tent is fun.	*Sleeping in any tent is fun.*

Contrasts Generic contrasts with 'specific'. An expression which refers to some specific thing(s) or person(s) is specific in its meaning. The underlined parts of these **sentences** are specific in meaning. Compare their meanings with those of the same expressions above.

- *The whale thrashed the water with its tail.*
- *In the street, women were queueing for bread.*
- *We climbed a mature oak tree.*
- *This smoked salmon is delicious.*
- *Greg slept in a tent every night when he was young.*

Relationships The kinds of expressions about which one can say that they are used in a generic sense are **noun phrases**. One does not usually speak of other kinds of **phrase** or other **parts of speech**, such as **verbs** and **adjectives**, being used generically. The main exception to this is bare **gerunds**, as in *Jogging is too energetic for me*, which are usually generic in meaning; this is not really out of line with the general link between genericness and **noun phrases**, because **gerunds** (though forms of **verbs**) are, by definition, used as **nouns**.

As the examples above show, in English, genericness is not exclusively signalled by any particular grammatical kind of **noun phrase**. Generic **noun phrases** can have a **definite article** (e.g. *the whale*), or an **indefinite article** (e.g. *a mature oak tree*), or no **article** at all (e.g. *AIDS sufferers* or *water*, as in *Water is wet*).

Similarly, either **singular** or **plural noun phrases** can be used generically, as shown by the examples already given.

In English, the **perfect** and **progressive** forms of **verbs** are usually odd with generic expressions, if they can be used at all. So, for example **The whale has been a mammal* and **I am adoring smoked salmon* are odd. This is presumably because statements applied generically are true in a 'timeless' way, and the **perfect** and **progressive** indicate specific points or periods in time.

Exercise Identify the expressions used generically in the following.

1 *High-pitched noises set my teeth on edge.*
2 *High-pitched noises were coming from behind the sofa.*
3 *In the realm of furniture, the sofa is a peculiarly English concept.*
4 *Teeth are vulnerable to sugar.*

Genitive case

Explanation English **possessives** are sometimes said to be in the genitive case, but, as English does not have a rich system of **cases**, the term is actually not very useful for describing English. The term is much more useful for describing languages with rich **case** systems, such as German, Latin or Russian.

Examples In the following **sentences**, the underlined **words** and **phrases** might be said to be in the genitive case.

- *John's mother is my aunt.*
- *The rain's acid content is killing our trees.*

Contrasts Genitive, as a **case**, contrasts with other **cases**, such as **nominative, accusative** and **dative**.

Relationships Unlike the main **cases, nominative, accusative** and **dative**, which relate to the structure of whole **sentences**, the genitive case plays its role primarily inside **noun phrases**. As it is much more useful to talk about genitive case in connection with a language with a richer **case** system than English, we will illustrate from German.

The man's book would be translated into (rather formal) German as either of the following:

das   Buch   des   Mannes
the+NOM *book* *the*+GEN *man*+GEN

des   Mannes   Buch
the+GEN *man*+GEN *book*

Here the genitive case signals a relationship between the man and his book. The expression referring to the possessor (the man) takes the genitive case; the expression referring to the thing possessed (the book) can take whatever **case** its role in the larger **sentence** requires (assumed to be **nominative** in the first example above).

As with **possessives** generally, the term 'genitive' should not be identified too closely with ideas of ownership or actual possession or belonging. The genitive case signals a structural grammatical relationship between a **noun** and a **noun phrase**, and the actual relationship between the things referred to by the **nouns** may simply be some kind of loose association. Below is another German example, meaning *the foundations of evolution*. Obviously evolution doesn't actually possess, or own, foundations, as a man may possess a book.

Die   Grundlagen der   Evolution
the+NOM *foundations* *the*+GEN *evolution*

(German marks **case** mainly on **articles** and **adjectives**, and only in some instances on the **nouns** themselves.)

The central, or prototypical, use of the genitive case in any language which has it is to express possession. In any language, use of a particular **case** to express possession is what makes a grammarian label this **case** 'genitive'. But the point was made above that the genitive case can also express a range of other meanings, some of which have little or nothing to do with possession. The English preposition *of* has a wide range of meanings, very comparable to the range of meanings conveyed by the genitive case in many languages.

For interest   The following parallelisms between English *of* and Latin genitive case are noteworthy. Although the three concepts expressed are very different from possession, or ownership, and from each other, both languages express all three concepts with the same construction, i.e. English uses *of*, and Latin uses the genitive case.

Latin 'Genitive of Material', e.g. *cup (made) of gold*

poculum auri
cup   *gold*+GEN

Latin 'Genitive of Description', e.g. *a man of small wisdom*

vir parvae   sapientiae
man small+GEN *wisdom*+GEN

Latin 'Objective Genitive', e.g. *love of praise*

amor laudis
love praise+GEN

One interesting, rather offbeat, use of the genitive is found in Russian. The Russian genitive singular of the noun for *table* is *stolá*; this can mean *of a table*. But this genitive singular *stolá* is also the form found after just the numerals for 2, 3 and 4. After other numerals, the genitive plural of the noun is used. So we have a pattern like the following:

dva stolá	*two tables*	(literally *two of a table*)
tri stolá	*three tables*	(literally *three of a table*)
četirye stolá	*four tables*	(literally *four of a table*)
piat' stolóv	*five tables*	(literally *five of tables*)
ščest' stolóv	*six tables*	(literally *six of tables*)

Exercise   Which parts of the following sentences might be said to be in the genitive case?

- *Excuse me, but you're standing on my foot.*
- *Her father left her his medals.*
- *It's turning its head this way.*
- *They're over there playing with their sister.*
- *The orbit of Halley's comet is elliptical.*

Gerund

Explanation   A gerund is a form of a **verb** used as a **noun**. As such, it functions as a **subject** or **object** of a **clause**, and acts as the **head** of a **noun phrase**. In English, a gerund ends in the **suffix** *-ing*.

Examples   The underlined forms in the following **sentences** are gerunds.

- *Rosie's <u>swimming</u> has improved enormously.*
- *<u>Reading</u>, <u>writing</u> and arithmetic are known as 'the three R's'.*
- *Felix has switched from pompous <u>boasting</u> to pathetic <u>whining</u>.*
- *Felix has switched from <u>boasting</u> pompously to <u>whining</u> pathetically.*
- *Does my asthmatic <u>wheezing</u> bother you?*
- *Does my <u>wheezing</u> asthmatically bother you?*

Contrasts   In English, a gerund has the same form, ending in *-ing*, as the **present participle** of a **verb**, but the two differ in their uses. A gerund is used as a **noun**, as in the examples above, whereas a **present participle** is the form of a **verb** that accompanies the **auxiliary** *be* in the **progressive**, as in *Phyllis was washing the dishes*. A **present participle**, but not a gerund, can also be used as an **adjective** as in *We were caught by the rising tide*.

Relationships   There are two slightly different constructions which use a gerund, and in one of these, the gerund is sometimes traditionally called a 'verbal **noun**'.

The verbal **noun** type of gerund takes the same kind of **modifiers** as a **noun**, such as **adjectives, possessives, demonstratives** and **prepositional phrases**. In the following examples, the gerunds (all of the verbal **noun** type) and their **modifiers** are underlined:

- *Heavy petting makes you blind.* (**adjective modifying** a gerund)
- *He's getting fanatical about his jogging.* (**possessive modifying** a gerund)
- *That kneeling was painful.* (**demonstrative modifying** a gerund)
- *The typing of the thesis is your responsibility.* (**article** and **prepositional phrase modifying** a gerund)
- *There were sixty killings in New York last week.* (**numeral modifying** a gerund)

In the last example, the gerund, true to its use as a **noun**, has the **plural** *-s* ending.

Verbs have **subjects** (and sometimes **objects**), and when a gerund is formed from a **verb** and used as a verbal **noun**, what would have been the **subject** of the **verb** is expressed by the corresponding **possessive**. Here are examples of such correspondences:

SENTENCE	PHRASE WITH (VERBAL NOUN) GERUND
I smoke.	*my smoking*
Fred snores.	*Fred's snoring*

In a similar way, **adverbs** in **sentences** correspond to **adjectives** in **phrases** with verbal **noun** gerunds; and the **objects** of **transitive verbs** correspond to **prepositional phrases** with *of*, as in:

SENTENCE	PHRASE WITH (VERBAL NOUN) GERUND
Amazingly, Ruby shot Oswald.	*Ruby's amazing shooting of Oswald*
You sang the carol tunefully.	*your tuneful singing of the carol*

When the gerund has the typical partners of a **verb** in a **sentence**, such as a **subject** or **object noun phrase** or an **adverb**, it is not so appropriate to call it a 'verbal **noun**', although it is still somewhat 'nouny' in its behaviour, because of the role it plays in a larger **clause**. Examples with the two types of gerund are set out together below for comparison.

'TRADITIONAL' GERUND	VERBAL NOUN GERUND
Ruby shooting Oswald	*Ruby's shooting of Oswald*
Rosie coughing constantly	*Rosie's constant coughing*
wasting time	*the wasting of time*

Notice that all of these examples could be used as **subjects** of a larger **clause**, as in *Ruby shooting Oswald shocked everyone*, or as **direct objects** of a larger **clause** as in *Calvin detested the wasting of time*. This is what makes gerunds (of both types) 'nouny'.

Gerunds behave very much like certain **infinitives**. Both are forms of **verbs**, remember. Note the following quite close paraphrases.

Killing time is a sin.	*To kill time is a sin.*
Lin's winning the 100m was incredible.	*For Lin to win the 100m was incredible.*
I love shopping.	*I love to shop.*

English gerunds always end in *-ing*. They are very similar in their distribution and use (especially when used as verbal **nouns**) to forms called 'nominalizations' by linguists. Nominalizations do not end in *-ing* and are formed in a variety of ways, not strictly predictable from the **verb**. Examples of corresponding gerunds and nominalizations are:

GERUND	NOMINALIZATION
destroying	*destruction*
arriving	*arrival*
establishing	*establishment*
referring	*reference*

Many English **verbs** have no corresponding nominalization distinct from a gerund. It is generally **words** derived from Latin roots which have distinct nominalizations.

For interest Some well-known examples in linguistics are:

- *Flying planes can be dangerous.*
- *Visiting relatives can be tedious.*

Each of these sentences is ambiguous, and in the same way. On one interpretation, a certain activity by unspecified people is described as dangerous, or tedious; on the other interpretation, certain things or people themselves are so described. It is either the flying of planes which is dangerous, or it is planes that fly which are dangerous. The interest in such examples for linguists lies in the fact that the ambiguity cannot be represented simply as a difference between two ways of dividing the sentences up into phrases. There is only one way to break these sentences up (to analyse them), and that is with *flying planes* (or *visiting relatives*) as subject, and *can be dangerous/tedious* as predicate.

This shows the need for a way of representing differences in meaning beyond merely showing 'what goes with what'. On either interpretation, *flying* goes with *planes*. What needs to be stated in addition to this is the relationship between these two adjacent words. In one interpretation, the relationship is that *planes* is the object of the verb *fly* from which the gerund *flying* is formed, and the subject is some unspecified person(s). In the other interpretation, the relationship is that *planes* is the subject of the present participle *flying* (used as an adjective). Somehow, a full description of English has to include the fact that *flying planes* is a paraphrase of either *to fly planes* or *planes that fly*.

Most languages have ways of treating the content of a sentence as either the subject or object of a larger sentence, which is what gerunds, in effect, allow you to do. But not all languages have such a highly structured way of doing it as English, with the detailed correspondences described in the previous section.

Exercise   Identify the gerunds in the following sentences. There are four in all.

1 *Shooting at moving targets is difficult.*
2 *Moving targets all day is making me a nervous wreck.*
3 *John's making a nervous wreck of me is worrying my mother.*
4 *He's having a big guilt trip about worrying my mother.*

Grammar

Explanation   The grammar of a language is a conventional system of rules for making and putting together the expressions (e.g. **sentences** and **phrases**) that belong to the language. The **sentences** and **phrases** put together by these rules are grammatical in the language concerned. In a slightly wider sense, the grammar of a language includes the system of connections between grammatical expressions and their meanings and uses.

The **word** 'grammar' is often used as a term for a kind of book, describing the rules followed by speakers in speaking their native language (that is, describing the grammar of the language). In practice, the rules followed by speakers (of any language) are so extensive and complicated that no book ever succeeds in describing more than the central and most frequent patterns. Grammar books present their information in different ways, depending on their purpose. There can be 'pedagogic', or teaching grammars, and reference grammars (see **Relationships** below).

Examples   Every language (and every **dialect**, or variety, of every language) has its own distinctive grammar, regardless of whether the grammar has been codified and written down in grammar books. So there is (standard) English grammar, Classical Arabic grammar, the grammar of Swahili speakers in Zaire, the grammar of West Greenlandic Eskimo, the grammar of the Black English of south central Los Angeles, and so on. The grammars of different languages can be strikingly different from each other in some ways, and yet there are some equally striking common patterns running through the grammars of all languages.

The most comprehensive reference grammar of English is *A Grammar of Contemporary English*, by R. Quirk, S. Greenbaum, G. Leech, and J. Svartvik. It is 1,120 pages long, and even at this length, it omits many tiny details of English grammar.

Contrasts   The grammar of a language is not the same thing as its vocabulary, or its pronunciation, although all three of these need to be known in order to speak a language as its native speakers do. The vocabulary of a language includes grammatical information about how the **words** go together to make **sentences**, for instance by stating what **part of speech** a **word** belongs to.

Linguists emphasize the following contrasts, not always traditionally respected.

Grammar is not the same as logic. Amongst other things, logic is the study of whether **sentences** are contradictory or not, or whether the meaning of one **sentence** can reasonably be inferred from the meaning of another, but logic does not deal with whether **sentences** are grammatical or not. Take the following example of a logical argument.

- *All men are mortal.*
- *Socrates is a man.*
- *Therefore, Socrates is mortal.*

All the **sentences** in this argument are grammatical in English, but the same logical chain of reasoning could be expressed in **sentences** that are ungrammatical in standard English, as shown below (assuming that the same meanings can be attached to these **sentences**).

- *★All men is mortal.*
- *★Socrates is man.*
- *★Therefore, Socrates am mortal.*

Of course, when conducting a logical argument, one normally uses expressions that are also grammatical, but this example makes the point that it is possible to separate grammar from logic.

Grammar also contrasts with meaningfulness, or sense. The grammatical rules of a language form **sentences**, but it is quite possible to compose grammatical nonsense. Here are some examples of such grammatical nonsense.

- *Colourless green ideas sleep furiously.*
- *Both of John's parents are married to aunts of mine.*
- *One fine day in the middle of the night*
  Two dead men got up to fight.

Grammar contrasts with style, or usage. That is, grammaticality and good style or elegant usage are not the same thing. A **sentence** can be perfectly grammatical but have very poor style. Here are some examples of grammatical, but stylistically poor, **sentences**, with some suggested reasons for the poorness of style in parentheses.

- *There are several arrangements which are now needed to be made by us.* (Unnecessary repeated use of the **passive**.)
- *Actually, Lesley said that he had actually done it, actually.* (Undue repetition of the same **word**.)
- *Back to the suburbs where he had come from earlier that day went John.* (Unusual inversion of **subject** and **verb**, combined with too much information piled up at the beginning of the **sentence**.)

Grammar contrasts with texts, such as books, articles or poems. Grammar is a major part of the system behind texts. You can use novels or newspaper articles to study the grammar of a language, because they are (usually!) written following the patterns and principles which are the grammar. Depending on one's choice of reading, this method of studying a language can be more or less systematic or thorough. All authors have their own particular biases in the grammatical patterns they use, and it is wise to study at least several contrasting texts, to see the range of grammatical devices available for different purposes in the language as a whole. Making explicit useful and interesting comparisons between the language of various texts requires familiarity with the terminology of grammar. Grammar is what written texts and spoken conversations are made with.

Relationships The most reliable authorities on what is grammatical in a language are the speakers themselves, who learn it swiftly and surely in early childhood. In speaking a language, speakers unconsciously follow the grammar learnt in childhood. The grammar learnt in childhood is not learnt from deliberate teaching, like school subjects such as arithmetic, spelling and history. Indeed, by the time they go to school, most children have already learnt most of the major grammatical constructions in their language. If they hadn't, they wouldn't be ready for the instruction they are to receive in school, as they wouldn't understand what the teacher says. (Naturally, if the language or **dialect** whose grammar they have learnt before attending school is different from that used in the school, they will have difficulty in any case.)

It may seem odd to say that anyone who speaks a language has learnt (and hence knows) its grammar, because many people feel they 'don't know any grammar'. This is because the practical skill of speaking a language is applied almost fully automatically, and without thinking consciously about grammatical rules. There is an analogy between speaking a language and performing any routine physical activity, such as walking. At first, the individual steps may take some concentration and mental effort, but after a while they become completely automatic, and people cannot describe the process of walking exactly in words, and certainly not in the technical words of physiologists. Knowing the grammar of a language, as all native speakers do unconsciously, is different from knowing the technical jargon for describing it.

Speakers sometimes make what they themselves recognize as mistakes in grammar, due to such factors as tiredness, distraction, drunkenness and nervousness. Such mistakes, which speakers of any **dialect** can make, are to be distinguished from patterns which are perfectly grammatical in one **dialect** (and therefore are not mistakes), but not grammatical in another.

Pedagogic, or teaching, grammars, are books for teaching other people (children or adults) a foreign language. These vary enormously in style; at one extreme, a teaching grammar can look (and be) as solidly informative (and as dull) as a railway timetable; at the other extreme, a modern foreign-language teaching grammar for use in schools can be hard to distinguish at a quick glance from a cartoon strip book. Teaching grammars typically start with very simple constructions, and proceed gradually to more complicated constructions, introducing measured quantities of vocabulary along the way.

Depending on their philosophy of teaching, such grammars may or may not use the technical terminology of grammar explained in this guidebook. Recently, the trend in language teaching has been away from the explicit use of grammatical terminology, and in favour of presenting the information about the organization of a language in terms of the kinds of contexts or situations where it will be used. To compare the two approaches, look at the following excerpts from the tables of contents of two teaching grammars. In the left-hand column are the first ten chapter headings from M. Fourman's *Teach Yourself Russian*, which takes an explicitly grammatical approach; in the right-hand column are the headings (translated into English) of the first ten lessons of *Deutsches Leben*,[5] a very successful textbook for German.

Teach Yourself Russian	*Deutsches Leben*
1 Nouns	Question and answer
2 Nouns (continued)	Colours
3 Adjectives	The family
4 Pronouns	The family; the class
5 Declension of Nouns, Adjectives and Pronouns	What children do. Revision 1
6 Genitive of Feminine Nouns	Numbers
7 Genitive of Neuter Nouns	Numbers
8 Dative of Masculine, Feminine and Neuter Nouns	At the seaside
9 Verbs	Telling the time; dates
10 Shortened Adjectives	The family at home. Revision 2

The title of the book, *Deutsches Leben*, means *German life*, even though the book is for teaching the German language. This perhaps reflects the philosophy that the language and its grammar are intricately bound up in the life of its speakers. Actually, the grammar of a language is to a large extent independent of the lifestyles of its speakers. There are lots of facts about German grammar which a learner must learn and which have little or nothing to do with any particular aspect of German life or culture. How Germans build their houses and where they go for their vacations has nothing to do with where they put the **verbs** in their **sentences** and whether **adjectives agree** in **gender**. In fact, *Deutsches Leben* does use a lot of grammatical terminology, gently interleaved with passages about German life, but this interleaving is more for the purpose of motivating the readers, and independently portraying pictures of German life, than for showing any kind of parallels between German grammatical structures and German social habits and conventions.

Disputes about the use of grammar in language teaching can become very polarized and dogmatic. An approach which makes no explicit use at all of a framework of grammatical terms is likely to leave its users puzzled, and without a clear understanding of the general organizational principles of the language.

5 First published by Ginn, London, in 1931.

On the other hand, an approach which explains the organization of a language only by statements couched in terms of grammar is likely to be too abstract for a learner to turn easily to practical everyday use. A sensible compromise approach is best, tailored to the various learning styles and motivations of different kinds of learners.

A perennial tension exists between grammarians who emphasize form and those who emphasize function. A purely formal description of English would, for example, point out that there is a type of **sentence** in which the first **auxiliary verb** precedes the **subject** of the **sentence**, but would neglect to add that this type of **sentence** is typically used for asking questions. Of course, this is not useful, and in fact no grammar in common use is purely formal in this way. In practice, grammars tend either toward a formal emphasis or toward a functional emphasis. This is partly a matter of what information is selected (i.e. whether about **sentence** patterns or about their uses), and partly a matter of the organization of the grammar by topics. A formally oriented grammar will tend to have chapters on such topics as 'the **verb phrase**', '**relative clauses**' and '**agreement**', whereas a functionally oriented grammar will tend to have chapters on such topics as 'asking questions', 'referring to people and things' and 'expressing emphasis'.

There is no way that a functionally oriented grammar can avoid referring to the form, or patterns of organization, of a language. Its purpose is to relate these patterns to their uses, or functions. In all languages, the relationship between grammatical form (organization, pattern) and communicative function is complex. There is typically not a single way of communicating a particular kind of message – think of the different grammatical patterns that can be used for asking questions, or expressing **future** time, in English. Nor is a single grammatical pattern often used for just one purpose, or function – see, for example, the many meanings of the English simple **present tense**.

This discussion illustrates a general and quite fundamental point about all grammar and the uses to which it is put in communication. For any grammatical entity at all, in any language, it may have typical uses to which it is put, but it will also have other uses at best only loosely related to its prototypical uses. For example, **interrogative sentences** are typically used to ask questions, but they can be used for other purposes as well, such as dropping hints, making veiled threats and commanding. **Nouns** typically refer to concrete objects, but there are many **nouns** which do not. The **subject** of a **sentence** may typically pick out the doer of some action expressed by the **verb**, but for many **sentences** this is not the case. **Genitive case** is typically used to express possession, but it has a range of other uses as well. And so on, and so on, for any grammatical term explained in this dictionary, and many other, more technical, terms.

Reference grammars are used more like dictionaries, for dipping into, to find out about the details of any particular construction in a language. These are not meant to be read from beginning to end, and so, unlike teaching grammars, do not build up a picture of the grammar of a language from simple constructions to the most complicated ones. Each section of a reference grammar attempts to be relatively complete, and may present a full complicated account, without any of the gentle cumulative style of a teaching grammar. Reference grammars are useful for experts, such as teachers, who occasionally want to check up on details of the language they are dealing with, or to develop a finer and subtler knowledge of its grammar.

The grammarians who write both kinds of grammar books are basically describing a language as they find it spoken by its speakers, for the benefit of readers who have not had experience of it. It is not for the grammarian to invent rules of grammar, although one can find such 'prescriptive' statements in some grammar books written for native speakers.

When people complain about 'incorrect' grammar, what they usually have in mind is the grammar of a non-standard **dialect**, which differs in some respects from the grammar of the standard language. Using non-standard grammar in a social situation with standard speakers is in part like wearing the wrong kind of clothes to a formal social function; both may be described as in some sense 'incorrect', and the yardstick of correctness in both cases is a matter of convention. But we have conscious control over our choice of clothes, whereas speaking one's native language comes quite automatically, so to stigmatize the use of non-standard grammar as 'incorrect' is to intrude on a more private aspect of behaviour. Of course, speaking is usually a public act, carried out with the intention of communicating, and if any speaker fails, through differences in grammar, to communicate, then some adjustment, in either speaker or hearer, ought to be made. But misunderstandings and failures of communication due to differences in grammar are remarkably rare between most English speakers.

The basic building blocks of grammar are similar in all languages, including such items as **clauses**, **verbs**, **nouns** and **subjects**, to mention the most commonly encountered ones. The items explained in this guidebook are just 'what grammars are made of'.

The grammar of spoken language is often somewhat different from that of written language. For instance, in conversation you might say, talking about some object, *It's a pretty one that, isn't it?*, or *Yes, 'cause remember it had a hole in it*. Such utterances are quite normal in standard English speech, but one would not write them (unless trying to represent speech).

'Syntax' is a term used by linguists in a sense synonymous with 'grammar'. 'Syntax' is derived from two Greek forms *syn* (= *together*) and *taxis* (= *putting*), which is entirely appropriate, because syntax, that is grammar, is the putting together of **words** to make **sentences**.

Head

Explanation A **word** is the head of a **phrase** if it is in some sense grammatically the central or most important **word** in that **phrase.** Not all **phrases** have heads, but most do. The head **word** in a **phrase** determines what kind of **phrase** it is, and hence what kinds of position it can occupy in whole **sentences**. The head **word** in a **phrase** can never be dropped without drastically changing the meaning or grammaticality of the **phrase**.

Examples   NOUNS (underlined) AS HEADS OF NOUN PHRASES
- *the star-spangled <u>banner</u>*
- *the little <u>house</u> on the prairie*
- *seven <u>dwarfs</u>*

ADJECTIVES (underlined) AS HEADS OF ADJECTIVE PHRASES
- *rather <u>formidable</u>*
- *<u>rotten</u> to the core*
- *not <u>wide</u> enough for me*
- *as <u>tough</u> as nails*

VERBS (underlined) AS HEADS OF VERB PHRASES
- *<u>ran</u> out of the house*
- *<u>seems</u> wrong*
- *might have been <u>teasing</u> you*
- *sometimes <u>takes</u> life too seriously*

ADVERBS (underlined) AS HEADS OF ADVERB PHRASES
- *very <u>softly</u>*
- *most <u>impertinently</u>*
- *more <u>often</u> than might be expected*

In modern linguistics, it is also common to treat a **preposition** as the head of its **prepositional phrase**. Thus, for example, *on* would be treated as the head of the **phrase** *on the table*.

Contrasts   Head contrasts with **modifier**, although the two concepts are interdependent. If a **word** is the head of a particular **phrase**, it cannot simultaneously be a **modifier** in that **phrase**; a **word** plays one role or the other, head or **modifier** in a **phrase**, but not both.

'Head' contrasts with all **part of speech** terms, such as 'noun', 'verb', 'adjective' and 'preposition'. To illustrate, *room* is a **noun** in both *a dark room* and the larger **phrase** *in a dark room*, but it is only the head of the former.

The **head–modifier** relationship is distinct from certain other relationships that exist between parts of **sentences**, such as the **subject–predicate** relationship, and the relationship of **agreement**.

Relationships   'Head' indicates a relationship between a **word** and a **phrase** which contains it. A **word** which acts as the head of one **phrase** might not act as the head of another **phrase** it occurs in. For example *handsome* is the head of the **adjective phrase** *very handsome*, but is not the head of the larger **noun phrase** *a very handsome black cat*. Similarly, *table* is the head of the **noun phrase** *a wooden table*, but is not the head of the **prepositional phrase** *on a wooden table*.

Compound words have heads, too. For example, *shelf* is the head of *bookshelf*, and *book* is the head of *textbook*.

The terms 'head' and '**modifier**' are interdependent. If one **word** in a **phrase modifies** another, the **modified word** is the head of the **phrase**. The relationship between heads and **modifiers** is not symmetrical. **Modifiers** need heads to **modify**; without a head, there can be no **modifiers**. But a head does not necessarily have **modifiers**; in a one-**word phrase**, the single **word** is its head. Examples of such one-**word phrases**, of which the single **word** acts, simultaneously, as a **phrase** and as its head are:

PROPER NOUN AS (HEAD OF) NOUN PHRASE	*John*
PRONOUN AS (HEAD OF) NOUN PHRASE	*they*
INTRANSITIVE VERB AS (HEAD OF) VERB PHRASE	*disappeared*
ADJECTIVE AS (HEAD OF) ADJECTIVE PHRASE	*nice*

Not all **phrases** have heads. The most important type of headless **phrase** is one formed by conjoining, or coordination. Examples are:

- *Jane and her uncle*
- *Rubens, Rembrandt and Renoir*
- *happy and glorious*
- *jumped on his horse and rode off into the sunset*
- *either maliciously or negligently*

In such examples, there is a kind of balance between the conjoined parts, so that neither one can be said to be more central than the other. One would not want to say which of *Rubens, Rembrandt* and *Renoir* was more important in the second example. And, clearly none of these **words modifies** any of the others. For this reason, such **phrases** are judged not to have a head at all.

Note, however, that a headless **phrase** can contain **phrases** which do have heads. An example is the fourth one given above; here *jumped* is the head of *jumped on his horse*, and *rode* is the head of *rode off into the sunset*. But the whole coordinate **phrase** *jumped on his horse and rode off into the sunset* has no head.

Exercise Identify the head of each of the following phrases.

1 *our successful meeting in Cambridge in September*
2 *those persons responsible for administering the system*
3 *absolutely marvellous*
4 *the employee's last name*
5 *proceeds to the next task*
6 *go round in circles*

Imperative

Explanation An imperative **sentence** is of the sort typically used to give a command, or order. In English, imperatives are normally missing a **subject**, though all other normal parts of the **sentence** are present. The **verb** in an English imperative is the bare form of the **verb**, without endings of any kind, thus identical to a 2nd **person**, **present tense** form.

Examples Here are some imperative **sentences**.

- *Call me Ishmael.*
- *Look out!*
- *Please clear the table when you have finished breakfast.*
- *Note that this sentence has no explicit subject.*

Contrasts Imperative contrasts with the two other main types of **sentence**, namely **declarative** and **interrogative**. Imperatives differ from these two by the absence of a **subject**. Imperative, **declarative** and **interrogative** are called 'moods' by grammarians, so one will come across references to the 'imperative **mood**'.

Relationships As noted, English imperatives lack **subjects**, but in them an implicit 2nd **person subject** *you* is normally understood. If I say *Please go away*, the person I am speaking to naturally understands that he or she is the person who is to go away, even though I haven't said *you*.

The relationship of imperatives with *you* appears in various restrictions on other parts of the **sentence**. With imperatives, the only **reflexives** that can occur are *yourself* and *yourselves*. So, while *Shoot yourself!* and *Get a grip on yourself!* are fine as imperatives, examples like *Shoot myself!* and *Get a grip on themselves!* are not interpreted as imperatives. These last can only be understood as possibly **elliptical** responses to previous parts of a dialogue, as in *What is there left for me to do? Shoot myself!*

The relationship between imperatives and *you* also appears in what linguists call 'tag questions', little reduced questions tagged onto the end of a **sentence**, as in *Get lost, will you?* and *Please don't be late, will you?* After an imperative, the **pronoun** in such a tag is always *you*. So *Get lost, will she?* is not an imperative.

With **negative** imperatives, the **auxiliary** *do* is used, as in *Don't drink the water.*

There are no different **tense** (e.g. **past** versus **present**) forms of imperatives.

Imperatives are normally used to give commands, and there are certain things that, normally, you can't realistically command people to do, such as change the past, or change their stature, or know things they don't know. For this reason, imperatives cannot normally occur with elements such as the following:

- **auxiliary** *have*, e.g. *＊Have gone to London!*;
- **modal verbs**, such as *can* and *would*, e.g. *＊Can go!* (meaning *Be able to go*);

- **passives**, e.g. **Be kissed by Mary!*;
- certain **adjectives** describing states over which a person usually has no immediate control, e.g. **Be tall!*;
- certain **verbs** describing states over which a person usually has no immediate control, e.g. **Belong to the Boy Scouts!*, or **Know the answer!*;
- certain **nouns** describing states over which a person usually has no immediate control, e.g. **Be a genius!*, or **Be a Sicilian!*

It must be said, however, that these restrictions can be flouted, to achieve some striking or dramatic effect, as in *Be a man!*, or to give a command relating to a more distant future, as in *Be an architect*, or where some kind of pretence is to be involved, as in *For the fancy dress party, be Napoleon!*

Another restriction on imperatives is that they do not occur in **subordinate clauses**, which **declaratives** and possibly **interrogatives** do. A report of a command, as in *I told him to go away*, does not differ in any clear way from a report of a desire or an expectation, as in *I wanted him to go away*, or *I expected him to go away*.

For interest In all languages, the imperative is mainly associated with the second person (singular or plural), expressed in English as *you*. But in some languages, there are sentences that clearly pattern like other imperatives, but involve other persons. French is such a language, as it has first person plural imperatives, as illustrated below.

Voyons!
See+1ST+PLUR   (= *Let's see.*)

Finissons   *notre repas.*
Finish+1ST+PLUR *our   meal*   (= *Let's finish our meal.*)

Partageons!
Share+1ST+PLUR   (= *Let's share.*)

Note how the English translations of these have to use a fossilized 2nd person imperative form, *let's*, abbreviated from *let us*. *Let us go* does not now mean the same thing as *Let's go*. The first is a command or request (to a person who will not be going) to be allowed to go, like *Release us*; the second is a suggestion that the speaker and the hearer go together, and so in meaning is very like the French 1st person imperatives above. In poetry, of course, *Let us go* can still have the meaning of *Let's go*, as in:

- *Let us go then, you and I,*
  When the evening is spread out against the sky
  Like a patient etherized upon a table.

Despite (or possibly because of) the normal association of the imperative with 2nd person, the verbs in imperatives in most languages are in a bare form, with no indication of person. But familiar European languages, such as German, Italian and French, are a partial exception to this. The French plural imperative *Allez!*, meaning *Go!*, addressed to several people, has the *-ez* ending, indicating

2nd person plural agreement. And the German familiar plural imperative *Kommt!*, meaning *Come!*, addressed to several people, likewise has the *-t* ending, indicating 2nd person plural agreement.

But even in French and German, imperatives have less marking of person and number than non-imperatives. The French singular imperative *Va!*, meaning *Go!*, addressed to one person, lacks the *-s* ending that occurs in declaratives, e.g. *Tu vas, You go*. And the German singular imperative *Komm!*, meaning *Come!*, addressed to one person, lacks the *-st* ending that occurs in declaratives, e.g. *Du kommst, You come*.

Exercise   In the following passages, there are seven imperative sentences or clauses. Identify them.

- *Look at this. Look! What a cheek. Look what I've found hidden away at the back of the bloody airing cupboard.*
- *'Now, what I want is, Facts. Teach these boys and girls nothing but Facts. Facts alone are wanted in life. Plant nothing else, and root out everything else. You can only form the minds of reasoning animals upon Facts: nothing else will ever be of any service to them. This is the principle on which I bring up my own children, and this is the principle on which I bring up these children. Stick to Facts, sir!'*

Impersonal

Explanation   An impersonal **sentence** is one in which, by a variety of devices, the identity of the main actor (i.e. 'who does it') in the situation described is kept unmentioned. The crucial ingredient of an impersonal **sentence** is that it seems to avoid assigning responsibility. The term 'impersonal', applied to **sentences**, is not tied down with any great precision – it is used with a certain amount of freedom.

An impersonal **pronoun** is one which is used to avoid referring to any specific person, while still giving the impression that a person is involved; here the term 'impersonal' is used more strictly.

Examples
- The **pronoun** *one* in *One doesn't like to be difficult, but this is going too far* is impersonal.
- The **pronouns** *you* and *they*, when not used to refer to specific people or things, are impersonal, as in:
  - *When you fall off your horse, you just have to dust yourself off and get on again.*
  - *They are always fighting in the Balkans.*

Though the term is not applied with great precision, the following **sentences** would be counted as impersonal by most grammarians.

- *A large bomb was detonated today in Whitehall.*
- *It is raining.*
- *It is not easy to intimidate Ellen.*
- *Fighting broke out.*
- *Intimidating Ellen is a piece of cake.*
- *To spread gossip at a time like this is unforgivable.*

Contrasts

An impersonal **sentence** is not necessarily one which does not mention any people. For instance, *The satellite orbited the earth* mentions no people, but would not be called 'impersonal'.

The impersonal **pronoun** *one* contrasts with the **personal pronouns** *I*, *you*, *he*, *she*, *it*, *we* and *they*; and the impersonal uses of *you* and *they* contrast with their **personal** uses to refer to specific people and things.

The impersonal **pronoun** *one* contrasts with the **numeral** *one*, and, more subtly, with the **indefinite pronoun** *one* as in *I was hoping for a drink, but nobody offered me one.*

Relationships

In English, the main ways of keeping a **sentence** impersonal are:

- by the use of the **passive**, with no **phrase** starting with the **preposition** *by*, as in *This will not be tolerated*;
- by the use of the impersonal **pronouns** *one* (more formal) and *you* and *they* (less formal), as above;
- by the use of the various kinds of **sentence** in which the **subject** is the neutral, or 'empty' **pronoun** *it*, not referring to any particular thing, as in:
  - *It's blowing a gale out there.*
  - *Is it hard to get to St Andrews from here?*
- by the use of **gerunds** and **infinitives** with no **subjects**, as in:
  - *Eating people is wrong.*
  - *To dislike London is to dislike life.*

For interest

Not surprisingly, every language has ways of avoiding assigning responsibility, of making sentences impersonal. This is one of the main uses of the English passive. Although the canonical passive sentences that grammarians talk about usually have the *by*-phrase, in fact over 95 per cent of English passive sentences in use do not have it. So sentences like *The tree was felled* are vastly more frequent than sentences like *The tree was felled by the woodsmen*. English passive sentences without the *by*-phrase are called 'agentless passives' by linguists.

In French and German, agentless passives, and passives generally, are not so common as in English, and it is customary to translate such English sentences into French and German using the equivalents in these languages of the impersonal pronoun *one*, namely French *on* and German *man*. Thus the following are natural translations of each other.

- *Siegfried was killed.*
- *On a tué Siegfried.*

- *Man hat Siegfried getötet.*

Exercise

1 Identify the impersonal pronouns, or pronouns used impersonally, in the following. There are six of them in all.

(a) *When one has lost one of one's children, life is never the same.*

(b) *Fred is one in a million – they don't make them like that any more.*

(c) *You can't get AIDS from doorhandles.*

(d) *I can't give you anything but love, baby, as they say in the song.*

2 Which of the following sentences are impersonal?

(a) *Jimmy's leaving broke Hazel's heart.*

(b) *Parting is such sweet sorrow.*

(c) *The Romanovs were executed by the Bolsheviks.*

(d) *These temples were built around 700 BC.*

(e) *To tell the Dean about it would be stupid.*

(f) *John told the Dean about it.*

Indefinite

Explanation

The English word *a* (and its variant *an*) is traditionally known as the indefinite **article**.

It is also useful to speak of indefinite **noun phrases**. Many of these are introduced by *a* or *an*, while others have the word *some* or no **article** at all, where one would have been possible. The meanings of such indefinite **noun phrases** vary in quite subtle ways, but fall under two broad cases. Indefinite **noun phrases** either

- refer to specific things (in the widest sense of *things*), but there is no assumption that the hearer already knows about these things; or
- do not refer to any particular thing(s) at all, but just indicate what type of thing is being talked about.

Examples

A and *an* are the only examples of the indefinite **article**, in English.

The underlined **phrases** in the **sentences** below are indefinite, referring to specific things (a kitten, a tomcat, some food, two mice), but without any presupposition that the hearer already knows about these things,

- *Look out, there's a kitten on that chair.*
- *A handsome elderly tabby tomcat ambled down the path.*
- *I gave him some food, but he still went out and caught two mice.*

The underlined **phrases** in the **sentences** below are indefinite, not referring to specific things at all.

- *I wish I had a kitten.*
- *But I can't even find an elderly tomcat.*
- *All I need is some food.*

- *Two mice couldn't squeeze into that space.*

To clarify, in the first of the last four examples, there is no particular kitten that I am talking about (referring to); any kitten will do. In the last example, the speaker is not referring to two particular mice, but just making a statement about any two mice.

Contrasts The indefinite **article** *a* contrasts with the **definite article** *the* in English.

Indefinite **noun phrases** contrast with **definite noun phrases**. With the use of the latter, there is generally both some particular thing(s) being referred to, and a presupposition that the hearer knows of its (or their) existence, whereas indefinite **noun phrases** are typically used when there is no such assumption, when something is being referred to for the first time, or indeed when nothing is actually being referred to.

Relationships To bring out the perhaps subtle difference mentioned above between the two kinds of meanings carried by indefinite **noun phrases**, compare the following two **sentences**:

- *Miriam is a teacher.*
- *Miriam saw a teacher.*

The second **sentence** mentions a teacher, whom we can later sensibly refer to as *the teacher that Miriam saw*. But after hearing *Miriam is a teacher*, we can't similarly use **the teacher that Miriam is*. This is because **predicate noun phrases**, the ones used after *be*, don't actually refer to people or things; they just describe some property of the **subject**, in the same way that **adjectives** do, as in *Miriam is tall*. So indefinite **noun phrases** after the **verb** *be*, as in *She is a teacher*, have the 'non-referring' kind of meaning mentioned above.

Indefinite **noun phrases** are the only kind normally used after so-called 'existential' expressions *there is* (or *there are*) in English, as in *There's a vulture on the back of your chair*, or *There are some grey hairy things at the back of the fridge*. This is exactly what we would expect, given that the *there is* construction is used to state the existence of something. If you are telling someone about the existence of something, you obviously don't assume they know about it already. Some linguists test for whether a **noun phrase** is indefinite or not by seeing if it can be used after the *there is/are* construction.

The **pronouns** *someone, somebody* and *something* are indefinite. They can be used after *there is*, e.g. *There is something throbbing upstairs*.

It seems reasonable to regard the word *some*, pronounced unstressed (like [sm] as in the last syllable of *handsome*), as an indefinite **article** that can go with **plural** or **mass nouns**, as in *I took some [sm] bowls to the party* or *I took some [sm] rice to the party*. Here *some bowls* and *some rice* are indefinite **noun phrases**, as the speaker does not assume that the hearer knows which particular bowls or which rice were taken to the party.

Noun phrases with **common nouns** but no **article** at all, where an **article** could have been used, are indefinite in English. Examples are *lions* and *oil*, as in

There are lions in Africa and *There is oil on the floor*. Both *lions* and *oil* can be used with an **article** as in *the lions* and *the oil*.

Abstract mass nouns, such as *pity, fear, love, communism* and *literature* do not normally occur with **articles**, but it is not clear whether such **nouns** are **definite** or indefinite; this is an area of uncertainty, or indeterminacy, in **grammar**.

Indefinite **noun phrases** are frequently used in questions, as in *Would you like some shortbread?* This is because questions, more often than statements, involve referring to things that a hearer is not assumed to know about specifically. In the example just given, for instance, the speaker is probably mentioning shortbread for the first time in the conversation.

Indefinite **noun phrases** often occur in **conditional clauses**, such as *If I had a car, I'd lend it to you*. This kind of **clause** is used to express a condition contrary to fact, so, in the example given, the speaker does not actually have a car. Therefore the **phrase** *a car* cannot refer to a specific car, because there isn't one (that the speaker has).

Quite similarly, indefinite **noun phrases** are often found in **negative** contexts, as in *I don't have a car*. As **negative sentences** often describe the absence, or non-existence, of particular sorts of things, naturally there is often no actual thing that both the speaker and the hearer have in mind. In the example just given, there is no specific car which the speaker is telling the hearer he or she doesn't have. In saying *I don't have a car*, I am not referring to a particular car that I don't have; I'm saying that I don't have any car, or that there is no car that I have.

The word *any* corresponds to *some* and is often used instead of it in **interrogatives**, and in fact must (for many speakers) be used instead of it in **negative** contexts. For example, *Would you like any shortbread?* is very similar in meaning to *Would you like some shortbread?* And for many speakers, **We don't have some rice* is odd or even ungrammatical, whereas *We don't have any rice* is fine. The *some/any* relationship applies to the pairs *someone/anyone, somebody/anybody* and *something/anything*, too, with the *any* ones occurring more frequently in **interrogative** and **negative** contexts.

Indefinite **noun phrases** are common in the context of **verbs** which deal with things entertained in the mind, **verbs** such as English *like, want, imagine* and *dream of*. Examples of natural uses of indefinite **noun phrases** with such **verbs** are:

- *Jody likes bald men.*
- *Lulu wants an ice cream.*
- *Imagine a miniature elephant.*
- *I'm dreaming of a white Christmas.*

The **impersonal pronoun** *one*, used in rather formal styles, as in *One can't find decent housemaids anywhere these days* should be counted as indefinite also, because it doesn't refer to any specific person.

One also occurs in **sentences** such as *I've been looking for fossils here for years, but I've never found one*. This instance of *one* is also indefinite.

For interest

Try to put your finger on the exact difference in meaning (if you feel there is one) between *Would you like any shortbread?* and *Would you like some shortbread?* Do they reflect different expectations on the part of the speaker about whether the hearer will say *Yes* or *No*? If so, which way round is it, *any* anticipating *Yes* and *some* anticipating *No*, or vice versa?

Why does *Please can I have some lemonade?* sound right, but *Please can I have any lemonade?* sound odd? If you left the *Please* off the second sentence, would it make any difference to the oddness? Why?

Exercise

Pick out the indefinite noun phrases in the following sentences. There are seven in all, including one inside another.

1 *On a very hot evening at the beginning of July a young man left his little room at the top of a house in Carpenter Lane, went out into the street, and, as though unable to make up his mind, walked slowly in the direction of Kokushkin Bridge.*
2 *On the pleasant shore of the French Riviera, about half way between Marseilles and the Italian border, stands a large, proud, rose-colored hotel.*
3 *But, you may say, we asked you to speak about women and fiction — what has that got to do with a room of one's own?*

Indicative

Explanation

Indicative forms of **verbs** are **finite** forms used to describe situations or events, with no hint in the **verb** form itself that they are in any sense unreal or hypothetical. In English, the indicative is the form of the **verb** used almost all of the time, and so the term is seldom needed for discussing English examples. (See under **Contrasts** below.)

Examples

All the **verbs** (underlined) in the following **sentences** are indicative.

- *When I went home last night, Bugsy followed me.*
- *I hope it happens again.*
- *I told him he had no chance.*

Contrasts

Indicative contrasts mainly with **subjunctive**. Below are some **sentences** in parallel, illustrating the difference between indicative and **subjunctive verbs**, with the relevant **verbs** underlined.

INDICATIVE	SUBJUNCTIVE
If I am your brother, who is this?	*If I were your brother, I'd disown you.*
We suggest that he is a crook.	*We recommend that he be excluded.*

Both indicative and **subjunctive** are said to be 'moods' of the **verb** (although the term '**mood**' is in fact somewhat inconsistently and confusingly applied by traditional grammarians). In English, **subjunctives** are rare.

Both indicative and **subjunctive** forms of **verbs** are **finite**, and so **indicative** also contrasts with **infinitive**, as illustrated below, with the relevant **verb** forms underlined (and apologies for the slight mangling of *Hamlet*).

INDICATIVE (hence FINITE)	INFINITIVE
That is the question.	*To be or not to be.*
Whether 't is nobler in the mind	*to suffer the slings and arrows*

Indicatives, being **finite** forms of **verbs**, contrast with **participles**, such as *driving, driven, taking* and *taken*.

Since traditional grammarians sometimes apply the term '**mood**' to types of **sentence**, such as **declarative**, **interrogative** and **imperative** (rather than to forms of **verbs**, as above), and since in some languages **imperative sentences** require a particular form of the **verb**, the term 'indicative' sometimes gets contrasted with '**imperative**' as well.

Relationships   In English, as indicative is overwhelmingly the normal form for **verbs**, indicatives combine very freely with all other grammatical types. Indicatives occur in both **declarative** and **interrogative** sentences, but, for some (see immediately above), by definition not in **imperatives**. Indicatives may be used with either **active** or **passive voice**, and they may occur in **main** or **subordinate clauses**.

Indicatives are the **verb** forms (**main** or **auxiliary**) in **sentences** that receive **tense**. So the indicative forms in the following are the ones underlined.

- *Christmas comes but once a year.*
- *I was hoping that it had snowed.*
- *I hear you have been looking for me.*

Exercise   Identify the indicative verbs in the following. There are four of them in all.

- *When I reached 'C' Company lines, which were at the top of the hill, I paused and looked back at the camp, just coming into full view below me through the grey mist of early morning.*

Indirect object

Explanation   Some **verbs** can take two **object noun phrases**, both a **direct object** and an indirect object. The indirect object in a **clause** with such a **verb** is typically the **noun phrase** referring to the person or thing for whose benefit the action concerned was carried out.

As with **direct object**, it is convenient to apply the term 'indirect object' to the **nouns** and **pronouns** which are the **heads** of indirect object **noun phrases**.

Examples

In the following, the indirect object **phrases** are underlined.

- *Herod gave <u>Salome</u> a nice present.*
- *Bertie bought <u>his aunt</u> a box of chocolates.*
- *I sent <u>the tax inspector</u> my book receipts.*
- *Herod gave a nice present to <u>Salome</u>.*
- *Bertie bought a box of chocolates for <u>his aunt</u>.*
- *I sent my book receipts to <u>the tax inspector</u>.*

Contrasts

Indirect objects contrast most immediately with **direct objects**, and less immediately with **subjects**.

Relationships

The **verbs** which can take an indirect object are a subset of **transitive verbs**, and known as 'ditransitives'. For English, such ditransitive **verbs** include *give, send, lend, lease, rent, hire, sell, write, tell, buy* and *make*.

In English, where the two **object noun phrases** are adjacent, just after the **verb**, with no intervening **preposition**, the indirect object is the first of these two **noun phrases**. In other cases, the indirect object is marked by the **preposition** *to*, and, less often, by *for*. For most of the relevant **verbs**, both these constructions are possible, giving rise to corresponding pairs, as above, and below.

I lent Sue my Bible.	*I lent my Bible to Sue.*
Julia wrote Dom a 'Thank you' note.	*Julia wrote a 'Thank you' note to Dom.*
Pete told the kids a story.	*Pete told a story to the kids.*
Did Jim make himself a coffin?	*Did Jim make a coffin for himself?*
Noel built his family a house.	*Noel built a house for his family.*

With some verbs which take indirect objects, one or other of these two constructions is not possible. For example, *Ethel said 'Hello' to me* is fine, but **Ethel said me 'Hello'* is not grammatical. And we can have *Dick donated £1,000 to the Conservative Party*, but **Dick donated the Conservative Party £1,000* is odd for older speakers, but not so odd for younger speakers, reflecting an ongoing change in English **grammar**.

Often, the indirect object of a **verb** is optional and can be left out, as in *I wrote a letter, He made a coffin* and *They built a house*.

In languages with **case** systems, indirect object corresponds to **dative case**. An English **sentence** with an indirect object would typically be translated into such a language by a **sentence** with the corresponding **noun phrase** in the **dative case**.

For interest

A language which clearly has indirect objects (or dative case) is Japanese. But Japanese works in a strikingly different way from English and most European languages. In basic Japanese sentences the verb always goes at the end, and is preceded by a number of noun phrases, in more or less any order. These noun phrases express the subject of the verb, the direct object, if there is one, and the indirect object, if there is one. But if these phrases can go in any order, how can a Japanese listener tell which is subject, and which is object (direct or indirect)? After all, in English, it is largely the relatively fixed order of phrases that identifies subject and object. Japanese does it by marking noun phrases with an explicit marker of their role. These markers are little words, called 'postpositions' placed at the end of each noun phrase, so that, wherever it occurs in the sentence, whether at the beginning, in the middle or near the end, you can tell whether a noun phrase is to be understood as subject, as direct object or as indirect object. The postposition markers are as follows:

Subject (or nominative)	*ga*
Direct object (or accusative)	*o*
Indirect object (or dative)	*ni*

Here are some example sentences with these markers. These sentences could all be translated as *Taro gave that book to Hanako.*

> taroo ga   hanako ni   sono hon o   yatta
> *Taro* NOM *Hanako* DAT *that book* ACC *gave*

> hanako ni   taroo ga   sono hon o   yatta
> *Hanako* DAT *Taro* NOM *that book* ACC *gave*

> taro ga   sono hon o   hanako ni   yatta
> *Taro* NOM *that book* ACC *Hanako* DAT *gave*

These sentences all describe exactly the same situation, despite the difference in the order of phrases. The only difference is a matter of emphasis. Some of these different orderings are a bit more awkward than others, but all are allowed in suitable contexts.

Exercise   Identify the indirect objects in the following.

1   *The World Bank lends money to Third World countries.*
2   *Western countries sell them arms.*
3   *They can't repay the money to the bank.*
4   *This brings those poor people nothing but ruin and starvation.*
5   *America is dealing death, not only to people in other lands, but also to its own people.*

Indirect speech

Explanation   A passage is said to be in indirect speech (otherwise known as reported speech) if it clearly reports someone's words or thoughts, but without deliberately using exactly the original words.

Examples   In the examples below, passages in indirect speech are underlined.

- *My wife told me <u>I would find you here</u>.*
- *The lieutenant informed the men <u>that their leave had been cancelled</u>.*
- *Philip asked <u>whether anyone had sent him a letter</u>.*
- *Kirstie wondered <u>what had become of the statuette</u>.*
- *The lieutenant instructed the men <u>under no circumstances to leave the camp</u>.*

Contrasts   Indirect speech contrasts with **direct speech**, in which the actual **words** used by the original speaker are quoted verbatim. Neither **direct** nor indirect speech are involved in many **sentences**, in which no report is made of what someone has said or written.

Relationships   Passages in indirect speech always constitute **subordinate clauses**. These **subordinate clauses** are usually understood as the **direct objects** of **verbs** such as *say, tell, inform, ask, enquire* and *order*.

The **subordinate clauses** expressing indirect speech may be based on any of the three basic types of **sentence**, or **moods**, namely **declarative**, **interrogative** and **imperative**, to report statements, questions and commands, respectively. The examples below show the parallels between **declaratives**, **interrogatives** and **imperatives** in **direct** and indirect speech.

DIRECT DECLARATIVE	INDIRECT DECLARATIVE
John said, 'I'm coming.'	*John said that he was coming.*

DIRECT INTERROGATIVE	INDIRECT INTERROGATIVE
John asked, 'Are you coming.'	*John asked whether she was coming.*
John asked, 'Where is Mary?'	*John asked where Mary was.*

DIRECT IMPERATIVE	INDIRECT IMPERATIVE
John told Bill, 'Clean my boots.'	*John ordered Bill to clean his boots.*

As the above examples show, when speech is reported indirectly in this way, there are certain systematic changes to the original **words**. These involve **personal pronouns** and **tenses**. When the reporting is by someone other than the original speaker, the changes involving **personal pronouns** are these:

- *I* becomes *he, she* or *you*.
- *we* becomes *they* or *you*.
- *you* becomes *he, she* or *I*.
- *he* and *she* need not change, but may become *I* or *you*.
- *they* need not change, but may become *we* or *you*.

The precise changes chosen depend on who the original speaker was referring to. *It* does not change from **direct** to indirect **speech**. (As an exercise, try to think of examples of each one of the above possibilities.)

When the reporting is of **words** spoken or written in the past, the main changes involving **tenses** are these:

- **present tense** becomes **past tense**
  e.g. *John said, 'I am exhausted'* becomes *John said that he was exhausted.*

- **past tense** and **perfect** become **pluperfect**

  e.g. *John said, 'I saw Mary'* and *John said, 'I have seen Mary'* both become *John said that he had seen Mary.*

For interest The grammatical label 'indirect speech' suggests that a language will have a particular construction specially devoted to the reporting, without quoting verbatim, of people's words. In fact this appears not to be the case, at least for English, and many other languages. To take examples from English, the grammatical constructions that are used to convey indirect speech can all be used for other purposes as well. This is illustrated below.

The most common English construction for representing indirect speech is a subordinate clause introduced by *that*, as in *He said that John was in the bedroom.* But this construction also occurs with verbs that have little or nothing to do with vocal acts, as in *Nobody knew that John was in the bedroom.*

Indirect questions are expressed in English by a *wh-* interrogative word, such as *whether, why, when* or *where*, introducing a subordinate clause, as in *He asked whether anyone had seen him.* But again, this construction can also be used in cases which have nothing to do with any reported question, as in *He didn't care whether anyone had seen him.*

Indirect imperatives are expressed in English by an infinitive clause, as in *He ordered the players to leave the field.* This construction also can be used for purposes which have no clear connection with the reporting of speech, as in *He expected the players to leave the field.*

'Indirect speech', then, is not a term that identifies any well-defined grammatical phenomenon, in terms of grammatical construction. There are a number of different, though related, constructions, that, as it happens, can be used for the purpose of reporting speech indirectly. But all of these constructions can be used for quite other purposes as well, so there is no single grammatical pattern that we can identify as existing expressly for the indirect reporting of speech.

Devices confined to the reporting of speech do in fact occur in some languages. A 'logophoric pronoun' is defined[6] as a 'specialized pronominal form always and only embedded under a verb of saying, thinking or perception and referring to the person whose speech, thoughts or perceptions are reported. Such pronouns are especially frequent in West African languages. In the following examples from Yoruba, the first shows an ordinary pronoun [o] in the embedded clause, the second a logophoric pronoun [oun]:'

o	ri	pe	o	ni	owo	
he	saw	that	he	had	money	(= He saw that he (someone else) had money.)

o	ri	pe	oun	ni	owo	
he	saw	that	he	had	money	(= He saw that he himself had money.)

6 The information given here on logophoric pronouns is taken from Larry Trask's *A Dictionary of Grammatical Terms in Linguistics*, (Routledge, London, 1993).

Exercise Identify the clauses in indirect speech in the following sentence, and for each such clause provide the probable exact words of the original utterance.

- *When anyone asked Frensic why he took snuff he replied that it was because by rights he should have lived in the eighteenth century.*

Infinitive

Explanation An infinitive is a form of a **verb** with no marking for **tense**, and usually (but not always) with no **agreement** with any **subject**. In English, the word *to* before the bare form of the **verb** marks it as infinitive. In many languages, the infinitive form of the **verb** is marked by a special **affix**. Italian infinitives, for example, all end in *-are*, *-ire*, *-ere* or *-rre*, French infinitives all end in *-er*, *-ir* or *-re*, and German infinitives all end in *-en*. In Turkish, infinitives are marked by the **suffix** *-mak* or *-mek* stuck onto the **verb**.

An infinitive **clause** is simply a **clause** whose **verb** is in the infinitive form.

Examples The infinitive forms of **verbs** are underlined in the following **sentences**.

- *Do you want to go for a walk?*
- *I prefer to stay at home.*
- *To tell you the truth, I haven't written to her for weeks.*
- *To be such a bad letter-writer embarrasses me.*

Contrasts Infinitives contrast with **finite** forms of **verbs**, which show **tense** and **agree** with their **subjects**. Infinitives are thus non-**finite** forms of **verbs**, along with, and differing from, other non-**finite** forms of **verbs**, such as **participles** and **gerunds**.

Relationships A **subordinate clause** with an infinitive often acts as the **subject** or **object** of the **main clause**. In the following examples, the whole infinitive **clause** (underlined) is understood as the **subject** of *is human*, *is decadent* or *was unnecessary*

- *To err is human.*
- *To drink Martinis before noon is decadent.*
- *For Mervyn to redirect Maggie's mail was unnecessary.*

And in the following examples, the whole infinitive **clause** (again underlined) is understood as the **direct object** of *hates*, *loves* and *expected*.

- *Jim hates to wash his car.*
- *Rosie loves to plan parties.*
- *Phil expected Martha to stay at home all day.*

In case this is not obvious at first, you can test this by answering questions such as *What does Jim hate?* (answer: *to wash his car*), or *What did Phil expect?* (answer: *Martha to stay at home all day*).

These statements above concern the relationship between a whole infinitive **clause** and the **main clause** outside it. Now we'll mention the relationships inside the infinitive **clause** itself. It is the **subjects** of infinitives which are most interesting. Ask yourself what (or who) is understood as the **subject** of the **verb** *to get married* in the following:

- *Tess wanted to get married.*
- *Tess expected to get married.*
- *Tess hoped to get married.*

The answer is *Tess*. Not only is Tess 'doing the wanting', or the expecting, or the hoping, in these examples, but she is also the one who is to 'do' the getting married, in her desires, expectations and hopes. These sentences are equivalent to *Tess wanted Tess to get married*, or *Tess expected that she (Tess) would get married*, and so on. But, presumably to avoid repetition, the second *Tess* is omitted, although it remains understood as the **subject** of the infinitive **verb**. And the infinitive form of the **verb** signals in these cases that its **subject** has been left out.

Now we'll look at a closely related case, with **sentences** like:

- *Fred wanted her to leave.*
- *She expected him to leave.*

Who is understood to be the **subject** of *to leave* here? Clearly *her* in the first case, and *him* in the second. But there is a puzzle with this, because *her* and *him* also seem to be the **direct objects** of the **verbs** *wanted* and *expected* in the **main clauses**. (Otherwise why would *her* and *him* be in the **accusative case**?) What seems to be happening is that the **main-clause verb** has 'borrowed' the **subject** of the following **subordinate clause** to be its **object**. The infinitive form of the **verb** in the **subordinate clause** is a signal that this 'borrowing' from one **clause** to another (or 'sharing' between **clauses**) is going on.

In the cases we have just looked at, the **subject** of the infinitive **clause** can be identified with someone or something actually mentioned in the **sentence** as a whole. There are other cases where the **subject** of an infinitive is simply understood as some anonymous, unmentioned party. For example, the **sentence** *To lie in court is perjury* is not about any particular identified person lying in court, but about anyone, whoever he or she may be, who might lie in court. The sentence is roughly equivalent to *For anyone to lie in court is perjury* or *For someone to lie in court is perjury*. These uses of the infinitive are **impersonal**.

Infinitives, being non-**tensed** forms of **verbs**, cannot express meaning in the dimension of time, and so other devices are used with infinitives for this purpose. This is the motivation for a relationship in English between infinitives, the **past tense**, and the **perfect**, as in *It seems that someone was here* compared with *Someone seems to have been here*.

For interest Contemplate for a moment, if you will, the horror (in some people's view) of the English 'split' infinitive. A split infinitive is an infinitive form of a verb whose *to* has been separated from the verb by some other word (or even a whole phrase). Examples are *to boldly go* and *to slowly but surely sink into oblivion*. There is an old-fashioned view that it is bad grammar, or at least bad style, to split infinitives in this way. So the examples just given should, in this view, be rendered rather as *boldly to go* and *slowly but surely to sink into oblivion*. In these cases, putting the *to* next to the verb can be done with no problem. But there are cases where splitting an infinitive is needed to resolve ambiguity and make meaning clearer. Take the following examples.

1 *She solemnly promised to perform.*
2 *She promised solemnly to perform.*
3 *She promised to solemnly perform.*
4 *She promised to perform solemnly.*

The different positions of the adverb *solemnly* here allow the expression of two different meanings. In one case the sentence is about a solemn promise; in the other case, a (promised) solemn performance is being talked about. Let's label these 'solemn promise' and 'solemn performance' meanings SOL-PROM and SOL-PERF for short. Now let's look at two different dialects of English, which we'll call the 'SPLIT-RESISTANT' and the 'SPLIT-TOLERANT' dialects. The SPLIT-RESISTANT dialect, which resists split infinitives, is statistically more common among older and more educated people; and the SPLIT-TOLERANT dialect, which tolerates split infinitives, is statistically more common among younger and less educated people. The following table sets out how the two dialects assign the two meanings to these four sentences.

	SPLIT-RESISTANT DIALECT	SPLIT-TOLERANT DIALECT
She solemnly promised to perform.	SOL-PROM only	SOL-PROM only
She promised solemnly to perform.	both meanings	SOL-PROM only
She promised to solemnly perform.	ungrammatical	SOL-PERF only
She promised to perform solemnly.	both meanings	both meanings

To sum up this table in words, the first sentence can only have the 'solemn promise' meaning, for all speakers; the second sentence can only be interpreted by speakers of the SPLIT-TOLERANT dialect as being about a solemn promise, but for speakers of the SPLIT-RESISTANT dialect, it can have both meanings, because they use it deliberately to avoid splitting the infinitive; the third sentence cannot be used by speakers of this SPLIT-RESISTANT dialect, because it has the split infinitive, while for speakers of the SPLIT-TOLERANT dialect, this sentence can only have the 'solemn performance' meaning; finally, for both dialects, the last sentence can have both meanings, although the 'solemn performance' meaning is probably the preferred meaning for both dialects.

This shows that both dialects have a way of expressing the 'solemn promise' meaning unambiguously (via the first sentence). Both dialects also have a way of keeping the meaning ambiguous if desired (via the fourth sentence). But only·

the SPLIT-TOLERANT dialect has a way of expressing the 'solemn performance' meaning unambiguously, via the third sentence, with its split infinitive, which speakers of the SPLIT-RESISTANT dialect cannot bring themselves to utter.

Another good example of how splitting an infinitive can actually make a meaning clearer is:

- *This theory has failed to fully explain the facts.*

If, to avoid the split infinitive here, one were to write or say *This theory has failed fully to explain the facts*, it would not be clear whether one meant that there had been a full failure to explain or merely a failure to explain in full.

Exercise   Identify the infinitive forms of verbs in the following passage. There are three altogether.

- *Doctor, the pills are good for nothing – I might as well swallow snow-balls to cool my reins – I have told you over and over, how hard I am to move; and at this time of day, I ought to know something of my own constitution.*

Interjection

Explanation   Interjection is a minor **part of speech** used for **words** which can often stand alone as exclamations, typically followed in writing by an exclamation mark.

Examples   *Ouch!, Golly!, Gosh!* (these last two are now quite old-fashioned), *Christ!, Shit!, Blast!, Hey!, Shoo!, Hush!, Shhh!* and *Hullo!* are interjections.

Yes, *no* and *eh?* are also sometimes classified as interjections.

Contrasts   'Interjection' contrasts with terms for other minor **parts of speech**, such as **article**, **modal** and **pronoun**. And of course it also contrasts with terms for major **parts of speech**, such as **noun**, **verb** and **adjective**.

Relationships   As they are mainly used as one-**word** utterances, interjections are not well integrated into the **grammar** of languages, that is, into the rules for building **sentences**. When they do occur inside **sentences** it is often in **direct speech**, marked by quotation marks, as *'Oh!', she gasped.*

There are a few longer expressions that might be called 'compound interjections', such as the old-fashioned *Golly Moses!* or the profane *Jesus H. Christ!*

Some exclamations are not interjections at all, but either **clauses** or **phrases**, formed more or less according to normal grammatical rules. Examples of such **clausal** exclamations are *God damn it!* and *Damn and blast it!* Examples of **phrasal** exclamations are *For Pete's sake!* and *Up yours!* Some of the simple one-**word** interjections, like *Damn!* may have arisen through shortening of these longer exclamations.

Some interjections also have pronunciations which are not well integrated into the general pronunciation rules of their language. In many **dialects** of English, there are colloquial equivalents of *Yes* and *No* made with nasal sounds interrupted either by a voiceless, breathy *h*-like interval (for *Yes*) or by a glottal stop (for *No*). English spelling usually represents both of these as something like *Uhuh* or *Mmhmm*, failing to capture the crucial difference between them. These particular interjections, though falling outside the general grammatical system and usual sound patterns of English, are very useful in emergencies when a *yes/no* answer is required of a speaker whose mouth is full, or who might, for example, be holding a pin between the lips.

The interjection *Shhh!*, for telling people to be quiet, is phonetically strange, too, as it contains no vowel. There are also various interjections used by English speakers with clicking noises, not found elsewhere in the language, for expressing disapproval (sometimes spelt *tut tut* or *tsk tsk*), or getting a horse to move (the '*Gee up*' noise).

Many interjections are taboo **words**, not used in polite conversation. The examples above included a couple of the less offensive taboo interjections. See how many more you can think of.

In summary, interjections are marginal in many ways, grammatically, phonetically and socially.

Exercise   Which of the following English words are interjections? *A, aha, alas, an, blimey, blind, coo-ee, cow, oops, ooze, pow, powder.* (They might normally be spelt with a capital letter and be followed by an exclamation mark.)

Interrogative

Explanation   An interrogative **sentence** is a type of **sentence** most typically used to ask a question. In English, interrogatives normally have an **auxiliary verb** placed before the **subject**.

English interrogative **words** form a mixed bag of **words** used specially in some interrogative **sentences**. They are sometimes known informally as 'question **words**'. Almost all of them begin with the letters *wh-*. When they occur they usually go at the very front of an interrogative **sentence**.

Examples   All these are interrogative **sentences**.

- *Has anybody here seen Kelly?*
- *Did you feel the earthquake this morning?*
- *Who killed Cock Robin?*
- *What does he do for a living?*
- *Where are the next Olympic Games?*
- *When does daylight-saving time start?*

English interrogative **words** are *who, whom, whose, what, which, when, how, where* and *why*.

Contrasts

Interrogatives contrast with **declaratives** and **imperatives**, the other two basic types of **sentence**.

In English, **relative clauses** can begin with some of the same **words** as interrogative **sentences**, such as the **words** *who, whom, which* and *when*. And in fact some interrogative **sentences** are identical in shape to some **relative clauses**. For instance, *who killed Cock Robin* in the **phrase** *the person who killed Cock Robin* is a **relative clause**, and not an interrogative **sentence**.

Adverbial **clauses** can also begin with some of the same **words** as interrogative **sentences**, in particular the **words** *when* and *where*. The final **clause** in *There was a fight where John lives* is an adverbial **clause**, and not an interrogative **sentence**.

Some exclamations begin with the **words** *what* and *how*, which are also interrogative **words**. Examples of their use in exclamations are *What a lovely baby that is!* and *How prettily it gurgles!* But these are not interrogative **sentences**.

Relationships

Interrogative is a **mood**, or **sentence** type, along with **declarative** and **imperative**. An interrogative **sentence** might be called a 'sentence in the interrogative **mood**'.

In English there are two basic types of interrogative, which linguists call '*yes/ no* interrogatives' and '*wh-* interrogatives'.

Questions asked with *yes/no* interrogatives expect a simple answer *Yes* or *No*. Examples are:

* *Is she feeling well?*
* *Did they sleep well?*
* *Does your chewing gum lose its flavor on the bedpost overnight?*
* *Have you ever seen a dream walking?*
* *Could you pass the salt?*

For every such *yes/no* interrogative, there is a corresponding **declarative**, such as *They did sleep well* or *They slept well*.

Questions asked with *wh-* interrogatives expect more informative answers. They ask for some piece of missing information, whose place is signalled by the *wh-***word**, to be given by the hearer. So, for example, the interrogative *Who is your legal guardian?* invites the hearer to supply the **subject** X in a **sentence** with a 'blank' in it, *X is my legal guardian*. The answer could be a full **sentence**, such as *Lord Owen is my legal guardian*, or, **elliptically**, a simple **noun phrase**, such as *Lord Owen*, 'filling in the blank'.

Similarly, the interrogative *Whose pigeonhole did he put it in?* invites the hearer to supply the **possessive** *X's* in *He put it in X's pigeonhole*. A reply might be *The Prime Minister's*.

The main correspondences between grammatical positions or **parts of speech** and English *wh-***words** are as follows:

113

Subject (person)	*who*
e.g. *Who is your guardian?*	*Lord Owen (is my guardian).*
Object (person)	*whom* in formal style, *who* otherwise
e.g. *Whom does it concern?*	*(It concerns) your uncle.*
Possessive (person)	*whose*
e.g. *Whose box did he put it in?*	*(He put it in) the PM's (box).*
Subject, object or **object**	
of a **preposition** (thing)	*what* or *which*
e.g. *What did you find?*	*(We found) some razorshells.*
Article, demonstrative	
or other **modifier** of a **noun**	*what* or *which*
e.g. *Which book did you borrow?*	*(I borrowed) the big black one.*
Adverb of time	*when*
e.g. *When did they come?*	*(They came) on Monday.*
Adverb of manner	*how*
e.g. *How did he die?*	*(He died) painfully.*
Adverb of place	*where*
e.g. *Where did he put it?*	*(He put it) in the fridge.*
Adverb of reason	*why*
e.g. *Why did he give up?*	*(He gave up) because he was unfit.*

There is a correspondence in English between these interrogative **words** and the **words** introducing **relative clauses**. In fact *who, whom, whose, which, when, where* and *why* do double duty as interrogatives and as **relative pronouns**, as shown below.

who	*the man who saw me*
whom	*the man whom I saw*
whose	*the man whose bike I stole*
which	*the book which I borrowed*
when	*the year when the Berlin Wall came down*
where	*the place where I was born*
why	*the reason why I did it*

The two interrogative **words** missing here are *what* and *how*. *What* corresponds to the **relative pronoun** *that*, as in *the book that I borrowed*. But notice that *the book what I borrowed* is grammatical in some non-standard dialects. *How* corresponds to *in which*, as in *the way in which I did it*, or *that*, as in *the way that I did it*.

Words identical to these interrogative words also introduce abbreviated or '**head**less' **relative clauses**, as (triply) in *What matters is not what you know, but who you know.*

And the interrogative **words** corresponding to **adverbs**, *when* and *where*, coincide with subordinating **conjunctions** used to introduce adverbial **clauses**, as in *They were waiting for him when he came home*, or *She crashed where the road is shaded by trees.*

English interrogative **sentences** are characterized by the **auxiliary** placed before the **subject** in the **main clause**. Interrogatives with this characteristic order of **auxiliary** and **subject** do not occur in **subordinate clauses**, but there are **subordinate clauses** which resemble **main clause** interrogatives in being introduced by *wh*-**words**, as in *They asked me what I was doing*, or *Sally wondered when Colin would come back*. Linguists call these **subordinate clauses** 'embedded questions' or '**indirect** questions' (see INDIRECT SPEECH). In fact there are embedded questions corresponding to *yes/no* interrogatives, too, and these are introduced by *whether* or *if*, as in *They asked me whether I wanted an interview*, or *They asked me if I wanted an interview*.

For interest

The way English forms its interrogative sentences, with the inversion of the subject and an auxiliary, is rather exotic. Few other languages form interrogatives in this way, although, near to home, German does, and so, to some extent, does French.

Some French interrogative sentences are formed somewhat like English interrogatives, with inversion of the subject, if it is a pronoun, and a verbal element, but not the auxiliary. So we find:

Vous allez		*Allez vous*
You go (= *You are going*.)		Go you (= *Are you going?*)
Elle vient		*Vient elle*
She comes (= *She is coming*.)		Comes she (= *Is she coming?*)

But this method of forming interrogatives doesn't work if the subject is not a pronoun. So you can't say **Vient Marie?* (literally **Comes Mary?*) for *Is Mary coming?* Instead, you can put a special interrogative marker *est-ce-que*, best regarded as a single word pronounced [esk], in front of the corresponding declarative sentence, and say *Est-ce-que Marie vient?* Imagine the word *est-ce-que* being the equivalent in words of the question mark punctuation '*?*', and placed, not at the end of the sentence, but at the beginning. (In fact Spanish punctuation puts its question marks both at the beginning and at the end of question sentences.)

Many languages form interrogatives in a way similar to French, with a special question word (or phrase) either at the beginning or at the end of the sentence.

Kinyarwanda, a Bantu language spoken by the inhabitants of the central African republic of Rwanda, forms questions, like French, by putting a special word *mbesé* at the beginning of a sentence.[7] For instance:

	muzaajya i	*Kigalí ejó*	
	you-go to	Kigali tomorrow	(= *You go to Kigali tomorrow*.)
mbesé	*muzaajya i*	*Kigalí ejó*	
QUES	you-go to	Kigali tomorrow	(= *Are you going to Kigali tomorrow?*)

---

7 These facts about Kinyarwanda are from *Apprendre la langue Rwanda* by C. M. Overdulve (Mouton, The Hague, 1975).

Japanese forms a question by putting the question word *ka* at the end of a sentence. Chinese has several ways of forming questions. One way, in Beijing (Mandarin) Chinese, is to put the question word *ma* at the end of a sentence. (Chinese and Japanese are quite unrelated languages, by the way.)

Even English has a colloquial way of forming interrogatives by putting a special word at the end of a sentence, as in *You're leaving tomorrow, right?* German has a tag phrase *nicht wahr?* (literally *not true?*), which it can put at the end of sentences to express questions.

Although interrogatives are typically used to ask questions, there is no one-to-one correspondence between interrogative sentences and actual utterances asking questions. In English, as is well known, one need not vary the actual grammar of a declarative sentence to ask a question; one can just add a questioning, rising intonation. And some sentences which are grammatically interrogative, with the inversion of subject and auxiliary, are not spoken with the intention of asking a question, but rather of making a request (a polite command), as in *Could you pass the salt?* A simple *Yes* or *No* answer to this, without any action, would be uncooperative, but the sentence is still grammatically an interrogative.

Exercise In the following sentences, which of the words *who, whom, whose, what, which, when, how, where* and *why* are used as interrogative words (rather than, say, relative pronouns or subordinating conjunctions)?

1 *When did you last see your father?*
2 *What was happening where I left you last night?*
3 *When we were in town yesterday, why wouldn't you speak to the lady whose car you dented?*
4 *Which of you saw the person who picked up my jacket?*

Intransitive

Explanation An intransitive **verb** is one which takes only a **subject**, and no (**direct** or **indirect) object**.

Examples Some English intransitive **verbs** are *arrive, blink, come, dive, go, jump, sleep, sneeze* and *snore*.

Contrasts Intransitive **verbs** contrast with **transitive verbs**, which can take **objects**. The contrast between **transitive** and intransitive is generally restricted to **verbs**.

Relationships Some **verbs** which are really **transitive** allow their **objects** to be omitted, thus giving the impression that these **verbs** are intransitive. For example, in *John smokes*, we understand an omitted **direct object**, such as *cigarettes* or *a pipe*. And in *Brenda drinks too much*, we understand an omitted **direct object**, such as *booze* or *alcohol*. But *smoke* and *drink* are not intransitive, but **transitive**. With genuine intransitive **verbs**, such as *sleep* and *come*, there is no understanding of any implicit **object**. For example, in answer to *John smokes*, I can ask *What does he smoke?*, but in answer to *John sleeps*, it makes no sense to ask *What does he sleep?

For some **verbs**, we have to say that they come in two versions, one intransitive and the other **transitive**. This happens in several different ways. One kind of example is with **verbs** such as *jump*, *dance*, *hum* and *sing*. For each of the activities described by such **verbs**, they can be done in a rather undirected or formless way. For example, you can just jump, in the air, without there being any particular thing (fence, rope, flowerbed) that you are jumping. So *jumped* in *Freda jumped* is the intransitive version of *jump*. Likewise with *sing*; you could be just singing, either tunelessly, or unselfconsciously warbling some meandering idiosyncratic medley of your own − not singing anything, just singing. In such a case, the *sing* in *Freda was singing* is the intransitive version. But you could, more directedly, jump a fence, or sing the hymn 'Jerusalem'. The versions of *jump* and *sing* in *Freda jumped the Empire State Building* and *Freda sang the soprano part of Verdi's Requiem* are **transitive**.

Another type of **verb** which comes in two versions, an intransitive and a **transitive**, is the type like *break*, *drop*, *sink*, *lift*, *open*, *close*, *bend*, *move* and *turn*. Compare the following pairs of **sentences**, in which intransitive versions of **verbs** are put beside **transitive** versions.

INTRANSITIVE	TRANSITIVE
The glass broke.	*Mavis broke the glass.*
Something dropped on my head.	*Phil dropped something on my head.*
The Titanic sank.	*An iceberg sank the Titanic.*
The handle turned.	*Maud turned the handle.*

Notice that the **subjects** of the intransitive versions correspond to the **direct objects** of the **transitive** versions. In all these cases, the **transitive verbs** are what linguists call the 'causatives' of the intransitive **verbs**, because the **transitive verbs** all contain an element of causing to do something in their meanings. For instance, *Mavis broke the glass* is a quite close paraphrase of *Mavis caused the glass to break*, and *Maud turned the handle* paraphrases *Maud caused the handle to turn*.

In **sentences** like *Liz ran a mile* and *Lucifer slept a sound sleep*, it might seem as if the **verbs** *run* and *sleep* are **transitive**, because they seem to have **direct objects** (*a mile* and *a sound sleep*). It might be better to regard these **phrases**, not as **direct objects**, but as **adverb phrases**. The **sentences** can indeed be paraphrased by **sentences** with **adverb phrases**, such as *Liz ran for a mile* and *Lucifer slept soundly*.

These are in fact only some of the different types of 'amphibious' **verbs**, i.e. **verbs** which can be either **transitive** or intransitive.

For interest The causative relationship, mentioned above, between some intransitive verbs and their transitive counterparts, is not signalled in English by any difference in the shape of the verb. That's why we had to speak of different 'versions' of the same verb. Thus the same verb, *break*, is sometimes intransitive and sometimes transitive, depending on the sentence it is used in. There are a few pairs of different verbs in English which have this causative relationship between them. Examples are:

INTRANSITIVE	TRANSITIVE	
rise	*raise*	meaning *cause to rise*
fall	*fell* (as in *Dan felled a tree*)	meaning *cause to fall*
lie	*lay* (as in *We laid a carpet*)	meaning *cause to lie*
sit	*seat* (as in *We seated twenty guests here*)	meaning *cause to sit*

In some other languages, however, there is a much more clearly organized relationship between intransitive verbs and their causative, transitive counterparts. Well-known languages in which this happens are Turkish, Japanese and Arabic.

Turkish systematically forms causative verbs by adding a suffix such as *-dür* or *-dir* to the stem of an intransitive verb. For example:

> *öl = die*   *öldür = kill* (i.e. *cause to die*)

Japanese also forms causative transitive verbs from intransitive verbs by changing the word, in this case by inserting either *-su-* or *-sasu-*. Examples are:

yukaru	=	*go*	*yukasuru*	=	*send* (i.e. *cause to go*)
nemuraru	=	*sleep*	*nemurasuru*	=	*put to sleep*
taberu	=	*eat*	*tabesasuru*	=	*feed* (i.e. *cause to eat*)
ukeru	=	*receive*	*ukesasuru*	=	*give* (i.e. *cause to receive*)

Exercise Identify the intransitive verbs in the following. There are nine altogether, but not every sentence below has one.

1 *The sun had not yet risen.*
2 *Will they ever raise the Titanic?*
3 *The sergeant marched the squad across the square.*
4 *The squad marched tiredly and raggedly.*
5 *Peter trudged home, went upstairs, undressed and slept till noon.*
6 *The kittens were playing on the stairs while I was cleaning them.*
7 *The boss wanted me to work on Saturday.*
8 *The computer wouldn't work.*
9 *I had to work it for him.*

Main clause

Explanation The main clause of any **sentence** is the 'outside', or 'containing' **clause**. Where a **sentence** has only one **clause**, the whole **sentence** itself is the main clause; for such simple **sentences**, 'main clause' is synonymous with '**sentence**'. For more complicated **sentences**, a main clause is any **clause** which is not contained inside any other **clause**, that is, any **clause** which is not **subordinate**. Several main clauses can be joined together by **conjunctions**.

Examples
- The following simple **sentences** are all (also) main clauses.
  - *Mellors watered the roses.*
  - *Mellors, the gardener, has been watering the roses in the oval flowerbed since ten o'clock this morning.*
  - *Charlie is dead.*
  - *Charles James McDuff has duly shuffled off this mortal coil.*
- In the following **sentences**, which contain **subordinate clauses**, each whole example **sentence** is, technically, a main clause (but see **Contrasts** and **Relationships** below, for an important practical qualification to this).
  - *Mellors, who had been watering the roses, peered over the hedge.*
  - *It was a pity that Mr McDuff passed away without seeing our exam results.*
- In these **sentences**, where several **clauses** are joined together by a **conjunction**, the main clauses are underlined.
  - *Charlie died and Mellors put roses on his grave.*
  - *Charlie, who was a teacher, died and Mellors, who was a gardener, buried him.*
  - *Charlie died, Mellors grieved, Madame emigrated and the roses withered.*

Contrasts Main clause contrasts with **subordinate clause**. Since a **subordinate clause** is always contained in, or a part of, a main clause, any part of a **subordinate clause** is also a part of the containing main clause. But for convenience, when we talk about parts of the main clause of a **sentence**, it is implied that we are talking about those parts which are just parts of the main clause, and not part of any **subordinate clause**. For example, a grammarian might mention 'the **verb** in the main clause of *I told her you wanted to see him*'; in this case, the grammarian would certainly be referring to the **verb** *told* (and not *wanted* or *see*). Similarly, when we speak of 'the **subject** of the main clause' of a sentence such as *I told her you wanted to see him*, we would be referring to the **pronoun** *I* (and not *you*).

Thus, in practice, 'main clause' is used to refer just to those parts of a **sentence** which do not belong to any **subordinate clause**, for example, the underlined parts of the following **sentences**.
- *I told her you wanted to see him.*
- *It was a pity that Mr McDuff passed away without seeing our exam results.*
- *Charlie, who was a schoolteacher, died.*

119

Main clauses, understood in this way, do not express the whole content of the **sentences** they belong to, but rather provide a kind of frame or template, into which the **subordinate** elements of the **sentence** fit.

Relationships Like all **clauses**, a main clause always contains a **verb**. The **verb** in an English main clause is always **finite**. The other central parts of a **clause** are a **subject** and, depending on the **verb**, a **direct object** and possibly an **indirect object**. As for these parts, a main clause always either contains them or has a place for them, filled by some **subordinate clause**. For example, compare these pairs of **sentences**, in which the main clauses, as practically referred to by grammarians, are underlined.

John said it.   *John said that Kennedy had been shot.*
It shocked the world.   *That Kennedy had been shot shocked the world.*
Bobby suggested it to Lyndon.   *Bobby suggested to Lyndon that they appoint Mitchell.*

In these examples, there is either the **pronoun** *it* or a full **subordinate clause**. The **pronoun** *it* plays a role, such as **subject** or **object**, in the main clause; where this **pronoun** is 'filled out' or replaced by a whole **subordinate clause**, it is the **subordinate clause** itself that plays the role of **subject** or **object** of the main clause. But since the purpose of the term 'main clause' is essentially to contrast with '**subordinate clause**', grammarians tend to regard the main clause as everything that is not **subordinate**, as the underlinings above show.

Where the **subject** or **object** in a main clause are not themselves whole **subordinate clauses**, these may be either bare simple **noun phrases** or **noun phrases** modified by one or more **relative clauses**. As **relative clauses** are **subordinate clauses**, nothing in them counts as part of the main clause; only the **head noun** (and any other, non-**clausal modifiers**, such as **adjectives**) belong to the **main clause**. This is shown in the following examples, where the main clauses are underlined.

- *I know a man who speaks Basque.*
- *Basque is a language that has no known relationship to other languages.*
- *The man whose picture we had seen introduced us to John.*

In a similar way, a main clause can have either simple **adverbs** or adverbial **phrases** containing **subordinate clauses**. When a main clause contains an adverbial **phrase** with a **subordinate clause**, nothing in the **subordinate clause** is counted as belonging to the main clause. This is shown in the following examples, where the main clauses are underlined.

- *When he had finished, he collapsed into an armchair.*
- *The armchair likewise collapsed, as Fred has been using it for a sawhorse.*
- *Picking himself up, he moved gingerly, in case he had broken some bones.*

As many of the examples given above tend to show, the information expressed by the main clause in a **sentence** is often by no means the main information conveyed by that **sentence**. In more complex **sentences**, especially, much of the significant content of a **sentence** is contained, not in the main clause, but in its **subordinate clauses**.

Clauses joined together by **conjunctions**, such as *and*, *but* and *or*, are not **subordinate** to each other. Therefore, a number of main clauses can be joined by such **conjunctions** to form a **compound sentence**. This is the only case where a **sentence** has more than one main clause. In the following, the main clauses, as practically referred to by grammarians, are underlined.

- *She looked for him, but he wasn't there, or he was hiding.*
- *She saw him later, and he asked where she had been.*
- *After she had explained it all, he bought her a cream bun, and they went to their class as if nothing had happened.*

For interest   All languages have clauses as their central grammatical units, and ways of putting clauses inside each other. Any clause that happens not to be put inside any other is a main clause.

When one clause is put inside another, certain changes may be apparent in the inner, or subordinate, clause. Typically, these changes have to do with engineering the linkage between the outer, main, clause, and the inner, subordinate, clause, so that the meaningful role that the inner clause (and its parts) plays within the outer clause is clear enough to a hearer. But apart from that, main and subordinate clauses are remarkably similar. They all have the same basic ingredients, and tend to put them all in the same basic order. It is rare to find a language that has one rule for subordinate clauses, and a different rule for main clauses (apart from the rules connected with the actual embedding of one clause within another). For example, in any language, if adjectives go before their nouns in main clauses, then almost certainly adjectives will go before their nouns in subordinate clauses, too. And if verbs go at the end of their clauses in subordinate clauses, that's where they will go in main clauses, too, by and large.

German (along with other related, Germanic languages, such as Dutch and Swedish) seems to present a counterexample to this general similarity between main and subordinate clauses. In German, finite verbs occur after the second phrase in a main clause (i.e. not necessarily at the end of the clause), but in subordinate clauses a finite verb must go at the end of its clause. Here are some examples.

Das Fenster war offen	*Er sagte, dass das Fenster offen war*
The window was open	He said that the window open was
	(= He said that the window was open.)
Das Fenster war offen	*Er zitterte, weil das Fenster offen war*
The window was open	He shivered because the window open was
	(= He shivered because the window was open.)
Das Fenster war offen	*Er schliess das Fenster, das offen war*
The window was open	He closed the window which open was
	(= He closed the window which was open.)

German and the other Germanic languages that behave like this are unusual, however, among the languages of the world, in giving their main clauses a different basic structure from their subordinate clauses.

Exercise   Underline the main clauses, as practically referred to by grammarians (i.e. not underlining any part of a subordinate clause), in the following sentences.

1 *Holmes had read carefully a note which the last post had brought him.*
2 *Mr Sherlock Holmes, who was usually very late in the mornings, save upon those not infrequent occasions when he was up all night, was seated at the breakfast table.*
3 *It is a most singular thing that a problem which was certainly as abstruse and unusual as any which I have faced in my long professional career should have come to me after my retirement.*
4 *It was pleasant to Dr Watson to find himself once more in the untidy room of the first floor in Baker Street which had been the starting point of so many remarkable adventures.*

Main verb

Explanation   The main verb in any **clause** is the **verb** which is not an **auxiliary**, and which, in English, follows any other **verbs** in its **clause**.

Examples   In the following examples, the main verbs are underlined.

- *When Danny came home from the army he learned that he was an heir and an owner of property.*
- *Flambeau and his friend the priest were sitting in the temple gardens about sunset; and their neighbourhood or some such accidental influence had turned their talk to matters of legal process.*
- *Father Brown was walking home from Mass on a white weird morning when the mists were slowly lifting – one of those mornings when the very element of light appears as something mysterious and new.*

Contrasts   Main verb contrasts with **auxiliary verb**. A **verb** in a given **clause** cannot simultaneously be both the main verb and an **auxiliary**.

'Main verb' does not mean 'verb in a main clause'; there are **main verbs** in both **main** and **subordinate clauses**.

Relationships   The main verb of a **clause** can appear in various forms, including **finite**, participial and **infinitive**, as detailed below.

In English, main verbs occur in **finite** forms, showing **tense** and **agreement**, only when there is no **auxiliary verb** in the **clause**, as in these examples, where the main verbs are underlined.

- *The sun rose gradually above the bank of clouds on the horizon.*

- *I understand that you are a friend of my sister's.*

In English, **present participle** and **past participle** forms of a main verb occur with the **auxiliaries** *be* and *have* as in:

- *Grandfather was sitting in a rocking chair on the verandah.*
- *He had smoked a pipeful of his favourite tobacco.*
- *We hadn't realized that he was waiting for us.*

Bare forms of a main verb occur after **modal verbs**, as in *You can laugh* and *I might buy you an ice cream.*

Infinitive forms of a main verb occur after **verbs** such as *want, try, decide, ought* and *need,* and in certain **subordinate clauses**, as in these examples (where only the **infinitive** main verbs are underlined):

- *I want you to put your arms around me.*
- *Fred persuaded Mary to knit him a sweater.*
- *I never expected her to agree to it.*

With **passive clauses**, the **verb** in the **past participle** form would usually be called the **main verb**, as in *Caesar was assassinated in the Forum.*

The English **verbs** *have* and *be* can be used as main verbs, as in *Ponsonby was Britain's most dangerous criminal* and *I have a nephew in Spain.*

Main verbs can be joined by **conjunctions**, in which case there can be several main verbs in a single **clause**. Here are some examples, with all the main verbs underlined.

- *Charles the First walked and talked.*
- *I looked but found nothing at all.*
- *He runs down the left wing, dodges three defenders, looks for support and sends a high arching crossfield pass to Humberstone.*

Except when the main verb is omitted by **ellipsis**, as in *Oh, yes, I can...*, every **clause** has a main verb.

For interest   It is not always easy to tell a main verb from an auxiliary verb. There are borderline cases, and in fact many auxiliary verbs are historically derived from forms which were once used only as main verbs. Consider first some uses of the verbs *go* and *come*, as discussed below.

- *I'm going to stay here tonight.*
- *That boy is going to be very tall when he grows up.*
- *I'm coming to think you don't love me.*
- *He's coming to look more like his mother.*

In these examples, the verbs *go* and *come* clearly don't have their normal meanings involving physical motion in space. Instead, *go* has taken on the meaning of 'future time', and seems to be becoming like an auxiliary expressing future time. Similarly *come* is used in these examples to express the beginning of some action or state of affairs, a meaning that in some other languages (e.g. Russian) is marked by an affix on the main verb.

On the other hand, there are some English constructions where *go* and *come* have their normal meanings (expressing movement to or from the speaker), but seem to be squeezed into the same clause as another verb, giving two main verbs in one clause (with no conjunction), which goes against the traditional European understanding of the term 'main verb'. These are examples like the following:

- *Go tell your father.*
- *Wait while I go get my coffee.*
- *Why don't you come sit by the fire?*
- *Come see what I've found.*

In these sentences (which are grammatical in some, though not all, English dialects), there are none of the usual markers of subordinate clauses, like an infinitive or participial form, or a subordinating conjunction such as *that*; the conjunction *and* is not present, either, although these sentences are understood more or less as if it were present. Grammatically, we seem to have two verbs looking like main verbs squeezed into one clause. Interestingly, the verb forms involved are all 'bare verbs', that is either imperatives or finite forms with no explicit agreement or tense markers. If one tries to find forms corresponding to these examples with 3rd person present tense, or past tense, marked on both verbs, they are much less grammatical in these dialects. This is shown below, where more grammatical equivalents are also given in parentheses.

★He went told his father.   (*... went to tell...*)   (*... went and told...*)
★Wait while she goes gets her coffee. (*... goes to get...*)   (*... goes and gets...*)
★They came sat by the fire.   (*... came to sit...*)   (*... came and sat...*)
★He comes sees what I've found.   (*... comes to see...*)   (*... comes and sees ...*)

This English non-standard dialectal *go*+VERB construction is somewhat similar to the 'serial verb' constructions found in languages in many parts of the world. But in many of these languages, where it is regularly possible to squeeze two or more different verbs into one clause, all these verbs can take agreement and show tense, unlike the situation with auxiliaries and main verbs in English and familiar European languages. Here is an example from Lango, an Eastern Sudanic language spoken in Uganda.[8]

Dákɔ́	òpòyò	òcègò	dɔ̀gòlá
woman	remembered	closed	door
	+3RD+SING	+3RD+SING	(= *The woman remembered to close the door.*)

Note that the English free translation has a finite verb followed by an infinitive (... *remembered to close*...), whereas the Lango sentence allows a succession of two finite verbs.

Here is another example, from another language, Gã, spoken by about 50,000 people in Upper Volta.

---

8 This example and the next are adapted from 'Complementation', by Michael Noonan, in *Language Typology and Syntactic Description*, Volume II: *Complex Constructions*, edited by Timothy Shopen (Cambridge University Press, 1985).

mínyɛ̃́	*míbá*
be able	come
+1ST+SING	+1ST+SING
+PERF	+PERF	(= *I have been able to come.*)

mínyɛ̃́ɔ́	*míbàà*
be able	come
+1ST+SING	+1ST+SING
+HABIT	+HABIT	(= *I am (usually) able to come.*)

Again, note that both verbs carry the tense and 1st person singular markings, so that the distinction between main and auxiliary verb appropriate for European languages does not apply to these languages.

Exercise   Identify the main verbs in the following. There are twelve altogether (including repetitions).

1 *I don't think that any of my adventures with Mr Sherlock Holmes opened quite so abruptly, or so dramatically, as that which I associate with The Three Gables.*

2 *Holmes had read carefully a note which the last post had brought him.*

3 *It may have been a comedy, or it may have been a tragedy. It cost one man his reason, it cost me a bloodletting, and it cost yet another man the penalties of the law. Yet there was certainly an element of comedy. Well, you shall judge for yourselves.*

Mass noun

Explanation   Mass nouns refer to stuff or unsegmented material (which may be abstract) dealt with as an indivisible mass.

Examples   *Air, benzene, excrement, hatred, intertextuality, rice, soil, spaghetti, water* and *weather* are all mass nouns.

Contrasts   Mass nouns contrast primarily with **count nouns**. Being a kind of **common noun**, they also contrast with **proper names**, and, more distantly, with other **parts of speech** such as **verbs** and **prepositions**.

Relationships   Concrete mass nouns can, in unusual contexts only, be **pluralized** and used with **numerals**, or used with the **indefinite article**, but when this happens, their meanings are altered to something like *units of* X or *kinds of* X, or else their meaning is changed to something even less commonplace. Thus *two beers* means either two measures (e.g. glasses) of beer, as one might order in a pub, or two different kinds of beer, such as Budweiser and Tartan Special. *Waters* is used only for discrete units of water (e.g. glasses, ordered in a restaurant), or in somewhat idiomatic **phrases** such as *the waters of the Amazon*.

Abstract mass nouns, on the other hand, are used, in English at least, without an article, and have no normal plural form. So *Eddie showed courage* is grammatical, but *Eddie showed the courage, *Eddie showed a courage and *Eddie showed courages are not grammatical. Other examples of abstract mass nouns are *envy, intelligence, patience, literacy, education, grumpiness, democracy* and *welfare*. Thus we cannot normally have *two envies, *five intelligences, *a literacy or *the grumpiness.

Apart from articles, mass nouns can be modified by most of the usual modifiers of common nouns, such as adjectives (e.g. *auburn hair*), demonstratives and certain quantifiers (e.g. *all that noise*), prepositional phrases (e.g. *art in America*), and relative clauses (e.g. *publicity which might harm us*).

For interest   Things which would be named by count nouns in English are in some other languages referred to by mass nouns. In Arabic, for instance, the words for *onions, peaches, figs, bananas, dates, ants* are all in fact mass nouns, taking singular agreement. To refer to just one onion or just one peach, you have to put a special ending onto the mass noun, with a meaning something like *one of*.

In Middle English (the English spoken roughly between 1066 and 1500) there was a mass noun *pease*, which behaved like the Modern English word *rice*, so that you couldn't say, for example, *three pease. Over time, this word got reanalysed by English speakers, and taken to be a plural form of a presumed singular word *pea*, although in fact no such singular form *pea* had hitherto existed. The singular *pea* was historically formed from the mass noun *pease* by a process known as 'back-formation'.

Many languages, including some close to home, like French and German, use articles with mass nouns. In many contexts, the French translations of English *love, reason* (or *rationality*), *wine* and *beer* are *l'amour, la raison, le vin* and *la bière*, with articles. The translations into German also generally require articles, as in *die Liebe, die Vernunft, der Wein* and *das Bier*.

Exercise   Identify the nouns used as mass nouns in the following sentences. There are nine of them in total.

1 *January weather in Edinburgh is awful – nothing but drizzle, sleet and biting winds.*
2 *The California climate is superb, if you can stand the smog.*
3 *Aluminium, steel and glass can be recycled, but paper can't be remade into trees.*

Modal verb

Explanation   A modal verb is a kind of **auxiliary verb** that, in English, precedes a bare form of the following **verb**. In other languages, such as German, modal verbs precede **infinitives**. Many languages do not have a clear class of modal verbs, although Latin did, which probably accounts for the continued familiarity (relatively speaking) of the term in traditional **grammar**.

Examples   There are a handful of modal verbs in English. The clear cases are:

can   could
may   might
must
shall   should
will   would

Contrasts   Modal verbs contrast directly with all other kinds of **verbs**, including **main verbs** and other **auxiliaries**. Modal verb is a **word**-class, and so contrasts with all other **word**-classes and **parts of speech**. If, in a given **sentence**, a **word** is a modal verb, it cannot be any other **word**-class or **part of speech**.

Relationships   In English, a modal verb, if one is used, precedes all other **verbs**, such as **auxiliaries** *have* and *be*, if they are used, and **main verbs**. The **verb** immediately following a modal is in its bare form, that is, is not a **participle** of any kind, or an **infinitive** with *to*. This is shown below, where the modal verbs are underlined.

- *You may take the rest of the day off.*
- *They must have been drinking for a long time.*
- *This lid can be removed by unscrewing in a clockwise direction.*
- *Mary's sister will be coming to lunch.*

Modals are the first **verbs** to occur in a **clause**, if they occur at all. Thus, when they occur in **interrogatives**, they are the **verbs** which are inverted with the **subject** of the **clause**, as in these examples (with modals again underlined).

- *May I take the rest of the day off?*
- *Must they have been drinking?*
- *How can this lid be removed?*
- *What will Mary's sister be coming to?*

For the same reason, modals, when they occur, are the **verbs** which take the **negative** marker *not* or *-n't*, as shown below.

- *You may not take the rest of the day off.*
- *You must not drink while on duty.*
- *This lid cannot be removed by unscrewing in a clockwise direction.*
- *Mary's sister won't be coming to lunch.*

English modal verbs are unlike other English **verbs** in not showing 3rd **person singular present tense**, with an *-s*. So, though we get *he has, she is,* and *it goes,* for example, with modals there is no *-s,* and we get simply *he may, she can* and *it will.* We don't get such forms as **he mays, *she cans* and **it wills.*

In the examples of English modals given first above, they were presented in pairs *can/could, may/might,* and so on (except for *must* which has no paired form).

It might be tempting to think of these pairs as corresponding **present** and **past tense** forms. To some extent this is indeed how these forms alternate in English **grammar**, as in the changes that take place in **indirect speech**, for example, so that *John said, 'I can go'* becomes *John said that he could go* in reported **(indirect) speech**. But in most cases, the forms in the second column above are not proper **past tense** forms, in the sense of describing some action or event that took place before the time of speaking. Look at the following examples and see whether you think any of them describe things that happened in the past.

- *If you come to the office tomorrow, you could meet Tom.*
- *It might rain soon.*
- *You should never talk to strangers.*
- *If I had enough for myself, I would lend you some.*

None of these **sentences** describe things which happened in the past, despite the occurrence of *could*, *might*, *should* and *would*, which might possibly, at first, seem like **past tense** forms. In particular, although *You can meet Tom* means *You are able to meet Tom*, in the example above . . . *you could meet Tom* does not mean . . . *you were able to meet Tom*. And similarly, although *It may rain* means *It is possible that it will rain* above, *It might rain* does not mean *It was possible that it will rain*.

There are a small number of **verbs** which behave rather like modal **auxiliaries**, but which require an **infinitive** form (with *to* on the **main verb** after them. These are **verbs** such as *ought*, *have (to)*, and *used (to)*, underlined in the following examples.

- *You ought to see a psychiatrist.*
- *I have to get home by four o'clock.*
- *They used to go to London by ship.*

Notice that the *have* here is not the usual *have*, as it is pronounced differently, with an '*f*' sound (sometimes represented as *hafta*). Similarly the *used* in *used to* is not the same as the **main verb** in, for example, *We used a shovel to clean it up*. The *used* in *used to* is pronounced with a voiceless '*s*' sound, as in *noose*, rather than a voiced '*z*' sound, as in *news*.

In English, the **verbs** *need* and *dare* behave partly like modals, in being inverted in **interrogatives** and taking **negative** markers, as in:

- *Dare I do it?*
- *I dare not do it.*
- *Need you make all that noise?* (not acceptable in all dialects)
- *You needn't pretend you're so innocent.*

But these same **verbs** also behave like non-modal verbs, as in

- *Do I dare to do it?*
- *I don't dare to do it.*
- *Do you need to make all that noise?*
- *You don't need to pretend you're so innocent.*

For interest The interaction of negation with the English modals is interestingly inconsistent. When there is a negative element, such as *not* or *-n't*, between a modal and a following verb, sometimes the negative meaning is applied to the modal, and sometimes to the following verb, depending on which modal is being used. With some English modals, it is the modal which is negated. Note the paraphrases and non-paraphrases in the following, paying special attention to the position of the *not*.

	MEANS	DOES NOT MEAN
I cannot go.	*I am not able to go.*	*I am able not to go.*
You may not go.	*You are not permitted to go.*	*You are permitted not to go.*

Thus, with the modals *can* and *may*, the force of the negative *not* applies 'backwards' to the modal itself, and not to the following verb. But now look at the following examples, again paying attention to the position of the *not*.

	DOES NOT MEAN	MEANS
It might not rain.	*It is not possible that it will rain.*	*It is possible that it will not rain.*
You must not go.	*You are not obliged to go.*	*You are obliged not to go.*
We shall not move.	*We are not determined to move.*	*We are determined not to move.*

So with the modals *might*, *must* and *shall*, the negation applies 'forwards' to the following verb. Work out for yourself which way the negation applies with the modals *would*, *should* and *could*, which have not been illustrated.

Exercise Identify the modal verbs in the following. There are six in total.

1 *The fundamentalists might have won power, if the military hadn't staged a coup.*
2 *The military might of the government can have no effect on the people's religious beliefs.*
3 *Food from a punctured can can make you ill.*
4 *I shall leave these shares to you in my will.*
5 *How much wood would a woodchuck chuck if a woodchuck could chuck wood?*

Modify, modification

Explanation Modifiers typically make the meaning of the whole **phrase** more specific. Most **phrases** consist of a **head** and optional modifiers of the **head**; modifiers or modifying elements may or may not be present in a **phrase**. Modifiers may be single **words** or may themselves be **phrases**. A large part of the **grammar** of any language consists in stating what kinds of **words** and **phrases** can modify what other **words** and **phrases**. Modification is the relationship between the **head** and its modifier(s).

Examples   MODIFIERS (underlined) OF HEAD NOUNS IN NOUN PHRASES

ADJECTIVE	the <u>old</u> tree
ADJECTIVE PHRASE	a tree <u>heavy with fruit</u>
	a <u>better than average</u> year
NUMERAL	<u>five</u> trees
	the <u>third</u> street
DEMONSTRATIVE	<u>those</u> apples
POSSESSIVE	<u>our</u> lessons
PREPOSITIONAL PHRASE	the house <u>on the hill</u>
VARIOUS	<u>that</u> <u>sarcastic</u> <u>young</u> man <u>in the corner</u>

MODIFIERS (underlined) OF HEAD ADJECTIVES IN ADJECTIVE PHRASES

INTENSIFIER OR	<u>very</u> hot
DEGREE MODIFIER	<u>rather</u> overweight
	<u>too</u> easy
	strong <u>enough</u>
INTENSIFIER PHRASE	<u>ever so slightly</u> crooked
	fresh <u>as a daisy</u>

MODIFIERS (underlined) OF HEAD VERBS IN VERB PHRASES

ADVERB	ran <u>fast</u>
	<u>savagely</u> beat him
PREPOSITIONAL PHRASE	sank <u>to the bottom</u>
ADVERBIAL PHRASE	hit it <u>as hard as he could</u>

Contrasts Modifier contrasts with **head**. If a **word** or **phrase** in a construction is its **head**, it cannot simultaneously be a modifier in that construction. But, as we have seen, an **adjective**, for example, may be a **head** of one **phrase** and simultaneously a modifier in a different **phrase**. In *very hot soup*, for example, *hot* is the **head** of the **adjective phrase** *very hot* (modified by *very*) and simultaneously the modifier of the **noun** *soup*. (We pass over the technical question of whether it is just the **adjective** *hot* or the whole **adjective phrase** *very hot* which modifies the **noun** *soup*; grammarians differ on this fine point.)

Modifier and **head** are complementary sides of the modifier–**head** relationship which exists between specific parts of specific **sentences**. Thus 'modifier' contrasts with all **part of speech** terms, such as **verb**, **noun** and **adjective**, which do not directly describe relationships between parts of a **sentence**.

The modifier–**head** or modification relationship between parts of a **sentence** is different from certain other relationships between parts of **sentences**, in particular:

- The **subject–predicate** relationship. In traditional terms, the **subject** of a **sentence** is neither a modifier nor a **head** in relation to its **predicate**.
- **Agreement**. Although (in languages with **agreement**) modifiers sometimes **agree** with their **heads**, they do not always do so, and there can be an **agreement** relationship between elements other than **heads** and modifiers.

Relationships   Modifiers modify **heads**. The concepts of modifier and **head** are interdependent. A **phrase** without a **head** (and there are some – see HEAD) can have no modifiers, as there is nothing to modify.

The definitions of the various **parts of speech** often include conditions involving modification. For instance, part of the definition of an **adjective** is that it can modify a **noun**. And part of the definition of an **adverb** is that it can modify a **verb**. Examples have been given above.

Exercise   Identify the modifiers in the following phrases; there are eight in all, including a repetition.

1 *hot spicy soup*
2 *those three houses*
3 *very very ugly*
4 *rich enough*
5 *drives dangerously*

Mood

Explanation   The term 'mood' is used in two somewhat different ways by traditional grammarians, a fact which detracts from its usefulness.

On the one hand, different types of **sentence** or **clause**, such as **declarative**, **interrogative** and **imperative**, are said to be in these different moods. This is probably the sense in which 'mood' is most often used when discussing English.

On the other hand, different forms of **finite verbs**, such as **indicative** and **subjunctive**, are said to be in these different moods. As **subjunctives** are rare in English, 'mood' is not so often used in this sense when discussing English. But when discussing languages with a more productive **subjunctive**, such as French, 'mood' is more often used in this sense.

Examples   Examples of statements with 'mood' used in the sense of '**sentence** (or **clause**) type':

- *Christmas Day was a Thursday last year* is a **sentence** in the **declarative** mood.
- *What's up, Doc?* is a **sentence** in the **interrogative** mood.
- *Get out of here!* is a **sentence** in the **imperative** mood.

Examples of statements with 'mood' used in the sense of 'form of a **finite verb**':

- The **verb** in *I am so sleepy* is in the **indicative** mood.
- The second **verb** (a form of the **verb** *be*) in *I wish I were not so sleepy* is in the **subjunctive** mood.
- In French, *soit* is a form of the **verb** *être* in the **subjunctive** mood.
- In German, *wäre* is a form of the **verb** *sein* in the **subjunctive** mood.

131

Contrasts In the sense of '**sentence** type', mood contrasts with 'voice', which has to do with the distinction between **active** and **passive**. Every **sentence** is in some mood or other (**declarative/interrogative/imperative**), and simultaneously in some voice or other (**active/passive**).

In the sense of 'form of a **finite verb**', mood contrasts with **tense**. Every **finite verb** is in some mood or other (**indicative/subjunctive**), and simultaneously in some **tense** or other (**past/present/** . . .).

Relationships The link between the two senses of 'mood' is to be found in the **imperative**, which is in many languages a distinct type of **sentence** requiring a specific form of the **verb**. In such languages, one can talk about the '**imperative** mood', beside the **indicative** and **subjunctive** moods mentioned above.

In English, both voice (**active/passive**) and mood in the sense of '**sentence** (or **clause**) type' involve substantial changes in the basic shape of the **clause**. Here are some examples:

SENTENCE	MOOD	VOICE
The Dodgers will beat the Giants.	Declarative	Active
Will the Dodgers beat the Giants?	Interrogative	Active
The Giants will be beaten by the Dodgers.	Declarative	Passive
Will the Giants be beaten by the Dodgers?	Interrogative	Passive

Both **tense** and mood (in the sense of '**verb** form') typically involve changes to the form of the **verb**. Here are some examples from French, in which the **subjunctive** mood is in greater use than in English. These are all forms of the irregular **verb** *être*, meaning *be*:

VERB	MOOD	TENSE
est	Indicative	Present
soit	Subjunctive	Present
était	Indicative	Imperfect
fut	Subjunctive	Imperfect

For interest While a basic function of clauses in all languages is to express factual information about situations and events, languages provide devices for putting a variety of different 'slants' or perspectives on their expression of such information. The basic distinction is between what linguists call 'realis' and 'irrealis', or 'factual' and 'non-factual'. Different languages use grammatical constructions to distinguish different kinds of non-factuality, and speakers' attitudes to it, in ways such as the following.

- Something might be the case, but the speaker doesn't know whether it is or not, and asks the hearer to tell him/her.
- Something is not the case, but the speaker wishes it were, and places an obligation on the hearer to make it so.
- Something is not the case, but the speaker wishes aloud that it were, without placing any obligation on the hearer to make it so.

- Something may or may not be the case, and the speaker wonders aloud about the possible consequences of it being so.
- Something will happen, but is not yet 'factual', because it has not yet happened.
- Something probably happened at some time in the past, but the evidence for it is lost or not available.
- Something is not the case, but it ought to be.
- Something is not definitely known to be the case, but all the evidence points in that direction.

Probably no language distinguishes all of these different kinds of non-factuality by specific grammatical constructions, but these are some of the distinctions that are found among the languages of the world. The grammatical devices used to distinguish them vary quite widely, and may include both changes to clause structure and changes in the shape of verbs. It is this general area of meaning, the area of factuality versus non-factuality, that is associated with the term 'mood', but as there are quite different ways of expressing it, often intertwined with other aspects of meaning such as time/tense, the term 'mood' itself is not securely associated with any one type of grammatical device.

Exercise   Below are four statements about grammar. Two are correct, and two are incorrect. Identify the correct statements.

1 The sentence *Houdini escaped from the sack* is in the passive mood.
2 The sentence *Did Houdini escape from the sack?* is in the interrogative mood.
3 The French verb *soit* is in the present mood.
4 The French verb *soit* is in the subjunctive mood.

Negative

Explanation   A negative **clause** or **sentence** expresses the absence or non-existence of some state of affairs, or the falsity of some proposition. In English, negation is most commonly expressed by *not* or *-n't*, but *never* is also used to negate **clauses**.

Typically, negative **words** are formed from other **words** to give some kind of opposite meaning. In English, the most common way of forming such negative **words** is by adding the **prefix** *un-*, but other **affixes** such as *in-*, *a-*, *dis-*, *mis-*, *ab-*, *de-* and *-less* also form **words** sometimes called 'negative' (with more or less justification – see **Relationships** below).

Negative **phrases** are usually the parts of negative **clauses** on which the negative information is focussed. A **clause** containing a negative **phrase** is often equivalent in meaning to a whole negative **clause**. In English, negative **phrases** can be signalled by such **words** as *no*, *none*, *neither* and *nor*.

Naturally, it can be problematic to have a term that applies to so many rather different things, such as **clauses**, **phrases** and **words**. Some linguists tend to prefer to restrict application of the terms 'negative' and 'negation' just to **clauses**.

Examples In the following examples, the negative **clauses** are underlined. (Where a **main clause** is negative, the whole **sentence** is underlined.)

- *Things ain't what they used to be.*
- *I am not a bimbo.*
- *He said he would not do it.*
- *I asked them not to do it.*
- *Never say 'Die'.*

The following English **words** could be said to be negative **words**: *unhappy, untruth, untie, nondescript, non-aligned, careless, misbehave, misuse, mistrust, disentangle, distrust, disprove, de-louse, deconsecrate.*

In the following examples, there are underlined negative **phrases**.

- *Yes, we have no bananas.*
- *I have neither harmed him nor taken any of his possessions.*
- *Neither of the above examples is positive.*
- *None of my friends knew where I was.*
- *We phoned you not just once, but three times.*

Contrasts Negative contrasts with **positive**. The **positive**/negative axis, or dimension, is not the same as 'voice' **(active/passive)** or mood **(declarative/interrogative/imperative)**.

Relationships Virtually all possible combinations of **tenses**, voices and **moods** can occur in both negative and **positive clauses**. Here are a few examples, all with negative **clauses**.

	TENSE	VOICE	MOOD
We did not find any trace of poison.	Past	Active	Declarative
Wasn't any trace of poison found?	Past	Passive	Interrogative
Don't be taken for a ride!	Present	Passive	Imperative

As mentioned above, the basic unit affected by negation is the **clause**. In English, the marker of negation, typically the word *not* or its contraction *-n't*, goes with the **auxiliary verb** (or a kind of 'dummy' **auxiliary** form of *do*, as in *don't* or *didn't*). This may make it seem at first sight as if the verbal part of the **clause** is the focus of the negation. But in fact, any part of a **clause** can be responsible for the 'negativeness' of what is being expressed. This can be shown by considering **negative clauses** with emphasis placed on different elements. In these examples, capital letters are used to convey an emphatic pronunciation with heavy stress or a marked intonation contour. It might help to say them aloud.

THE PROFESSORS didn't sign the petition yesterday. (Someone else signed it.)

The professors didn't SIGN the petition yesterday. (They did something else to it.)

The professors didn't sign THE PETITION yesterday. (They signed something else then.)

The professors didn't sign the petition YESTERDAY. (They signed it some other time.)

In fact, all these meanings can also be expressed in **sentences** with negative **phrases**, as shown below, with the negative **phrases** underlined.

- *Not the professors, but someone else, signed the petition yesterday.*
- *The professors didn't sign, but did something else to, the petition yesterday.*
- *The professors signed not the petition, but something else, yesterday.*
- *The professors signed the petition not yesterday, but some other time.*

(These **sentences** are grammatical, although taken out of context they may sound a little stilted.)

The negative **words** *no, none, nothing, nobody, nowhere* and *never* are typically used to shift the focus of negation in a **sentence** away from the verbal elements, and onto some other **phrase**. So the following are rough paraphrases.

Lawrence did not take any prisoners.	*Lawrence took no prisoners.*
The houses did not withstand the quake.	*None of the houses withstood the quake.*
Mummy, I don't have anything to do.	*Mummy, I have nothing to do.*
She did not go there ever again.	*She never went there again.*

So-called negative **words** are actually rather a mixed lot, and the sense in which they involve negation is often rather loose. First, here are some examples which are genuinely negative: *untrue* (= *not true*), *unlikely* (= *not likely*), *improbable* (= *not probable*) and *impossible* (= *not possible*).

But the following examples are not quite perfectly negative: *unhappy* (which doesn't quite mean *not happy*, because a person (or perhaps an animal) can be said to be neither happy nor unhappy), *unpleasant* (for a similar reason) and *unlucky* (likewise).

And the following examples of what might be called 'negative **words**' are certainly not just simply the negations of the **words** from which they are formed: *untie* (= *reverse the effects of tying*), *misplace* (= *place in the wrong position*) and *dismember* (= *remove the members (limbs) of*).

Finally, some 'negative **words**', such as *uncouth, unkempt, dismantle* and *dishevelled*, have no corresponding **positive** forms at all (at least not in all **dialects** – some Welsh **dialects** have *couth*).

There are some **words** which are felt to have a negative element in their meanings, although they contain no overtly negative **affix**. These are **words** such as *hardly, scarcely, barely, doubt, ignore, criticize* and *without*. Although many people agree that these are in some sense negative, it is hard to devise a precise demonstration of how they all relate to the kind of negation that is applied to **sentences** and **clauses**.

For interest   In standard English, there can normally only be one negative element per clause, precluding 'double negation'. In many non-standard English dialects, however, multiple negation is quite grammatical, as in these examples.

- *I don't have no money.*
- *We ain't none of us goin' there again, never.*

There is no 'logical argument' against such multiple negatives on the grounds that 'two negatives make a positive'. Clearly, in these dialects two negatives do not make a positive; speakers who say *I don't have no money* do not mean that they have some money. If there is any communication problem with double negatives, which there hardly ever is, it arises at least as much on the part of the hearer as on that of the speaker; speaker and hearer simply speak different dialects, which treat negatives differently.

What is happening in these dialects which allow multiple negatives is something like agreement. In a clause with negation (in these dialects) certain elements may or must agree in negativeness, across the whole clause, so that we get a repetition of negative elements.

In standard Italian, there is something like double negation. Simple negation is expressed by the word *non* (= *not*) before the verb, as in *Non vogliamo andare* (= *We don't want to go*). Words and constructions such as *niente* (= *nothing*), *nessuno* (= *nobody*) and *né ... né* (= *neither ... nor*) are all clearly negative, and yet can occur after *non* without being cancelled out by it. So *Non c'è nessuno*, meaning, in standard English, *There isn't anybody*, is actually closer in form to the non-standard doubly negated *There isn't nobody*. Another example is *Non dire niente!*, meaning *Don't say anything!*, but literally closer to *Don't say nothing!* Even the Italian equivalent of the English *neither...nor* construction can be preceded by *non*, as in *Non è né nero né grigio*, literally *It is not neither black nor grey*, but actually translated into English as *It is neither black nor grey*. But Italian is not criticized for 'illogicality'.

Some interesting ambiguities arise in cases where it is not clear which element of a complex sentence is the focus of negation. This happens particularly, but not only, with adverbial clauses and phrases. Here are some examples – try varying the pronunciation (the intonation in particular), or inserting a comma, to get the different meanings.

He doesn't beat her because he loves her.	(Does he beat her, or not?)
She didn't appeal as her lawyer advised her.	(Did she appeal?)
Nothing happened as Frans had predicted.	(Did anything happen?)
All of the audience couldn't hear.	(How many could hear?)

Exercise The following sentences all contain negative phrases. For each one, give a negative sentence, with *not* or *-n't* attached to a verbal element, with a roughly identical meaning. The first one is done for you, to show what is wanted.

1 *I see no ships.* Answer: *I don't see any ships.*

Now you do the rest:

2 *You saw nobody.*
3 *There was nothing in the box.*
4 *I have had neither food nor sleep since yesterday.*
5 *In no circumstances can I tolerate this.*

Nominative case

Explanation   In European languages such as Latin, German and Russian, the **subject** of a **verb** is said to be in the nominative case. These languages identify **subjects** (and other positions in a **sentence**) with special forms (often **affixes**).

For English, the **case** terminology is not of great use, as only a few forms, all **pronouns**, have nominative case forms distinct from other **case** forms. Sometimes the terminology of **case** is stretched to English, and then the terms '**subject**' and '**noun (phrase)** in the nominative case' are virtually synonymous.

Examples   The English **pronouns** *I, he, she, we, they* and (in some dialects) *who* are distinctively nominative. These **pronouns** can only be used as **subjects**; you can say, for instance, *I like her*, but not **Me like she*. Other **pronouns**, *you, it* and *one*, are not distinctively nominative, that is, these forms can serve as **objects**, or, in **case** terminology, in the **accusative case** as well.

Stretching the terminology of languages with extensive **case** systems, such as Latin, to English, one could say that the underlined **words** and **phrases** in the following **sentences** are in the nominative case, since they are all **subjects**.

- *We hold these truths to be self-evident.*
- *The United States has the most powerful economy in the world.*
- *This sentence is six words long.*
- *Where are my glasses?*

Contrasts   Nominative contrasts with other **cases**, such as **accusative** and **dative**. If a **word** or **phrase** in a **clause** is in the nominative case, it cannot also be in any other case, such as **accusative** or **dative**. For English, at least, the two-way nominative/**accusative** contrast is equivalent to the two-way **subject/object** contrast.

Relationships   Nominative case, like all other **cases**, is assigned primarily to **nouns, pronouns** and **noun phrases**, as only these can be **subjects** of **verbs**. In languages with extensive **case** systems (e.g. Latin, Russian), other **parts of speech**, such as **demonstratives, articles**, and **adjectives** can also receive **case** markings, including **nominative**, by **agreement** with **nouns**.

All kinds of **verbs**, both **transitive** and **intransitive**, occur with items in the nominative case, as all have **subjects**. (By contrast only **transitive verbs** can take items in the **accusative case**, as only they have **objects**.)

For interest   In familiar European languages with case systems, we are used to a basic nominative/accusative organization of the case system, where the following correspondences hold.

CASE	FUNCTION IN CLAUSE
Nominative	Subject of transitive verb
Nominative	Subject of intransitive verb
Accusative	Direct object of transitive verb

The first two lines here emphasize the point that nominative case in these languages does double duty, signalling the subject in both transitive and intransitive clauses. The accusative case signals only one function, that of direct object (only transitive clauses have direct objects). To illustrate with Latin, the *-us* endings below mark nominative case, and the *-um* ending marks accusative case.

Romulus videt Remum
Romulus sees Remus
NOM   ACC   (= *Romulus sees Remus*)

Romulus it
Romulus goes
NOM   (= *Romulus goes*)

But other languages work, at least partly, in a different way. In such languages, we have what linguists call an 'ergative/absolutive' case system. 'Ergative' and 'absolutive' are the names of cases in these languages, and they correspond to subjects and objects as follows (compare to the nominative/accusative correspondences above).

CASE	FUNCTION IN CLAUSE
Ergative	Subject of transitive verb
Absolutive	Subject of intransitive verb
Absolutive	Direct object of transitive verb

What is interesting about these languages is that they group together, for the purposes of case-marking, the subject of an intransitive sentence and the direct object of a transitive sentence. Here are some examples from an Australian aboriginal language called Warrgamay. Warrgamay was spoken until recently in an area of North Queensland, but its last living speaker died a few years ago.[9]

ngulmburu gagama
woman   will go
ABS   (= *The woman will go*)

maal gagama
man will go
ABS   (= *The man will go*)

ngulmburu-ngu ngundalma maal
woman   will see   man
ERG   ABS   (= *The woman will see the man*)

maal-du ngundalma ngulmburu
man   will see   woman
ERG   ABS   (= *The man will see the woman*)

9 The Warrgamay examples are adapted from R. M. W. Dixon's *The Languages of Australia* (Cambridge University Press, 1980).

There are many languages, in different parts of the world, as far apart as Australia and northern Canada, with ergative/absolutive case systems. In western Europe, the only language with such a system is Basque; the more familiar European languages have nominative/accusative case systems. The existence of ergative/absolutive systems shows us how different languages can encode quite basic aspects of experience rather differently. It should be said, however, that languages with ergative/absolutive systems are usually not completely thorough about it, and they often also contain some traces of a nominative/accusative system.

Actually, one can even find traces of an ergative/absolutive system in English. Consider noun phrases constructed out of whole clauses by forming a verbal noun, such as *arrival* (from the intransitive verb *arrive*) and *destruction* (from the transitive verb *destroy*). Linguists call such nouns formed from verbs 'nominalizations'. We can have phrases such as the following. Note the function of the prepositions *of* and *by* in these phrases, in terms of the understood subjects and objects of the original verbs *arrive* and *destroy*.

The arrival of the army	(*of* signals subject of *arrive*)
The destruction of the city by the army	(*of* signals direct object of *destroy*, *by* signals subject of *destroy*)

Here the preposition *of* is acting rather like an absolutive case marker, signalling the subject of a nominalized intransitive verb (*arrival*) and the object of a nominalized transitive verb (*destruction*), while *by* acts like an ergative case marker, signalling only the subject of a nominalized transitive verb.

Exercise   Applying the terminology of case to the following English sentences, identify the words and phrases that could be said to be in the nominative case.

1 *We secretaries were getting tired of all the new arrangements.*
2 *The new arrangements were annoying everybody.*
3 *Someone had even phoned the* Glasgow Herald *about it.*
4 *Through the fence, between the curling flower spaces, I could see them hitting.*
5 *An unassuming young man was travelling, in midsummer, from his native city of Hamburg to Davos-Platz in the Canton of the Grisons, on a three weeks visit.*

Noun

Explanation   A noun is any **word**, other than a **pronoun**, that can serve as the **subject** of a **sentence**. Many nouns denote persons, places and things, as the traditional definition says. These are the most typical, or basic, nouns. They denote either whole classes (kinds) of physical objects, such as cats, people, tables, clouds, houses, trees, fish, atoms, stars and so on, or particular individual objects; in the latter case, the objects are most typically people and places, such as Einstein, Billy or London. Nouns can also be used for a great variety of other kinds of concept, such as stuff (i.e. substances), actions, emotions, times, distances, songs, ideas and ideologies. Nouns denoting such concepts can appear in the same positions, in relation to other kinds of **words**, as the more typical nouns denoting physical objects.

What binds nouns together as a class of **words** is their common grammatical behaviour, that is, the positions they can take in relation to other **words**, and the roles (such as **subject**) they can take in **clauses**. In English, most nouns can occur immediately after the **word** *the*, the **definite article**. (See also under **Relationships** below.)

Nouns indicate many 'things' which are not really things, in the sense that you can touch them. You can't touch fear, you can't pick up a mile and put it in your pocket, and Monday can't literally fall on you and hurt you. But *fear*, *mile* and *Monday* are nouns. Nouns do seem to have the effect of making us talk about 'things' as if they somehow really were concrete. So one might say, adapting the old definition, that a noun is a **word** that indicates anything just as if it were a person, place or thing.

Examples All the following are nouns in English: *cat, person, table, cloud, house, tree, fish, atom, star, Einstein, London*. These, because they denote physical objects, are the most central cases of nouns. Other nouns, so classified because they can occur in all the same grammatical positions as these, include **words** such as *example, game, activity, song, modesty, love, gravity, language, society, mind, revelation, French, Chinese, kick, fear, Monday* and *mile*.

Contrasts Noun is a **part of speech** and so contrasts with all other **parts of speech**. If a **word** in a particular **sentence** is a noun, then it cannot simultaneously belong to any other **part of speech**. The **part of speech** most closely related to the nouns are the **pronouns**, but the two kinds of **word** are distinct; a **pronoun** is not a noun.

The basic contrast between the two primary **parts of speech**, namely noun and **verb**, is found in all languages.

Relationships The statements about nouns below are mostly true of nouns in all languages.

There are two main subtypes of nouns, **common** nouns and **proper names**. The former, e.g. *cat, table, ambition, game*, denote classes of things in general, whereas the latter, e.g. *London, Spain, Napoleon*, denote particular individual things (counting people as things). Beside the subdivision into **common** and **proper** nouns are also classified into **count** versus **mass**, and concrete versus **abstract**.

Common nouns can normally be **modified** by many other kinds of **words**, **phrases** and **clauses**, as shown below:

EXAMPLE	MODIFIER
the mountain	**Definite article**
a hill	**Indefinite article**
those languages	**Demonstrative**

Ronald Reagan's memory	**Possessive phrase**
three songs	**Numeral**
pleasant weather	**Adjective**
children dancing	**(Present) participle**
fish swimming in the sea	**Participial phrase**
love in a cold climate	**Prepositional phrase**
people who live in glass houses	**Relative clause**

In addition, nouns may **modify** other nouns, to form what are called 'compound nouns'. Examples of such **compound** nouns, which can reach considerable lengths, are _tractor driver, river Thames, Colorado river, palm tree, ocean current, window frame, sash window, window frame maker, sash window frame maker, crocodile skin shoes_ and so on.

Nouns (and **pronouns**) are the basic **parts of speech** which carry **number (singular/plural)**. In languages which have systems of **gender**, nouns (and **pronouns**) are also the basic **parts of speech** which carry **gender (masculine/feminine/** . . . **)**.

Nouns (and **pronouns**) are the items which stand in the relationships of **subject, direct object** and **indirect object** to **verbs**. Correspondingly, in languages with **case** systems, nouns (and **pronouns**) are the basic **parts of speech** which receive **case** markings, e.g. for **nominative, accusative, dative, genitive**, etc., assigned to them by **verbs** and **prepositions**.

In languages with **agreement** systems, other **parts of speech**, such as **adjectives** and **verbs**, may **agree** with nouns and **pronouns** in such categories as **number, gender** and **case**.

The basic nouns, as we have seen, denote physical objects, and these are typically not formed from other **words**. But many nouns, some with more **abstract** meanings, are formed using **affixes** or more complex changes from other **words**. Some examples are:

arrival, destruction, establishment	Denoting actions, derived from **verbs**
dryness, coolness, warmth, chastity	Denoting qualities, derived from **adjectives**
baker, driver, manufacturer, beggar	Denoting agents, derived from **verbs**

In addition, some **words** of other **parts of speech** can simply be taken and used as nouns, with no change to their shape. So we can have _the good, the bad, the reds_ and _the blues_, using **adjectives** as nouns. We also have **phrases** like _a loud purr, a long run, a silly walk_ and _a disastrous crash_, using **verbs** as nouns.

Statistically, in most and probably all languages, **nouns** are the most common **part of speech**; that is, there are more nouns in the vocabulary of any language than there are **words** of any other **part of speech**.

For interest What would a language be like that did not have the basic distinction between nouns and verbs? As the noun/verb distinction is the most basic part-of-speech distinction in language, we can assume that such a language, if it existed, would in fact not have any distinct major parts of speech, i.e. nouns, verbs, adjectives, prepositions and adverbs, at all. That is, all major words would simply belong to one grand 'part of speech' – though this actually takes most of the meaning out of the term 'part of speech'. Perhaps such a language would still have a basic distinction between these major words, on the one hand, and a class of 'functional' or 'grammatical' words, on the other hand, expressing things like definiteness, tenses, gender, number and the like.

We have seen above how English can take a word of one part of speech (e.g. *run*, a verb) and use it as a noun, in, for example, *a long run*. Our hypothetical language without a noun/verb distinction would be able in this way to use any major word in any way, in combination with any of the grammatical or function words. Let's make up a specific example of such an apparently weird language, using English words, but allowing ourselves to put them in unorthodox positions, i.e. to do grammatically anything we like with them, but still using them meaningfully. Is this possible? Let's see. Here is a suggested mini-vocabulary. In it, we prefix every word of the hypothetical nounless language with a *x*- just to identify it clearly as belonging to this hypothetical language.

xman = *a man, to be a man, manlike, in a manlike way*
xrun = *a runner, to run, like a runner, running*
xJohn = *John, to be called John, like John*
xsend = *a sender, to send, sending*
xbook = *a book, to be a book, booklike, in a booklike way*

-ed = marker of past tense
-um = marker of direct object
-o = marker of indirect object

So that's some of the vocabulary of our hypothetical language. Now here are some actual sentences, with their English translations.

xman xsend-ed xJohn-o xbook-um	(= *A man sent John a book*)
xsend xman-ed	(= *The sender was a man*)
xman xsend-ed	(= *The man sent (something)*
	or *The man was the sender*)
xsend xwork-ed	(= *The sender worked*
	or *The sender was a worker*)
xJohn xwork-ed	(= *John worked* or *John was a worker*)
xwork xJohn-ed	(= *The worker was called John*
	or *The working one was called John*)

The basic idea is that any of the 'major' words *xman, xwork, xJohn, xsend, xbook* can be combined with any of the grammatical suffixes *-ed, -um* and *-o*. The order of words is fixed to subject–verb–object(s). The main limitation on what can be said is what makes sense. So you see that it is possible in principle for a language not to have the basic distinction between nouns and verbs – any word can function either as what we would call a noun or as what we would call a verb, and these functions are marked by various suffixes.

Now the question arises whether in fact any real language is like this. It has been claimed that some American Indian languages spoken in British Columbia, Canada are in fact like this. Nootka is one such language. Here is a mini-vocabulary for this real language, Nootka.[10]

mamuk	=	*worker, to work*
qu?as	=	*man, to be a man*
-ma	=	marker of present tense
-?i	=	marker of definiteness

In Nootka, these grammatical markers, the suffixes -*ma* and -*?i* are very versatile, and can be added both to words that we would translate (depending on the context) into English as nouns, and to words that we would translate as verbs (again depending on the context). The point about the context is vital, because the very same word can often be translated either as a noun or as a verb, depending on the sentence it occurs in. Here are two Nootka sentences, to illustrate the point.

mamuk-ma   qu?as-?i
work+PRES *man*+DEF   (= *The man is working.*)
qu?as-ma   mamuk-?i
man+PRES *work*+DEF   (= *The working one is a man.*)

In fact, however, although Nootka does not make such a clear distinction between nouns and verbs as English and familiar European languages do, there are still some small differences between forms like *mamuk* (*work*) and those like *qu?as* (*man*), in terms of exactly where they can occur in sentences. So, for instance, *mamuk* (*work*) cannot function in a 'nouny' way as subject of a sentence unless it has a suffix attached, but the same is not true for *qu?as* (*man*).

As far as we can tell at present, all human languages make a basic distinction between nouns and verbs, although some, like Nootka, mark the difference in far fewer ways than familiar European langugaes.

Exercise   Identify the nouns, both common and proper, in the following sentences. There are eighteen in total.

1 *The lean mother bear couldn't bear to lean against the tree.*

2 *When I travel, I wear my suit, in case I forget my case.*

3 *The wear and tear of travel doesn't suit me.*

4 *I was on a flight from Miami on Wednesday, and I have a meeting in Singapore next week.*

5 *I'll give up my career as an applied linguist and retire to a country retreat.*

10   This data is taken from Paul Schachter's article 'Parts-of-speech systems', in *Language Typology and Syntactic Description*, volume I: Clause Structure, edited by Timothy Shopen (Cambridge University Press, 1985).

Number

Explanation

Nouns and **pronouns** all have a certain grammatical number, and in English this number can be either **singular** or **plural**.

A **noun** or **pronoun**'s number almost always reflects its meaning, so that individual people and things are usually referred to by **singular nouns** or **pronouns**, and collections of things are usually referred to by **plural nouns** or **pronouns**.

Examples

The number of the following English **nouns** and **pronouns** is **singular**: *person, window, celebrity, sky, water, animosity, pleasure, I, he, she, it*.

The number of the following English **nouns** and **pronouns** is **plural**: *people, windows, celebrities, skies, waters, pleasures, we, you, they*.

Contrasts

Number (**singular/plural/. . .**) contrasts with **person** (1st/2nd/3rd), **gender** (masculine/feminine/neuter/. . .) and **case (nominative/accusative/dative/. . .)**. These are all intersecting (crosscutting) dimensions, and a **noun** or **pronoun** may possess a value on any of them.

Number, a dimension including **singular** and **plural**, and categorizing **nouns** and **pronouns**, is different from **numeral**, which is a class of **words**, such as *two, six* and *thousand*.

Relationships

Number only affects **parts of speech** other than **nouns** and **pronouns**, e.g. **verbs** and **adjectives**, indirectly, typically through **agreement**. So, for example, the **verb** *be* is inherently neither **singular** nor **plural**, that is, it has no inherent **number**. The choice of *is* (**singular**) or *are* (**plural**) arises from **agreement** with its **subject**.

★You is is ungrammatical in standard English. The **pronoun** *you* always takes the **plural** form *are*, which is why *you* was listed among the **plurals** in the examples above. But there is a slight problem. **Reflexives** generally **agree** in number, and *you* can be followed by a **singular reflexive** *yourself* (as well as *yourselves*), as in *Aren't you ashamed of yourself?* This is an instance where the straightforward rules of grammar are not consistent with each other.

Noun phrases take their number, whether **singular** or **plural**, from the **nouns** they are built around, that is, from their **head nouns**. So the **noun phrase** *three men in a boat* is **plural**, because its **head noun**, *men*, is **plural**.

When two or more **singular noun phrases** are conjoined by *and*, the resulting larger **noun phrase** is **plural**. So, though *John* and *Mary* are both **singular**, the **phrase** *John and Mary* is **plural**.

The dimension of number intersects, as noted, with other grammatical dimensions, such as **gender** and **person**. **Pronouns**, in particular, can have various combinations of values on these dimensions.

There are some irregular **nouns**, whose grammatical number is at odds with their meaning. In English, *scissors* and *trousers* are **nouns** of this sort; they denote single objects, but are grammatically **plural**. A converse case is *bikini*, which denotes a pair of separate objects, but is a **singular noun**.

Queen Victoria reputedly said *We are not amused*, with the **plural** *we* referring to her royal but singular self. This use of the 'royal *we*' persists for formal occasions, such as the opening of Parliament. It is also common in the formal style of some academic journals and newspaper editorials, where it is known as the 'authorial' or 'editorial *we*'.

Some languages have not only **singular** and **plural** but also 'dual' (denoting just two things) and even 'trial' (denoting just three things) (see PLURAL).

Exercise In the following sentences, identify the number (singular/plural) of each of the underlined words. There are fifteen underlined words in all.

1 *The woman who wrote all those books is a genius.*
2 *Who knows what secrets lie in the hearts of men?*
3 *The police are undermanned.*
4 *Sticks and stones may break my bones.*
5 *Mud sticks.*

Numeral

Explanation A numeral **word** is a **word** used for counting, or expressing the number of items in a collection of things (**cardinal** numeral), or expressing the position of an item in a sequence of things (**ordinal** numeral). Complex numeral expressions, for expressing higher numbers, are constructed out of numeral **words**.

Examples *One, two, three, . . . , nine, ten, eleven, . . . , nineteen, twenty, thirty, . . . , ninety, hundred, thousand, million* are (**cardinal**) numeral **words**.

First, second, third, . . . , ninth, tenth, eleventh, . . . , nineteenth, twentieth, thirtieth, . . . , ninetieth, hundredth, thousandth, millionth are (**ordinal**) numeral **words**.

Twenty-five, eleven hundred, four hundred and seventy-six thousand are complex (**cardinal**) numeral expressions.

twenty-fifth, eleven hundredth, four hundred and seventy-six thousandth are complex (**ordinal**) **numeral** expressions.

Contrasts Numeral contrasts primarily with other classes of **word** that can **modify nouns**, such as **articles**, **demonstratives**, **possessives** and **adjectives**. Although numerals, like **adjectives**, can occur as **modifiers** before **nouns**, numerals are nevertheless distinct from **adjectives**.

Do not confuse numeral with **number**. In grammatical terminology, **number** is a dimension, with values such as **singular** and **plural**, mainly affecting **nouns** and **pronouns**; whereas numeral is a class of **words** and longer expressions distinct from **nouns** and **pronouns**.

145

Relationships Numerals are unique among **words** in being ordered in a sequence, independently of their use in any particular **sentence**. Thus it makes sense to ask, out of the blue, '*What comes after six?*' (Answer: *Seven*), '*What comes after two hundred and fifty two?*' Answer: *Two hundred and fifty three*). And so on. But we cannot similarly ask, without reference to any particular **sentence**, '*What comes after the* **verb** *dig?*' Perhaps this makes sense in the context of a dictionary, where **words** are listed in alphabetical order, but this is a different kind of ordering from that of numerals. For amusement, let's put the English numerals from *one* to *ten* in alphabetical order: *eight, five, four, nine, one, seven, six, ten, three, two*. This is plainly not their natural order as numerals. With any other kind of **word**, it is not even possible to talk of 'their natural order'. Numerals have this natural order, of course, because of their meanings, the arithmetic sequence of natural numbers, or positive integers.

(For other relationships involving numerals, see CARDINAL and ORDINAL.)

Exercise Identify the numeral expressions, both cardinal and ordinal, in the following. Some are single words and some are longer expressions. There are eleven in total.

1 *Nine out of ten housewives prefer Stork to butter.*
2 *The armistice was signed at the eleventh hour of the eleventh day of the eleventh month.*
3 *The first of the six runners in our second team finished the race in ninth position.*
4 *There are over two hundred and twenty words in the twenty third psalm.*

Ordinal numeral

Explanation Ordinal numerals are a subclass of the **numerals**, the other **numerals** being the **cardinals**. Ordinals are **words** and longer expressions used to express the order in which an item stands in a given sequence.

Examples *First, second, third, . . . , tenth, eleventh, twelfth, thirteenth, . . . , twentieth, thirtieth, fortieth, . . . , hundredth, thousandth, millionth, . . .* are all ordinal numeral **words**.

Contrasts Ordinal contrasts primarily with **cardinal**, the other kind of **numeral**. Ordinal numeral contrasts with all other **word**-classes and **parts of speech**, such as **noun**, **verb**, **adjective** and **preposition**. If a word in a given sentence is an (ordinal) **numeral**, it can't be any other **part of speech**.

English also uses its ordinal numeral forms to express fractions, a rather different meaning. Examples are *two thirds* and *five sixteenths*. When they express fractions, it is best to regard **words** such as *third* and *sixteenth* not as **ordinals**, but as **nouns**, because, like **nouns**, they form **plurals** with the **suffix** -*s*.

Relationships English ordinal numerals are formed from **cardinals** by a **regular** process, adding the **suffix** *-th* onto the end of the **cardinal**. For example, the **cardinal** *seventeen* gives the ordinal *seventeenth*. This works for longer **numerals**, too, as with, say, *five hundred and twenty-sixth*. The formation of the first few ordinals is **irregular**, so that there is no clear similarity in shape between *one* and its ordinal *first*, or between *two* and its ordinal *second*. After that, there are just a few minor oddities, like the shortening of the vowel in *fifth*.

Ordinal numerals are rather more like typical **adjectives** than their close relations the **cardinals**. Thus, you can use either an ordinal or an **adjective** as a **predicate** after the verb *be*, as in *Ben Johnson was second* or *Ben Johnson was fit*. And ordinals, like **adjectives**, can **attributively modify** a **noun**, as in *the third athlete* or *the fit athlete*.

Ordinals can to some extent occur either before or after other **adjectives modifying** a **noun**, as in

their fourth historic meeting   *their historic fourth meeting*
his first useful suggestion   *his useful first suggestion*

(Note the differences in meaning here.)

English ordinals distribute in a similar way to **superlatives**, before other **adjectives** and either before or after **cardinal numerals** as in:

ORDINAL   SUPERLATIVE
the three first people   *the three hungriest people*
the first three people   *the hungriest three people*

Ordinals occur almost exclusively with **definite noun phrases**. *The fifth day* is much more usual than *a fifth day*.

For interest Not all languages have distinct ordinal numerals, not even languages that do have cardinal numerals. In fact, English often uses its cardinal numerals to express ordinal meanings. So the following are paraphrases:

the first day   *day one*
the tenth exercise   *exercise ten*
the nineteenth chapter   *chapter nineteen*

In many languages, the ordinal corresponding to the cardinal numeral for 1 bears no resemblance to the cardinal numeral at all. For instance:

	CARDINAL	ORDINAL
ENGLISH	*one*	*first*
GERMAN	*eins*	*erste*
ITALIAN	*uno*	*primo*

Linguists call such irregular forms, which bear no resemblance to the forms from which one would expect them to be formed, 'suppletive'. Some languages have suppletive forms for the ordinals for 2 (and even 3), as well. An example is English *second*, which is nothing like *two*. Usually, higher-valued ordinals are expressed by a quite regular form derived from the corresponding cardinal. For instance:

147

		CARDINAL	ORDINAL
GERMAN (add -*te*)		*vier*	*vierte*
		neunzehn	*neunzehnte*
		hundert	*hunderte*
ITALIAN (add -*esimo*)		*undici*	*undicesimo*
		cento	*centesimo*
		mille	*millesimo*

It is interesting that some languages do, and some languages do not, use the suppletive forms in the higher-valued ordinals. German does, as in *hunderterste* (= *101st*), derived from *hunderteins* (= *101*); that is, German does not use **hunderteinste* for *101st*. But the Italian for *101st* is *centounesimo*, derived from *centouno* (= *101*); if Italian behaved like German, we would have expected something like **centoprimo*, which does not occur.

Question: Do English higher-valued ordinals behave like the German ones or like the Italian ones?

Exercise Identify the ordinal numerals in the following sentences (one of them is non-standard):

1 *I'll give you two thirds and eat the third piece myself.*
2 *The twenty-second runner finished twenty seconds after the first.*
3 *The First and Second World Wars took place in the twentieth century.*
4 *When Mr Bilbo Baggins of Bag End announced that he would shortly be celebrating his eleventy-first birthday with a party of special magnificence, there was much talk and excitement in Hobbiton.*

Part of speech

Explanation A part of speech is a collection of **words** that all behave in a similar way, or is the label for any such collection. The basic concept of **word**-classes (sets of dictionary **words**), which is at the heart of this definition of part of speech, is essential to the **grammar** of any language. Unfortunately, the traditional term 'part of speech' has acquired a rigid sense, according to which there are supposed to be, as an unrevisable 'fact', just eight (sometimes nine) parts of speech. Modern linguists prefer to use the term '**word**-class', which can be discussed undogmatically, and whose flexibility lends itself to application to a range of very different languages. A **word**-class is a collection of **words** in one language that all behave in a similar way.

Examples The most commonly mentioned parts of speech are **noun** and **verb**. Such central or major parts of speech are indispensable in the description of the **grammar** of any language, and modern linguists refer to them as '**word**-classes'. **Noun**, **verb**, **pronoun**, **adjective**, **preposition**, **adverb**, **article**, conjunction and **interjection** make up the traditionally recognized parts of speech. These will probably be known to people who have studied European languages. Not all languages have the same **word**-classes or parts of speech. The traditional set known to people familiar with the **grammar** of European languages is to some degree adequate for the description of these languages, but less familiar languages can have **word**-classes quite different from these well-known European ones. The **word**-classes which a language has must be decided on the basis of considerations from that language itself. Other **word**-classes, which are relevant to the description of some less well-known languages, include 'numeral classifier', 'politeness marker', 'mood marker', 'postposition', 'existential marker' and 'predicator'.

Contrasts   Part of speech contrasts with the system of roles such as **subject, direct object** and **indirect object**. For example, it makes sense to say simply that the English word *computer* is a **noun**, regardless of context, but we cannot say, out of context, whether *computer* is a **subject, direct object** or **indirect object**. For exactly the same reason, part of speech contrasts with **case** (e.g. **nominative, accusative, dative**, etc.).

A **word**'s part of speech indicates the main class of **words** that it belongs to. But within such **word**-classes, there can be subclasses, and even sub-subclasses. For example, **nouns** can be subdivided into **common nouns** and **proper names**; and **common nouns** can be further subdivided into **mass common nouns** and **count common nouns**. It is usual to reserve the term 'part of speech' for the highest-level label, in this case **noun**. It is less usual to see a subclass, such as **count common noun**, referred to as a separate part of speech. As another example, **verbs** can be subdivided into **transitive** and **intransitive**; and **transitive verbs** can be further subdivided into 'monotransitive' and 'ditransitive', depending on whether thay can take an **indirect object**. But though it would be usual to call '**verb**' a part of speech it would be less usual to apply the term 'part of speech' to a sub-subclass, such as 'ditransitive **verb**'.

The subclassifications of parts of speech can crosscut each other. As mentioned above, **nouns** can be subclassified into **proper** and **common nouns**; but in languages with a **gender** system, such as French, both **proper** and **common nouns** can be either masculine or feminine. Here are some examples from French.

	MASCULINE	FEMININE
PROPER NAMES	*Pierre, Paris*	*Marie, Athène*
COMMON NOUNS	*homme, voyage*	*femme, cage*

Grammatical categories or dimensions, such as **gender**, which crosscut other classifications in this way, are not themselves parts of speech. So part of speech contrasts with such dimensions.

Relationships   It has been traditional to define various parts of speech in terms of the meanings of the **words** belonging to them. For example, 'A **noun** is the name of a

149

person, place or thing.' But such traditional definitions are all notoriously difficult to apply with any consistency or usefulness, and they are supplemented in this dictionary with other information about the typical patterns of use of the **words** concerned. If a **word** belongs to more than one part of speech, like *list* in English, which can be either a **noun** or a **verb**, it has correspondingly different meanings (which may, however, be related).

An essential criterion in deciding what **word**-classes or parts of speech a language has, and what **words** belong to which, is the range of positions in which the **words** can occur in grammatical **sentences**. If two **words** can go in all the same positions in **sentences**, they belong to the same **word**-class. Unfortunately, **grammar** is seldom quite so clean and neat, and we find cases where two **words** can go in almost all, but not quite all, the same positions in **sentences**. There is no firm principle in grammatical theory stating how similar in their range two **words** have to be in order to qualify as belonging to the same **word**-class. And in most languages there are a handful of **words** which resist clear classification, each behaving in its own individual characteristic way (see **PARTICLE**).

The **word**-class system of any language involves a set of interlocking and interrelated definitions. Some parts of speech, such as **noun** and **verb**, are more basic than others, in almost all languages. Often in a language these two are defined partly in relation to each other. For example, the definition of a **noun** in some language might include 'can occur as **subject** of a **verb**'. And once such basic parts of speech as noun and verb are defined, the definitions of rather less basic parts of speech or **word**-classes, such as **adjective** and **preposition** often rest in part on a prior understanding of the more basic parts of speech, **noun** and **verb**.

The above talk of 'definitions' of various **word**-classes is somewhat misleading. An indispensable part of the characterization of any **word**-class in any language is also a fair-sized set of representative examples. An example-giving statement such as '**Adjectives** are **words** like *happy, nice, tall, French, asleep* and *inconsequential*' is an essential complement to a more definitional statement such as '**Adjectives** are **words** which can **modify nouns**.' Together, examples and definitions can give a reasonably clear idea of what is included in any particular part of speech.

As the term implies, the system of **word**-classes in any language applies primarily to the **words** (or in some languages **word**-stems) in the language. Thus units larger than **words**, such as **phrases** and **clauses**, do not belong to any **word**-class. But the classification of **phrases** is usually related to the **word**-classes of the **words** they are formed around. So a **phrase** built around a **noun** as its **head**, with various **modifiers** (e.g. **adjectives**, **demonstratives**, etc.), will generally be called a '**noun phrase**'. For instance, the **phrase** *poor old Joe* is a **noun phrase** because its **head word** *Joe* belongs to the part of speech '**noun**'. Other parts of speech which give their names to classes of **phrases** are **verb**, **preposition**, **adjective** and **adverb**, giving rise to **verb phrases**, **prepositional phrases**, **adjective phrases** and adverbial **phrases**, respectively.

Not all **word**-classes lend their names to classes of **phrases** (at least in traditional analysis). So, in the traditional terminology of grammar, there are no '**article phrases**' or '**demonstrative phrases**'. Linguists draw a broad distinction between major **word**-classes such as **noun, verb, adjective** and **adverb,** on the one hand, and those such as **demonstrative, auxiliary** and **article** on the other. The former type are called 'lexical classes', containing **words** known as 'content **words**', while the latter type are sometimes called 'grammatical classes', containing **words** known as 'function **words**'.

Some parts of speech or **word**-classes (typically those of 'content **words**' – see above) are open-ended, and new **words** can easily be added to them as the vocabulary of the language expands. The English language is constantly acquiring new **nouns** (by borrowing and coining), for example. But there is little chance of English developing a new **demonstrative** or a new **conjunction**, as these **word**-classes are characteristically not open-ended, but closed classes. Some parts of speech, such as **noun**, have very many members. Others have very few, even as few as two, as does the traditional part of speech '**article**' (*the* and *a* in English). At this level of detail traditional grammar and modern linguistics part company. Clearly the pair of **words** *a* and *the* behave very similarly to others such as *this* and *my*, and a more useful grouping includes all of these in a **word**-class known as 'determiner'.

The effect of adding an **affix** to a **word** is often (but not always) to change its part of speech. Thus in English, adding *-al* to some **verbs** (e.g. *arrive, refuse, dispose*) produces **nouns** (*arrival, refusal, disposal*). Adding *-ness* to some **adjectives** (e.g. *happy, careless, selfish*) produces **nouns** (*happiness, carelessness, selfishness*). **Affixes,** being units smaller than **words,** do not themselves belong to any part of speech.

For interest When linguists set out to describe languages, the organization of their descriptions (e.g. the resulting grammar books) necessarily reflects the organization of the languages themselves. A grammarian who takes a short cut, and writes the grammar quickly, may often not analyse the language deeply enough to realize how different its organization is from that of familiar European languages, and the description may be rather awkwardly organized in terms of the parts of speech originally devised to describe Latin.

There can often be substantial disagreement about the part-of-speech system of a language. Compare, for example, two analyses of Tamil, a language of south India now spoken by about 50 million people (the number has more than trebled this century). A grammar of this language written in 1906[11] is explicitly organized in terms of the following parts of speech: Articles, Nouns, Pronouns, Adjectives, Verbs, Adverbs, Postpositions, Conjunctions, Interrogatives, Emphatic Particles and Interjections. Note the similarities with familiar tradi-

11   *Tamil Grammar Self-Taught*, by Don M. de Zilva Wickramasinghe (E. Marlborough, London, 1906).

151

tional European grammar, and some important differences, e.g. Postpositions and Emphatic Particles, dictated by the nature of the Tamil language itself. By contrast, a modern linguist[12] radically reanalyses this: 'Although some grammars of Tamil list as many as ten parts of speech, all of them can be resolved into one of two formal categories: noun and verb.' Well, who is right? Does Tamil have eleven parts of speech, as the grammar of 1906 implies, or just two, as the modern linguist claims? The facts of the language are the same; the language itself cannot have changed so drastically in a matter of eighty years.

Some of the differences between grammarians can be reduced to questions of mere labelling. What is called a 'part of speech' by one grammarian may simply be called a 'subcategory' by another, but both will mention essentially the same grouping of words and describe its range of occurrence more or less equivalently. There is no getting away from the basic facts of the language concerned (i.e. what strings of words are grammatical or not, and what they mean), and provided the grammarian gets these basic facts right, some of the organization of the description can depend on the grammarian's purpose. The 1906 grammar of Tamil was intended for use by people familiar with European languages to teach themselves Tamil. The linguist writing in the late 1980s was more concerned with emphasizing the underlying formal simplicity and clear lines of the Tamil grammatical system, following the broad theoretical orientation of his day. But, even allowing some freedom for grammarians, depending on their purposes, every language has its own inherent system of grammatical organization that can hardly be distorted without falsifying the basic facts, which is why even the 1906 author had to mention some non-European parts of speech, such as 'Postposition' and 'Emphatic Particle'.

An in-depth analysis of the organization of a language will reveal both similarities with, and differences from, the familiar European pattern. (Do not jump to the conclusion, by the way, that all European languages use an identical part-of-speech system; they don't.) It is instructive to look at a few grammar books, to get an idea of what parts of speech their authors have analysed them as having. Here are some more lists of parts of speech, for various languages, as analysed by (relatively) modern linguists.

Yao, a Bantu language spoken in parts of Tanzania, Mozambique and Malawi, has, according to one grammarian[13] the following groupings of words: Variable words, including Nominal words and Verbs; Invariable words, including Pronominals, Numerals, Connectors, Interrogatives, Adverbials, Intensifiers, Ideophones, Expansors, Selectors, Pre-nominals and Interjections. In this language, according to this description, Adjectives, Possessives and Demonstratives are merely subspecies of the large class of words called 'Nominals'. Note again the similarities and differences in relation to the part-of-speech systems of familiar European languages. Pronominals,

---

12 Sanford B. Steever, 'Tamil and the Dravidian languages', in *The Major Languages of South Asia, the Middle East and Africa*, edited by Bernard Comrie (Routledge, London, 1990), p. 240.
13 W. H. Whiteley, *A Study of Yao Sentences* (Clarendon Press, Oxford, 1966).

Numerals and Adverbials seem familiar enough, but Ideophones, Expansors and Selectors are parts of speech for the Yao language without very close counterparts in English, French or German.

Ngiyambaa, a dying Australian aboriginal language, now spoken, if at all, by no more than a few dozen elderly speakers, has the following parts of speech:[14] Nominals, Pronouns, Determiners, Indeterminates, Verbs, Adverbs, Particles and Interjections.

The central core of the grammar of Acehnese, a language spoken by about a million and a half people in northern Sumatra, Indonesia, is described[15] in terms of these broad groupings of words: Verbs, Nominals, Epistemological Classifiers and Prepositions. The author explains in some detail why it is not appropriate to say that this language has adjectives; where English would use an adjective, Acehnese would use a form of a verb.

In all these lists, note that Verbs and Nouns (sometimes in the guise of 'Nominals') always occur (all languages have them), whereas Adjectives and Prepositions do not (some languages don't have them), and some languages have their own further, more or less idiosyncratic, parts of speech, or word-classes.

Exercise Below is a list of some of the grammatical terms explained in this dictionary. Which terms in this list identify word-classes? There are seven in total, of which five are the names of traditional parts of speech.

Accusative, active, adjective, adverb, affix, agreement, apposition, case, clause, conditional, conjunction, dative, declarative, demonstrative, ellipsis, nominative, noun, numeral, passive, tense, verb, voice.

Particle

Explanation 'Particle' is a term used of small **words** (and occasionally **affixes**) which do not easily fit into any clear **word**-class, such as **common noun**, **auxiliary**, **modal**, **article** or **preposition**. Particle is thus something of an 'escape (or cop-out) category' for grammarians. 'If it's small and you don't know what to call it, call it a particle' seems to be the practice; and a very useful practice it is, too, as it avoids pushing **words** into categories in which they do not properly belong.

Examples In English, the little **words** (here underlined) which form the second part of such two-**word verbs** as *take out*, *hand in*, *give up*, *wash down* and *push over* are

14 According to Tamsin Donaldson's book, *Ngiyambaa: the Language of the Wangaaybuwan* (Cambridge University Press, 1980).
15 By Mark Durie, in his *A Grammar of Acehnese on the Basis of a Dialect of North Aceh* (Foris, Dordrecht-Holland, 1985).

often called 'particles'. (Such two-**word verbs** are also known as 'phrasal **verbs**'.)

The English **negative word** *not* is sometimes called a '**negative** particle'.

Another candidate for the label 'particle' is the grammatically mysterious *rid* in the idiomatic *get rid of*. What exactly is this *rid*? Although it seems to be historically descended from a **past participle**, it is obviously quite special, a law unto itself, now; hence it might, for want of a better term, be called a 'particle'.

Contrasts Since the term tends to be chosen as a deliberate alternative to other terms such as '**auxiliary**', '**modal**', '**article**' or '**preposition**', it is implied that 'particle' contrasts with all these **word**-class terms. And of course 'particle' also contrasts with all the terms for major **parts of speech**, such as '**noun**', '**verb**' and '**adjective**'.

Do not confuse 'particle' with the similar-looking ' **participle**'; the latter has a much more well-defined application.

Passive voice

Explanation In a passive **clause**, the recipient of some action is typically expressed as the **subject** of the **clause**. The doer of the action may or may not be mentioned in the **clause**. In English, passives are formed by combining a form of the **auxiliary verb** *be* with the **past participle** of the **main verb**.

Examples The underlined **clauses** in the following examples are passive.

- *Joe <u>was kicked by a mule</u>.*
- *Joe felt <u>as if he had been kicked by a mule</u>.*
- *<u>Paul was converted to Christianity</u>.*
- *Everyone was surprised <u>that Paul was converted</u>.*
- *Nobody expected <u>Paul to be converted</u>.*

Contrasts Passive contrasts with **active**. Both passive and **active** are called 'voices'. If a **clause** is in the passive voice, it is not in the **active** voice.

In English, passives involve the **verb** *be* and a **past participle**, and since **past participles** can often function as **adjectives**, or **adjectives** can look like **past participles**, there can be **clauses** which seem very like passives but in fact are not. Here are some examples which are not passives, although they look like them. They clearly do not correspond to the hypothetical **actives** given alongside (for this correspondence, see **Relationships** below).

I am delighted to accept your offer.	★*Someone delights me to accept your offer.*
He was ashamed of his crimes.	★*Someone ashamed him of his crimes.*
Are you interested in trains?	★*Does someone interest you in trains?*

Some languages provide several ways of expressing the recipient of an action as the **subject** of a **clause**, and often only one such construction per language is known as its passive. The following English **sentences** are known as examples of a 'middle' construction, rather than the passive.

- *These woollens don't wash well.*
- *The meat had been cooking for forty minutes.*

Relationships The **verb** in a passive **clause** in English is generally a form of a **transitive verb**. This follows from the nature of the relationship between **active** and passive **clauses**, discussed below.

Generally speaking, for every passive **clause**, there is a corresponding **active clause**, with a roughly equivalent meaning. The relationship between **actives** and passives involves a regular 'change' from one grammatical role, **object**, to another, **subject**. (In languages with **case** systems, this would be reflected in a 'change' from **accusative case** to **nominative**.) This is shown below, with **actives** corresponding to the above passives.

- *A mule kicked Joe.*
- *Joe felt as if a mule had kicked him.*
- *Someone (or something) converted Paul to Christianity.*
- *Everyone was surprised that someone (or something) had converted Paul.*
- *Nobody expected anyone (or anything) to convert Paul.*

Passive **clauses** are a device for expressing **impersonal** meanings, that is, for avoiding identifying the person responsible for an action, as in *Kennedy was assassinated*, which does not mention the assassin. This explains why some of the **active clauses** above (especially the ones about Paul's conversion) are at least a little awkward. Putting such **clauses** in the **active** form involves identifying a doer of the action, to go in the **clause**'s **subject** slot, but it is not clear who or what actually did convert Paul, so the vague and awkward *someone (or something)* has to be used. This is why the passive, which avoids identifying the agent of the action, is less awkward here.

Passive **clauses** are also a device for 'foregrounding', or giving a certain kind of emphasis to, one part of a **clause** in relation to another. For example, the passive *John was run over by a bus* seems somehow to focus more attention on the unfortunate John than does the corresponding (and slightly callous-sounding) **active** *A bus ran over John.*

As noted, the **subject** in a passive construction corresponds to the **object** in an **active** construction. In English, and in some other languages, this correspondence can include both **direct** and **indirect objects**, provided that the **indirect object** is not signalled by the **preposition** *to*. This is shown below, with the **active objects** which become passive **subjects** underlined.

ACTIVE	PASSIVE
John gave Mary some books.	*Mary was given some books by John.*
John gave some books to Mary.	*Some books were given to Mary by John.*

155

Not all **active transitive clauses** have passive counterparts. In English, **active clauses** with **(transitive) verbs** such as *cost*, *weigh* and *have* (indicating possession) do not have corresponding passives, as shown by the ungrammaticality of the hypothetical examples on the right below.

This book costs twenty dollars.	*★Twenty dollars is cost by this book.*
This elephant weighs ten tons.	*★Ten tons is weighed by this elephant.*
The Duke has three castles.	*★Three castles are had by the Duke.*

Both **main** and **subordinate clauses** can be passive, as can be seen from the examples given earlier. In English, and in other languages with a clear passive construction, passives combine very freely with all types of **subordinate clauses**.

Since passives crucially involve the **subjects** of **clauses**, the processes which involve **subjects** also affect passives. For instance, in some **subordinate clauses**, the **subject** is omitted, or suppressed, and this applies equally to the **subjects** of **actives** and passives. In each of the following examples, the **subject** of the **subordinate clause** is missing, but these **clauses** are nevertheless passive, as shown by the presence of the **auxiliary** *be* and the **past participle**. These **subject**less passive **subordinate clauses** are underlined below.

- *Dan expected to be renominated.*
- *I want to be loved by you.*
- *This ticket seems to have been dunked in coffee.*

Sometimes both the **main** and a **subordinate clause** in a **sentence** can be passive, as in *It is known that Agatha was poisoned*, or *Agatha is known to have been poisoned*, or *Justice must be seen to be done*.

In English, passive voice can occur freely with **declarative** and **interrogative moods**, but is at least a little awkward in the **imperative mood**. This is shown by:

I was overtaken by a cyclist.	DECLARATIVE
Were you overtaken by a cyclist?	INTERROGATIVE
★Be overtaken by a cyclist!	IMPERATIVE

Some conventional passive **imperatives** do occur, especially in rather formal style, as in *Please be seated*.

For interest Some languages, from a wide range of areas in the world, have no passives. In such languages, the device used to avoid identifying the agent of an action is often an impersonal construction, rather like the French use of the impersonal pronoun *on*, as in *On danse* (literally *One dances*, which avoids saying who dances).

The English passive is formed by means of an auxiliary *be*. Other languages form passives by means of affixes, or even more complicated changes to the shape of a word. Latin forms its passives by adding the suffix *-ur* to the corresponding forms of the verb. Here is an example.

Romeo amat Juliam
Romeo loves Julia
NOM   ACC   (= *Romeo loves Julia.*

Julia amat-ur
Julia loves
NOM PASS   (= *Julia is loved.*

Egyptian Colloquial Arabic forms its passives with a prefix *it-*. Here is an example.

mohammad kasar il baab
Mohammed broke the door   (= *Mohammed broke the door.*)

il baab it-kasar
the door broke
PASS   (= *The door got broken.*)

Such examples help make the point that where the passive construction involves a change in the shape of any word (e.g. by a suffix), such a change typically, across the world's languages, affects the verb.

In some languages, there can be passives involving intransitive verbs. In German, for instance, the passive involves a special auxiliary verb *werden*, followed by a past participle. An example with an intransitive verb is *Es wurde getanzt*, literally *It was danced*. Here *es* does not refer to any particular dance, but is rather more like the fairly empty English *there* in *There was dancing*. This is a way of saying, in German, that there was dancing without saying who was dancing. This German construction is usually called the 'impersonal passive', which is not entirely appropriate, as many other passives, such as *Tee wurde gebracht* (= *Tea was brought*) are also impersonal.

Exercise   Identify the passive clauses in the following examples. Underline the whole clause in each case. There are five in all.

1 *I am being pursued by an integer.*
2 *Electromagnetism was discovered by Faraday after he had been released from tedious government research.*
3 *I can't bear to be taunted.*
4 *Coffee has been spilt over this keyboard and it has broken down.*
5 *Have you been to London yet?*

Past participle

Explanation   In English, the past participle is a form of a **verb** used for either of two purposes:

- with **auxiliary** *have*, to express the **perfect**;
- with **auxiliary** *be*, to express the **passive**.

Forms in other languages called 'past participles' are forms used for these and similar purposes.

The past participles of **verbs** in English are formed in various ways. The most **regular** way is to add a **suffix** -ed or -d to the **verb**; another method is to add the **suffix** -en to the **verb**, possibly also changing its vowel; there are also a few other less **regular** methods.

Examples The table below gives the past participles of a sample of English **verbs**.

VERB	PAST PARTICIPLE	VERB	PAST PARTICIPLE
scrub	scrubbed	scream	screamed
fix	fixed	talk	talked
need	needed	waste	wasted
take	taken	know	known
drive	driven	break	broken
swim	swum	begin	begun
hit	hit	come	come
bring	brought	teach	taught
do	done	be	been

Contrasts Past participles contrast with **past tense** forms of **verbs**, even though in English they often have the same spelling and pronunciation. The **past tense** and past participle forms of regular English **verbs** are identical, e.g. *probed, banged, typed, frothed, fretted, computed*. But in many other cases, especially involving more common **verbs**, past participle and **past tense** forms are distinct, as illustrated below:

VERB	PAST TENSE	PAST PARTICIPLE
write	wrote	written
bite	bit	bitten
sink	sank	sunk
drink	drank	drunk
see	saw	seen
sew	sewed	sewn

In some non-standard **dialects**, some **past tenses** and past participles which are not identical in standard English are the same. In such **dialects**, for example, one can say *I seen it* and *I done it*. These meanings would be expressed in standard English as *I saw it* and *I did it*. There is probably a historic drift slowly taking place in the language, by which **past tense** forms and past participles are becoming identical. Few people noticed, for instance, that the title of a recent popular movie, *Honey, I Shrunk the Kids*, used what would once have been thought of as a past participle, *shrunk*, in place of a **past tense** form, *shrank*.

Past participles contrast with **present participles**, but there is little risk of confusion, as **present participles** all end in -*ing*, which no past participle does.

Relationships   Some English **verbs** have alternative past participle forms, depending sometimes on **dialect** and sometimes on style. Examples are *dream – dreamed/dreamt,
burn – burned/burnt* and *lean – leaned/leant.*

Something seldom noticed by non-linguists, but one of the first things that is
learnt (or learned!) in a linguistics course, is that the past participle-forming
suffix spelt (or spelled!) *-ed* is actually pronounced in three clearly different
ways, depending on the nature of the preceding sound. The three different
pronunciations are:

1 a single consonant [d], as in *seized, frowned, chilled*;

2 a single consonant [t], as in *missed, tipped, asked;*

3 a syllable consisting of a short vowel plus a consonant, [ɪd], as in *mended,
boarded, rotted, patted.*

As English past participles can be used in both **perfect** and **passive** constructions, it can happen that two past participles are used together, one in each
of these senses, as in *We have <u>been discovered</u>. (Been* is the past participle of the
verb *be.*)

As noted above, English past participles can be used with the **auxiliary verb**
be to form **passives**. In this **passive** sense, the English past participle also takes
on a use like that of an **adjective**, either occurring before a **noun** and **modifying** it, or occurring in a **modifying** participial **phrase** after the **noun**. Here are
some examples:

NOUN WITH MODIFYING PAST PARTICIPIAL PHRASE	PAST PARTICIPLE MODIFYING FOLLOWING NOUN
a soldier wounded by the enemy	*a wounded soldier*
a letter copied by a secretary	*a copied letter*
a ceiling painted white	*a painted ceiling*
a duck strangled by the farmer	*a strangled duck*

This adaptation of past participles to an adjectival use applies only to the past
participles of **transitive verbs**, as only they occur in the **passive**. (There are
some rare exceptions to this rule, with the past participles of **intransitive verbs**
being put to this adjectival use, as in *a fallen tree, the risen dough.*)

For interest   The use of one common 'past participle' form to express both the perfect and
the passive is familiar from European languages. Both French and German, for
example, along with quite a few other European languages, put their so-called
'past participles' to just these two uses. But perfect and passive constructions
convey quite different meanings, and it is something of a puzzle why the same
form should be used for both in a number of languages.

Certainly, not all languages use the same form to express perfect and passive.
Arabic has what is best called a 'passive participle' used essentially like an
adjective, and always with the passive sense. Thus, some uses of the English
past participle (i.e. the passive uses) are translatable by the Arabic passive
participle, but other uses (the perfect ones) are not. Take an example. Arabic
maktuub means *written*, in the passive sense only. The word *maktuub* would be

used in a sentence meaning *It is written*, but not in a sentence meaning *He has written it*. Similarly, Arabic *maftuuḥ* means *opened*, and would be used in a sentence meaning, for example, *The door has been opened*, but not in a sentence meaning *Ali has opened the door*.

Exercise Identify the past participles in the following. There are eight in all.

1 *She was so deeply imbedded in my consciousness that for the first year of school I seem to have believed that each of my teachers was my mother in disguise.*
2 *This would never have been revealed, if you had not intervened.*
3 *He had fallen backwards when I hit him.*
4 *He fell backwards after I had hit him.*
5 *Bill could have come yesterday, but Fred can't come until tomorrow.*

Past tense

Explanation The past tense of a **verb** is a form typically indicating that the event or state of affairs expressed by the **verb** took place or existed before the present. ('The present' here is whenever the speaker or writer is actually speaking or writing.) In English, past tense forms are usually inflected with a **suffix** *-ed, -d* or, in rarer cases, *-t*, but there are also some common irregular **past tense** forms.

Many languages have not just one past tense, but several.

Examples Here is a sample of English **verbs** and their simple past tenses.

VERB	PAST TENSE	VERB	PAST TENSE
talk	*talked*	*laugh*	*laughed*
sail	*sailed*	*rhyme*	*rhymed*
invent	*invented*	*mind*	*minded*
hear	*heard*	*read*	*read* (pronounced [red])
bring	*brought*	*seek*	*sought*
grind	*ground*	*find*	*found*
be	*was/were*	*have*	*had*
go	*went*	*come*	*came*

Contrasts Past tense contrasts, in English, with **present tense**. Past and **present** are the only English simple **tenses**, using one-**word** forms of the **verb**. **Future** is expressed in English as a **compound tense**, with two **words**, using the **modal auxiliary** *will*, e.g. *will come*; the corresponding past tense *came* is just one **word**.

Past tense contrasts, in English, with another way of expressing pastness, namely the **perfect**, which uses the **auxiliary** *have* and a **past participle**. Here are some contrasting English past tenses and **perfects**.

PAST TENSE	PERFECT
came	*has/have come*
went	*has/have gone*
was/were	*has/have been*
rose	*has/have risen*

Note that in these **perfects**, the **auxiliary** *have* is itself in the **present tense**. (If the **auxiliary** *have*, used with a **past participle**, were itself in the past tense, giving *had come* or *had risen*, this would be a case of the **past perfect** or **pluperfect**.)

The simple past tenses of most English **verbs** happen to be the same as their **past participles**, often ending in the **suffix** *-ed* or *-d*. But past tenses and **past participles** do contrast. The one (the past tense form) is used on its own to express a completed action or state in the past, whereas the other (the **past participle** form) is used with an **auxiliary** *have* to express a rather different attitude to a past event or state. The previous table, comparing past tense with **perfect**, can also be used to compare past tenses with **past participles** – just ignore the *has/have*.

Relationships   In English, **tense**, including past tense, is shown on the first verbal element in a **clause**, whatever this happens to be, whether a **main verb** or an **auxiliary verb**. In the examples below, the past tense forms are underlined, to illustrate this.

- *She caught the bus at half past twelve, and was home by one o'clock.*
- *Nothing had gone wrong, until you arrived.*
- *My mother was always pouring gin down him.*
- *I could have danced all night.*

As the second and third of these examples show, English past tense can combine with the **perfect** and the **progressive**, with **auxiliary** *have* or **auxiliary** *be* showing the **tense**. When this happens, we have the so-called **past perfect** (or **pluperfect**) and the **past progressive**.

As the last of the above examples shows, English **modal verbs**, such as *can*, *shall* and *may* can be said to have past tense forms, since they all (apart from *must*) go in pairs which superficially resemble **present/past** pairings. The pairings are *can/could*, *shall/should*, *will/would* and *may/might*. From the purely grammatical point of view, it makes sense to call *could*, *should*, *would* and *might* 'past tense' forms, because of this neat pairwise patterning, just as happens with all other **verbs**. But clearly, from the point of view of meaning, these forms do not simply express versions in the past of the meanings of their apparently '**present**' counterparts. *She would do it*, for example, is not simply a 'pushing back' of *She will do it* into a time before the present. Similarly, *She might do it* does not describe a version before the present of *She may do it*.

English past tense **verb** forms do not, in general, show **agreement** with the **subject** of their **clause**. That is, English past tense **verb** forms are all the same, regardless of the **person** (1st/2nd/3rd) or **number (singular/plural)** of their

subjects. The single exception to this, in standard English, is the **verb** *be*. In standard English, only *be* shows **number (singular/plural) agreement** in the past tense. So we get *she was*, but *they were*. (In some non-standard **dialects**, this **singular/plural** distinction in the past tense of *be* is lost, and we find *was* used for both **singular** and **plural** (e.g. *we was, they was*) in London and the south of England. In other non-standard **dialects**, e.g. in the British Midlands and parts of the north of England, *were* is used for both **singular** and **plural** (e.g. *I were, she were*).)

In some non-standard English **dialects**, a few **verbs**, including *do, see* and *come*, have a past tense form identical to the standard **past participle**. So in these **dialects** we get, for example, *I done it, We seen it* and *He come yesterday*.

Just as with the **past participle**, the English past tense **suffix** which is written -*ed* or -*d*, actually has three different pronunciations. These are: [t] as in *walked, wished* and *wiped*; [d] as in *killed, died* and *sneezed*; and [ɪd] as in *landed* and *rented*.

The past tenses of most English **verbs** are formed in a **regular** way by adding the **suffix** -*ed* or -*d*. But there are about a hundred English **verbs** with irregular past tenses, which a foreign learner (for instance) must simply learn by heart. Examples of some such irregular past tenses are *made, sang, dreamt, taught, drove, took, sat, swam, flew, drew, wrote, bore*.

For interest English has only two simple (one-word) tenses, present and past. This does not mean that English cannot express the future, of course, merely that it does not use a simple tensed form of the verb to do it. As already noted, English expresses the future with a modal auxiliary, *will*.

German is like English in having only two one-word tenses, also present and past. This is not surprising, as English and German both belong to the same historic family of languages, Germanic. French, by contrast, has a rich range of different one-word tenses, including three different kinds of past tense.

A few languages use different past tenses to distinguish how far back in the past the event described took place. Here are two examples of such finely grained past tense systems.[16]

In the Wishram-Waco dialect of Chinook, a North American Indian language,[17] there are four past tenses, indicated by prefixes, as follows:

PREFIX	PAST TENSE MEANING	EXAMPLE	TRANSLATION
ni-	Far past	*ni-čiuχ*	*He did it long ago.*
ga-	Remote past	*ga-čiuχ*	*He did it some time ago.*

16 This data is from an article, 'Tense, aspect and mood', by Sandra Chung and Alan Timberlake, in *Language Typology and Syntactic Description*, volume III: *Grammatical Categories and the Lexicon*, edited by Timothy Shopen (Cambridge University Press, 1985).

17 Chung and Timberlake get this data from an article by Michael Silverstein, 'Dialectal developments in Chinookan tense–aspect systems: an areal-historical analysis', *International Journal of American Linguistics*, Memoir 29 (1974).

na-	Recent past	na-čiuҳ	*He did it recently.*
i-	Immediate past	i-čiuҳ	*He just did it.*

In the Bantu (African) language ChiBemba, there are also four distinct past tenses, indicated by infixes and suffixes, as these examples show.[18]

- remote past
  ba-àlí-bomb-ele
  They worked (before yesterday).
- removed past
  ba-àlíí-bomba
  They worked (yesterday).
- near past
  ba-àcí-bomba
  They worked (today).
- immediate past
  ba-à-bomba
  They worked (within the last three hours).

By complete contrast, Chinese has no past tense (and indeed no tenses) at all.

Exercise   Identify the past tense forms, of both main verbs and auxiliaries, in the following. There are ten in all, including some repetitions.

1 *I was born in the year 1632, in the city of York, of a good family, though not of that country, my father being a foreigner of Bremen, who settled first at Hull: he got a good estate by merchandise, and leaving off his trade, lived afterwards at York.*

2 *I was born in 1927, the only child of middle-class parents, both English, and themselves born in the grotesquely elongated shadow, which they never rose sufficiently above history to leave, of that monstrous dwarf Queen Victoria.*

3 *If you really want to hear about it, the first thing you'll probably want to know is where I was born, and what my lousy childhood was like, and how my parents were occupied and all before they had me, and all that David Copperfield kind of crap, but I don't feel like going into it, if you want to know the truth.*

Perfect

Explanation   'Perfect' is the label given to various forms of **verbs** in various languages, with somewhat different meanings, but always with some ingredient of pastness.

In English, the form called 'perfect' is the two-**word** form of a **verb** using the **auxiliary** *have* and the **past participle** of the **verb**.

---

18 Chung and Timberlake get this data from an article by Talmy Givon, 'Studies in ChiBemba and Bantu grammar', *Studies in African Linguistics*, Supplement 3 (1972).

Examples   In the English examples below, the perfect forms of **verbs** are underlined.

- *Who <u>has stolen</u> my pencil?*
- *The young men <u>have gone</u> away.*
- *I <u>had been</u> walking for three miles when Sheila came along.*

Contrasts   In English, perfect contrasts with the simple **past tense**. The perfect of a **verb** uses an **auxiliary**, whereas the simple **past tense** of a **verb** is a one-**word** form, as in *Who <u>stole</u> my pencil?* Both express kinds of pastness, but there is a subtle difference in meaning. The English perfect is said to express a more recent past, or a more 'currently relevant' past than the simple **past tense**. So, typically *Fred has stolen my pencil* would describe a very recent happening; by contrast *Fred stole my pencil* is more likely to describe an event more distant in time.

In English, perfect contrasts with another two-**word** form of the **verb**, the **progressive**, which uses the **auxiliary** *be* and a **present participle**, as in *Who is stealing my pencil?* The difference in meaning between *Fred has stolen my pencil* and *Fred is stealing my pencil* is clear.

The English perfect also contrasts with the **passive**, which it resembles, as they both use the **past participle** form of a **verb**. But whereas perfect uses the **auxiliary** *have*, the English **passive** uses the **auxiliary** *be*, as in *My pencil was stolen.*

Relationships   The perfect in English is traditionally labelled a '**compound tense**', as it consists of more than one **word**. Modern linguists more usually call the perfect a type of 'aspect'.

All three English constructions mentioned above as contrasting with the perfect can in fact be combined with it.

Perfect combines with **past tense** to produce the **past** perfect, or **pluperfect**. In this case the perfect's **auxiliary** *have* takes the **past tense**, as in *Someone had stolen my pencil.*

Perfect combines with **progressive** in examples such as *Someone has been stealing my pencils.* Here the **verb** which takes the **past participle** form is the *be* of the **progressive**.

Perfect combines with **passive** as in *My pencils have been stolen.* Here the **verb** which takes the **past participle** form is the *be* of the **passive**.

In fact, all four elements which have just been discussed, namely simple **tense** (**present/past**), perfect, **progressive** and **passive**, are mutually independent variables in English, which can co-occur in any combination.

The English perfect can be interrupted. That is, other **words** and **phrases** can intervene between the **auxiliary** *have* and the **past participle**, as in (separated parts of the perfect are underlined):

- *I <u>have</u> never in my life <u>seen</u> such a shambles.*
- *She <u>has</u> always <u>acted</u> in your best interest.*
- *<u>Have</u> you <u>been</u> snooping round my room?*

For interest
The grammars of other languages often use the term 'perfect' for some verb form with pastness in its meaning. But there is not necessarily a very direct correspondence between what is called 'perfect' in different languages.

Traditional Latin grammars identify a tense which they call 'perfect', but this is not always appropriately translated by the English form known (and discussed above) as 'perfect'. For instance, the perfect form of the Latin verb *duco*, meaning *I lead*, is *duxi*, and this may be translated, depending on the context, as either *I led* or *I have led*.

A similar situation exists with Arabic grammar, where grammarians identify a particular form of the verb with the label 'perfect'. Thus the Arabic word *katab* is a perfect form of the verb meaning *write*. But normally the best translation for *katab* is not the English perfect *has written*, but rather the simple past tense *wrote*. In fact there is a different Arabic verb form, which grammarians usually call a 'participle', rather than a perfect, which is more often the better translation of the English perfect form.

Standard German has a perfect form very like English, with a quite similar meaning, distinguished subtly, as in English, from the simple past tense. But there are dialects of German, particularly in Switzerland, in which the simple past tense has disappeared from the language completely, and has been replaced by the perfect, so there is in effect no longer any contrast in such dialects between the perfect and the simple past tense. Yet it is natural to continue to call the Swiss German form 'perfect', even though its meaning is broader than that of the standard German perfect.

In fact, British and American English differ in their use of the perfect. The perfect is more widely used in British English. Where a British speaker would tend to say *Have you seen Bill today?*, an American speaker would tend to say *Did you see Bill today?* Where a British English speaker would tend to say *I have just had breakfast*, an American speaker would tend to say *I just had breakfast*.

Exercise
Identify the perfect forms in the following:

1 *Mr Phillips, you have met Mr Squires, I believe.*
2 *Sherlock Holmes had been bending for a long time over a low-power microscope.*
3 *It had taken three men to shift the grand piano upstairs.*
4 *No stone had been left unturned in the search for Tilly's killer.*
5 *I would like to have experienced the whole thing myself.*

Person

Explanation
The dimension of person in **grammar** distinguishes between different kinds of **pronouns** and **noun phrases** in the following way:

- 1st person identifies expressions referring to the current speaker or writer, or to groups of people which include the current speaker or writer;

- 2nd person identifies expressions referring to the current hearer(s) or addressee(s);
- 3rd person identifies expressions referring to people other than the current speaker, writer, hearer(s) or addressee(s).

Examples English **personal pronouns** may be classified by person as follows:

PRONOUNS	PERSON
I, we	1st person
you	2nd person
he, she, it, they	3rd person

The **impersonal pronoun** *one* is 3rd person **(singular)**.
Most other **noun phrases** are 3rd person, for example:

- *The man on the Clapham omnibus*
- *Some friends that I ran into last night*
- *Mary*
- *Henry Fitzroy McLean*

These **noun phrases** are all 3rd person.

Contrasts The dimension of person (1st/2nd/3rd) contrasts with the dimensions of:

- **number (singular/plural)**;
- **gender** (masculine/feminine/ . . .);
- **case (nominative/accusative/dative/ . . .).**

Person, and its subdivisions, 1st, 2nd, 3rd, are not **parts of speech**, or **word**-classes, as they represent a dimension which can be applied to several different **parts of speech**.

Relationships The three other dimensions mentioned under **Contrasts** above, namely **number**, **gender** and **case**, can all combine freely with person. The most commonly mentioned combinations are of person with **number**. For example:

PRONOUN	PERSON–NUMBER COMBINATION
I	1st person **singular**
we	1st person **plural**
they	3rd person **plural**

Modern standard English makes no distinction of **number** in the 2nd person, so the pronoun *you* can refer either to just one person, or to several. Some **dialects** get around this by having a special 2nd person **plural** form, such as *youse* in Glasgow and parts of Ireland, and *y'all* in the south-eastern United States. A modern youthful variant, common across America, is *you guys*, which may be addressed to groups of males and/or females. If these forms are used regularly, then presumably *you* is by default the 2nd person **singular pronoun** in these **dialects**.

In earlier stages of the history of English, there was a **number (singular/plural)** distinction in 2nd person **pronouns**; *thou* and *thee* were **singular** forms and *you* and *ye* were 2nd person **plural** forms. But this situation was made more complicated by an additional dimension of familiarity or politeness, with *thou* being reserved for intimates and juniors.

The dimension of person can combine with the dimension of **gender**, so that, for instance, the **pronoun** *she* can be referred to as the 3rd person singular feminine **pronoun**. (In English, the dimension of **gender** is not very active, however.)

The dimension of person can also combine with the dimension of **case**, so that *him*, for example, may be described as the 3rd person **singular** masculine **accusative pronoun**; and *me* can be called 1st person **singular accusative**. (But the dimension of **case**, like that of **gender**, is not very active in English.)

Person is involved in **agreement**, to a very limited extent in English, but much more fully in some other languages. In English, the **present tense** of the **verb** *be* is sensitive to person in the **singular**, with the forms *am* – 1st, *are* – 2nd, and *is* – 3rd. *Be*, like other **verbs**, is not sensitive to person in the **plural**. The only person for which all other English **verbs** have a special **agreement** marker (the suffix -*s*) is 3rd person **singular**, and then only in the **present tense**, as in *She talks, he listens, and the dog sleeps.*

Full **noun phrases** built around **nouns** are generally 3rd person, naturally enough, as these are normally only used to refer to people other than the speaker or hearer. But in rare cases when such a **phrase** is in **apposition** to a non-3rd person **pronoun**, the non-3rd person **agreement** prevails. So we get, for example, *Richard Nixon stands accused of fraud*, but *You, Richard Nixon, stand accused of fraud.*

Imperatives, to the extent that they are associated with any person at all, are, rather naturally, associated with 2nd person. Thus in French, the **plural imperative** (e.g. *Allez!* – Go!) has a 2nd person **plural** ending; but the French **singular imperative** has no characteristic person ending (except in one or two unusual circumstances).

For interest As mentioned, full noun phrases built around nouns are generally 3rd person. Even the super-polite forms used to royalty, such as *Your Majesty*, take 3rd person agreement, as in *Does Your Majesty require anything else?* (i.e. not **Do Your Majesty require...*). This is a case of grammar overruling meaning, because *Your Majesty* clearly refers to the person being spoken to (the Queen, or whoever), and so should be 2nd person. Presumably, forms like *Your Majesty* originated in a need to avoid the direct (and perhaps blunt) form of address *you*, but it is ironic that the device does not really succeed, because the 2nd person *you* is still present, buried in the possessive *your*.

Many languages seem to have felt that 2nd person forms of address are excessively direct, and impolite, and have invented polite substitutes with the appearance of 3rd person expressions. The German *Sie*, now meaning *you* (polite), was taken from the pronoun meaning *they* (and given a dignifying capital letter!) and still takes agreement identical to that of a 3rd person plural form. In Italian, the polite pronouns of address are *Lei* and *Loro*, which are identical to the 3rd person forms for *she* and *they*; polite *Lei* and *Loro*, even though referring to the addressee(s), take 3rd person agreement.

The avoidance of specifically 2nd person, and also 1st person, forms has been taken relatively far in some East Asian languages, including Japanese, Thai and Malay. The transparent historical origins of some of these very polite forms in Japanese is interesting. In Japanese *denka*, now understood as either *Your Highness* (2nd person) or *His Highness* (3rd person), literally means (*he who lives*) *under* (i.e. *in*) *the pavilion*.[19]

In Japanese, there is an elaborate system at work in much of the vocabulary, distinguishing between 'honorific' forms and 'humble' forms. Honorific forms are used for anything connected with the hearer (and so are associated with 2nd person), and humble forms are used for anything connected with the speaker (and so are associated with 1st person). Even such a value-free action as is expressed by the English verb *go* has a distinct honorific form, *irassharu*, and a distinct humble form, *mairu*. *Irassharu*, being honorific, cannot refer to the 1st person, and *mairu*, being humble, cannot refer to the 2nd person.

Some languages make a distinction, not made in English, between 'inclusive' and 'exclusive' 1st person plural. Thus in Tagalog, the main language of the Philippines, there are pronouns as follows:

taju Inclusive 1st person plural (meaning *you and I*)

kami Exclusive 1st person plural (meaning *I and someone else, but not you*)

Exercise Supply the modern standard English pronouns which fit the following descriptions.

1 2nd person
2 3rd person plural nominative
3 1st person singular nominative
4 3rd person singular neuter
5 3rd person singular masculine accusative

Personal pronoun

Explanation Personal pronouns, like all **pronouns** are typically little **words** that can stand in place of **noun phrases**. Personal pronouns are used to refer to specific people or things.

19 The information here and below on Japanese is from *An Historical Grammar of Japanese*, by G. B. Sansom, Clarendon Press (Oxford, 1928).

Examples　The English personal pronouns are *I, me, you, he, him, she, her, it, we, us, they* and *them*. Note that *it* is generally counted as a 'personal' pronoun, when it refers to some specific thing.

Contrasts　Personal pronouns contrast with **impersonal pronouns**, such as English *one*, and the **impersonal** *it* as in such **sentences** as *It is a pity that it rained.*

Although **reflexive pronouns**, such as English *myself* and *themselves*, can refer to just the same range of people and things as personal pronouns, **reflexives** are not usually counted among the personal pronouns, and so contrast with them.

Personal pronouns contrast with **relative pronouns**, such as English *who, which* and *that.*

Personal pronouns contrast with **demonstratives**, such as English *these* and *that*, when these are used as **pronouns** (as just happened).

Personal pronouns contrast with **possessive pronouns**, such as English *mine, yours* and *theirs.*

Personal pronouns contrast with **possessives**, such as *my, your* and *their*, which are not **pronouns** at all, although they are systematically related to **pronouns**.

Relationships　Personal pronouns can stand in place of whole **noun phrases**. That is, just as a **noun phrase** consisting of an **article**, an **adjective** and a **noun**, such as *the last bus*, can act as **subject** or **direct** or **indirect object** in a **clause**, a personal pronoun can also act as any of these in a **clause**.

Personal pronouns in English differ according to **case** (**nominative/accusative**). Thus, when a personal pronoun is used as the **subject** of a **clause**, it is in the **nominative case**, as in <u>He</u> *bought a car* or <u>They</u> *sold a car*. When a personal pronoun is used as the **object** in a **clause**, it is in the **accusative case**, as in *Shirley met* <u>me</u> or *Fred saw* <u>them</u>.

Personal pronouns are usually **definite**.

Being **definite**, 3rd **person** personal pronouns are normally only used when the person or thing they refer to has already been mentioned in the conversation or written text. The **noun phrase** in the previous conversation or written text which refers to the same person or thing as the personal pronoun is called the **pronoun**'s 'antecedent'. In each of the examples below, the first underlined item is most naturally interpreted as the antecedent of the later personal pronoun, also underlined.

- <u>John</u> *came home late.* <u>He</u> *was drunk.*
- <u>Mary</u> *told John that* <u>she</u> *was leaving home.*
- *I saw John and* <u>Mary</u> *this morning.* <u>They</u> *seem to have made it up.*

Personal pronouns can normally be identified in terms of **person** (1st/2nd/3rd). Thus English *I* is 1st **person** and *you* is 2nd **person**.

Personal pronouns can usually be identified in terms of **number** (**singular/plural**). Thus English *she* is **singular** and *we* is **plural**.

And personal pronouns can often be identified in terms of **gender** (masculine/feminine/ . . .). Thus English *he* is masculine, and *her* is feminine.

For interest   Personal pronouns are interesting from the point of view of their meanings, which have been the subject of much discussion by philosophers and logicians, as well as by linguists and grammarians.

1st and 2nd person personal pronouns, such as *I* and *you*, carry their meanings in a special kind of way. When they are used, these pronouns pick out particular individual people in the world. When I use *I*, the pronoun identifies me; but when you use *I*, the same pronoun identifies a different person, namely you. This may seem trivial, but it is important to realize how unusual this situation is, in terms of the usual relations between words and their meanings.

To take a kind of word which carries its meaning in a quite different way from *I* and *you*, consider the proper name *Bill*. Now, there are many Bills in the world, but if you and I want to talk about one Bill in particular, we first ascertain which individual we are talking about, and then follow a convention whereby the word *Bill*, for the duration of our conversation, means just that person. If I start meaning another Bill, or even some other person or thing, such as the chair I am sitting on, when I say *Bill*, we will not communicate successfully (unless I warn you of the meaning-change). So, for people to communicate, it appears that the meanings of words have to be held constant between them.

But the personal pronouns *I* and *you* systematically change their meanings, according to who is speaking. When I say *I*, I mean me; when you say *I*, you mean you. Actually it sometimes takes children learning their native language a little while to figure this out, and for a period they are confused about the apparent contradiction that *I* can mean you and *you* can mean me. (Such words whose meanings shift to reflect the situation in which they are used are known as 'deictic' words.)

Exercise   Identify the personal pronouns in the following. There are fourteen in all, including repetitions.

1 *He walks down the street. The asphalt reels by him.*
   It is all silence.
   The silence is music.
   He is the singer.
   The people passing smile and shake their heads.
   He holds a hand out to them.
   They open their hands like flowers, shyly.
   He smiles with them.
   The light is blinding: he loves the light.
   They are the light.
2 *We settle down in our new home and I resolve to keep a diary. Tradesmen trouble us a bit, so does the scraper. The curate calls and pays me a great compliment.*

Phrase

Explanation   A phrase is a part of a **sentence** or **clause** which holds together as a meaningful unit on its own, and contributes in a unified way to the meaning of the whole **sentence** or **clause**. Phrases often consist of several **words** clustered around a particular **head word**, which in some sense carries the central idea in the meaning of the whole phrase. Phrases can be long, and may contain other phrases inside them.

Examples   Here are some simple English phrases, of various types:

- *might be coming*
- *ran away home quickly*
- *all the black horses*
- *extremely tall*
- *under the kitchen table*
- *not very convincingly*

These examples of phrases were, for simplicity, not given in the contexts of **sentences** that might contain them. In most contexts, the strings of **words** given above would indeed be phrases, but one can in fact only tell from its sentential context whether a string of **words** is a phrase. (See end of **Relationships** section below.)

Contrasts   Traditionally, 'phrase' contrasts with **word**, as a phrase is traditionally held to consist of more than one **word**. But in fact, linguists find it useful to talk of 'one-**word** phrases', and the term 'phrase' is in fact often used in this guide in a way which does not necessarily contrast with 'single **word**'.

Phrases contrast with **clauses**, which they do, however, resemble. None of the examples given above are **clauses**. The main feature of a **clause** is that it has all the components of a potentially independent **sentence**, namely a **verb** and usually a **subject**, and perhaps **objects**, too. A part of a **sentence** with just these components would be called a '**clause**', rather than a 'phrase'. A phrase can contain a **verb**, without its **subject**, or it may itself be the **subject** of some **verb**.

Phrases also contrast with **sentences**, for the same reasons as those involving **clauses** (see above), as **sentences** are essentially structured groupings of **clauses**.

Importantly, phrases contrast with random sequences of **words** arbitrarily cut out of **sentences**. Take a simple (but well-known) **sentence**, such as:

- *The quick brown fox jumped over the lazy dog.*

Now, if we were, completely haphazardly, say blindfolded and with a pin, to pick two points in this **sentence**, we might, say, divide it into three parts as follows:

The quick || brown fox jumped over the || lazy dog.

171

These three parts are not phrases, as they do not hold together as meaningful units on their own, or contribute in a unified way to the meaning of the whole **sentence**. So a phrase is not just any sequence of **words**; it is a unified sequence of **words** composed according to the rules of the language for putting meaningful 'chunks' together.

Relationships   There can be phrases inside other phrases, and this is in fact very common. This can happen in two ways:

1 'conjoining' smaller phrases by a **conjunction**, such as *and*, *but* or *or*;
2 'nesting' a smaller phrase inside a larger one, as an integral part of it.

Here are some examples of large phrases formed by conjoining smaller phrases; all the phrases are underlined here.

- *might be coming but won't sing*
- *all the black horses and a few white ones*
- *extremely tall and breathtakingly handsome*
- *under the kitchen table or somewhere silly*
- *very passionately but not very convincingly*

Note that such conjoined phrases are generally of the same type (see CONJUNCTION).

Here are some examples of a smaller phrase being 'nested' inside a larger one, as an integral part of it; all the phrases are underlined here.

- *might in all probability be coming*
- *ran away home quickly to his mother*
- *five extremely tall basketball players*
- *out from under the kitchen table*
- *is not very convincingly established*

There is in principle no limit on the depth to which phrases may be embedded inside each other in these ways. A very great range of possible combinations is available, and the possibilities are extensively exploited in the normal use of language. Virtually any **sentence** that you choose at random from a newspaper or book will have phrases inside others, often to a depth of three or four.

A general principle for the construction of complex phrases is that any single **word** of one of the major **parts of speech**, namely **noun**, **verb**, **adjective** and **adverb**, can be replaced by a longer phrase containing that or a similar **word**. Here are some examples; the single **word** underlined in the left-hand column is replaced by the phrase underlined in the right-hand column.

Alex sang.	*Alex sang songs.*
Alex sang.	*Alex sang hoarsely.*
Alex sang songs.	*Alex sang some old songs.*
Alex sang.	*The accordionist sang.*
Alex sang some old songs.	*Alex sang some really ancient songs.*
Alex sang hoarsely.	*Alex sang very hoarsely indeed.*

A phrase which can replace a single **word**, while itself being built around that **word** or a similar one, is named by linguists after the **part of speech** of that **word**. Thus, in the examples just given, we have seen:

Verb phrases built around a **verb**	(e.g. *sang songs* and *sang hoarsely*)
Noun phrases built around a **noun**	(e.g. *some old songs* and *the accordionist*)
An **adjective** phrase built around an **adjective**	(e.g. *really ancient*)
An **adverb** phrase built around an **adverb**	(e.g. *very hoarsely indeed*)

Clearly, there is a general principle here, and this kind of organization of phrases is found in languages across the world. The terminology of '**noun phrases**', '**verb phrases**' and so on is a development of modern linguistics, rather than of traditional grammar.

The **word** around which a phrase is built is known, by linguists, as the '**head**' of the phrase; the other **words** that make up the phrase are often called the '**modifiers**'.

Prepositions are often not classed as a 'major' **part of speech**, but it is useful to identify a class of **prepositional** phrases. A **prepositional** phrase consists of a **preposition** followed by a **noun** phrase (note again here the inclusion of one type of phrase inside another).

Here is an illustration of how a fairly complex structure can be built up by successively nesting phrases inside phrases. We start with the simple one-**word noun** *liberty*. Putting this after a **preposition**, we get:

- *for liberty* (a **prepositional** phrase)

Now we can make this the **modifier** in a **noun** phrase such as:

- *the struggle for liberty* (a **noun** phrase)

Now add another **preposition**, giving:

- *in the struggle for liberty* (a **prepositional** phrase)

And so on.

Clauses contain phrases, as in the example (the phrases are underlined):

- *All the first year students believed the story.*

And phrases, in their turn, can contain **clauses**. So we could put a (**relative**) **clause** after the **noun** *story*, giving:

- *All the first-year students believed the story that the student newspaper had printed.*

173

Languages (not just English) have the potential for expressing messages of unlimited richness and complexity, through this device of building phrases and **clauses** out of other simpler phrases and **clauses**.

As noted earlier, linguists entertain the possibility of single-**word** phrases as below:

you	**Pronoun**	or	Single-**word noun** phrase
John	**Proper noun**	or	Single-**word noun** phrase
runs	**Intransitive verb**	or	Single-**word verb** phrase
happy	**Adjective**	or	Single-**word adjective** phrase
today	**Adverb**	or	Single-**word adverb** phrase

The concepts of **subject** and **object** relate to phrases in a somewhat ambivalent way, though in practice hardly any confusion arises. Sometimes linguists and grammarians will speak of a whole phrase as being the **subject** or **object** of a **verb**; at other times they will speak of a single **word**, the **head** of the phrase concerned, being the **subject** or **object** of the **verb**. Usage among grammarians is somewhat inconsistent here, and (in the case of linguists at least) reflects somewhat different conceptions of **grammar** and **sentence** structure. This dictionary is in fact similarly inconsistent, although on the whole preferring the convention by which phrases, rather than their **head words**, are the **subjects** and **objects** of **verbs**.

We noted with the first examples in this entry that a sequence of **words** can only be judged to be a phrase in the context of a **sentence**, or at least some larger containing grammatical unit. Here are some examples in which the two-**word** sequence *extremely short* is not in fact a phrase.

- *Irene is extremely short-sighted.*
- *If you treat them extremely, short people can react with anger.*

In these examples, punctuation gives an obvious clue to the way **sentences** are built up. In other cases, punctuation does not clearly mark the edges of phrases (but intonation may help in speech). The three-**word** sequence *in the winter* is sometimes a phrase, and sometimes not, depending on context.

- *in the winter* USED AS A PHRASE
  - *They won't survive in the winter.*
- *in the winter* NOT USED AS A PHRASE (relevant meaningful units underlined)
  - Do you call the season that we're in the winter?
  - Sue gazed out and took in the winter scenery.
  - They won't survive in the winter weather.

In these last three examples, *in the winter* does not contribute in a unified way to the meaning of the whole **sentence**. Either *in* combines first meaningfully with the **words** before it, as in the first and second examples, or *the winter* combines with the **words** following, as in the second and third examples.

Exercise   In the following examples, identify all the noun phrases (except single-word phrases), including phrases inside phrases, by underlining, as in the text above. Do not underline any clauses or phrases other than noun phrases, such as prepositional phrases, verb phrases or adjective phrases. It will help to write the examples out with plenty of room on a large piece of paper. Don't guess – take it carefully, and be sure you get all the noun phrases inside bigger noun phrases.

1 *Sherlock Holmes was in a melancholy and philosophic mood that morning.*
2 *The ideas of my friend Watson, though limited, are exceedingly pertinacious.*
3 *Somewhere in the vaults of the bank of Cox and Co., at Charing Cross, there is a travel-worn and battered tin dispatch-box with my name.*

Pluperfect, past perfect

Explanation   'Pluperfect' and 'past perfect' mean the same thing.

The pluperfect or past perfect form of a **verb** is a combination of **past** and **perfect**, expressing a kind of pastness that is typically further back in time than what is expressed by the simple **past tense**, and expressing also the kind of completeness associated with the **perfect** aspect. In English, the pluperfect is a **compound tense** formed by using the **past tense** of the **auxiliary** *have* followed by the **past participle** of the **verb** concerned. English pluperfect forms thus always begin with the **word** *had*.

Examples   The pluperfects in the following examples are underlined. Note that they can be discontinuous, that is, interrupted by other **words**.

- *We had taken the high road.*
- *Phyllis had been taking Valium for years.*
- *Jane had already given the book back.*
- *Moriarty had cleverly disguised himself as a Turk.*

Contrasts   Pluperfect contrasts with other **tense** and aspect forms, as illustrated below by variations on simple examples.

SIMPLE PAST	*drove*	*went*	*was*
PERFECT	*has driven*	*has gone*	*has been*
PLUPERFECT	*had driven*	*had gone*	*had been*

Relationships   The examples just given showed contrasts in forms of the **main verbs** *drive* and *go* and the **verb** *be*, which can also be used as an **auxiliary**. The fact that in English and some other languages **auxiliaries** can take **compound tenses** gives rise to complex forms such as the following.

PLUPERFECT PROGRESSIVE (ACTIVE)	*had been seeing*
PLUPERFECT PASSIVE	*had been seen*
PLUPERFECT PROGRESSIVE PASSIVE	*had been being seen*

In these examples, 'PLUPERFECT' could be replaced by its synonym 'past perfect'.

Exercise   Convert each of the following examples into the corresponding pluperfect form.

1 *came*
2 *was coming*
3 *took*
4 *was taken*
5 *was being taken*

Plural

Explanation   A **noun** is usually plural if it denotes a collection of things (where 'things' can be concrete objects or abstract entities). Typical English plural **nouns** end in the suffix *-s* or *-es*, but there are other, irregular, plural forms.

There are also plural **personal pronouns**.

A small number of other **parts of speech** in English have forms explicitly showing **agreement** with a plural **noun** or **pronoun** – see **Relationships** below.

Examples   The following are **regular** plural **nouns** in English: *apples, bears, chrysanthemums, doorknobs, efforts, frivolities, ghosts, happenings, idiots, jerks*.

Some irregular English **plural nouns** are: *children, mice, men, women, geese, teeth, people, deer, sheep*.

The English plural **personal pronouns** are *we, you* and *they*.

Contrasts   Plural contrasts, in English and almost all other languages, with **singular**. In some languages, there is a further contrast, with the 'dual', a form used to denote pairs of things; and in a very few languages, there is even a further contrast with 'trial' forms, denoting trios of things.

Relationships   Plural **number** is essentially a property of **nouns** and **pronouns**, and other **parts of speech** acquire it by **agreement**. The test for whether a **noun** is plural is whether it takes plural **agreement**. In English, there are several **parts of speech** or **word**-classes which show plural **agreement**, illustrated below.

WORD-CLASS	PLURAL FORM	EXAMPLE
3rd **person present tense verb**	bare form, with no **suffix**	*Sheep graze.*
Verb *be*	*are, were*	*Sheep are stupid.*
Demonstrative	*these, those*	*those sheep*
'Quantifier'	*many, few, fewer*	*many sheep*

The **pronouns** *we*, *you* and *they* all take plural **agreement**, e.g. *We are the champions*, *You are nowhere*, even though *you* may sometimes only refer to one person. *You* is therefore always grammatically plural, if sometimes **singular** in meaning.

The English **definite article**, *the*, does not show plural **agreement**, unlike the **definite articles** of French and German. The **word** *some*, unstressed and pronounced [sm], is sometimes regarded as the plural of the **indefinite article** *a*, which is always **singular**.

In English, any **noun modified** by a **cardinal numeral**, other than *one*, is plural, e.g. *three mice*.

Only **common nouns** have frequently used plurals. Plural forms for **proper names**, e.g. *Kevins*, as in *How many Kevins do you know?*, are unusual.

Within the **common nouns**, the plural forms of **count nouns** simply denote collections of more than one thing. But the plural forms of **mass nouns** denote different kinds of stuffs (e.g. *five great wines from the south of France*), or measures of stuff (e.g. *Five beers for this table, please!*).

Some **adjectives** of nationality, such as *French*, *Chinese* and *British*, when used as **nouns**, are normally plural, e.g. *The British are coming!*

Singular nouns conjoined by the **conjunction** *and* make a plural **noun phrase**, as in *Socrates and Xanthippe were a happy couple*.

There are a few exceptional **nouns** which are grammatically plural, taking plural **agreement**, but which denote single objects. Examples are *trousers* (a single garment), *scissors* (a single instrument) and *billiards* (a single kind of game); these **nouns** have no **singular** forms. There is a traditional Latin label for such **nouns** – *pluralia tantum*.

In modern English, the plurals of certain **nouns** borrowed from Latin and Greek are less well known and used rather inconsistently. The standard **singulars** and plurals of some of these **nouns** are given below, but it should be noted that this is a very volatile area, where standard English itself is susceptible to change in the near future.

SINGULAR	PLURAL
criterion	*criteria*
medium	*media*
phenomenon	*phenomena*

Certain English expressions of quantity and measurement, though containing plural **nouns**, nevertheless take **singular agreement**; compare *Ten dollars is too much* with the definitely odd **Ten dollars are too many*.

For interest   As mentioned above, some languages have, in addition to the singular/plural distinction, the further category of 'dual' used to refer to pairs of things. Arabic is such a language. Here are some examples from Egyptian Colloquial Arabic.

SINGULAR	DUAL	PLURAL
kitaab − book	*kitab-een − 2 books*	*talat kutub − 3 books*
bint − girl	*bint-een − 2 girls*	*talat banaat − 3 girls*
walad − boy	*walad-een − 2 boys*	*talat ?awlaad − 3 boys*

A singular/dual/trial/plural distinction is reported for the personal pronouns of the language of Annatom Island, a Melanesian language.[20] Here is the system:

SINGULAR	DUAL	TRIAL	PLURAL
ainjak	*aijumrau*	*aijumtai*	*aijama*
(= I)	*(= we two* (EXCL.))	*(= we three* (EXCL.))	*(= we* (EXCL.))
	akaijau	*akataij*	*akaija*
	(= we two (INCL.))	*(= we three* (INCL.))	*(= we* (INCL.))
aiek	*aijaurau*	*aijaitaij*	*aijaua*
(= you (SING))	*(= you two)*	*(= you three)*	*(= you)*
aien	*arau*	*ahtaij*	*ara*
(= he)	*(= they two)*	*(= they three)*	*(= they)*

Exercise   Identify the plural nouns in the following. There are just six in all.

1 *He objects to the objects she ships back from her travels.*
2 *The ships she travels in have no sails.*
3 *She sails up the coast, and beaches her boat in the evenings.*
4 *The beaches here are safer than those overseas.*

Positive

Explanation   A **clause** or **sentence** is positive if it contains no **negative** grammatical element of any kind, such as English *not*, *no*, *none* or *never*. (Positiveness is so much the normal, or unmarked, state for **clauses** and **sentences** that the most natural definition is in terms of its opposite, **negation**.)

A **word** whose meaning is in some sense the opposite of the meaning of a **negative word** can also be called a 'positive' **word**.

Examples   The following are positive **sentences**:

- *Yuri Gagarin was the first man in space.*
- *John Wayne decided something had to be done.*
- *Now it all seems like a dream.*
- *Did it really happen?*

20   This data comes from Leonard Bloomfield's *Language* (Holt, Rinehart and Winston, New York, 1933).

The **words** in the left-hand column below can be said to be positive words:

POSITIVE	NEGATIVE
happy	*unhappy*
moral	*immoral*
enchanted	*disenchanted*
useful	*useless*
knowledgeable	*ignorant*

Contrasts Positive contrasts with **negative**.

Relationships The single-**word** reply *Yes* to a question such as *Did you put the garbage out last night?* can be called a 'positive answer', or an 'answer in the affirmative'. The two expressions are equivalent. The pair of **words** *Yes/No* provides the clearest example of the basic positive/**negative** opposition.

Typically, only positive **sentences** are preferred after *Yes*. So *Yes, I saw him* is natural, but **Yes, I didn't see him* is definitely less natural. This perhaps accounts for the quirky appeal of the song title 'Yes, we have no bananas'.

The positive/**negative** dimension combines freely with **mood** (**declarative/interrogative/imperative**), as these examples show:

POSITIVE	NEGATIVE	
Bogart did it.	*Bogart didn't do it.*	DECLARATIVE
Did Bogart do it?	*Didn't Bogart do it?*	INTERROGATIVE
Do it!	*Don't do it!*	IMPERATIVE

Notice that the negativeness of an **interrogative** does not seem to affect the real question being asked. So, in a situation where we know that in fact Bogart had done it (whatever it was), the truthful answer to either of the **interrogatives** above would be *Yes*. The truthful answers to the possible questions, given the two possible facts of the matter, are shown in the look-up table below.

	FACT OF THE MATTER	
	Bogart did it.	Bogart didn't do it.
QUESTION	ANSWER	
Did Bogart do it?	*Yes.*	*No.*
Didn't Bogart do it?	*Yes.*	*No.*

What this shows is that, in English at least, the positiveness or negativeness of an answer to a *Yes/No* question depends more on the positiveness or negativeness of the situation concerned (e.g. whether or not Bogart did it) than on the positiveness or negativeness of the original question. (But for some French speakers, for instance, things don't work this way. See **For interest** below.)

Whereas a **negative sentence** is signalled in English by a particular **word**, such as *not*, a positive **sentence** typically has nothing in the position of the *not*. But in some **dialects**, especially in America, there is the possibility of an emphatic positive, using either *so* or *too*, occupying the position where the *not* would occur in a **negative sentence**, i.e. just after the first **auxiliary** in the **clause**. Examples are:

- *He did SO do it!*
- *They did TOO do it!*

These would be used as emphatic denials of an allegation that someone hadn't done something. For these dialects, then, the **words** *so* and *too*, used in this position, are markers of positiveness, just as *not* is a marker of negativeness. Such markers of positiveness are unusual.

In many languages there are some **words** which have a preference for occurring in positive **sentences**, and such **words** can often be paired with **words** which prefer to occur in **negative sentences**. English examples are

	POSITIVE	NEGATIVE
too/either	*Her mother came too.*	*Her mother didn't come either.*
both/either	*I saw both of them.*	*I didn't see either of them.*
some/any	*I picked some apples.*	*I didn't pick any apples.*

Notice that *either* and *any* are definitely ungrammatical in positive (**declarative**) **main clauses**, as in **Her mother came either*, **I saw either of them* and **I picked any apples*.

This effect of negativeness stretches down into subordinate clauses. Thus, for example, **I have any, either* is ungrammatical as a **main clause**, i.e. as an independent **sentence**. But *I don't think that I have any, either*, where this same sequence of **words** appears as a **subordinate clause**, is perfectly grammatical. The words *any* and *either* in the **subordinate clause** are 'licensed' by the negativeness of the **main clause**.

For interest   French has two equivalents, *Oui* and *Si*, to English *Yes*, *Oui* for replying to positive sentences, and *Si* for replying to negative sentences. Here are some examples.[21]

L'avez vous dit? − Oui, monsieur.	*Did you say it? − Yes, sir.*
Venez! − Oui, oui, je viens.	*Come! − Yes, yes, I'm coming.*
Il ne va pas. − Si, il va.	*He is not going. − Yes, he is.*
Il ne vas pas? − Mais si.	*Isn't he going? − Yes, of course.*
Je n'irai pas. − Si, si, venez.	*I won't go. − Yes, yes, come on.*

Exercise   Of the following six sentences, three are grammatically positive. Which are they? Don't get confused between the grammar and the meanings of some of the sentences.

1 *I wonder whether you can help me.*
2 *Nobody said nothing had been done about it.*
3 *That was the most revolting meal it has ever been my misfortune to eat.*

---

21 Adapted from *Heath's Practical French Grammar* by W. H. Fraser and J.Squair (Harrap, London, 1966).

4 *The computer can't lie.*
5 *The answer to that question was negative.*
6 *The answer to the next question wasn't negative.*

Possessive

Explanation   The term 'possessive' is applied to three different (though closely related) kinds of English expression.

1 A **word**-class including such **words** as *mine*, *yours*, *ours* and *theirs*. Because these **words** can be used as substitutes for whole **noun phrases**, they are referred to in this guide as 'possessive **pronouns**'.

2 A different **word**-class including such **words** as *my*, *your*, *our* and *their*, which can occupy the same position in a **noun phrase** as the **definite article** *the*. Such **words** are referred to in this guide simply as 'possessives'.

3 **Possessive phrases**, formed by adding 'apostrophe *s*', the **suffix** -*'s*, to a whole **noun phrase**, i.e. **suffixing** -*'s* to the last **word** in the **noun phrase**. The range of occurrence of such **phrases** includes the range of occurrence of the simple possessives mentioned above. (**Phrase** here, as elsewhere in this dictionary, includes single-**word phrases**.)

Examples   1 The full set of possessive **pronouns** in English is *mine*, *yours*, *his*, *hers*, *its*, *ours* and *theirs*.

2 The full set of simple possessives in English is *my*, *your*, *his*, *her*, *its*, *our*, *their* and (in rather formal style) *ones*. (Note that two **words**, *his* and *its*, belong to both of these **word**-classes.)

3 Examples of English possessive **phrases** are:

John's	as in *This car is John's.*
the President's	as in *The President's brain is missing.*
romantic poetry's	as in *Keats was romantic poetry's most tragic figure.*
this car's	as in *This car's fuel consumption is high.*
my father's	as in *The farm used to be my father's.*

Contrasts   Possessive **pronouns**, such as *mine* and *yours*, contrast with the simple possessives, such as *my* and *your*. There is no context in which *mine* and *my*, for example, are interchangeable. Compare *This is mine* (grammatical) with ******This is my* (ungrammatical); or *My dog is asleep* (grammatical) with ******Mine dog is asleep* (ungrammatical); and so on.

English (simple) possessives, such as *my* and *your* are not **pronouns**, like *I*, *me* and *you*, because they cannot occur in the same positions as these (or any other) **pronouns**. Thus, while, for instance, *I like my dog* is grammatical, neither ******My like my dog* nor ******I like I dog* is at all grammatical. It would be seriously misleading to call these '**pronouns**'.

English (simple) possessives, such as *my* and *your*, are not **adjectives**, though the misleading term 'possessive **adjective**' is sometimes used by grammarians. These **words** do not have the same range of occurrence as typical **adjectives**, such as *big*, *red* and *pretty*. **Adjectives**, for example, go after **numerals**, as in *my three big brothers*, but (as this same example shows) possessives go before **numerals**. The opposite ordering of **adjective** and possessive, as in *★big three my brothers* is ungrammatical.

Possessive **phrases** contrast with **noun phrases**, by having the extra -'s on the end. Possessive **phrases** with this **suffix** can occur in the **noun-modifying** or **article** position, whereas **noun phrases** (without the **suffix**) cannot occur in this position. So, for instance, while both *The man's bike is outside* and *The bike is outside* are grammatical, *★The man bike is outside* is ungrammatical. But the contrast is not absolute; there are some positions which can be occupied by both possessive **phrases** and **noun phrases** (see **Relationships** below).

Relationships The temptation to call possessives, such as *my* and *your*, '**pronouns**' arises from the fact that there is a clear one-to-one correspondence between possessives and **personal pronouns**, as set out below.

POSSESSIVE	Corresponding PERSONAL PRONOUN
my	*I*
your	*you*
his	*he*
her	*she*
its	*it*
our	*we*
their	*they*

Now, such a correspondence does not entail that the **words** involved belong to the same **part of speech**. There is, for example, a similar correspondence between pairs of **adverbs** and **adjectives**, such as *happily/happy*, *morosely/morose* and *timidly/timid*, but one would not therefore say that all these **words** belong to the same **part of speech**.

The relationship between the possessives and their corresponding **personal pronouns** is the same as that between possessive **phrases** and the (-'s-less) **noun phrases** inside them. This latter correspondence can be set out in a way exactly parallel to the table just above.

POSSESSIVE PHRASE	Corresponding NOUN PHRASE
John's	*John*
the Mayor of Boston's	*the Mayor of Boston*
the Atlantic Ocean's	*the Atlantic Ocean*

It is as if the possessives were shorthand, or coded, forms for the **personal pronouns suffixed** by -'s. That is, it is as if *my* were code for *★I's*, and *your* were code for *★you's*, and *its* for *★it's*. As we see, this last hypothetical example is in fact close to the truth; the correspondence pointed out is no doubt what leads people into the spelling mistake of putting an apostrophe in the possessive *its*.

In English, both the single-**word** possessives and possessive **phrases** can occur in the position of the **definite article**, *the*, and **demonstratives**, such as *this* and *those*, as shown below:

my limousine	*the President's limousine*	*the limousine*
her hat	*Aunt Augusta's hat*	*that hat*
their opinions	*senior military personnel's opinions*	*those opinions*

This correspondence prompts linguists to set up a unifying **word**-class, called 'determiner', covering **articles**, **demonstratives** and possessives.

There is also a correspondence between the simple possessives, such as *my* and *your*, and the possessive **pronouns**, such as *mine* and *yours*. In this case, there are close paraphrases involving the **words** *one* and *ones*, as shown below.

POSSESSIVE PRONOUN	Paraphrasing POSSESSIVE + *one* or *ones*
mine	*my one, my ones*
yours	*your one, your ones*
his	*his one, his ones*
hers	*her one, her ones*
its	*its one, its ones*
ours	*our one, our ones*
theirs	*their one, their ones*

Examples in **sentences** would be *Yours is better than mine*, paraphrasing *Your one is better than my one*, or *His are smaller than ours* paraphrasing *His ones are smaller than our ones*. (These forms with *one* and *ones* may not be entirely acceptable in all English **dialects**; they seem somewhat marginal to standard English.)

The **word** *one* or *ones* in these examples is a substitute for a **singular** or **plural noun**, so *my one(s)* (= *mine*) could mean, depending on the situation, *my car, my cars, my pen, my pens, my house* or whatever else of the speaker's he or she might be referring to. This fits in with the behaviour of the possessive **pronouns** *mine, yours*, etc., which are substitutable for whole **noun phrases**. *My car* is a **noun phrase**, *my one* is a less specific version of it, interpretable from context, and *mine* is a kind of shortened form of *my one*.

The correspondence with forms involving *one* and *ones* also fits the fact that the possessive **pronouns** *mine, hers, yours*, etc. can be either **singular** or **plural**, as in *Ours has gone already* or *Mine are not ripe yet*.

The possessive **pronouns** are always 3rd **person**, despite the fact that some of them correspond with 1st and 2nd **person personal pronouns**. Thus, although we say *I am*, we cannot say **mine am*; because *mine* is 3rd **person**, we have to say *mine is* or *mine are*.

Possessive **phrases** can also, in some, but not all, positions, be paraphrased by versions with an added *one* or *ones*. Here are some examples:

The department's has been stolen.	*The department's one has been stolen.*
I prefer Picasso's.	*I prefer Picasso's ones.*

This shows that a possessive **phrase** can sometimes be left standing alone, when a *one* or *ones* on the end of a **noun phrase** is left off, by a kind of **ellipsis**.

Possessive **pronouns**, like *theirs*, *ours* and *yours*, are **definite**. A speaker who says *I've already got mine* presumes that the hearer will be able to identify the particular thing(s) that *mine* refers to.

Noun phrases introduced by a possessive, such as *my*, *his* and *their*, are also **definite**. A speaker who says *Have you seen his hat?* presumes that the hearer can identify the particular person whose hat is in question, and therefore presumably can identify that person's hat.

Noun phrases introduced by a possessive **phrase** can be either **definite** or **indefinite**, depending on the **definiteness** of the inner **noun phrase** inside the possessive **phrase**. Thus *the man's hat* is **definite** because *the man* is **definite**, while *a man's hat* is **indefinite** because *a man* is **indefinite**.

The English **word** *whose* is both a **relative pronoun**, as in *the man whose bike you stole*, and an **interrogative word** or *wh*-**word**, as in *Whose bike did you steal?* In both uses, *whose* is also clearly possessive, and can reasonably be called either the 'possessive **relative pronoun**' or the 'possessive *wh*-**word**'.

When the terminology of **case** is extended to English, the various possessive **forms** discussed above are said to be in the **genitive case**.

For interest In English, as seen above, possessives and possessive phrases occupy the position of the article or demonstratives. This makes it impossible to combine an article, or a demonstrative, with a possessive or possessive phrase in a neat way in English. So, for instance, we cannot say **the my son*, or **a my son*, or (even worse) **a this woman's son*; **this my son* is also ungrammatical in modern standard English, although it was once grammatical. Other nearby European languages do not have this limitation, because their possessives do not occupy the same position as their articles or demonstratives.

In Italian, an article (or a demonstrative) and a possessive can both appear together before a noun, so that we can have examples like;

> *il   suo libro*
> the his book   (= *his book*)
> *questa mia mamma*
> this   my   mother   (= *my mother here*)

In Arabic, the way of indicating possession is quite unlike that of English. Arabic uses suffixes on the noun, suffixes which are (for the most part) identical to those used to express pronoun objects of verbs. Here are some examples.

> *muhammad darab-ha*   *kitaab-ha*
> Mohammed hit-her   (= *Mohammed hit her.*)   book-her   (= *her book*)
> *muhammad darab-na*   *kitaab-na*
> Mohammed hit-us   (= *Mohammed hit us.*)   book-us   (= *our book*)

In Arabic, expressions like *kitaab-ha*, *her book*, are definite, and the definite article cannot appear with them, even though there is a position, before the noun, which it could occupy.

Exercise In the following, say whether the underlined items are possessive pronouns, possessives or possessive phrases.

1 *His is the one with the blue stripe.*
2 *Do you prefer Beethoven's sonatas to Mozart's?*
3 *Excuse me, but my purse is under your chair.*
4 *That's funny, because mine was under yours.*
5 *Am I my brother's keeper?*

Predicate

Explanation Predicate is used in two different, though closely related, senses.

1 The predicate of a **clause** is the core part of the **clause**, minus the **subject**. It is everything in the **clause**, barring its **subject** and, usually, barring any **adverb phrases modifying** the whole **clause**. Being a traditional grammatical term of considerable antiquity, 'predicate' has come to be used with rather differing shades of meaning (see **Contrasts** below).

2 In English and similar languages, a **noun** or **adjective** (or **noun phrase** or **adjective phrase**) after the **verb** *be* (or equivalent) is said to be a predicate **noun** **(phrase)** or predicate **adjective** **(phrase)**. Sometimes a **prepositional phrase** after the **verb** *be* (or equivalent) is said to be a predicate **prepositional** **(phrase)**.

These two (closely related) senses of 'predicate' are easily, and usually, kept distinct by using the full expressions, without abbreviation, e.g. 'predicate' versus 'predicate **noun phrase**' – a practice followed in this guide.

Examples 1 In the examples below, the predicates of **clauses** are underlined.

- *Mr Finch, the butcher, had ground the next day's mince.*
- *As it happened, the nurse was highly appreciative of Henry's efforts.*
- *An ugly knife lay buried in the heart of mad Carew.*
- *It was the vengeance of the little yellow god.*
- *Frankly, you are a blackguard, Sir.*

2 The underlined **phrases** in the examples below are of the predicate type indicated on the right:

John is a sociologist.	PREDICATE NOUN PHRASE
It was the vengeance of the yellow god.	PREDICATE NOUN PHRASE
John is very tall.	PREDICATE ADJECTIVE PHRASE
The nurse was highly appreciative of it.	PREDICATE ADJECTIVE PHRASE
John is behind the cocktail cabinet.	PREDICATE PREPOSITIONAL PHRASE

Contrasts Predicate contrasts primarily with **subject**. If a **word** or **phrase** belongs to the predicate of a **clause**, it cannot belong to the **subject**, and vice-versa. The division of a **clause** into two fundamental parts, **subject** and predicate, is one of the oldest themes in **grammar**.

For most grammarians, predicate contrasts with **verb** and **direct** and/or **indirect object** because the predicate of a **clause** actually contains the **verb** and any **objects**, as parts.

'Adjuncts' are **words** and **phrases**, like **adverbs** and **adverb phrases**, which are not completely central to the meaning of the **clause**; predicate contrasts with 'adjunct', although with some unfortunate inconsistency. For some grammarians, adjuncts are not a part of the predicate, so that for them a **clause** consists of **subject**, predicate and adjuncts. For others, perhaps the majority, adjuncts are a part of the predicate, so that the **clause** consists of just two parts, **subject** and predicate, with the predicate in turn containing, amongst other things, any adjuncts.

Predicate contrasts, rather trivially, with terms such as 'predicate **noun phrase**' and 'predicate **adjective phrase**'. The predicate of a **clause** with the **verb** *be* contains a predicate **noun phrase**, or a predicate **adjective phrase**, or a predicate **prepositional phrase**. Indeed, the twin senses of the term 'predicate' stem from a view that the **verb** *be* is somehow not a proper **verb**, or merely present to 'carry' **tense** (and possibly **agreement**) markers. If the **verb** *be* in a **clause** is overlooked, then the twin senses of 'predicate' merge into one.

For some grammarians, predicate also contrasts directly with **complement**, a term used in an unfortunately confusing variety of ways. When used in connection with predicate, '**complement**' can normally be understood as synonymous with 'predicate **noun phrase**', or 'predicate **adjective phrase**', or 'predicate **prepositional phrase**'. The thinking behind this is that the **verb** *be* is special, and cannot be said to have an **object** of any kind. What follows the **verb** *be* (and certain other **verbs** like it) is, then, not an **object**, but a **complement**. (But see the COMPLEMENT CLAUSE entry for a totally different and barely related sense of this term.)

Relationships In English, the predicate of a **clause** always contains its **verb**, and is almost always a **phrase** built around the **verb**. Hence, in relatively simple cases, in the absence of any of the factors raising disagreement, such as adjuncts, predicate is equivalent to **verb phrase**. So the underlined parts of the **sentences** below are both their predicates and **verb phrases**.

- *Mrs Kershaw poured herself another cup of tea.*
- *Grandpa snores.*
- *Harry is an awful bore.*

A difference between predicate and **verb phrase** is that a predicate is usually thought of, like a **subject**, in relation to a **clause**. That is, one generally talks of something being 'the predicate of' a **clause**, just as one talks of a particular **noun phrase** being 'the **subject** of' a **clause**. Predicate, then, refers to a role, or function, in a **clause** (just as **subject** does); **verb phrase**, on the other hand, refers to a kind of **phrase** which (as it just happens in English and some other languages) almost always occurs playing that role, or fulfilling that function in the **clause**.

The difference between predicate and **verb phrase** can be seen much more clearly in languages where there are **verb**-less **sentences** (see '**For interest**' in the entry for COPULA); in such cases, the predicate of a **clause** may be a **noun phrase**, an **adjective phrase** or some other kind of **phrase**.

Although the predicate of a **clause** can contain any kind of **verb**, there is a close conceptual link between predicate and the **verb** *be* (and its equivalents in other languages). In English, the **verb** *be* has three main uses.

1 In a predicative use, as in:
- *Joan is a linguist.*
- *Joan is quite short.*
- *Joan was in the garage.*

2 With the **progressive**, as in *Joan is trying hard.*

3 With the **passive**, as in *Joan was arrested.*

We are only concerned in this entry with the first of these uses of *be*, the predicative use, which occurs with predicate **noun phrases**, predicate **adjective phrases** and predicate **prepositional phrases**.

Predicate **noun phrases** are sometimes also called 'predicate nominals'.

Indefinite noun phrases after *be*, as in *Diana was a victim of the media* are predicate **noun phrases**.

But some grammarians would not extend the term 'predicate **noun phrase**' to **definite noun phrases** after *be*, as in *Sarah is the one with red hair*. The reason is that, with an **indefinite**, the **verb** *be* seems to have the same kind of meaning as it does before, say, an **adjective**, that is, associating some property (like being a victim of the media, or being glamorous) to the person or thing referred to by the **subject**. But with a **definite noun phrase** after *be*, the meaning seems to be equating two definite descriptions, e.g. *Sarah* and *the one with red hair*. Notice that a **definite noun phrase** after *be* can normally be interchanged with the **subject**, as in *The one with red hair is Sarah*. But this cannot easily be done with an **indefinite noun phrase** after *be*, as the oddness of **A victim of the media was Diana* shows.

Only certain **adjectives** can occur as, or in, predicate **adjective phrases**. Some **adjectives**, such as *mere* and *former*, for example, cannot occur in predicate **adjective phrases**, as can be seen by the ungrammaticality of **His misjudgements were mere* and **Her husband is former*. **Adjectives** which can occur in predicate **adjective phrases** are classified as predicative **adjectives**. Examples of predicative **adjectives**, which are the majority of **adjectives**, are *happy* and *delicious*, as in *Leon was ecstatically happy* or *That frog was quite delicious*. There are some English **adjectives** which can occur only predicatively. Examples are *asleep* and *alive*, e.g. *He is asleep*, but not **Let asleep dogs lie*, and *Elvis is alive*, but not **Elvis is an alive legend*.

The **verb** *be*, in its predicative use, is called the **copula** (Latin for *linker* or *coupler*); other **verbs** which, like *be*, can be followed by a **noun phrase** but are not **transitive**, are often called **copular verbs**. Such **verbs** include *remain, seem* and *appear*. The terms 'predicate **noun phrase**', 'predicate **adjective phrase**' and 'predicate **prepositional phrase**' can be applied to **phrases** following any **copular verb**, as in the examples below, where the underlined **phrases** are of the predicate type indicated on the right:

MacDonald remained <u>a committed socialist</u>.	PREDICATE NOUN PHRASE
Mellors remained <u>staunchly loyal</u>.	PREDICATE ADJECTIVE PHRASE
Mannering seems <u>in poor health</u>.	PREDICATE PREPOSITIONAL PHRASE

For interest The difference between the direct objects of transitive verbs and predicative noun phrases after a copula is clearer in French (and to some extent in German) than it is in English. In these languages there is no indefinite article after a copular verb. For example, in French, we have:

Je suis dentiste.
I am dentist.   (= *I am a dentist.*)

Elle est bergère.
She is shepherdess.   (= *She is a shepherdess.*)

This situation weakens the difference, in predicative phrases, between nouns and adjectives, since one of the things that distinguishes nouns from adjectives is their ability to take an article. In fact, in French, there are many more words than in English that can function either as a noun or as an adjective. This is reinforced by the fact that some words have both masculine and feminine forms. *Fou/folle – mad, crazy* is an example. It can look like a noun, with a preceding article, as in:

Ils ont trouvé un fou
They have found a mad+MASC   (= *They found a mad man.*)

Ils ont trouvé une folle
They have found a mad+FEM   (= *They found a mad woman.*)

And it can look like an adjective, following a noun, as in:

un homme fou
a   man   mad+MASC   (= *a mad man*)

une femme folle
a   woman mad+FEM   (= *a mad woman*)

But when it appears in predicative position, after the verb *être – be*, we can't tell whether it is a noun or an adjective, as can be seen from the alternative English translations below.

Il est fou
He is mad+MASC   (= *He is mad / a mad man.*)

Elle est folle
*She is mad+*FEM   (= *She is mad / a mad woman.*)

Thus in French, in predicative position, one of the major part-of-speech distinctions tends to dissolve. This happens in other languages, too, and is characteristic of predicative constructions.

Exercise   Identify the predicates of the following sentences.

1 *Birds evolved from reptiles.*
2 *Sixty-four million years ago, the dinosaurs died out.*
3 *Neanderthal Man survived into the modern era.*

Say what kind of predicate phrases (noun, adjective, prepositional) occur in each of the following sentences.

1 *The New York subway is very unhygienic.*
2 *The Mayor is a Democrat.*
3 *Ronnie was under the influence of an astrologer.*

Prefix

Explanation   A prefix is an **affix** attached to the front of a **word**.

Examples   Common English prefixes are: *pre-, post-, con-, dis-, re-, un-, in-, sub-* and *ex-*.

Contrasts   Prefixes contrast with **suffixes**, which are attached at the other end of **words**.
Prefixes also contrast, like **affixes** in general, with whole **words**. **Words** can stand on their own, but prefixes have to be attached to something. Prefixes are parts of **words**.

Relationships   Prefixes are somewhat less common than **suffixes**, across languages in general.
In English, whereas **suffixes** express some of the central grammatical features of the language, such as **tense (past/present)** and **number (singular/plural)**, there are no prefixes expressing such central features.
Prefixes can be attached to **words** of most of the major **parts of speech**, i.e.

- to **nouns**, e.g. *ex-husband, pro-abortion, subway*;
- to **adjectives**, e.g. *unhappy, dishonest, impossible*;
- to **verbs**, e.g. *re-enter, displace, undo*.

In English, the changes in meaning which are brought about by adding a prefix to a **word** are rather irregular and not exactly predictable. For instance, the prefix *sub-* has the different effects illustrated below:

subway   (= *a way below something*)
subhuman   (= *something below the human level*)

We can't state a general rule that *sub-X* is a paraphrase of *something below X* (as in *subhuman*), or conversely of *X below something* (as in *subway*); sometimes *sub-X* means one, and sometimes the other.

There are many **words** in English which look as if they begin with a familiar prefix, but in which it is not clear what meaning to attach either to the prefix or to the remainder of the **word**, in order to arrive at the meaning of the whole **word**. For example, *exercise* apparently has the prefix *ex-*, but what does **-ercise* mean? Again, *recruit* apparently has the prefix *re-*, but what does **-pose* mean? Other words with such fossilized parts are *prevail*, *promenade*, *subdue*, *conceal*, *expect* and *forfeit*.

For interest   Whereas, as noted, prefixes do not express central grammatical features in English, they do in some other languages.

Chipewyan is an American Indian language spoken, at a recent estimate, by about 5,000 people, in the region of the Great Slave Lake in Canada. In Chipewyan, person and tense are expressed by prefixes on the verb.[22]

The prefix *n-* indicates 2nd person singular.
The prefix *uh-* indicates 2nd person plural.
The prefix *ye-* indicates Perfective tense.
The prefix *ywa-* indicates Future tense.

The prefixes can get piled up on each other, so that we get the following versions of the verb meaning *cry*, whose stem is *-tsay*.

	PERFECTIVE	FUTURE
2nd person singular	*ye-n-tsay*	*ywa-n-tsay*
2nd person plural	*ye-uh-tsay*	*ywa-uh-tsay*

(These forms undergo some further changes in pronunciation, apparently, so that the prefixes are somewhat disguised in the language as spoken.)

Exercise   Some of the following words contain prefixes and some do not. Identify all the prefixes; there are eight in all.

unfortunate, untimely, superfluous, superb, reappear, really, miser, misfortune, inkstand, injustice, encourage, enemy, explain, Exeter.

Preposition

Explanation   A preposition is a (typically small) **word** that occurs before a **noun phrase**, making another **phrase** (a prepositional **phrase**) with it. The term itself reflects the grammatical place of prepositions, 'positioned before' **noun phrases**.

---

22 This data comes from *Morphology: an Introduction to the Theory of Word-structure*, by P. H. Matthews (Cambridge University Press, 1974). The primary source cited is Li Fang-Kuei's article 'Chipewyan', in *Linguistic Structures of Native America*.

Prepositions typically express relationships in time or space between things and events.

Examples Examples of English prepositions are *to, in, at, by, for, with, under, over, below, near, from, before, after* and *since*.

Contrasts Preposition is a **part of speech**, and so contrasts with all other **parts of speech**. If a **word** in a given **sentence** is a preposition, it is not any other **part of speech**.

Some, but not all, English prepositions can also occur as subordinating **conjunctions**, that is, as the little **words** that introduce **subordinate clauses**. **Words** which can play this double role include *after, before* and *since*. The two different uses are illustrated below:

PREPOSITION	SUBORDINATING CONJUNCTION
You have to register before October.	*You have to register before they print the list.*
After ten o'clock, they went out.	*After I had gone to bed, they went out.*
It's all happened since Easter.	*It's all happened since Daisy was born.*

Some English prepositions also occur as **adverbs**, as does *above* in *Above, all was calm*.

Relationships In any language, there are relatively few prepositions, compared to some other **parts of speech**, such as **nouns** and **verbs**. Prepositions, like **auxiliaries** and **demonstratives**, form a 'closed class' of words – it is hard to imagine English borrowing a new preposition into the language, whereas new **nouns** are borrowed frequently.

In English, there are some two-**word** (and even three-**word**) sequences which act just like single-**word** prepositions. Examples are *instead of, next to* and *in front of*. From the point of view of **grammar**, these sequences behave like single **words** and are best regarded as being prepositions.

A preposition forms a prepositional **phrase** with a following **noun phrase**. The following are all prepositional **phrases** (with the prepositions underlined): *for me, under the sofa, since the January sales, before the Second World War* and *with his mother*.

Prepositions typically express relationships between things and events, and so prepositional **phrases** can **modify** both **nouns** and **verbs** or whole **clauses**.

When prepositional **phrases modify nouns**, they form new, larger, **noun phrases** with them, as below (where the prepositions are again underlined):

PREPOSITIONAL PHRASES MODIFYING NOUNS, TO FORM NOUN PHRASES
the only girl for me
a tissue under the sofa
the period since the January sales
a conference after the Second World War
the boy beside his mother

Prepositional phrases in this position, **modifying nouns**, are often equivalent to longer **relative clauses** with the **verb** *be*, as in *a tissue which was under the sofa*, or *the boy who was beside his mother*.

Prepositional **phrases** modifying **nouns** can be embedded inside other prepositional **phrases**, as in this example, which contains four prepositions, and accordingly four embedded prepositional **phrases**

- *a boy beside his mother on the sofa at the back of the room*

When prepositional **phrases** modify **verbs** or whole **clauses**, they are often interchangeable with, and occur in the same position as, **adverbs**, as in these examples (with prepositional **phrases** and their possible **adverb** equivalents underlined):

PREPOSITIONAL PHRASES MODIFYING VERBS OR CLAUSES, LIKE ADVERBS

They live near here.	*They live nearby.*
It crawled behind the sofa.	*It crawled there.*
We have relaxed during the sales.	*We have relaxed recently.*
She was born before the war.	*She was born then.*
Marco came in a spectacular way.	*Marco came spectacularly.*

Prepositional **phrases** can also be used predicatively (i.e. as **predicate** prepositional phrases), with the **verb** *be* (or any other **copular verb**, such as *remain*, *seem* or *become*), as in these examples, where the prepositional **phrases** are underlined: *Your marble is under the sofa, Morecambe is by the sea* and *Paul is with his mother*.

Some English prepositions have closely corresponding **adverbs**. Some pairs related in this way are *under/underneath, over/overhead, before/beforehand* and *after/afterwards*.

In many languages, there is a close connection between prepositions and specific **cases**. In English, three specific prepositions, namely *of, to* and *by*, play roles closely integrated with **case** and the grammatical structure of **clauses**. Thus:

- *of* is associated with a variety of **possessive** or (loosely speaking) '**genitive**' constructions, as in *the book of the teacher, the arrival of the ferry* and *the mortification of the flesh*.
- *to* is a marker of **indirect objects** or 'dative case', as in *We donated our earnings to the Dog and Cat Home.*
- *by* marks the **noun phrase** in a **passive clause** corresponding to the **subject** of the related **active clause**, as in *We were ruined by the currency speculators* or *Our ruination by the currency speculators.*

As noted, prepositions occur before **noun phrases** and form prepositional phrases with them. This is quite parallel to **transitive verbs** occurring before **noun phrases** and forming **verb phrases** with them. Thus the two types of **phrases** shown below are closely parallel in structure.

PREPOSITIONAL PHRASE	TRANSITIVE VERB PHRASE
on the ball	*see the ball*
to the man	*hit the man*
for the money	*find the money*
with some food	*take some food*

There are **words** in English, with similar meanings to prepositions, sometimes rather vaguely called '**particles**'; these are **words** like *up, down, out* and *along*. These can in fact be used before **noun phrases**, like the prepositions discussed above, but they can also occur without a following **noun phrase**. It is tempting to see these **words**, in their use without a following **noun phrase**, as '**intransitive**' prepositions, on the analogy of **intransitive verbs**, which also do not take a following **noun phrase**. The two patterns of use are shown below.

USE AS 'TRANSITIVE' PREPOSITION	USE AS 'INTRANSITIVE' PREPOSITION
He went down the stairs.	*He went down.*
She sauntered along the street.	*She sauntered along.*
We climbed up the mountain.	*We climbed up.*

For interest We have just seen a parallel between prepositions and verbs, in the possibility of talking about 'intransitive' prepositions. There are further parallels between prepositions and verbs, which recur again and again in the languages of the world. One similarity is that prepositions and verbs are the main parts of speech that assign case (other than genitive, i.e. accusative, dative, etc.) to nouns.

To express another parallel between verbs and prepositions, we have to introduce a new term, namely 'postposition'. A postposition is just like a preposition, except that it follows its noun phrase, rather than preceding it. Typically, a given language has prepositions and few or no postpositions, or vice versa. That is, languages tend to be either thoroughly prepositional or thoroughly postpositional. Here are some examples from a postpositional language, Panjabi,[23] spoken by about 20 million people in north-west India and Pakistan. (Panjabi is an Indo-European language, and therefore distantly related to English.)

janvarī nū̃
January in   (= *in January*)

ghar tõ
house from   (= *from the house*)

manje ute
bed   on   (= *on the bed*)

---

23 The Panjabi data comes from *The Panjabi Language: a Descriptive Grammar*, by N. I. Tolstaya, translated by G. L. Campbell (Routledge and Kegan Paul, London, 1981).

In other words, Panjabi speakers express *on the bed* with words like **bed on*, and so on. The Panjabi words *nū̃*, *tõ* and *ute* here are postpositions.

There is a very striking correlation, across the languages of the world, between prepositions or postpositions and the position of the verb in the clause. If a language puts the verb at the end of the clause (like Panjabi, Turkish and Japanese, for example), almost certainly that language has postpositions, rather than prepositions. Conversely, if a language puts the verb at the beginning of the clause (like Welsh, Tagalog and Classical Arabic), almost certainly that language has prepositions, rather than postpositions. (Classical Latin, with verb at the end but prepositions, is a rare counter example.)

Languages (like English and French) which put the verb in the middle of the clause, are less predictable in whether they have prepositions or postpositions. In fact, English has mainly prepositions, but it does have one postposition, namely *ago*, which goes after its noun phrase, as in *four years ago*.

It is sometimes said to be bad English style to end a sentence with a preposition. By way of comment on this prescription, we present some well-known relevant examples. The first, attributed to Winston Churchill, is:

- *That is something up with which I will not put.*

This is clearly more awkward than the alternative, which ends with a preposition (in fact two):

- *That is something that I will not put up with.*

The following example discovered by a linguist (reputed to be Professor Frank Palmer) actually manages to end a sentence with no less than five prepositions.

- *What did you bring that book that I didn't want to be read to out of up for?*

Say it. It's not so bad, given the right intonation, although you might think it better to say:

- *Why did you bring up that book that I didn't want to be read to out of?*

But this still ends with three prepositions. How can we get rid of them? Here's how to get rid of two of them.

- *Why did you bring up that book out of which I didn't want to be read to?*

But this is really quite awkward, and still ends with one preposition (which is not the source of the awkwardness). Let's face it; it's sometimes hard to avoid using a preposition to end a sentence with.

Exercise   Pick out the prepositions in the following passage. There are twelve of them altogether.

- *He lay flat on the brown, pine-needled floor of the forest, his chin on his folded arms, and high overhead the wind blew in the tops of the pine trees. The mountainside sloped gently where he lay; but below it was steep and he could see the dark of the oiled road winding through the pass. There was a stream alongside the road and far down the pass he saw a mill beside the stream and the falling water of the dam, white in the summer sunlight.*

Present participle

Explanation   A participle is a form of a **verb** used like an **adjective**. In English, the present participle is the form of a **verb** used primarily with the **auxiliary** *be* to form the **progressive**, and also in adjectival and adverbial ways. English present participles are all formed by adding the **suffix** *-ing* to the base form of the **verb**.

Examples   The underlined **words** in the following examples are all present participles.

- *The boss is <u>looking</u> for you.*
- *Al Capone might just have been <u>joking</u>.*
- *When the Queen sat down, her courtiers remained <u>standing</u>.*
- *John was like a <u>raging</u> bull this morning.*
- *He greeted me <u>going</u> to work.*

Contrasts   In English, present participles and **gerunds** are identical in shape, both ending in *-ing*. But they contrast: a present participle is a **verb** form behaving like an **adjective**, whereas a **gerund** is a **verb** form behaving like a **noun**. In particular, present participles can be used like **adjectives**, to **modify nouns** (see **Relationships** below).

English present participles contrast with **past participles**. Both are forms of the **verb**, but they differ in shape (the present participle always ends in *-ing*), they go with different **auxiliaries** (the present participle goes with *be*), and they express different meanings.

Despite the term 'present', so-called English present participles have little specific connection with present time. (Similarly, English **past participles** have little specific connection with past time.) The pairing apparent in the traditional terminology is misleading; present and **past participles** are not systematically linked to **present** and **past tenses**.

Both present and **past participles** contrast with **finite** forms of the **verb**, which carry **tense (past** or **present)** and can show **agreement** with a **subject**. In many languages, forms known as 'participles' have no **tense**, and in English at least (though not in French and German), participles show no **agreement**.

Relationships   The primary use of the present participle in English is with the **progressive**, in which it is accompanied by the **auxiliary** *be*, as in *Maria was <u>flying</u> a kite* and *John is <u>building</u> a tree-house.*

Present participles, especially of **intransitive verbs**, can often be used as **adjectives, modifying** a following **noun**, as in:

- *A <u>flying</u> kite zoomed across the sky.*

- *It is hard to hit a <u>moving</u> target.*
- *Let <u>sleeping</u> dogs lie.*

In such cases, there is a straightforward correspondence with a **clause** in which the **modified noun** is the **subject** of the **verb** whose present participle is involved, as in these examples (where the (adjectival) present participle is underlined):

NOUN MODIFIED BY PARTICIPLE AS ADJECTIVE	NOUN AS SUBJECT OF PARTICIPLE AS VERB
a *flying* kite	*A kite was flying.*
the *moving* target	*The target is moving.*
sleeping dogs	*Dogs are sleeping.*

When such an **intransitive verb** is **modified** by a following adverbial **phrase**, its present participle can still be used as an **adjective**, but now as the **head** of an **adjective phrase** following the **modified noun**, as shown by these correspondences (where the participial, or adjectival, **phrases** are underlined):

NOUN MODIFIED BY ADJECTIVAL (PARTICIPLE) PHRASE	NOUN AS SUBJECT OF PARTICIPLE AS VERB
a kitten *playing with some string*	*A kitten was playing with some string.*
a land *flowing with milk and honey*	*A land is flowing with milk and honey.*
dogs *barking in the night*	*Dogs are barking in the night.*

The present participles of **transitive verbs** can be used in **adjective phrases** following a **noun**, and here again there is a correspondence between the **noun modified** by the participial, or adjectival, **phrase** and the **subject** of the participle in its more **verb**like position. This is illustrated below.

NOUN MODIFIED BY ADJECTIVAL (PARTICIPLE) PHRASE	NOUN AS SUBJECT OF PARTICIPLE AS VERB
a man *planting potatoes*	*A man was planting potatoes.*
ladies *telling jokes*	*Ladies were telling jokes.*
guards *patrolling the border*	*Guards are patrolling the border.*

This construction can be extended to include the **passive**, in which case the present participle of the **auxiliary** *be* is used, as in:

a story <u>being followed by millions</u>   *A story is being followed by millions.*

Participial **phrases** built around present participles can modify **verbs** and whole **clauses**, in which case they behave like adverbial **phrases**, with much of the positional mobility of **adverbs**. Examples are:

- *<u>Fuming at his infidelity</u>, she raced back to the house.*
- *She raced, <u>fuming at his infidelity</u>, back to the house.*
- *She raced back to the house, <u>fuming at his infidelity</u>.*
- *<u>Leaping to his feet</u>, he shouted 'I've got it!'*

Such adverbial participial **phrases** can also be constructed out of **perfect** forms, as in:

- *<u>Having waited all night</u>, he was first in line when the box office opened.*

For interest With some adverbial phrases formed around present participles, there is an ambiguity regarding who or what the assumed subject of the participle is supposed to be. For instance, in *Anne met Philip going to work* it is not clear who is going to work, Anne or Philip. If we put the participial phrase at the beginning of the sentence, as in *Going to work, Anne met Philip*, it will probably be agreed that it is Anne who is going to work.

There are other cases where the position of the participial phrase makes a difference to the interpretation. Compare these two sentences:

> *Anne saw Philip mending the fence.* (Almost certainly Philip is mending the fence)
> *Mending the fence, Anne saw Philip.* (Most probably Anne is mending the fence)

So in English the ordering of the participial phrase in relation to the rest of the sentence affects the interpretation of the subject of the present participle.

The situation is very different in Ancient Greek, where the order of words and phrases is very free, but words are more heavily marked than in English for features like number, gender and case. In Ancient Greek, just as in English, there are participial phrases modifying the whole clause in an adverbial way (like *going to work* or *mending the fence* above). But Ancient Greek solves the problem of the ambiguities we have noted, not by the position of the phrase, as can happen in English, but by marking the participle itself with the number, gender and case of the noun phrase which is to be understood as its subject. Here are some examples, in which for clarity, only the case (nominative/dative) marking is mentioned.[24]

The following sentences all mean *Klearchos met Philip while Klearchos was leaving*, despite the various positions of the participle *apio:n – leaving*.

Klearchos	*ape:nte:se*	*Philippo:i*	*apio:n*
Klearchos+NOM	met	Philip+DAT	leaving+NOM
Klearchos	*ape:nte:se*	*apio:n*	*Philippo:i*
Klearchos+NOM	met	leaving+NOM	Philip+DAT
Klearchos	*apio:n*	*ape:nte:se*	*Philippo:i*
Klearchos+NOM	leaving+NOM	met	Philip+DAT
apio:n	*Klearchos*	*ape:nte:se*	*Philippo:i*
leaving+NOM	Klearchos+NOM	met	Philip+DAT

Wherever the participle *apio:n* is placed, whether at the front, in the middle, or at the end of the sentence, it is clear that its subject is *Klearchos*, because it has the same case marking (Nominative) as *Klearchos*. Similarly we could express *Klearchos met Philip while Philip was leaving* by using the form of the participle *apionti*, which is Dative, agreeing with *Philippoi*, in any position.

Exercise Identify the present participles in the following sentences, including those used as adjectives.

---

24 These Ancient Greek examples are adapted from Avery Andrews' article 'The major functions of the noun phrase', in *Language Typology and Syntactic Description*, volume I: *Clause Structure*, edited by Timothy Shopen (Cambridge University Press, 1985).

1 *Lok was running as fast as he could.*
2 *Mr Tench went out to look for his ether cylinder, into the blazing Mexican sun and the bleaching dust.*
3 *Thirty years ago, Marseilles lay burning in the sun, one day.*
4 *Squire Trelawney, Dr Livesey, and the rest of these gentlemen having asked me to write down the whole particulars about Treasure Island, from the beginning to the end, keeping nothing back but the bearings of the island, and that only because there is still treasure not yet lifted, I take up my pen in the year of grace 17–, and go back to the time when my father kept the Admiral Benbow inn, and the brown old seaman, with the sabre cut, first took up his lodging under our roof.*

Present tense

Explanation
Present tense forms of **verbs** are the forms whose range of meanings typically includes description of events happening at the time at which the speaker or writer is actualy speaking or writing. In English, the present tense of a **verb** is the bare form, with no inflections or **suffixes**, except for the 3rd **person singular**, which takes the **suffix** -*s* or -*es*.

Examples
The following are all English present tense forms of **verbs**: the second member of each group is the 3rd **person singular** form. *am/is/are, have/has, go/goes, come/comes, weep/weeps, stride/stride, gamble/gambles, fornicate/fornicates, blaspheme/blasphemes, bother/bothers, find/finds, hit/hits, save/saves.*

Contrasts
In English, present tense contrasts most directly with **past tense**. In fact, present and **past** are the only two simple **tenses** in English; a simple **tense** form is a one-**word** form produced by the addition of **affixes** or by other changes internal to the **word** itself. Because the range of meanings of the English 'present tense' is so great (see **For interest** below), some grammarians have preferred to refer to it simply as 'non-**past**'.

Using the above **verbs** again as examples, now with **past tense** forms added in for contrast, the present/**past** contrast can be illustrated with: *am/is/are//was/ were, have/has//had, go/goes//went, come/comes//came, weep/weeps//wept, stride/ strides//strode, gamble/gambles//gambled, fornicate/fornicates//fornicated, blaspheme/ blasphemes//blasphemed, bother/bothers//bothered, find/finds//found, hit/hits//hit, save/saves//saved.*

The present tense in English (along with the **past tense**) is a simple **tense**, formed from a single **word**, in contrast to so-called **compound tenses**, **perfect** and **progressive**, formed by a combination of an **auxiliary** (either *have* or *be*) and a **(past or present) participle** of the **verb**. But present tense also combines with **perfect** and **progressive** (see **Relationships** below).

Present tense contrasts, in English, with **present participle**, which is not specifically connected with the present tense at all, but rather with the **progressive** (again, see **Relationships** below).

Relationships Present tense combines with both **perfect** and **progressive** in that the **auxiliaries** associated with these forms (*have* and *be*) can be in either the present or the **past tense**. And, as will be seen, **perfect** and **progressive** also combine with each other, in either present or **past tense**. The possible combinations are illustrated below (where the **tensed** forms are underlined):

	PERFECT	PROGRESSIVE	PERFECT PROGRESSIVE
PRESENT	*has gone*	*is going*	*has been going*
PAST	*had gone*	*was going*	*had been going*

Present tense **verb** forms are **finite**, since they show **tense**, which is one of the criteria for being **finite**.

English present tense **verb** forms show **agreement** with their **subject** only in the 3rd **person singular**.

The English 3rd **person singular** present tense **suffix** spelt as *-s* or *-es* is pronounced in three distinct ways, depending in the preceding sounds, that is:

- as [s] in **verbs** like *hits, flips, laughs* and *takes*;
- as [z] in **verbs** like *climbs, goes, lives, rides* and *sags*;
- as [iz] in **verbs** like *buzzes, watches, misses* and *judges*.

The English present tense is almost entirely **regular**. Irregular forms occur only for **verbs** which can act as **auxiliaries**, e.g. *do/does, have/has, be/am/is/are*. No English **verb** which can only act as a **main verb** has an irregular present tense.

For interest As mentioned, the English simple present tense has a wide range of meanings and uses, some of which are given below:

- ETERNAL STATEMENTS, as in
  Every odd number is the sum of two primes.
  Beauty is truth.
- ENDURING STATES, as in
  Books cost an arm and a leg these days.
  This book belongs to Steve.
- HABITUAL, as in
  I go to Mass every Sunday.
  The manager walks her dog after work.
- CONFIDENTLY FORESEEN FUTURE, as in
  The next Olympic Games are in Atlanta.
  Sue's train gets in at midnight tonight.
- CONDITIONAL FUTURE, as in
  If he comes, he'll get a surprise.
  If you make me a cup of tea, I'll wash the dishes.

- VIVID DESCRIPTION OF THE PAST, as in

  Last night, this man <u>comes</u> up to me and <u>starts</u> insulting me.
  HURRICANE <u>MISSES</u> MIAMI!

Notice that few, if any, of these meanings are very narrowly tied to the present time.

Exercise   Identify the present tense verb forms (including forms of auxiliaries) in this passage. There are seven in all.

> *August, 1931 – The port town of Veracruz is a little purgatory between land and sea for the traveler, but the people who live there are very fond of themselves and the town they have helped to make. They live as initiates in local custom reflecting their own history and temperament, and they carry on their lives of alternate violence and lethargy with a pleasurable contempt for outside opinion, founded on the charmed notion that their ways and feelings are above and beyond criticism.*

Progressive

Explanation   In English, the progressive is a two-**word** form of a **verb**, consisting of the **auxiliary** *be* followed by the **present participle** of the **verb**. It is typically used to express ongoing, or continuing, action or activity. The progressive is sometimes also called the 'continuous'.

Examples   The following **sentences** contain examples of the progressive (underlined).

- *Kim <u>was watching</u> the tigers through his binoculars.*
- *They <u>were sleeping</u>.*
- *I <u>am going</u> to show you how to do this.*
- *We had <u>been intending</u> to visit Benares.*

Contrasts   The English progressive contrasts with the **perfect**. The progressive uses the **auxiliary** *be* and the **present participle**, whereas the **perfect** uses the **auxiliary** *have* and the **past participle**. But the two can combine (see **Relationships** below).

In English, the progressive is a two-**word** form (or **compound tense**), using an **auxiliary**, whereas **present** and **past tenses** are both one-**word** forms of a **verb** (or simple **tenses**). Again, **progressive** can combine with these two **tenses** (see **Relationships** below).

The English progressive contrasts with any sequence of **words** in which a **gerund** just happens to come after the **verb** *be*, as in *My favourite pastime is playing the tuba*. Obviously this should not be understood with *my favourite pastime* as the **subject** of *play*. That is, this example can be paraphrased by *Playing the tuba is my favourite pastime*, and not by **My favourite pastime plays the tuba*.

Relationships Progressive, like **perfect**, is often traditionally called a '**compound tense**', but is more often referred to as an 'aspect' by modern linguists.

When the progressive combines with the **perfect**, the **perfect** is 'applied' to the progressive, so that the **auxiliary** *be* of the progressive appears in **past participle** form (i.e. as *been*) after the *have* of the **perfect**. Examples are:

- *Cleopatra had been trailing Caesar for some time.*
- *I have been reading this play for two weeks.*

Progressive combines with **present** and **past tenses** by putting its **auxiliary** *be* in either one of these **tenses**, as in:

I am thinking. PRESENT PROGRESSIVE
I was thinking. PAST PROGRESSIVE

The English progressive is odd, or even ungrammatical, with certain **verbs** describing states, such as *know, weigh, belong* and *cost*. Hypothetical examples are: **Billy was knowing the answer, *This book is weighing two pounds, *Her dress was costing ninety dollars* and **I am belonging to the Philological Society.*

For interest We tend to think of actions and activities as being primarily expressed by verbs, and of 'aspects' such as the English progressive and perfect as naturally combining with verbs to express different perspectives (e.g. 'ongoing' or 'completed') on these actions and activities. Although this picture is in fact typical of languages, it should be remembered that all the participants in an action contribute to, and are affected by, the perspective on the action, so that, in principle, it should be possible for different perspectives on an action to be expressed, not by forms of the verb, but by different forms of the subjects and/or objects of the clause. Such a thing actually happens in Finnish.

Finnish has a large number of cases for its nouns, including the familiar Nominative and Accusative, but also a 'Partitive'. In some situations, putting a noun in the partitive case means exactly what the name suggests – referring to just a part of the thing referred to by the noun. But in other situations, putting the object of a verb in the partitive case is the way of expressing that an action is/was not completed, or that it is/was ongoing. The concepts of 'completedness' or 'ongoingness' are not expressed by any change affecting the verb. Compare these two examples[25]:

> *liikemies   kirjoitti kirjeen   valiokunnalle.*
> *businessman wrote   letter+ACC committee-to.*
> (= *The businessman wrote a letter to the committee.*)

---

25 This data on Finnish is taken from Paul Hopper and Sandra Thompson's article 'Transitivity in grammar and discourse' in the journal *Language*, 56, 2, (1980).

liikemies   kirjoitti kirjettä   valiokunnalle.
businessman wrote   letter+PART committee-to.
(= The businessman was writing a letter to the committee.)

Notice the two free English translations. One uses *wrote*, to convey that the writing was finished, while the other uses the progressive form *was writing*, conveying that the writing was not finished, at the time referred to. But the verb in the two Finnish sentences is the same, *kirjoitti*, and the difference in meaning is actually conveyed by an alternative form of the object noun.

Exercise   Identify the progressive forms in the following. For each progressive form that you find, underline the two words that make it. And watch out! – There is a trick.

1 *We were waiting for you in the wrong place.*
2 *What were you and Evie doing in the raspberry patch?*
3 *What you are doing is a big mistake.*
4 *His greatest achievement was winning the New York Marathon.*
5 *My problem is that I am being pursued by an integer.*
6 *The Time Traveller (for so it will be convenient to speak of him) was expounding a recondite matter to us.*

Pronoun

Explanation   A pronoun is typically a little **word** that stands in place of a **noun phrase**. There are various ways in which this can happen, and correspondingly various different types of pronoun. The main types of pronoun (all of which are dealt with more fully in separate entries) are:

- **Personal** pronouns: these are the most familiar type, and can occur in almost all the positions where **noun phrases** can occur. They usually refer to people or things.
- **Impersonal** pronouns: these can also occur in almost all the positions where **noun phrases** can occur. They are relatively rare, and are used specifically to avoid referring to particular people or things.
- **Reflexive** pronouns: these refer to people or things, but typically only to people or things which have been explicitly mentioned within the same **clause**. Hence, their range of occurrence is quite limited.
- **Possessive** pronouns: these refer to people or things, of a type which has been previously mentioned in the conversation or text, and which can be identified through belonging, in some sense, to some other person or thing.
- **Relative** pronouns: these are the little **words** used to introduce **relative clauses**. They stand, inside their **relative clauses**, for understood **noun phrases**.

- **Interrogative words**: some **interrogative words** are sometimes called 'interrogative pronouns'. These, in English, are the **words** used to ask a question which expects as an answer an expression referring to a person or thing.

Examples English examples of these various types of pronoun are:

- **Personal** pronouns: *I, you, them*.
- **Impersonal** pronouns: *one*.
- **Reflexive** pronouns: *myself, yourself, themselves*.
- **Possessive** pronouns: *mine, yours, theirs*.
- **Relative** pronouns: *who, that, which, whose*.
- **Interrogative words** also classed as **interrogative** pronouns: *who?, what?, which?*.

Contrasts Pronouns contrast with **nouns**. **Nouns** can take a range of **modifiers**, such as **articles** and **adjectives**, but pronouns stand on their own, and (with a handful of exceptions) take no **modifiers** before them. This is what one would expect from the fact that pronouns stand for whole **noun phrases**.

As 'pronoun' is a **part of speech**, pronouns contrast with all other **parts of speech**. If a **word** in a given **sentence** is a pronoun, it isn't any other **part of speech**.

Relationships The traditional formula, that 'a pronoun stands in place of a **noun**', is wrong. In fact, a pronoun stands in place of a whole **noun phrase**. Take a typical **sentence**, containing a **noun phrase** with some **modifiers**, such as perhaps an **article** or an **adjective**, and try replacing just the **noun** with an appropriate pronoun; the result will almost certainly be ungrammatical. Here are some examples of such attempted replacement of a single **noun** by a pronoun.

SENTENCE WITH NOUN (underlined)	NOUN REPLACED BY PRONOUN
We found the poor boy waiting outside.	**We found the poor him waiting outside.*
Many fungi are poisonous.	**Many they are poisonous.*
I went past your old house today.	**I went past your old it today.*

As you see, the results of replacing a single **noun** by a pronoun are usually ungrammatical (as indicated by the asterisks). In fact, pronouns stand in place of whole **noun phrases**, as shown by the parallel examples below.

SENTENCE WITH NOUN PHRASE (underlined)	NOUN PHRASE REPLACED BY PRONOUN
We found the poor boy waiting outside.	*We found him waiting outside.*
Many fungi are poisonous.	*They are poisonous.*
I went past your old house today.	*I went past it today.*

The examples just given were **personal** pronouns replacing whole **noun phrases**, but the same message also applies to other kinds of pronouns. Pronouns stand for **noun phrases**, not for **nouns**.

PRONOUN FOR NOUN PHRASE	PRONOUN FOR NOUN	TYPE OF PRONOUN
We found ourselves outside.	**We found the poor ourselves outside.*	REFLEXIVE
We found ours outside.	**We found the poor ours outside.*	POSSESSIVE

Pronouns can be the **subjects** and (**direct** or **indirect**) **objects** of **clauses**, and the **objects** of **prepositions**. This follows from the fact that pronouns can stand on their own in place of whole **noun phrases**.

There are **noun phrases** built around **nouns**, and **adjective phrases** formed around **adjectives**, and so on. But there are not, and cannot be, 'pronoun **phrases**', as pronouns already stand for whole **noun phrases**. This is essentially the same fact as the fact that pronouns generally take no **modifiers** at all.

The few cases where a pronoun takes a **modifier** before it, as in *Poor you!* and *little me*, are clearly quite exceptional. But pronouns can take **modifying phrases** after them, as in *we who are about to die*, or *you at the back*, or *him with the hat on*.

We are following a definition of 'phrase' which permits one-**word phrases**, and in this sense a pronoun in a **sentence** actually constitutes a **noun phrase**. For example, in the **sentence** *He loves Brahms*, the **subject** is a **noun phrase** consisting of a single **word**, the pronoun *he*. (It is no contradiction to say that a pronoun both 'stands for' and 'is' a **noun phrase**.)

Certain types of pronoun are closely connected with specific grammatical constructions or positions. The three main connections between types of pronoun and specific features in English **grammar** are as follows:

Reflexive pronouns are connected with **direct** and **indirect object** positions
Relative pronouns are connected with **relative clauses**
Interrogative words are connected with **interrogative sentences**

These connections are dealt with in more detail in the entries for REFLEXIVE, RELATIVE PRONOUN and INTERROGATIVE.

Personal pronouns also show some characteristic behaviour which can be attributed to their being little or 'lightweight' **words**. Some effects plausibly due to these pronouns being 'lightweight' (i.e. short to pronounce) are mentioned below.

Look at the positions of the underlined **noun phrases** in the examples below:

Jackie took the garbage out.   *Jackie took out the garbage.*
Joe looked the mysterious words up.   *Joe looked up the mysterious words.*

In such **sentences**, full **noun phrases** can go either before or after **particles** such as *out* and *up*. Now try replacing these **noun phrases**, in both positions, by **personal** pronouns. What we get is:

Jackie took it out.   **Jackie took out it.*
Joe looked them up.   **Joe looked up them.*

This shows that English **personal** pronouns, as opposed to the full **noun phrases** they replace, cannot occur isolated out to the right-hand side of **particles** such as *out* and *up*.

For interest The 'lightweight' behaviour of personal pronouns, tending to avoid positions near the end of a sentence, and to prefer positions nearer to the beginning of a sentence, is more evident in some nearby languages, such as French and Italian.

In French, as in English, personal pronouns stand for whole noun phrases. In French, as in English, a direct object noun phrase follows the verb. So we have word-for-word correspondences like the following between some English and French sentences.

Je vois le   chemin
*I see the+*MASC *path*   (= *I see the path.*)

Je vois la   route
*I see the+*FEM *road*   (= *I see the road.*)

But if the direct object of a French verb is a personal pronoun, it has to go before the verb, as in:

Je le   vois
*I it+*MASC *see*   (= *I see it.*)

Je la   vois
*I it+*FEM *see*   (= *I see it.*)

In Italian, the process of treating personal pronouns as 'lightweight' is, in some situations, taken one step further, and they even cease to be independent words, and become suffixes on verbs. Thus the single Italian word *vederlo* means, in English, *to see it* (or *him*), with the *-lo*, meaning *it* or *him*, attached as a suffix, or 'clitic', to the verb *veder*, meaning *to see*. Other examples are *vederla* – *to see her* and *vederci* – *to see us*.

This kind of treatment of personal pronouns is very common in languages. In many languages, it is possible to omit personal pronouns from subject position altogether. Again, Italian is like this. The single word *vengo* can stand as a sentence on its own, meaning *I am coming*, with the subject pronoun simply 'understood' rather than explicitly present in the sentence. Of course, it helps comprehension that, in Italian, verbs show agreement for person and number.

You have probably noticed that, in French and Italian, the personal pronouns (in object position) are similar, or even identical, to the definite articles. Thus French *le*, *la* and *les* are all definite articles, and also all object personal pronouns. Such a correspondence between personal pronouns and definite articles is also quite common in languages.

Exercise In the examples below, one or two pronouns in each example are underlined. For each underlined pronoun, say what type it is, i.e. whether personal, impersonal, reflexive, relative, possessive or interrogative.

1 *Who do you think you are?*
2 *Which is mine?*
3 *The one which just ran away was yours.*
4 *It hurt itself on the wire.*
5 *But one shouldn't worry about it.*
6 *I don't worry myself over such things.*

Proper name

Explanation   A proper name, or proper **noun** (the two terms are equivalent), is a **word** (or sequence of several **words**) identifying some particular individual person, place, event or thing. A proper name can stand on its own as a **noun phrase**. Typically, English proper names are spelt beginning with capital letters.

Examples   These are some English proper names: *John, Henry, Helsinki, Hurford, Fido, Rover, Dobbin, Fluffums, New York, San Francisco, Robert Louis Stevenson, Alec Guinness, 1066* (the date), *Watergate, Waterloo, Mars, Alpha Centauri, Chitty Chitty Bang Bang, Hamlet, Romeo and Juliet* (the play), *Fidelio, R2D2* (a robot).

Contrasts   Proper names contrast with **common nouns**, the other major kind of **noun**. A **common noun**, such as *dog*, on its own does not identify a particular individual thing, whereas the proper name *Fido* picks out one individual.

As proper name is a **word**-class, it contrasts with all other **word**-classes or **parts of speech**. If a **word** in a given **sentence** is a proper name, it cannot belong to any other **word**-class or **part of speech**.

Relationships   Proper names can stand on their own as whole **noun phrases**. This means that they can act as **subjects** and **direct** or **indirect objects** of **clauses**, as in *New York is wilder than London*, or *Lady Margaret visited Saudi Arabia*.

Proper names are always **definite**.

Proper names are almost always **singular**, as can be seen from the **agreement** of **verbs** used with them, as in *Omaha is a swinging town*. Even expressions which, if not taken as proper names, would be **plural** are **singular** when used as proper names, as in *Romeo and Juliet is a sexist masterpiece*, or *The Carpetbaggers is my favourite novel* or *Sex and the Single Girl was pretty boring*. There are rare exceptions, such as *the Bahamas*.

The most typical proper names don't contain any of the possible **modifiers** of **nouns**, such as **articles**, **adjectives** and **numerals**. There are plenty of exceptions to this tendency, however, as in: *the Sahara, the Bahamas, the Caribbean, Key West, Knott's Landing* and *Twenty-nine Palms*.

If, in unusual circumstances, an **article modifies** what is usually a proper name, or if the proper name is pluralized, it becomes effectively a **common noun**, not referring any longer to a single individual. For instance, in *I know* *three Robins*, the **plural** form *Robins* is synonymous with *people named 'Robin'*. Similarly, in *That's not the Robin I'm talking about*, the **word** *Robin* is essentially used as a **common noun**, meaning *person called 'Robin'*.

But some **adjectives** can **modify** proper names without changing their status, as in *big John* or *poor old Joe*. Proper names may be **modified** by non-restrictive **relative clauses**, as in *John, who I had met before, ignored me*. But proper names may not be **modified** by restrictive **relative clauses**, as in *John that I had met before ignored me*★.

Some proper names are (semi-)fossilized **definite noun phrases**, like *the Great Barrier Reef* and *the Rocky Mountains*.

Proper names are the **words** most easily and frequently borrowed from other languages. That is why the 'senses' of proper names are often obscure. For instance, what 'is' a Bahama? or What 'is' a Himalaya?

Adjectives and derived **common nouns** can often be formed from proper names, sometimes in rather idiosyncratic ways, as in: *Spain/Spanish/Spaniard, Glasgow/Glaswegian, Peking/Pekinese* and *London/Londoner*.

Exercise   Identify the proper names in the following passages. There are eight in all.

> *On an evening in the latter part of May a middle-aged man was walking homeward from Shaston to the village of Marlott, in the adjoining vale of Blakemore, or Blackmoor.*
>
>   *Kinraddie lands had been won by a Norman childe, Cospatric de Gondeshil, in the days of William the Lyon, when gryphons and such-like beasts still roamed the Scots countryside and folk would waken in their beds to hear the children screaming, with a great wolf-beast, come through the hide window, tearing at their throats.*

Reflexive

Explanation   In English, reflexive **pronouns** are used to show that the **object** in a **clause** refers to the same person or thing as the **subject**. English reflexive **pronouns** all end in *-self* or *-selves*.

Examples   The English reflexive **pronouns** are: *myself, yourself, himself, herself, itself, ourselves, yourselves, themselves* and, in rather formal language, *oneself*.

Contrasts   Reflexive **pronouns** contrast mainly with **personal pronouns**, such as *I, me, she* and *him*. Such non-reflexive, personal pronouns are interpreted as not referring to the same person or thing as some other **noun phrase** in the **clause**. But use of a reflexive **pronoun** definitely indicates sameness of reference. For example, in *Alice kicked herself*, the reflexive **pronoun** *herself* must refer to Alice, but, by contrast, in *Alice kicked her*, the **personal pronoun** *her* can in fact refer to any (female) person except Alice.

Reflexive **pronouns** also contrast with other kinds of **pronouns**, such as **possessive pronouns** (e.g. *mine, yours*) and **relative pronouns** (e.g. *who, which*), but there is little danger of confusion with these.

Relationships   Like **pronouns** generally, a reflexive **pronoun** constitutes a (one-**word**) **noun phrase**. Like **pronouns** generally, they do not take any **modifiers**, such as **adjectives** or **articles**. So expressions like **the real himself* are ungrammatical.

Reflexives, like **pronouns** generally, stand in the place of whole **noun phrases**. They are understood as picking out exactly the same person(s) or thing(s) as are referred to by some preceding **noun phrase** in the same **clause**. For instance, the **sentences** with reflexives on the left below are understood as the hypothetical **sentences** on the right.

The old grey mare shook herself.	**The old grey mare shook the old grey mare.*
The hill road turns back on itself.	**The hill road turns back on the hill road.*
Your parents should blame themselves.	**Your parents should blame your parents.*

The preceding **noun phrase** referring to the same person or thing as the reflexive **pronoun** is known as its 'antecedent'. Reflexive **pronouns** and their antecedents are always in the same **clause** (except for a few tricky cases that linguists know about). Compare the following **sentences**.

- *Mary urged Jane to smarten herself up.*
- *Mary urged Jane to smarten her up.*

In the first example here, the person meant by *herself* can only be Jane, because *Jane* is in the same **clause** as *herself*. In the second **sentence** the person referred to by *her* cannot be Jane, because *Jane* is in the same **clause** as *her*.

Reflexives cannot be **subjects**, because **subjects** cannot have any antecedent in the same **clause**, as **subjects** occur first in a **clause**. That is why, for example, **Myself will shoot me* is not grammatical. For the same reason, a hypothetical **sentence** like **I told John that myself would do it* is ungrammatical; here the **word** *that* marks the boundary between **clauses**, and *I* is in one **clause** (the **main clause**) and *myself* is in another (the **subordinate clause**).

Reflexive **pronouns** occur as **direct** or **indirect objects** of **verbs** or as **objects** of **prepositions**, as illustrated below.

Politicians always praise themselves.	DIRECT OBJECT
Hilary bought herself a tool kit.	INDIRECT OBJECT
We did it by ourselves.	OBJECT OF PREPOSITION

English reflexive **pronouns** show **person** (1st, 2nd, 3rd), **number** (**singular/plural**) and **gender** (masculine/feminine), as follows.

	PERSON	NUMBER	GENDER
myself	1st	Singular	–
yourself	2nd	Singular	–
himself	3rd	Singular	Masculine

herself	3rd	Singular	Feminine
itself	3rd	Singular	Neuter
ourselves	1st	Plural	–
yourselves	2nd	Plural	–
themselves	3rd	Plural	–

English reflexive **pronouns agree** in **person, number** and **gender** with their antecedents. So a reflexive whose antecedent is *the grand old man* can only be *himself*; and a hypothetical example such as **The man threw ourselves at the door* is ungrammatical, because of the lack of **agreement**.

Reflexive **pronouns** are **definite** (apart from *oneself*, which is **indefinite**).

Reflexive **pronouns** can also be used in English to add emphasis to, or focus attention on, a particular **noun phrase**. Such emphatic reflexives are illustrated below.

- *I myself don't own a car.*
- *I don't own a car myself.*
- *You will have an opportunity to meet the Pope himself.*
- *You will have an opportunity to meet the Pope yourself.*

Note that these emphatic reflexives are quite mobile, rather like **adverbs**, able to occur at several different places in the **sentence**.

For interest   Transitive verbs have a subject and an object, which usually refer to different people or things, so that two different individuals are involved in the action. In *Ruby shot Oswald*, for example, two people are involved, the shooter and the shot. But in sentences with reflexive pronouns, such as *Jimmy shot himself*, only one person is mentioned, but twice; there is a single, rather complex action, involving just one person.

Doing something to oneself is often a quite different kind of action from doing it to someone else, and it is not surprising that in many languages there are special intransitive reflexive verbs for expressing what in English would be expressed by a transitive verb with a reflexive pronoun object. In Russian, for instance, the suffix *-sja* or *-s'* attached to a transitive verb makes it into an intransitive reflexive verb. Here are some examples.

mat' pomyla rebenka	
mother washed child	(= *The mother washed the child.*)
mat' pomyla-s'	
mother washed+REFL	(= *The mother washed (herself.*))
ja umyvaju rebenka	
I am-washing child'	(= *I am washing the child.*)
ja umyvaju-s'	
I am-washing+REFL	(= *I am washing (myself.*))

There are two different forms of the Russian verb for *wash* here. Both of them are 'reflexivized' in the same way, by the addition of the suffix *-s'*.

Reflexivizing a verb in this way turns a transitive verb into an intransitive verb. There can be other reasons, besides the need to express reflexive meaning, for converting a transitive verb to an intransitive one. Another type of meaning, closely related to the reflexive, is 'reciprocal'. In English, reciprocal meaning is expressed by a transitive verb (e.g. *meet*) with a special object, *each other*, as in *They met each other*. But, although several people are involved when people meet each other, the event could be seen as a single event involving one group of people (formed by the meeting itself). And this is rather how Russian treats it, with an intransitive verb (taking no object), formed from a transitive verb, again by the addition of the suffix *-sja* or *-s'*. Here is an example.

oni vstrechajut sestru
they meet   sister   (= *They meet the sister.*)

oni vstrechajut-sja
*they meet+*REFL   (= *They meet each other.*)

Interestingly, Russian also uses this same suffix *-sja* or *-s'* to form some passive verbs, as in:

nakhodit' to find	*nakhodit'sja to be found (situated)*
otkryvat' to open	*otkryvat'sja to be opened*
zakryvat' to close	*zakryvat'sja to be closed*

Thus, Russian uses the same suffix for three different meanings, reflexive, reciprocal and passive. What these three meanings have in common is that they all involve the reduction of an action or event seen as involving two entities to an action or event seen as involving just one. In the case of the passive, this means omitting the agent of the action (the person who did it).

The connection between these meanings can be seen in other languages, too. In French, the so-called 'reflexive pronoun' is used for genuine reflexives, but also for reciprocals, as shown below.

ils se   reculent
they REFL/RECIP *withdraw*   (= *They retreat* or *retire* literally
                                        They withdraw themselves.)

ils se   battent
they REFL/RECIP *fight*   (= *They fight each other.*)

Exercise   Identify the reflexive pronouns, including emphatic reflexives, in the following.

1 *John has a self-destructive streak; he often criticizes himself.*
2 *Mary was annoyed at herself for breaking her shelf.*
3 *For him, self-denial is a virtue in itself.*
4 *May I introduce myself?*
5 *She introduced me to the Rabbi himself.*
6 *She introduced me to the Rabbi herself.*

Regular, irregular

Explanation **Words** are **regular** if they are combined with the usual **affixes** of the language in the same predictable way as most other similar **words**. **Words** which have their own unusual or peculiar ways of combining are irregular.

Less often, the terms 'regular' and 'irregular' are applied to types of **phrase** or **sentence**. A regular **phrase** or **sentence** is one that is formed to exactly the same pattern as many other similar **phrases** or **sentences**, so that, for example, one could substitute other **words** without making the **phrase** or **sentence** ungrammatical. An irregular **phrase** or **sentence** is one which is formed according to a pattern seen in no (or few) others.

Examples English **nouns** which form their **plurals** by simply adding -*s* or -*es* are regular. Such regular **nouns** (or more precisely, **nouns** with regular **plurals**) include *apple, building, couch, disaster, effect, yacht* and *zero*. By contrast, **nouns** such as *mouse, tooth, man, woman* and *criterion* have irregular **plurals** (*mice, teeth, men, women* and *criteria*), which are not formed in the usual way, by adding –*s* or -*es*.

English **verbs** can be regular or irregular in the formation of their **past tenses** and **past participles**. The regular **verbs** add -*d* or -*ed* to make both these forms, as in *attend/attended, believe/believed, crawl/crawled, walk/walked, Xerox/Xeroxed* and *yawn/yawned*. English irregular **verbs** include *buy/bought, catch/caught, do/did/done, go/went/gone, sit/sat* and *take/took/taken*.

Other comparisons between other regular and irregular English forms are given below:

	REGULAR	IRREGULAR
CARDINAL and ORDINAL NUMERALS	*four/fourth*	*one/first*
	six/sixth	*two/second*
ADJECTIVES and their COMPARATIVES	*warm/warmer*	*good/better*
	strong/stronger	*bad/worse*

An example of an irregular **sentence** in English is the idiomatic greeting *How do you do?* This is odd, because the **main verb** *do* usually takes a **direct object** after it. Notice that you can't say, for example, **When do you do?* or **Why do you do?*

Another irregular construction is with the (somewhat colloquial) *How come?*, with a meaning similar (but not identical) to *Why?*. In questions formed with *How come*, the **subject** does not get inverted with an **auxiliary verb**, as in normal English **interrogatives**. Compare carefully the order of the **words**, especially the underlined ones, in the following:

How come Frances took my book?   *Why did Frances take my book?*
How come nobody loves me?   *Why does nobody love me?*
How come Kirsty can't hear me?   *Why can't Kirsty can hear me?*

The term 'irregular' might sometimes be applied to a **word** such as *umbrage*, whose occurrence is very restricted; it only occurs with the **verb** *take*. You can't even **give umbrage!*

Contrasts 'Regular' contrasts, of course, with 'irregular'. If a form is not regular, it is irregular.

Relationships In English, most **auxiliary verbs** are irregular.

The **part of speech** most prone to irregularity, at least in familiar European languages, is the **verb**. Many such languages have long lists of irregular **verbs** but relatively few irregular **nouns**, **adjectives** and **adverbs**.

There can be sub-**regularities**. That is, there can be small groups of **words** which behave in a way different from the dominant pattern, but in a way which is consistent with the behaviour of other members of the group. An example of such a sub-**regularity** in English would be the small number of **nouns** ending in an *'f '* sound, whose **plurals** change this *'f '* to a *'v'* sound, **nouns** such as *wife/wives, roof/rooves, hoof/hooves, knife/knives, life/lives, elf/elves* and *shelf/shelves*.

There is some correlation between frequency and irregularity. Irregular forms are found among the more frequently used **words** in a language (such as **auxiliaries**).

Idioms are often, but not always, irregular in construction. An example is *in the main*, as in *In the main, Jackie works hard*. *Main* is an **adjective** and, as a general rule, you can't use an **adjective** after *the* without a **noun**, or unless some **noun** is understood. So you can't say, for example, **In the principal, Jackie works hard*, or **In the general, Jackie works hard* or **In the usual, Jackie works hard*. *In the main* is an irregular idiom.

A case of an idiom which is grammatically regular is *kick the bucket*, meaning *die*; this is formed according to a quite normal pattern of **transitive verb** plus **noun phrase**, as in *wash the dishes, climb a tree* and *write a letter*.

For interest When learning a language, either as a child or when learning a second language as an adult, the irregular forms always impose a disproportionate burden on the memory. If languages were intentionally designed for ease of learning, there would be no irregular forms. But in fact, all languages have at least some irregularities of some kind. So it is a universal that languages are not optimally designed, at least for learning. (There might be some argument that having a few irregularities helps communication, but that is another matter.)

Children learning English usually go through a stage in which they spontaneously produce their own regularized (and incorrect) forms of irregular nouns and verbs. Here are some examples:

CHILD'S REGULARIZED FORM	ADULT FORM
Billy goed home.	*Billy went home.*
Sharon taked my teddy.	*Sharon took my teddy.*
Lizzy hitted me.	*Lizzy hit me.*

Lizzy hurted me.   *Lizzy hurt me.*
We've got some gooses.   *We've got some geese.*

Children seem particularly resistant to being corrected (if the adults bother) on such overgeneralizations. In their own time, they learn the adult form and drop these spontaneous regularizations. But it is not without some confusion. Often, when a child realizes that there is something wrong with saying *goed*, realizing as well that an *-ed* ending should be involved, he or she produces **wented*, which is a kind of blend of the correct form and the original over-generalized form. Another common example is *tooken* instead of *taken*. Perhaps the child makes some association between past tense and past participle, and realizing that the past tense of *take* is *took*, and that many irregular past participles end in *-en*, produces a blend of all these properties, namely *tooken*.

Exercise   In each of the following two lists of English words, half are regular, and half are irregular (of course). Identify the irregular nouns and verbs.

> Nouns: *hand, foot, boy, child, cow, ox.*
> Verbs: *come, comb, spank, speak, strike, stroke, make, chase.*

Relative clause

Explanation   A relative clause is a type of **subordinate clause modifying** a **noun** and giving detailed information about the person or thing the **noun** refers to. In English, relative clauses follow the **nouns** they **modify** and are usually introduced by a **relative pronoun**, such as *who*, *which* or *that*.

Examples   In the following **sentences**, the relative clauses are underlined.

- *The man who broke the bank at Monte Carlo was an engineer.*
- *We have visited the casino that banned him.*
- *I hate pencils that other people have chewed.*
- *The lady whose dog I kicked panicked.*
- *I will sue the lady whose dog bit my child.*
- *The official to whom I protested was fired.*
- *There is a tall building, at the back of which is a car park.*
- *That's the place where I was robbed.*

Contrasts   Relative clauses contrast with other kinds of **clause**. There is little danger of confusing them with **main clauses**. But there are a number of other kinds of **subordinate clause** which closely resemble relative clauses, and which in fact contrast with them. These resemblances and differences are explained below.

Relative clauses should not be confused with *wh*-**interrogatives**, which begin with many of the same **words** (e.g. *who, whom, which*) as relative clauses. A *wh*-**interrogative**, such as *Who did you see?*, is a **main clause** and

213

can stand on its own as a **sentence**, whereas a relative clause, such as ... *whom you saw*, is a **subordinate clause** and needs a **noun** to be attached to, as in *the person whom you saw*. Some relative clauses and *wh*-**interrogatives** are in fact identical, apart from punctuation, e.g. ... *who saw you* (relative clause) versus *Who saw you?* (*wh*-**interrogative**).

In a similar way, **indirect** questions, that is **subordinate interrogative clauses**, can be very similar in form to relative clauses, as both can begin with such **words** as *who*, *which* and *whose*. In the examples below, the same **clause** (underlined) is used once as a relative clause and once as an **indirect** question.

The day <u>when I was moving</u> came.	RELATIVE CLAUSE, **modifying** the **noun** *day*
They enquired <u>when I was moving</u>.	INDIRECT QUESTION (= *When are you moving?*)
He took the kitten <u>which we wanted</u>.	RELATIVE CLAUSE, **modifying** the **noun** *kitten*
He asked <u>which we wanted</u>.	INDIRECT QUESTION (= *Which do you want?*)
The boy <u>who wants this</u> is here.	RELATIVE CLAUSE, **modifying** the **noun** *boy*
I wonder <u>who wants this</u>.	INDIRECT QUESTION (= *Who wants this?*)

English relative clauses introduced by *when* and *where* are sometimes identical in shape to adverbial **clauses**. In the examples below, the same **clauses** (underlined) are used, once as a relative clause, and once as an adverbial **clause**.

The day <u>when I had my test</u> was wet.	RELATIVE CLAUSE, **modifying** the **noun** *day*
It rained <u>when I had my test</u>.	ADVERBIAL CLAUSE OF TIME, **modifying** **main clause** *It rained.*
Have you seen the area <u>where he lives</u>?	RELATIVE CLAUSE, **modifying** the **noun** *area*
<u>Where he lives</u>, dogs patrol.	ADVERBIAL CLAUSE OF PLACE, **modifying** **main clause** *Dogs patrol.*

The distinguishing feature of the relative clauses here is that they **modify nouns**.

Relationships Any **noun** in any position in a **clause** (i.e. **subject**, **direct** or **indirect object**, etc.) can be **modified** by a relative clause. This is illustrated below by taking a simple **sentence**, *The woman mentioned the man to the boy*, and putting the same **relative clause** after each **noun**, *woman*, *man* or *boy*. The relative clause we will use is *that we suspect*.

	RELATIVE CLAUSE MODIFIES
The woman <u>that we suspect</u> mentioned the man to the boy.	*woman*
The woman mentioned the man <u>that we suspect</u> to the boy.	*man*
The woman mentioned the man to the boy <u>that we suspect</u>.	*boy*

A relative clause is a **clause**, and therefore itself contains a **verb** and a **subject** and quite possibly a **direct** and **indirect object**, too. Any **noun** position in the relative clause can be 'shared' with the **noun** which is being **modified**. Let's say we want to use a relative clause to **modify** the **noun** *dog* in the **noun phrase** *the lazy dog*. Now, what do we want to say about this lazy dog? Here are some of the possibilities.

	It ACTS AS
It has fleas.	**Subject** of an **active clause**.
The cat chased it.	**Direct object** of an **active clause**.
It was chased by the cat.	**Subject** of a **passive clause**.
The cat was chased by it.	**Object** of the **preposition** *by* in a **passive clause**.
Polly gave it a bone.	**Indirect object** of the **clause**.
Its collar is loose.	Part of a **Possessive**, *its*, **modifying** a **noun**, *collar*.
Matty took a photo of it.	**Object** of the **preposition** *of*

For each of these possibilities (and more), we can construct a different relative clause **modifying** *dog* in *the lazy dog*. The results are as follows.

- ... *the lazy dog that has fleas* ...
- ... *the lazy dog that the cat chased* ...
- ... *the lazy dog that was chased by the cat* ...
- ... *the lazy dog that the cat was chased by* ...
- ... *the lazy dog that Polly gave a bone* ... (not grammatical for all speakers)
- ... *the lazy dog whose collar is loose* ...
- ... *the lazy dog Matty took a photo of* ...

We have illustrated great versatility of relative clauses in two aspects:

- **Nouns** in various positions can be **modified** by relative clauses.
- Various positions inside the relative clause can be 'shared' with the **modified noun**.

The choice of which **relative pronoun** to use at the beginning of a relative clause in English is somewhat complex. (See **RELATIVE PRONOUN**.)

As relative clauses are **subordinate clauses**, and there is no limit in principle to how many **subordinate clauses** can go inside each other, there can be embedded relative clauses. Examples (with each relative clause underlined) are:

- *The boy who shouted 'Beaver' at the man who paints the ladies' faces*

  is just passing by.

- *This is the dog*

  that chased the cat that caught the mouse that lay in the house that Jack built.

In English, certain relative clauses beginning with *who is/are* or *which is/are* can be reduced to adjectival or **participial phrases** by omission of the *who is/are* or *which is/are*. Here are some examples:

WITH FULL RELATIVE CLAUSE	WITH 'REDUCED' RELATIVE CLAUSE
a man who was asking the way to Glasgow	*a man asking the way to Glasgow*
a character who is subject to hallucinations	*a character subject to hallucinations*
a child who is afraid of the dark	*a child afraid of the dark*
the soap which is preferred by housewives	*the soap preferred by housewives*

There is an exceptional kind of relative clause that does not **modify** any **noun**, but simply stands on its own as a **noun phrase**. Such 'headless' relative clauses are underlined in the examples below:

- *Whoever planned this party was brilliant.*
- *I'd like to congratulate whichever person made this pudding.*
- *Take whichever you like, and give it to who you like.*

In English and some other languages, there is a difference between what are called 'restrictive' and 'non-restrictive' relative clauses. **Modification** of a **noun** by a restrictive relative clause narrows down the possible set of people or things the **noun** could be referring to. Non-restrictive relative clauses simply add new information about the person or thing referred to by the **modified noun**, without helping to specify him, her or it more closely. Non-restrictive relative clauses are often written with a comma, or pronounced with a slight pause before them. Here are some examples:

The dog that lives next door is called Alphonse.	RESTRICTIVE
The dog, which lives next door, is called Alphonse.	NON-RESTRICTIVE
My neighbour who breeds turtles is a bank manager.	RESTRICTIVE
My neighbour, who breeds turtles, is a bank manager.	NON-RESTRICTIVE

To take the second pair of examples, involving the turtles and the bank manager, use of the restrictive relative clause assumes that the hearer knows that the speaker has several neighbours, but that just one of them breeds turtles. Using the non-restrictive relative clause assumes that the hearer knows which neighbour the speaker is talking about, and gives the added information that he or she breeds turtles.

Proper names can only be **modified** by non-restrictive relative clauses, as in *Somalia, where there is drought, needs help.* The **relative pronoun** that can only introduce restrictive relative clauses, so, for instance, **Bill, that is my friend, arrived early*, is odd or even ungrammatical.

For interest Most, though not all, languages have relative clauses. While, in languages like English, relative clauses follow the noun they modify, in languages where the verb comes at the end of the sentence relative clauses typically precede the noun. Japanese is such a language, putting the verb at the end of clauses, and relative clauses before the modified noun, as in these examples.

Taroo ga	*katta*	*hon*	
Taroo NOM	*bought*	*book*	(= *the book which Taroo bought*)
Yamada-san ga	*kodomo ni*	*yatta hon*	
Yamada-Mr. NOM	*child*	DAT *gave book*	
			(= *the book which Mr Yamada gave to the child*)

Exercise Identify the relative clauses in the following. There are seven in all.

1 *People who live in glass houses shouldn't throw stones.*
2 *We picked the apples which the others had left.*

3 *The man who married your sister is the brother of the girl you married.*
4 *The idea really came to me the day I got my new false teeth.*
5 *The pilots who shot down the planes they were chasing were given medals.*

Relative pronoun

Explanation A relative pronoun is a special **pronoun** used to introduce a **relative clause**. In English it generally comes immediately after the **noun modified** by the **relative clause**.

Examples The English relative pronouns are *who, whom, whose, which, that, when, where* and *why*. (The **words** *when, where* and *why* can be used to introduce **relative clauses modifying nouns,** and so it is useful to group these with the relative pronouns, though this is not so often done by traditional grammarians; they are included among the relative pronouns in this guide.)

Contrasts All of the **words** which are English relative pronouns also belong to other **word**-classes or **parts of speech**, in particular as

- **interrogative words**, introducing:
- **direct** *wh*-questions, or
- **indirect** *wh*-questions.
- subordinating **conjunctions**, introducing:
- adverbial **clauses**, or
- **complement clauses**.

These contrasts are illustrated below.

The key feature of a relative pronoun, which distinguishes it from all these other uses, is that every relative pronoun introduces a **relative clause** (though not all **relative clauses** are introduced by a relative pronoun). For each English relative pronoun, its use as a relative pronoun is contrasted with other possible uses below.

WORD AND EXAMPLE	USED AS
who	
This is the man who met me.	RELATIVE PRONOUN
Who met you?	(DIRECT) INTERROGATIVE WORD
He asked who had met me.	(INDIRECT) INTERROGATIVE WORD
whom	
This is the man whom I met.	RELATIVE PRONOUN
Whom did you meet?	(DIRECT) INTERROGATIVE WORD
He asked whom I had met.	(INDIRECT) INTERROGATIVE WORD

whose

This is the man *whose* bike I took.	RELATIVE PRONOUN
Whose bike did you take?	(DIRECT) INTERROGATIVE WORD
He asked *whose* bike I had taken.	(INDIRECT) INTERROGATIVE WORD

which

This is the bike *which* I took.	RELATIVE PRONOUN
Which bike did you take?	(DIRECT) INTERROGATIVE WORD
He asked *which* bike I had taken.	(INDIRECT) INTERROGATIVE WORD

that

This is the man *that* met me.	RELATIVE PRONOUN
He says *that* I took his bike.	SUBORDINATING CONJUNCTION, INTRODUCING COMPLEMENT CLAUSE

when

That was the day *when* I took his bike.	RELATIVE PRONOUN
When did you take his bike?	(DIRECT) INTERROGATIVE WORD
He asked *when* I had taken his bike.	(INDIRECT) INTERROGATIVE WORD
He was angry *when* I took his bike.	SUBORDINATING CONJUNCTION, INTRODUCING ADVERBIAL CLAUSE

where

The place *where* I put it was safe.	RELATIVE PRONOUN
Where did you put it?	(DIRECT) INTERROGATIVE WORD
He asked *where* I had put it.	(INDIRECT) INTERROGATIVE WORD
He couldn't find it *where* I put it.	SUBORDINATING CONJUNCTION, INTRODUCING ADVERBIAL CLAUSE

why

I forget the reason *why* I took it.	RELATIVE PRONOUN
Why did you take it?	(DIRECT) INTERROGATIVE WORD
He asked *why* I had taken it.	(INDIRECT) INTERROGATIVE WORD

Relationships   The choice of which relative pronoun to use after a particular **noun** depends partly on the meaning of the **noun** itself, partly on the position which the **noun** 'shares' in the **relative clause**, and is partly a matter of style. These factors, as they affect each relative pronoun, are set out below.

MEANING OF MODIFIED NOUN	'SHARED POSITION' IN RELATIVE CLAUSE	STYLE
who mainly humans	Subject or object	any style
whom mainly humans	Objects only	formal style
whose anything	Possessive	any style
which non-humans	Subject or object	any style
that anything	Subject or object	any style
when period or moment	In adverbial phrase	any style
where area or position	In adverbial phrase	any style
why reason	In adverbial phrase	any style

In more complicated cases, the relative pronoun occurs in a short **phrase** introducing the **relative clause**. Here are some examples, with the short **phrases** containing relative pronouns underlined:

- *You are a person on whom I can rely.*
- *He found an envelope on the back of which someone had drawn a cat.*
- *We came to a field at the far corner of which stood a barn.*

The relative pronoun *that* cannot occur in any such **phrases** introducing **relative clauses**. If *that* is used, the **relative clauses** themselves are re-arranged in ways illustrated by the following, roughly paraphrasing the above.

- *You are a person that I can rely on.*
- *He found an envelope that someone had drawn a cat on the back of.*
- *We came to a field that a barn stood at the far corner of.*

(These are not very elegant.)

That is the only English relative pronoun that is not spelt with an initial *wh-*. It stands out from the others in other ways, too, described below.

Not every **relative clause** is introduced by a relative pronoun. The relative pronoun can be omitted altogether anywhere where *that* can be used, except when the 'shared' position inside the **relative clause** is the **subject** position. For example, all these **sentences** have **relative clauses** (underlined) with no introducing relative pronoun.

- *This is the man I met.*
- *This is the man I gave a book to.*
- *This is the man I took a picture of.*

In all these examples, one could use a *that* before the **relative clause**. Note that in *This is the man that saw me*, the relative pronoun cannot be omitted, giving *★This is the man saw me*.

Linguists make a distinction between 'restrictive' and 'non-restrictive' **relative clauses** (see RELATIVE CLAUSE). The relative pronoun *that* is the only one that cannot occur in 'non-restrictive' **relative clauses**. Compare these two examples, in the second of which there is an attempt to use *that* with a 'non-restrictive' **relative clause**.

1 *Bill, who had come earlier, was talking to Sue.*

2 *★Bill, that had come earlier, was talking to Sue.*

In some non-standard English **dialects**, *what* and *as* can be used as relative pronouns, as in *I met a bloke what owed me five quid* and *A man as I know grows carrots a yard long.*

For interest In English, there are some things which it is quite awkward to say with a relative clause, but where a relative clause still seems to be the most appropriate construction to use. In such rather complicated cases, speakers sometimes leave an extra pronoun inside the relative clause itself. Examples, with the 'extra' pronoun underlined, are:

219

- *There are lots of things in that cupboard that I don't know what <u>they</u> are.*
- *This is the man who Bill asked me if anyone knew <u>him</u>.*

Certainly these are not stylistically elegant, and are on the margins of standard English. Linguists call the 'extra' pronoun in such cases a 'resumptive pronoun'. Many languages make it a rule to use a resumptive pronoun inside all (or almost all) of their relative clauses. Here are some examples from Arabic:

il   walad illi šuf-t-u
the boy   that saw-I-him   (= the boy that I saw)

il   bint illi šuf-t-aha
the girl that saw-I-her   (= the girl that I saw)

il   fasatiin illi ištaree-t-hum
the dresses that bought-I-them   (= the dresses that I bought)

Exercise   Identify all the relative pronouns (used as such) in the following. There are six in all.

1 *I said that that was the one that I wanted.*
2 *When can you name a time when you'll be able to see me?*
3 *Who asked who had seen the secretary who just started this morning?*
4 *Which is the witch whose shoes Dorothy borrowed?*
5 *Whose shoes did Dorothy find at the spot where she landed?*
6 *Where is there a witch that I can rely on when I want one?*

Sentence

Explanation   In written English, a sentence begins with a capital letter and ends with either a full stop (period), a question mark (query) or an exclamation mark; a stretch of **words** that ends with a colon or semi-colon is also best regarded as a sentence, in which case the following sentence does not normally begin with a capital letter.

Punctuation is often used creatively, however, and there are many acknowledged uses of full stops, question marks, exclamation marks, colons and semi-colons for purposes other than marking the ends of sentences. So not everything that appears in writing between such punctuation marks is a sentence.

The sentence is the largest unit that traditional **grammar** deals with. **Grammar** books typically go into great detail about the formation of sentences and of the smaller units (such as **clauses** and **phrases**) that they contain, but say very little, if anything, about how sentences fit in with larger units such as paragraphs and chapters. Grammarians would point, with much justification, to the following two reasons why they concentrate on the structure of units at or below the level of the sentence.

- In any language, the rules for the formation of sentences and lower-level units (e.g. **clauses**, **phrases**) are clearer and more strictly applicable than rules relating to putting sentences together into larger units. In other words, **grammar** is (at least somewhat) more amenable to exact statements than is the study of style.

- The rules for the formation of sentences and smaller units differ markedly from one language to another (e.g. some languages put **verbs** at the beginnings of sentences, some put them in the middle, and some put them at the end), but the principles of good style are more uniform from one language to the next.

In recent years, there has been a countercurrent to these views, and the study of units larger than the sentence has begun to become articulated in more detail. But a general consensus remains that the sentence represents some kind of upper limit, or boundary between a field with rather clearly defined structures (i.e. **grammar**) and the study of style, discourse and conversation.

Examples   Here is a dialogue between two characters, Catherine and Raina. The speeches are made up partly of sentences and partly of other units, such as **phrases** and single **words**. Below, just the sentences are underlined.

> CATHERINE: *Raina – Raina – Why, where –*
> *Heavens! Child, are you out in the night air instead of in your bed?*
> *You'll catch your death. Louka told me you were asleep.*
>
> RAINA: *I sent her away. I wanted to be alone. The stars are so beautiful!*
> *What is the matter?*
>
> CATHERINE: *Such news. There has been a battle!*
> RAINA: *Ah!*
> CATHERINE: *A great battle at Slivnitza! A victory! And it was won by Sergius.*
> RAINA: *Ah! Oh, mother! Is father safe?*
>
> CATHERINE: *Of course: he sent me the news.*
> *Sergius is the hero of the hour, the idol of the regiment.*

Contrasts   Sentences contrast with **clauses**, **phrases** and single **words**. All four are significant units of the grammatical structure of languages, and the sentence is the largest of these, containing the other three. A sentence contains at least one **clause**; a **clause** contains at least one **phrase**; and a **phrase** contains at least one **word**.

Units of language larger than the sentence do exist, namely paragraphs, chapters, discourses and conversations, but these are all very loosely structured, by comparison with the grammatical units, sentence, **clause**, **phrase**, **word** (and **affix**).

Relationships   As the example above (which is quite true to life) shows, people do not always speak in sentences. The sentence is more adhered to as a unit of structure in written language, especially when authors are not making any attempt to imitate speech or thought.

The traditional definition of a sentence as 'expressing a single idea' is notoriously circular; no-one has a single reliable idea about how to identify 'a single idea'.

The shortest sentences consist of single **clauses**, which are, then, their **main clauses**. Any number of **main clauses** may be conjoined by coordinating **conjunctions** (*and*, *or* or *but*) to yield longer **compound** sentences, as in *Bill went, and we all laughed, but he came back, and we scowled*. Often, of course, many of the **conjunctions** except the last are omitted.

Since it contains at least one **main clause**, a sentence always contains at least one **finite verb**, and in most cases also (in English at least) a **subject**. A **main clause** may have any number of **subordinate clauses** successively embedded in it, as in *Mary said that I had told her that you wanted to try to persuade her to go with you*. This again yields potentially very long sentences. And the potential for unlimited recombination of conjoining and **subordination** creates the Byzantine complexity that we find in the sentences of the world's languages. Notice that, though sentences in a language may be very complex, this does not mean that the **grammar** of the language is necessarily complex. In the case of embeddings, all the **grammar** says is 'Embed any **clause** inside another (in any of a small number of specified ways).' This a not in itself a complicated statement; it just can lead to complicated results, rather as some very simple mathematical formulae can generate some extremely complex structures (e.g. fractals).

In spoken language, especially, people use sequences of **words** shorter than full sentences, but these can often be understood as if they had been reduced from full sentences by the process of **ellipsis**. Some of the non-sentences in the excerpt from the play above can reasonably be interpreted as full sentences, as shown below.

ELLIPTICAL NON-SENTENCE	INTERPRETATION AS A SENTENCE
Such news.	*There is such news!*
A great battle at Slivnitza!	*There has been a great battle at Slivnitza!*
A victory!	*There has been a victory!*
Of course:	*Of course father is safe.*

It is much harder, if not impossible, to suggest reasonable full-sentence interpretations for utterances such as *Raina – Raina – Why, where, Heavens!*, *Ah!* and *Oh, mother!*

Many languages provide a pair of special one-**word** sentences for giving **positive** or **negative** answers to questions. In English, these **words** are *Yes* and *No*. They are an exception to the general rule that sentences are made up of **clauses**. It does not seem sensible to try to find any **clause**-like structure, with **subject**, **verb**, etc. in *Yes* and *No*. (See **INTERJECTION**.)

For interest   We are encouraged to write in full sentences. In formal situations, such as giving a talk to an audience or at an interview, it is often thought desirable even to speak in complete sentences. But it is generally recognized that nobody speaks all the time in complete sentences. If, as traditional school grammar often insists, a sentence is the expression of a 'complete idea', presumably anyone who ever has a complete idea in their head somehow has something corresponding to a complete sentence in it. It is not hard to see how problematic this view is.

In many languages, including English, fully grammatical sentences are said, even by traditional grammarians, to omit elements which are 'understood'. Examples of such 'understood' elements are:

- the subjects of English imperative sentences (e.g. *Please go away*), understood as *you*;
- the subjects of many declarative sentences in Italian (e.g. *Ho invitato Giovanni* – (*I*) *have invited Giovanni* or *E venuta* – (*She*) *has come*), which can usually be interpreted either from the context of use or by the agreement features present on other parts of the sentence;
- the missing objects of English verbs like *smoke* and *drink*, as in *He smoked and she drank, but they both lived to a ripe old age*. These verbs are conventionally understood as having objects such as *cigarettes* and *alcohol*.

Now, if a sentence is supposed to 'express a complete idea', surely, in each of the cases just mentioned, since something essential to the understanding of the sentence has been left unexpressed, the constructions concerned cannot be full or proper sentences. But traditional grammar usually counts these as complete sentences. There is a traditional doublethink in saying a sentence expresses a complete idea, but that some parts of that idea, apparently, can simply be 'understood'.

Here are some extracts from a diary:

- *Got home at half-past three and went straight to bed. Woke up late with splitting headache and had to phone to cancel piano lesson. Mr Fifer not very pleased as this the third time this year.*

By the normal conventional definition of a sentence, there are no fully grammatical sentences in this excerpt. The stretch before the first full stop (period) has no subject for either of the verbs *got* and *went*. The stretch up to the second full stop is similarly lacking in subjects for its verbs *woke* and *had*. The stretch after that, to the end of the excerpt, though it has subjects (*Mr Fifer* and *this*), has no verbs: we understand some form of the verb *be* here. And yet this passage is as easily and completely understood as any passage made up of conventionally grammatical sentences.

Exercise In the following two passages, which of the stretches between full stops, colons, or semicolons are full sentences?

- *A squat grey building of only thirty-four storeys. Over the main entrance the words, CENTRAL LONDON HATCHERY AND CONDITIONING CENTRE, and, in a shield, the World State's motto, COMMUNITY, IDENTITY, STABILITY.*

- *I will tell you in a few words who I am: lover of the humming bird that darts to the flower beyond the rotted sill where my feet are propped; lover of bright needlepoint and the bright stitching fingers of humorless old ladies bent to their sweet and infamous designs; lover of parasols made from the same puffy stuff as a young girl's underdrawers; still lover of that small naval boat which somehow survived the distressing years of my life between her decks or in her pilothouse; and also lover of poor dear black Sonny, my mess boy, fellow victim and confidant, and of my wife and child. But most of all, lover of my harmless and sanguine self.*

Singular

Explanation   A singular **noun** or **pronoun** in a language typically refers to just one thing or person, or to a mass of stuff, rather than to a collection of things or people. Other **nouns** which occur in the same grammatical patterns as typical singular **nouns** may be classified as grammatically singular.

Examples   Some singular **nouns** in English are *waiter, inability, objection, cat, frostbite, garlic, refusal, gatepost, hair* and *region.*

The English **personal pronouns** *I, he, she* and *it* are singular.

Contrasts   Singular contrasts with **plural**. A **word** cannot simultaneously be both singular and **plural**.

Relationships   Singular and **plural** in a language belong to its system of **number**. It is common in languages for singular to be the unmarked member of the system, and for **plural nouns** to have some special marker, such as a **suffix**; this is true of English, where, for instance, the **noun** *dog* is singular, and its **plural** is formed by adding an *-s*. The singular is rarely formed by adding something in this way.

The basic **parts of speech** to which singular applies are **nouns** and **pronouns**; other **parts of speech** or **word**-classes may be marked as singular by **agreement** with a singular **noun** or **pronoun**. In English, only **verbs** and **demonstratives** show this **agreement**; *this* and *that* are singular **demonstratives**, and *is* and *was* are forms of the **verb** *be* which show singular **agreement**.

Among the **nouns, mass nouns** are always singular. So we may say *This stuff is sticky* and *That wine tastes of bananas*. **Count nouns** show the distinction between singular and **plural**. Thus we have **singular/plural** pairs such as *tree/trees, diagram/diagrams* and *burial/burials*. **Proper names** are almost always singular. Even **proper names** formed from **plural common nouns**, such as *the United States*, tend to be singular, as in *The United States is ready to defend its vital interests*.

The English **indefinite article** *a* is singular; the **definite article** *the* can be either **singular** or **plural**.

There are some **nouns** which are (or can be) singular, even though they refer to collections of people or things, which is what **plural nouns** usually do. Examples of such 'collective' **nouns** are *crowd, flock, group, committee, government* and *team*. There is a difference between American and British English here. In British English, **sentences** such as *The crowd <u>have</u> moved down the street* and *If the committee <u>vote</u> for change, I'll resign* are grammatical, if perhaps not preferred, but these are distinctly odd in American English. In American English, these **nouns** generally take singular **agreement** in **verbs**.

In English **compound nouns**, such as *paper weight, leg work, page turner, mountain climber* and *paperback writer*, the first **noun** is almost always singular. We don't call a person who climbs mountains a **mountains climber*.

Of the **numerals**, only the first, in English *one*, is singular, at least in meaning.

For interest

As implied just above, higher-valued numerals, such as English *ten, sixteen, forty* and *eight thousand*, are not singular in meaning. But in many languages (unlike the situation in English), such higher-valued numerals take a specifically singular noun. Even more curiously, perhaps, some languages use plural nouns with the first series of numerals, but then switch back to singular nouns for the higher numerals, which one might think were even less singular in meaning. Arabic is an example. It uses a plural noun after numerals from 3 to 10, and after that, for numerals from 11 upwards switches back to singular nouns.

> *talat rigaala*
> *three men*(PLUR) (= *three men*)
> *talatiin raagil*
> *thirty man*(SING) (= *thirty men*)

Exercise

Identify the singular nouns in the following. There are twenty-two in all, including proper names and nouns inside compound nouns.

> • *Two years have gone by since I finished writing the long story of how I, Tiberius Claudius Drusus Nero Germanicus, the cripple, the stammerer, the fool of the family, whom none of his ambitious and bloody-minded relatives considered worth the trouble of executing, poisoning, forcing to suicide, banishing to a desert island or starving to death – which was how they one by one got rid of each other – how I survived them all, even my insane nephew Gaius Caligula, and was one day unexpectedly acclaimed Emperor by the corporals and sergeants of the Palace Guard.*

Subject

Explanation   The subject of a **clause** or **sentence** is the **noun** or **noun phrase** that typically (but not in all cases) refers to the doer of the action expressed by a **transitive verb** in an **active sentence**, or to the main person or thing involved in the event or state expressed by an **intransitive verb**. With **transitive verbs** not expressing actions, the subject is the **noun** or **noun phrase** in an analogous position to the subjects of action-expressing **transitive verbs**.

The traditional definition of subject as referring to the 'doer of the action' (or 'agent'), though it is adequate for central or typical cases, will not work for all cases. For example, in **passive sentences**, such as *John was attacked*, the subject is *John*, but John is certainly not the 'doer' of the attacking. Again, not all **sentences**, even those with **transitive verbs**, express any action. Examples are *This book cost fifty francs* and *I loathe relativism*. But such **sentences** have always traditionally been held to have subjects (in these cases, *this book* and *I*).

Many languages have special grammatical rules that apply to the central cases of a **noun phrase** referring to the doer of an action expressed by a **transitive verb**. Often these same rules are also applied to a number of other cases of **noun phrases**, even though they do not refer to doers of any action. What we see, then (as so often in grammar) is a clustering of grammatical properties around a central or typical set of real-world circumstances (i.e. being the doer of an action), but with these grammatical properties extended beyond the central cases to other, rather different, sets of real-world circumstances. The **noun phrases** to which the rules typically affecting doers of actions apply are identified as 'subjects'.

Examples   In the following examples, the underlined **noun phrases** are the subjects of **main clauses**.

- *We believe these truths to be self-evident.*
- *All men are created equal.*
- *Has your old Ford broken down again?*
- *This book belongs to the Edinburgh City Library.*
- *Tragically, the wagon train was attacked by bandits.*
- *Nobody spoke.*

In the following examples, the underlined **noun phrases** are the subjects of **subordinate clauses**. (The subjects of the **main clauses** are not underlined.)

- *We never thought that John would do it.*
- *It is a pity that none of his friends could be here.*
- *When the red revolution comes, there'll be free beer for all the workers.*
- *This is the table that Napoleon used in St Helena.*

Contrasts   Subjects contrast with **direct** and **indirect objects**. A **noun phrase** which is the subject in a **clause** cannot be **direct** or **indirect object** in that **clause**.

Subject, **direct object** and **indirect object** all contrast with **part-of-speech** terms such as **noun**, **verb** and **adjective**. A particular **word** may be a **noun** or a **verb**, but this fact is not relative to any particular **clause**. But **nouns** and **noun phrases** are subjects and **objects** only in relation to particular **clauses**. 'Subject' is thus a relational term; a particular **noun** or **noun phrase** can be said to be the subject of a **clause**.

Relationships   In English, as in many languages, the subject is an obligatory element of a **clause**. With a few exceptions, mentioned below, every English **clause** must have an explicit subject.

English even uses 'empty' **words** as subjects. This happens in cases where there simply is no person or thing involved, as with some **sentences** describing the weather, such as *It is raining* and *It snowed yesterday*. The empty **pronoun** *it* is the subject of both these **sentences**.

The basic traditional division of a **clause** is into its subject and its **predicate**. In some views, at least, the **predicate** of a **clause** is everything in it except its subject, a view which emphasizes the primary importance of subjects in the structure of **sentences**.

The subjects of **clauses** are involved in a number of specific grammatical processes, of which the main ones are described below.

In English, **imperative sentences**, such as *Get lost!* and *Please stand aside*, have no overt subjects, although they have an 'understood' subject, referring to the hearer.

In English and many other languages, the **finite verb** in a **clause agrees** with the **subject** of the **clause**, as in *I am glad to hear it* and *Are you coming?*

In English, **interrogative sentences** are formed from **declaratives** by reversing the order of the subject and the first **auxiliary**, as in *Have the workmen been here today?*

The relationship between **active** and **passive clauses** crucially involves the subjects of both types of **clause**. The subject of an **active clause** is either omitted altogether from a corresponding **passive**, as in *John was attacked*, or found in a 'demoted' position, such as after the **preposition** *by*. The subject of a **passive clause** corresponds to the **object** in a corresponding **active clause**.

In English, the **infinitive** form of a **verb** often signals that its subject has either been omitted by some process rather like **ellipsis** or has been 'borrowed' into a neighbouring **clause**. Examples are:

John learned to swim.   SUBJECT OF *swim* OMITTED (John)
It is easy to annoy John.   SUBJECT OF *annoy* OMITTED (someone)
Mary was persuaded to marry John.   SUBJECT OF *marry* OMITTED (Mary)

With the **gerund** forms of **verbs** in English, the **noun phrase** which is understood as the subject of the **verb** occurs as a **possessive** or **possessive phrase**, as in *his* leaving town or *the milkman's* incessant yodelling.

Subject position in a **clause** is closely associated with **nominative case**. As some English **pronouns** have specific **nominative case** forms, e.g. *I*, *he*, *she*, *we*, *they*, these **pronouns** are, then, reserved for subject position.

For interest   Subject position in a clause is a very special position. In many languages, there are special processes applying just to the subjects of clauses. Some of these have been seen above, in connection with English. As the discussion showed, the subject of a clause does not always refer to the doer of some action. Linguists call the doer of an action the 'agent' of the action.

In English, subjects tend to come first in sentences, and in other languages, too, they often tend to have a prominent position. But there is another grammatical function reserved for the first position in sentences, which is distinct from 'subject'. Linguists call this function 'topic'. The topic of a sentence is what the sentence is about, and contrasts with the sentence's 'comment', which is the part which gives new information about the topic.

So now we have three different concepts, as follows:

- Agent: noun phrase referring to the 'doer of the action';
- Subject: noun phrase affected by a particular cluster of grammatical rules (such as omission in imperatives and agreement);
- Topic: noun phrase referring to the person or thing that the sentence is about, typically something mentioned before.

In the most bland everyday unremarkable sentences describing actions, these three concepts converge on a single noun phrase. So, for example, in *The farmer has killed the duckling*, the noun phrase *the farmer* is all three at once, for these reasons:

- Agent: because the farmer has done the killing;
- Subject: because *the farmer* is before the verb, *has*, which agrees with it;
- Topic: because the definite article *the* indicates that we know the farmer, and the sentence seems to be telling us something about him.

But agent, subject and topic are separate matters, and it is possible for the agent in a sentence to be distinct from the subject (and the topic). This is what typically happens in passive sentences. Here is an example, with the parts labelled:

SUBJECT
TOPIC   AGENT
The duckling was killed by the farmer.

It is possible for the subject of a sentence not to be its topic. Many dialects of English allow a noun phrase to be pulled to the front of a sentence, leaving the rest of the sentence intact (except for a pronoun or a 'gap' where the extracted noun phrase came from). Examples would be *Poor Mickey, he fell downstairs!*, and *That Brer Rabbit, he always tricks them*. In such sentences, topic and subject do not coincide, as shown by another labelled example, below.

SUBJECT

TOPIC   AGENT

The poor duckling, the nasty farmer killed it.

So far in these examples, subject has always coincided either with topic (in *The duckling was killed by the farmer*) or with agent (in *The poor duckling, the nasty farmer killed it*).

It is possible to have an example in which all three functions, agent, subject, and topic, are separate, as in:

TOPIC SUBJECT   AGENT

That poor duckling, it was killed by the farmer.

Exercise Identify the subjects in the following sentences, in both main and subordinate clauses. There are ten in all.

1 *After he had finished, she congratulated him.*
2 *This is the picture that Peter likes.*
3 *What did you say they wanted?*
4 *Her grandmother was a Stuart and her aunt won the Derby.*
5 *I know someone whose mother lives in Panama.*

Subjunctive

Explanation A subjunctive is a special form of a **verb** used in some languages to indicate a condition differing somehow from plain fact, such as a degree of uncertainty, or a hypothetical case, or a wished-for situation. French and German, for instance, have such forms. In English, there are a small number of cases where an unusual form of a **verb** is used to express some such non-factual situation, and these are also sometimes called 'subjunctives'. Grammarians agree, though, that the term 'subjunctive' is of quite limited use for describing English.

Examples In English, subjunctive forms occur (in what is perhaps becoming a rather old-fashioned style) in contexts such as:

EXAMPLES WITH SUBJUNCTIVES	(RATHER THAN)
The doctor recommended that I be excused work.	... I am ...
We suggest that you be more careful in future.	... you are ...
I insist that the students be notified of this error.	... the students are ...
Wash the wound carefully, lest it become infected.	... so that it does not become ...
If your father were here, he would be proud.	... your father was here ...

In French, some (**present tense**) subjunctive forms of the **verb** *être (to be)* are as follows, paired up with corresponding English subjunctive forms.

FRENCH	ENGLISH
je sois	*I be*
elle soit	*she be*
vous soyez	*you be*

Here is a German sentence containing two subjunctives (underlined).

Wenn Du ein Auto hättest, könnten wir Tante Maria besuchen
If   you a car   had,   could   we aunt Mary visit
(= *If you had a car, we could visit aunt Mary.*)

The corresponding non-subjunctive forms of these German **verbs** would be (*Du*) *hattest* and (*wir*) *konnten*, without the umlaut marks (the two dots over the vowel). As the English translation of this sentence makes clear, the corresponding English forms are not special in any way – they are not subjunctive.

Contrasts Subjunctive contrasts with **indicative**. The **indicative** form is the normal form for **verbs** in English; the use of the subjunctive is rare. Some contrastive examples are given below.

EXAMPLES WITH SUBJUNCTIVE	EXAMPLES WITH INDICATIVE
My lawyer insists that I be silent.	*My lawyer will insist that I am innocent.*
I suggest that you be careful.	*I suggest that you are ill.*
I recommend that he wear a toupee.	*I believe that he wears a toupee.*

In these examples, the use of the subjunctive is required in standard English to express hypothetical or **future** states of affairs introduced by **verbs** such as *insist*, *suggest* and *recommend*.

In other cases, the difference is a matter of style (formal versus informal); in the contrastive pairs below, the **sentence** with the subjunctive expresses the same thought as the **sentence** with the **indicative**, but more formally.

EXAMPLES WITH SUBJUNCTIVE	EXAMPLES WITH INDICATIVE
Whether it be fine or wet, he whistles.	*Whether it is fine or wet, he whistles.*
If your father were here, he would smile.	*If your father was here, he would smile.*

Relationships The English 'present' subjunctive (to the extent that it is used) is the bare form of the **verb**, with no ending, and thus shows no apparent **agreement** with its **subject**. For this reason, the English **present** subjunctive is only recognizably distinct from the **indicative** in two situations:

- with the **verb** *be* (which has distinctive **agreement** forms for various different **subjects**);
- with other **verbs**, only with 3rd **person singular subjects**. (**Verbs** with 3rd **person singular subjects** generally take an *-s* **suffix** in the **present tense**.)

An example of the latter type would be *I demand that he apologize*; other relevant examples were given above. But note that the term '**present**' is actually quite inappropriate to describe the meanings carried by these forms. In fact they express hypothetical or non-existent situations, and not situations that actually exist in the present. They are typically used with **verbs** expressing some kind of desire or intention about a future state of affairs, such as *demand*, *suggest*, *advise* and *recommend*.

As the English '**present**' subjunctive is the bare form of a **verb**, it is identical to the **infinitive**, but lacks the **word** *to* which marks **infinitives**. Even though it is a bare form of the **verb**, the subjunctive is a **finite** form of the **verb**, occurring in more or less the same general types of **subordinate clauses** as other **finite verbs**, e.g. after *that*, as in *I suggest that you <u>be</u> patient*.

The English '**present**' subjunctive of a **verb** also happens to be identical to its **imperative** form, having no ending at all.

English has a single **word** which grammarians call a '**past**' subjunctive. This is the **word** *were*, used with **singular subjects** in **conditional sentences** and also with the subordinating **conjunctions** *as if* and *as though* and a few **verbs** such as *suppose* and *imagine*. Examples are:

If I <u>were</u> you, I'd keep quiet about it.   *Imagine it <u>were</u> true.*
He acted as if he <u>were</u> my boss.   *Suppose he <u>were</u> a Martian, . . .*

Such examples with this subjunctive *were* are called 'counterfactual', because they always imply that the situation described is actually not the case. Thus, when I say *He acted as though he were my boss*, I imply that he is not my boss.

The subjunctive, along with its contrasting **verb** form, the **indicative**, is known as a **mood**. Although it is not very useful for English, we can talk of '**verbs** in the subjunctive **mood**' and '**verbs** in the **indicative mood**''.

For interest   Between the seventeenth and the twentieth century, the English subjunctive declined severely in use. This change (along with many other changes in grammar) can be seen by comparing versions of the Bible from the two periods.

In the 'Authorized King James' version of the English Bible, a translation dating from 1611, the subjunctive was used as the norm in finite clauses introduced by conjunctions such as *if*, *before*, *except*, *lest*, *though*, *that* (meaning *in order that*), and *till*. Note that all these conjunctions are typically used to introduce clauses expressing non-factual, e.g. conditional, hypothetical or future, propositions. Some examples are given below, paired with the corresponding translations from the modern 'Good News Bible', published in 1966 (New Testament) and 1976 (Old Testament). In these passages, the subjunctives in the King James version are underlined.

Here are some quotations (with subjunctives underlined) from Christ's words just before his arrest.

KING JAMES VERSION, 1611	GOOD NEWS BIBLE, 1966
Before the cock <u>crow</u>,	*Before the cock crows tonight,*
thou shalt deny me thrice.	*you will say three times that you do not know me.*
O my Father, if it <u>be</u> possible,	*My Father, if it is possible,*
let this cup pass from me:	*take this cup of suffering from me.*

And here is how the 127th Psalm begins in the two versions (subjunctives again underlined).

KING JAMES VERSION, 1611	GOOD NEWS BIBLE, 1976
Except the Lord <u>build</u> the house,	*If the Lord does not build the house,*
they labour in vain that build it:	*the work of the builders is useless.*
Except the Lord <u>keep</u> the city,	*If the Lord does not protect the city,*
the watchman waiteth but in vain.	*it is useless for the sentries to stand guard.*

Exercise Identify the verbs in the subjunctive form in the following examples. There are five of them altogether.

1 *Lodge suggested that White show it in strict confidence to Balfour, Clemenceau, and Nitti.*
2 *If music be the food of Love, play on!*
3 *I wish I were dead.*
4 *Although it was quite dark, he was driving as though it were broad daylight.*
5 *Some pundits on style prescribe that one use the subjunctive in contexts such as this.*

Subordinate clause

Explanation A subordinate clause is a **clause** inside another **clause**, usually playing some role, such as **object** or **modifier**, in the containing **clause**. In English there are three main types of subordinate clause:

1 **Complement clauses**: a **complement clause** acts as the **subject** or **direct object** of the **verb** in its containing **clause**.
2 **Relative clauses**: a **relative clause modifies** a **noun** in its containing **clause**.
3 Adverbial **clauses**: an adverbial **clause modifies** the **verb** in the containing **clause** or the whole containing **clause** itself.

Examples Examples of the three main types of English subordinate clause are given below, in the contexts of containing **main clauses**. The subordinate clauses themselves are underlined; there are some double underlinings, showing one subordinate clause inside another.

- **Complement clauses**:
  - *Some people claim <u>that Ancient Egyptians visited America</u>.*
  - *Everyone expected <u>Dan to resign</u>.*
  - *Would you like <u>me to arrange <u>for you to be met by a taxi</u></u>?.*
- **Relative clauses**:
  - *The man <u>who shot Liberty Valance</u> never existed.*
  - *Nobody doublecrossed the crooks <u>that Al Capone hung out with</u>.*
  - *These are the people*
    <u>on whose efforts the success <u>that has been achieved</u> is founded</u>.

- Adverbial **clauses**:
  - *While we are waiting, you can make me a cup of tea.*
  - *Please describe, as if you were directing a stranger, the route to Old College.*
  - *There is a civil war where I was stationed when I was in the army.*

Finally, here is an example of a **complement clause** inside a **relative clause** inside an adverbial **clause**:

- *As we trusted the man who told us Ned Barney was dead,*
  we printed the obituary.

Contrasts   Subordinate clauses contrast with **main clauses**. Every **sentence** has at least one **main clause**, but there can be (simple) **sentences** without any subordinate clauses at all. A **main clause** can contain a subordinate clause, but not vice-versa.

Subordinate clauses contrast with coordinate **clauses**, that is whole **clauses** joined together by a coordinating **conjunction**, such as *and*, *or* or *but*. Coordinate **clauses** are **clauses** placed side by side; subordinate clauses are **clauses** placed inside other **clauses**.

Subordinate clauses, as **clauses**, contrast with **sentences** (which contain **clauses**), and with **phrases** (which **clauses** contain).

Relationships   In general, there is relatively little restriction on which kinds of subordinate clauses can occur inside which other types. A general restriction involves excessive complexity of nested subordinate clauses at the front or in the middle of **sentences**. For example, in the **sentence** below, there are two **complement clauses** (underlined) inside each other at the beginning of the **sentence**.

- *That for John to leave was a pity was agreed by all.*

This **sentence** is hard to understand, but it can be done, if one thinks about it in the right frame of mind, and imagines the right intonation. But the following alternative, which means the same thing, and has the **complement clauses** accumulated at the other end of the **sentence**, is much more straightforward to understand.

- *It was agreed by all that it was a pity for John to leave.*

Subordinate clauses typically have most of the main components of any **clause**, e.g. a **verb**, a **subject**, and perhaps **objects** and other parts.

The essential **clause** components, the **verb** and the **subject** in particular, may take somewhat different forms in a subordinate clause from the forms they take in a corresponding **main clause**. For example, non-**finite** forms of **verbs**, such as **infinitives** and **participles**, are typical of subordinate clauses.

In English, most subordinate clauses are introduced by a characteristic introducing **word**, which gives a clue to the type of subordinate clause involved. For example:

- **Complement clauses** are introduced by subordinating **conjunctions** or 'complementizers', such as *that*.
- **Relative clauses** are introduced by **relative pronouns**, such as *who, which* and *that*.
- Adverbial **clauses** are introduced by other subordinating **conjunctions**, such as *when, after, if, since* and *because*.

There is also a parallelism between the three main types of subordinate clause mentioned and particular **parts of speech**. Thus

- **Complement clauses** are parallel to **nouns** or **noun phrases**, in that they can be **subjects** and **direct** or **indirect objects** of their containing **clauses**.
- **Relative clauses** have an adjectival function, in that both **relative clauses** and **adjectives modify nouns,** and restrict their meanings in similar ways.
- Adverbial **clauses** have an obvious similarity to single-**word adverbs** in that both the single **words** and the **clauses** can **modify** whole **clauses**, or **verb phrases**.

Note that, interestingly, there is no type of subordinate clause which in any way parallels the **verbs**.

Exercise Identify all the subordinate clauses in the following. There are two in each example, including subordinate clauses inside other ones.

1 *The girl I spoke to said it was raining in Glasgow.*
2 *I expected it to be where I had left it.*
3 *When you come, can you bring that book that I lent you.*
4 *The rules permit members whose spouses have died to pay half-fees.*
5 *As he had brought his suitcase, we expected that he would stay.*
6 *The old man that Eve objected to because he swore is actually quite nice.*

Suffix

Explanation A suffix is an **affix** attached after the stem of a **word**. A **word** may contain several suffixes, in which case they follow each other at the end of the **word**.

Examples Here are some English suffixes, with examples of the **words** in which they occur.

SUFFIX	EXAMPLES
-ed (PAST TENSE)	*talked, hummed, shouted*
-s (PLURAL)	*cats, dogs, horses*
-'s (POSSESSIVE)	*Bert's, London's, church's*
-s (3RD PERSON SINGULAR)	*talks, hums, hisses*
-ing	*coming, going*
-er (COMPARATIVE)	*happier, stiffer, softer*

-er (AGENT)	*writer, reader, diver*
-ness	*happiness, fruitfulness*
-al (NOUN-FORMING)	*dismissal, arrival, recital*
-al (ADJECTIVE-FORMING)	*practical, feudal, musical*
-ic	*cyclic, psychic*
-able, -ible	*readable, inevitable, responsible, edible*
-ful	*fruitful, careful*
-less	*careless, harmless*
-ize	*organize, sodomize, proselytize, propagandize*
-ate	*decimate, estimate, designate, asphyxiate*

Contrasts   A suffix is a kind of **affix**, so suffixes contrast with **words**. A suffix cannot stand 'free' on its own, without the support of a **word** (or stem) to which it is attached. Suffixes contrast with **words** in a further respect, in that suffixes are never complex, i.e. composed of further parts; a suffix, like any **affix**, is a single 'atomic' element, whereas some (but not all) **words** are clearly composed of several parts, some of which may well be suffixes.

Suffixes contrast with **prefixes** in their position of attachment; **prefixes** go at the front of a **word**, and suffixes at the end.

Relationships   Suffixes, like **affixes** generally, tend to separate into two rather different kinds.

1 Inflections: inflectional suffixes have several typical characteristics.

(a) They are closely intertwined with aspects of the **grammar** of whole **sentences**, for example by being involved in the **agreement** of **subject** and **verb**, like English 3rd **person singular** -*s*, or by being used in particular grammatical forms, like English -*ing*, used to form the **progressive**, or the -*er* used in **comparative** constructions.

(b) Inflections are also typically fairly productive, or **regular**. If a particular inflectional suffix can occur on one **word** of a particular **part of speech**, it can usually occur on all (or most) other **words** of that **part of speech**. For example, English -*ing* and 3rd **person singular** -*s* can occur on all **main verbs**.

(c) Inflections typically do not change the **part of speech** of the **word** they are attached to. For example, *talk, talks* and *talking* are all **verbs**.

2 **Word**-forming suffixes (called 'derivational' suffixes by linguists): typical characteristics are these:

(a) They are not heavily involved in the **sentence**-forming rules of **grammar**. For instance, the fact that some English **noun** happens to be formed with -*al* or -*ance* or -*ment* is not relevant to how that **noun** fits into **sentences** – all that matters is that it is a **noun**. There are, for example, no special **agreement** rules affecting only **nouns** ending in the suffix -*al*.

(b) **Word**-forming suffixes are erratic and unpredictable in the **words** to which they can be attached. For example, English -*al* can be attached to form **nouns** from *arrive, approve, deny* and *retrieve*, but not from the very similar-sounding **verbs** *connive, prove, reply* and *receive*; **connival, *proval, *replial* and **receival* do not exist (instead, we have *connivance, proof, reply* and *receipt*, amply demonstrating how quirky these **word**-formation processes are). **Word**-forming suffixes also quite often have an effect on the pronunciation of the stem to which they are attached. Thus, for example, the letter '*c*' in *music* is pronounced as a '*k*', but in *musician* it is pronounced like '*sh*'; the letter '*c*' is pronounced as a '*k*' in *electric*, but as an '*s*' in *electricity*; the first vowel in *nation* is not the same as the corresponding vowel in *national*.

(c) **Word**-forming suffixes often change the **part of speech** of the **word** to which they are attached. For example, one kind of *-al* changes a **verb** to a **noun**, as in *arrive – arrival, approve – approval, deny – denial, retrieve – retrieval*, and another kind of *-al* changes a **noun** to an **adjective**, as in *office – official, cause – causal, intention – intentional, nation – national*.

Suffixes of both kinds can pile up on each other, but when they do, the inflectional suffixes always go after the **word**-forming suffixes. This ordering, and the composition of some complex **words** with suffixes is show by underlining in the examples below.

nationalities	nation — al — ity — s
fictionalizing	fiction — al — ize — ing
facilitated	facile — it — ate — ed

Of course, both suffixes and **prefixes** can occur on the same **word**, as in *prevaricated, posthumously, disenfranchised* and *disconfirmation*.

Exercise Identify all the suffixes in the following words. There are ten in all. (Some of them are slightly modified in shape by their surroundings.)

1 *conclusions.*
2 *indebtedness.*
3 *terrorized.*
4 *unreasonableness.*
5 *neo-colonialism.*

Superlative

Explanation The superlative is a form of an **adjective** or **adverb**, expressing a value at the extreme limit of its normal meaning, in some assumed context. In English, superlative **adjectives** and **adverbs** are either marked by the **suffix** *-est* or preceded by the **word** *most*.

Examples *Brightest, tallest, warmest, nastiest, most delightful, most suspicious, most user-friendly, most happily* and *fastest* are all superlatives in English.

Contrasts Superlatives contrast primarily with **comparatives** and the basic forms of **adjectives** and **adverbs**. The three kinds of terms make a natural progression, as in:

BASIC	COMPARATIVE	SUPERLATIVE
big	*bigger*	*biggest*
tight	*tighter*	*tightest*
expensive	*more expensive*	*most expensive*
glamorous	*more glamorous*	*most glamorous*

Relationships Only **adjectives** and **adverbs**, and not all of them, have superlative forms. Other **parts of speech**, such as **nouns**, **verbs** and **prepositions**, do not have superlative forms.

The **adjectives** and **adverbs** that have superlative forms are those indicating some scale along which there can be variation, a scale which is implied to have extreme ends. It is such extreme ends of a scale that are indicated by superlatives. Thus **adjectives** with familiar superlative forms include *hot/hottest, cold/coldest, short/shortest, dark/darkest, heavy/heaviest* and *light/lightest*.

On the other hand, **adjectives** which do not indicate scales, and which therefore do not have superlative forms in normal use, include *French, mineral, primary, legal, interstellar, wooden, unique* and *identical*. Hypothetical superlatives of these, such as *Frenchest, ?most French, *most mineral, *most primary, ?most legal, *most interstellar, *most wooden, ?most unique* and *most identical* are only used, if at all, in ways which stretch the normal meanings of the **adjectives** concerned. Something is either primary or it is not, and to say something is 'most primary' is to stretch the meaning of the **word**. Likewise, something is either identical to something else or it is not, and to use the hypothetical form *most identical* would seriously stretch the usual meaning of *identical*.

Generally, if an **adjective** or **adverb** has a superlative, it also has a **comparative**.

Superlative **adjectives**, when used before a **noun**, are almost always used with the **definite article**, as in *the finest tobacco, the shortest route to India* and *the worst day of my life*. The use of superlatives with **indefinite** expressions, as in *?some finest tobacco*, *a shortest route to India* and *a worst day of my life*, is decidedly odd.

The **definite article** can be left out, but still seems to be implied, when superlatives occur after the **verb** be, as in *This tobacco is (the) finest, This route is (the) shortest* or *That day was (the) worst*.

This connection of superlatives with **definiteness** is natural, since superlatives indicate an extreme end of a scale, and typically such scales have only one clear extremity, which is thus unique.

When, occasionally, an **indefinite** is used with a superlative, as in, for example *I saw a most interesting programme on the television* or *Harriet is a most delightful person*, the meaning is rather different, and the **word** *most* is being used as a rough synonym of *very*. There is a subtle difference (say for a teacher writing

237

a school report) between *Daniel is a most energetic boy* and *Daniel is the most energetic boy*. Notice that you cannot say *Daniel is a most energetic boy of all, whereas *Daniel is the most energetic boy of all* is fine.

In their tendency to occur with **definite** expressions, superlatives are like **ordinal numerals**, which also tend strongly to occur with **definites**. The similarity between superlative and **ordinals** goes further, in that they can occur in a very similar range of positions, as shown below.

EXAMPLE WITH SUPERLATIVE	EXAMPLE WITH ORDINAL NUMERAL
the <u>best</u> three entries	the <u>first</u> three entries
the three <u>best</u> entries	the three <u>first</u> entries
That entry was (the) <u>best</u>.	That entry was (the) <u>first</u>.
Judith performed <u>best</u>.	Judith performed <u>first</u>.

Whether the superlative of an **adjective** or **adverb** is formed with the **suffix** *-est* or by the **word** *most* in front of it is largely a matter of the length of the **word** in syllables. The rough rule, to which there are exceptions, is that all one-syllable **words** and some two-syllable **words** can take the **suffix** *-est*, whereas longer **words** must form their superlatives with *most*. Here are some examples:

	BASIC WORD	SUPERLATIVE
ONE SYLLABLE	old	oldest
	young	youngest
	fresh	freshest
TWO SYLLABLES	juicy	juiciest
	simple	simplest
	modern	most modern (not *modernest)
	careless	most careless (not *carelessest)
MORE SYLLABLES	democratic	most democratic (not *democraticest)
	horrible	most horrible (only jokingly *horriblest)

In English, there are a few irregular superlatives, such as *best* (from *good*), *worst* (from *bad*), *eldest* (from *old* used of people) and *innermost, outermost, leftmost* and *rightmost* (from the basic **adjectives** *inner, outer, left* and *right*).

For interest Some languages don't have superlatives or don't distinguish the superlative from the comparative. French barely distinguishes the superlative from the comparative. To form a superlative, French adds a marker of definiteness (a definite article) to its comparative, as shown.

un marchand plus riche
a   merchant more rich   (= *a richer merchant*)

le   marchand le   plus riche
the merchant the more rich   (= *the richest merchant*)

Il   est plus riche
He is more rich   (= *He is richer.*)

Il   est le plus riche
He is the more rich   (= *He is the richest.*)

Exercise   Identify the superlatives in the following passages. There are six in all.

- *In the second century of the Christian aera, the empire of Rome comprehended the fairest part of the earth, and the most civilized portion of mankind.*
- *One of the most fateful errors of our age is the belief that 'the problem of production' has been solved.*
- *Idle reader, you can believe without any oath of mine that I would wish this book, as the child of my brain, to be the most beautiful, the liveliest and the cleverest imaginable.*

Tense

Explanation   The different tense forms of **verbs** are forms used primarily to express the time at which an event occurred, or at which some state of affairs held.

It is conventional, in everyday talk about language, to assume that there are just three basic tenses, namely **past**, **present** and **future**. But when one looks at the different ways in which languages express distinctions related to time, one generally finds a more complicated picture, and often a picture that does not reflect the simple **past/present/future** division.

Traditional grammarians and modern linguists have approached this complicated area of languages with slightly different terminological conventions. What many traditional grammarians label as various kinds of 'tense', modern linguists split into two different ideas, namely:

- Tense, which is strictly to do with WHEN something happened or was the case;
- Aspect, which is concerned with factors such as the DURATION or COMPLETENESS of events and states of affairs.

For English, this difference of terminology comes out mainly in relation to the **perfect** and the **progressive**, which many traditional grammarians would treat as part of the system of tense, but modern linguists treat as belonging to the system of aspect.

In this dictionary, we keep to the traditional grammarian's terminology. But 'tense' is an area in which the traditional terminology is indeed quite crude. The more modern distinction between **tense** and aspect is a valuable refinement, and advanced detailed work on languages must make this distinction.

Examples   English has just two simple tenses (**present** and **past**), plus **compound** tenses for **perfect**, **progressive** and **future**. The English **compound** tenses always combine with one or the other of the simple tenses, **present** or **past**. In addition, these **compound** tenses can combine with each other to form even more complex tense forms. This is illustrated below, with variants (3rd **person singular**) of the verb *go*.

SIMPLE TENSES

PRESENT	*goes*
PAST	*went*

PRIMARY COMPOUND TENSES

	PRESENT	PAST
PERFECT	*has gone*	*had gone*
PROGRESSIVE	*is going*	*was going*
FUTURE	*will go*	*would go*

COMBINATIONS OF TWO COMPOUND TENSES

PAST PERFECT PROGRESSIVE	*had been going*
FUTURE PERFECT	*will have gone*
FUTURE PROGRESSIVE	*will be going*

COMBINATION OF THREE COMPOUND TENSES

FUTURE PERFECT PROGRESSIVE	*will have been going*

Contrasts
Tense contrasts with 'voice' (**active/passive**), although both are variant formations of **verbs**. Tense is primarily a matter of the time at which an event occurred, whereas voice is a matter of whether the focus of attention is on the doer of the action (the 'agent') or on its recipient.

Tense contrasts with **mood** (**indicative/subjunctive**). **Mood** typically has to do, not with time, but with the degree of certainty with which some statement is expressed.

As mentioned above, tense contrasts, for modern linguists, with 'aspect'. Tense involves the basic location in time of an event or state of affairs, in relation to the time of speaking (or writing), while aspect relates more to the internal nature of events and states of affairs, such as whether they are (or were) finished, long-lasting, instantaneous, repetitive, the beginning of something, the end of something, and so on.

Tense contrasts with **person** (1st/2nd/3rd), **number** (**singular/plural**) and **gender** (masculine/feminine/neuter). Although **verbs** in many languages may be marked for some or all of these, they essentially arrive on the **verb** by the process of **agreement**, typically having their origin in the **subject** of the **clause**. But tense markings primarily 'start' on **verbs**.

Relationships
In all languages, tense involves primarily the **verbs**, and in most languages it involves only the **verbs**. In some languages, there are, for example, **adjectives** that carry tense.

The distinction between simple and **compound** tenses corresponds to the distinction between **affixes** and **words**. A simple tense form of a **verb** is a single **word**, usually augmented by a **suffix** (less often a **prefix**). A **compound** tense form consists of several **words**, at least one of them an **auxiliary**. The work done by the **affix** in a simple tense form and the **auxiliary** in a **compound tense** form is broadly the same; it expresses some distinction in the general area of time.

Tense and voice (**active/passive**) typically combine freely with each other. Here are some English examples:

	ACTIVE	PASSIVE
SIMPLE PAST	*took*	*was taken*
PRESENT PERFECT	*had taken*	*had been taken*
FUTURE PROGRESSIVE	*will be taking*	*will be being taken*

What is potentially confusing here is the fact that English, like many European languages, uses the **past participle** (e.g. *taken*) both for the **perfect** (a **compound** tense) and for the **passive** voice. Note that the English **passive** is formed in a way quite parallel to the formation of **compound** tenses, i.e. with an **auxiliary** and a **participle**. But, of course, **passive** is not a tense.

In languages which make distinctions of **mood**, such as the **indicative/ subjunctive** distinction in French, tense interacts in a somewhat limited way with **mood**. Often, there are fewer different tense forms in the **subjunctive mood** than in the **indicative mood**.

For interest Different languages have different numbers of tenses. The range of English tenses was shown above. French has five simple tenses in the indicative mood and two in the subjunctive mood (thus seven simple tenses in all), plus another seven corresponding (perfect) compound tenses. Chinese has no tenses at all.

How does a language manage with no tenses? Often, the context alone is enough to make it clear whether the speaker is referring to the past, the present, or the future. But when there is need to be more clear or specific, Chinese can use adverbs, like English *yesterday*, *today* and *tomorrow* to express the necessary distinctions. Note how the verb *lái* in the following three examples stays the same, even though it clearly indicates different times, past, present and future.

wǒ zuótiān   lái
I   yesterday come   (= I came yesterday.)

wǒ jīntian lái
I   today   come   (= I am coming today.)

wǒ míngtiān lái
I   tomorrow come   (= I will come tomorrow.)

(These examples are from modern standard Chinese, previously called 'Mandarin'.)

Exercise Given below are five example English sentences. Each one uses a different tense, sometimes a simple tense and sometimes a compound tense. The five tenses used are simple present, simple past, future, present perfect and future perfect progressive. Match the examples with these tenses. (Pay attention only to the forms of the verbs – do not be distracted by other words in the sentences.)

1 *Sue will be fifty next year.*
2 *Robin has won more games than Louise.*
3 *The Dodgers play the Giants on Thursday.*
4 *Next month, we will have been dating each other for seven months.*
5 *It all began last summer.*

Transitive

Explanation   A transitive **verb** is one which takes a **(direct** or **indirect) object**. So typically, in English, a transitive **verb** is followed by a **noun phrase**. (In English, a transitive **verb** can never take an **indirect object** on its own; if an **indirect object** is present, so is a **direct object**.)

Examples   Some English transitive **verbs** are *hit, see, kiss, hear, know, arrange, believe, put off, postpone, include, make, give, keep* and *burn*.

Contrasts   Transitive **verbs** contrast with **intransitive verbs**, which do not take **objects**. The contrast between transitive and **intransitive** is generally restricted to **verbs**.

Transitive **verbs** contrast with the **verb** *be* and other **copular verbs**. Although *be* and **copular verbs** may also have a **noun phrase** after them, as in *Geraldine is a bright student*, or *It seems a pity*, such **noun phrases** are not held to be the **direct objects**, but rather the **complements** of these **verbs**.

Relationships   Sometimes the **direct objects** of transitive **verbs** can be omitted, as in *Can you see?* or *They can't hear* or *I know*. In these cases, it is usually possible to interpret an understood object from the context, so the **sentences** just mentioned might be understood as, for example, *Can you see it?* or *They can't hear you* or *I know what you have in mind*. This distinguishes genuinely transitive **verbs** from **intransitive** ones, where there is no possibility of filling in any understood **object** in this way. For example, if you hear *Can she go?*, you don't understand **Can she go something?*, because *go* is not a transitive **verb**. (This and other cases of 'amphibious **verbs**' (**verbs** which can appear in both transitive and **intransitive** guise) are also discussed under INTRANSITIVE.)

There are two main kinds of transitive **verb**, called 'monotransitive' and 'ditransitive'. As these labels suggest, the difference has to do with how many objects the **verbs** take. A ditransitive **verb** can take two **objects**, one **direct** and one **indirect**, as in *Evie bought Edward a kitten* or *Stefano set Evie a good example*. Often, in such examples in English, the **indirect object**, but not the **direct object** can be omitted, giving, for example, *Evie bought a kitten* or *Stefano set a good example*. A monotransitive **verb** can only take a single **object**, a **direct** one, as in *Wellington thrashed Bonaparte* or *Edith unwrapped the parcel*.

Verbs fall into different subclasses, according to what other main parts of a **clause** must, or may, occur with them. The difference between monotransitive and ditransitive **verbs** is an instance of this. Another subclass of transitive verbs, sometimes called 'locative' **verbs**, includes the **verb** *put*, which requires both a **direct object** and a **prepositional phrase** expressing some location in space, as in *Hannah put the lasagna in the oven* or *Michael put his thesis in the dustbin.* Neither **Hannah put the lasagna* (which omits the locative **phrase**) nor **Michael put in the dustbin* (which omits the **direct object**) is grammatical.

The **direct object** of certain transitive **verbs** can be another **clause** embedded in the larger one containing the **verb**. Examples of such transitive **verbs** are *know, say, explain, report,* and *hear,* as in *Masha knew it was dangerous* and *Sasha heard that Yeltsin had dissolved parliament.*

In most languages, including English, only transitive **verbs** are found in **passive clauses**. In English, **passive clauses** involve putting what would normally (in an **active clause**) be the **direct object** of the **verb** in the **subject** position, and using the **past participle** of the **verb**, as in *The lasagna was put in the oven (by Hannah)* or *The parcel was unwrapped (by Edith).*

Some English **verbs**, many of them transitive, consist of two **words**, of which the second can often also be used as a **preposition**. Examples are *pick up, take out, fence off* and *push over.* These transitive **verbs** can be split, or interrupted by their **direct objects**, as in *Hamish picked his suitcase up* or *The cats have pushed the bookends over.* Such **verbs** are known as 'phrasal **verbs**'.

Such phrasal **verbs** are slightly different from another kind of two-**word verbs**, such as *look for, look at, listen to* and *consist of.* These cases can be analysed either as two-**word** transitive **verbs** or as one-**word intransitive verbs** which insist on being followed by particular kinds of **prepositional phrase**. The difference between these **verbs** and the phrasal **verbs** is that the **preposition**-like **word** (e.g. *up, over, to, of*) cannot be separated from its **verb**. So you can't say, for example, **Sasha was listening the radio to* or **The lesson today consists three parts of.*

Because of the ways in which English **interrogative sentences** and **relative clauses** are formed, transitive **verbs** in these constructions can sometimes appear without a following **noun phrase**. Examples are:

- *What are you reading?*
- *Who did you see?*
- *That is the book that I am reading.*
- *That is the person I saw.*

In these examples, the **verbs** *read* and *see* are still transitive, because these constructions are formed by regular processes which move or omit whole **noun phrases** from their normal positions in **clauses**.

Transitive **verbs** can occur in all the usual different forms of **verbs**, including **finite** forms (those with markers of **tense** and **agreement**) and non-finite forms (such as **participles, infinitives** and **gerunds**).

Exercise Identify the transitive verbs in the following. There are nine altogether.

1 *Katy flunked her German course.*
2 *Wesley wouldn't hurt a fly.*
3 *I found her raiding the ice box.*
4 *I told John not to tease his sister so.*
5 *Your lawyer will brief you about what to tell the judge.*
6 *Celia was judged best hockey player in her year.*

Verb

Explanation The most typical verbs are **words** expressing actions or states. A verb is usually the conceptually most important **word** in a **clause**, and there is almost always exactly one (**main**) **verb** per **clause**. Less typical verbs may express meanings such as events, habits, tendencies, and relationships between people and things.

Examples Examples of English verbs are: *run, sleep, buy, sell, eat, drink, marry, adjudicate, think, open, shut, expect, consolidate, do, organize, know, believe, own, belong* and *be*.

Contrasts Verb is a **part of speech**, and so verbs contrast with other **parts of speech** such as **nouns**, **adjectives** and **prepositions**. If a **word** in a given **sentence** is a verb, it cannot simultaneously belong to any other **part of speech**.

Verb and **noun** are the two most basic **parts of speech**, in any language. Languages tend to sort many of their **words** into groups which either typically refer to actions and states (these are the verbs) or typically to concrete objects (these are the **nouns**). The contrast between **nouns** and verbs is the most basic **part of speech** contrast in any language.

In English, because of its lack of a rich system of endings on verbs and other **words**, the same written form may often belong to two different **parts of speech** (but not, of course, used in the same **sentence**). For example, *list* is a verb in *Please will you list all your belongings on this sheet*; but *list* is a **noun** in *He gave me a long list of his troubles*. Likewise, *comfort* is a verb in *It is a nurse's job to comfort the sick*; but *comfort* is a **noun** in *I did it in the comfort of my home*.

Relationships The same verb may occur in different (though usually very similar) forms, due to variation according to such factors as **tense**. Thus, the separate forms on each line below are forms of the same basic verbs.

alphabetize, alphabetizing, alphabetized, alphabetizes
send, sending, sent, sends
write, writing, wrote, written, writes
be, being, was, were, been, am, is, are

A grammarian might say, for example, that *send* and *sent* are 'different forms of the same verb'. And similarly, *is* and *were* would be said to be 'forms of the verb *be*'.

In English, and in many other languages, there is a small subclass of **verbs** which may act as **auxiliaries**. **Auxiliary verbs** are 'helping' verbs used to indicate shades of meaning (such as **past**, **present** or **future** time, or possibility or necessity) on other, '**main**' verbs. In English, the various forms of *be* and *have* and the **modal verbs** can act as **auxiliaries**, although *be* and *have*, in particular, can also act as **main verbs**. Where a verb is the only verb in its **clause**, it is a **main verb**. On the other hand, an **auxiliary** verb is almost always one of at least two verbs in a **clause**. Here are examples with the **main** and **auxiliary verbs** underlined in their respective columns.

MAIN VERB	AUXILIARY VERB
We always <u>buy</u> a Sunday paper.	We <u>haven't</u> bought a paper for weeks.
I <u>dream</u> of Jeanie.	I <u>am</u> dreaming of a white Christmas.
We <u>had</u> muffins for tea.	We <u>have</u> had muffins every day.

Verbs in English may be **finite** or non-**finite**. A **finite** verb shows **agreement** with the **subject** of its **clause**, and may be marked to indicate **tense**, whereas a non-**finite** verb does neither of these things. Non-**finite** forms of verbs include **infinitives** and **participles**. Here are some examples with the same **verbs** (underlined) in both **finite** and non-**finite** forms.

FINITE	NON-FINITE
He <u>plagiarized</u> his essay.	He was foolish to <u>plagiarize</u> his essay.
The sun <u>sank</u> in the West.	The sun was <u>sinking</u> in the West.
I <u>am</u> not a proud man.	I used to <u>be</u> a proud man.

Verbs have an important influence on the overall shape of their **clauses**. **Main verbs** can be grouped into subtypes, according to what other parts of a **clause** they require to be present. The main traditional division is into **intransitive** and **transitive**. An **intransitive** verb is one which takes no grammatical **object** of any kind, such as the verbs *sleep, die, come, fall* and *sneeze*. A **transitive** verb is one which takes a grammatical **object**, and perhaps even two (a **direct object** and an **indirect object**); examples of **transitive** verbs are *kill, share, read, devour* and *befriend*. In fact many further important distinctions between types of verb may be made on the basis of what other parts of a **clause** they require or are permitted to occur with. A few examples of these further subdivisions of the class of verbs are given below.

- Verbs which may take a **subordinate clause** expressing some proposition and beginning with the **word** *that*: these include verbs such as *say, believe, think, declare, expect* and *persuade*.
- 'Weather' verbs, whose **subject** in English is always the **impersonal pronoun** *it*: these include the verbs *rain, snow* and *drizzle*.
- Verbs which can take an **adverb** of manner, such as *put, see, disintegrate, arrive*. (Some other verbs, such as *belong*, cannot occur with an **adverb** of manner.)

- Verbs which can occur in the **passive** form, such as *drive, take, write, break* and *give*. These are a subset of the **transitive** verbs. (Some **transitive** verbs which do not occur in the **passive** form are *cost* and *weigh*, as in the ungrammatical **Six kilos are weighed by this cat.*)
- 'Collective' verbs whose **subjects** must be **plural** (or be understood as **plural**), such as the **intransitive** verb *gather* as in *The storm clouds gathered.* Note that you cannot say (with this meaning) **John gathered.*

In the basic division of a **sentence** or **clause** into its two fundamental parts, the **subject** and the **predicate**, the verbs always belong to the **predicate**, and often the meaning of the verb is central to the understanding of the **predicate** as a whole. But where the verb *be* is used to link its **subject** with an **adjective**, **noun** or **prepositional phrase**, the verb *be* scarcely carries any meaning at all, beyond indicating **tense**; unusually, the most informative part of such **predicates** is not the verb, but the **adjective**, **noun** or **prepositional phrase** which follows it.

In the examples below, the **predicates** of the **sentences** are underlined, and the **verbs** inside them are doubly underlined.

- *We all live in a yellow submarine.*
- *It's been a hard day's night, and I've been working like a dog.*
- *The hills are alive with the sound of music.*
- *The predicate of this sentence is short*

Verbs are the basic carriers of **tense**. This is shown, in English and many other languages, by means of specific **suffixes**. In English, **main verbs** can only be **suffixed** for two **tenses**, namely **past** and **present**, with the **suffixes** *-ed* and *-s*, respectively. (**Future** time is expressed in a different way, by the **modal auxiliary** *will* placed before the verb.) Some other languages (e.g. French) have many more different **tense** variants of verbs than English.

Most English verbs are single **words**. But there is a significant number of English verbs which are actually made up of more than one **word**. Some examples are *take out, put up with, get rid of, make do with* and *take place*. Grammarians call such multi-**word** verbs 'phrasal verbs'; their behaviour is actually quite complicated and there are several different patterns into which such verbs may fall.

For interest Every human language has a class of words easily identifiable as verbs by their typical meanings and their essential role in clauses. Linguists classify languages in terms of the position of the verb in basic sentences. In relation to the other main parts of a (transitive) sentence, namely the subject and the object, there are three possible places to put the verb, namely:

1 At the beginning of the sentence, giving the basic order verb–subject–object. Linguists call this basic word order 'VSO' for short. The Celtic languages (e.g. Welsh and Gaelic) and the Polynesian languages (e.g. Maori, the native language of New Zealand, and Hawaiian) are VSO languages, as shown in these examples.

HAWAIIAN
Ua   aloha au iāia
PRES *love   I   her*   (= *I love her.*)

WELSH
Clywsom ni y gwcw
heard   we the cuckoo   (= *We heard the cuckoo.*)

2 In the middle of the sentence, between the subject and the object. This is the normal word order in English and in many familiar European languages. It is also the predominant order in Chinese, as this example shows.

Wǒ gěi nǐ júzizhī
I   give you orange-juice   (= *I give you orange-juice.*)

3 At the end of the sentence, after the object. Japanese and Turkish are well-known languages of this type, as the following examples show.

JAPANESE
Sensei wa   gakusei ni enpitsu o   agemashita
Teacher SUBJ *student to pencil* OBJ *gave*   (= *The teacher gave the student a pencil.*)
TURKISH
Müdür mektubu imzaladi
Director letter   signed   (= *The director signed the letter.*)

Exercise   Identify all the verbs, both main and auxiliary, in both main and subordinate clauses, in the following passage. There are ten altogether.

- *I first met Dean not long after my wife and I split up. I had just gotten over a serious illness that I won't bother to talk about, except that it had something to do with the miserably weary split-up and my feeling that everything was dead.*

Word

Explanation   The word 'word' might seem to be the least technical of terms in **grammar**. Everyone thinks they know what a word is, and indeed, for everyday practical purposes, we talk successfully about such factual matters as whether or not something is a word, how many words there are in an essay, and how many words a two-year-old child knows. But in fact we use 'word' in clearly different ways. It is worth distinguishing:

1 Word in a text. In the sense of 'word in a text', the traditional definition of 'sequence of letters without any spaces' is as useful a starting point as any other for written language, though not for speech (but, as we will see, this definition runs into many problems). In the sense of 'word in a text', every word that you can put a circle around in a printed or written passage is different from every other such word. The third word in this **sentence** that you are reading is a different word from the fourteenth word, and

247

from the eighteenth, and also from the last word. Words in a text follow each other in sequence.

2 Word in a language. In the sense of 'word in a language', a useful starting definition is 'item listed separately in an ordinary dictionary' (but this has its problems, too). In this sense of 'word in a language', the same word can occur more than once in a **sentence** (like the words *in, this, a, the, word* and *sentence* in this **sentence**). The only sense in which words in a language might be said to 'follow each other', i.e. alphabetical order, is quite different from the way words in a text follow each other. The alphabetical ordering of words in a dictionary is not really part of the system of a language itself, but is merely a convenience adopted by the dictionary writer. In a sense, the words in a language all coexist simultaneously, whether they are being used in texts or not.

The very slippery technical problems that linguists encounter in trying to formulate an exact definition for 'word' stem largely from the misfit between the two senses we have identified.

Examples   The **sentence** *Men like women like men* contains five words in the sense of 'word in a text'; but the same **sentence** only contains three words in the sense of '**word** in a language', *men, like* and *women*.

Contrasts   In both senses, word contrasts with **phrase**, **clause** and **sentence**, which describe larger units (of text and of language), and with **affix**, which describes a smaller kind of unit. A **phrase** in a text can consist of many words, but a word in a text can never contain many **phrases**. Likewise, the **phrases** that the **grammar** of a language allows are constructed out of the words that it has. Linguists find it useful, however, to define **phrase** in such a way that there can be one-word **phrases**.

Relationships   A word is often said to be the smallest unit of language that can stand alone as a single utterance. A person who makes a one-word utterance, such as *Yes* or *Blast!* can be said to be creating a spoken text consisting of a single 'word-in-a-text'; and to do it, the speaker draws from the repertoire of words in the language (the vocabulary) which he or she knows. Thus, in this commonly repeated view, the basic relationship between the two senses of 'word' is that a word in a language is the smallest POTENTIAL text. While this view does hold true for many words, there are several problems with it, discussed below.

As mentioned, the definition of 'word in a text' as any string of letters between spaces only works for written language. When we speak, we generally don't leave any pauses between many of the words, so we can't substitute 'pauses' for 'spaces' to try to make the definition work for speech.

In fact, if we didn't have a writing system, many of the items we are in the habit of calling 'words' would not seem to us to be units that can be used on their own. This is especially true of 'function words', little words like *a, an, the, and*, *of* and *to* that do not belong to the major **parts of speech** such as **noun**, **verb**, **adjective** and **adverb**. Have you ever heard, or can you imagine using, an utterance consisting of just one of the 'words' *a*, *an*, *the*, *and*, *of* or *to* on its own? Only in a rather artificial situation, where we are discussing language itself might we use one of these on its own, as in:

Q: *What's the definite article?*
A: *The.*

Children learning their native language from hearing the speech around them usually come up with at least some wrong guesses about what exactly is separable out as a word and what is not. A child I know repeated *a long time ago* as **a long time of go*, not realizing that *ago* is, in the written language, and to an adult, a single word. Children learning to write often write *might have* in some way such as *mightof, without a space, indicating (amongst other things) that it is not clear from speech just where the 'spaces between words' are. In fact, in speech, there are hardly any spaces between words.

Some strings of letters are rather irrationally written as single words in English; they really work in the language as sequences of several words. Examples are: *another* and *cannot*, which it would be just as sensible to write as *an other* and *can not*. The same lack of system in what we write as one word and what we write as two can be seen in many compound words, of which a few examples are given below.

WRITTEN AS ONE WORD	WRITTEN AS TWO WORDS
skyscraper	*sky writing*
bookseller	*book dealer*
countryman	*country person*
screwdriver	*bus driver*
airliner	*ocean liner*
textbook	*exercise book*
wallpaper	*art paper*
suitcase	*pencil case*

There is a tendency to write such expressions as two words when one of the parts is more than one syllable long, but there are many exceptions to this tendency (as can be seen in this table).

Sometimes grammarians will say that all of a group of forms varying only by the addition of certain **affixes** are actually the same word, especially where they all belong to the same broad **part of speech**. So such grammarians, for example, might say that the **verbs** *talked*, *talking*, *talks* and *talk* are all, in some sense, the same word. This way of talking about words is, however, less common nowadays.

A word almost always belongs to some word-class or **part of speech** or other, and possibly to several. In the dictionary entry for a word, you will find mentioned all the possible **parts of speech** that it can belong to. So, for example, in a dictionary, we might find:

> *fast*: **Noun**
> *fast*: **Verb**
> *fast*: **Adjective**
> *fast*: **Adverb**

Such cases of homonymy raise the question of whether, for example, *fast* the **noun** is in fact the same word as *fast* the **verb**, or *fast* the **adjective**, or whether belonging to a different **part of speech** makes a form, by definition, a different word. Practices differ on this, and, provided always that it is clear what definition one is assuming, little important confusion can arise.

There are problematic words which are difficult to allocate to grammatical word-classes. Often such words are merely labelled as 'particles'.

In a given **sentence**, the sense of a word is often narrowed down to just one of the senses or **parts of speech** listed for it in a dictionary. Thus, in *This is a very fast car*, the word *fast* can only be an **adjective**.

Words can be formed from other words by the addition of **affixes** (and other kinds of change, in some languages). Often when this happens, a word belonging to one **part of speech** is used as a basis to form a word of another **part of speech**. In English, this is very common, and a word of any major **part of speech** can be used to make a new word of almost any other major **part of speech**. Examples are:

arrive–arrival	(**verb** to **noun**)
bake–baker	(**verb** to **noun**)
organ–organize	(**noun** to **verb**)
divine–divinity	(**adjective** to **noun**)
red–redness	(**adjective** to **noun**)
care–careful	(**noun** to **adjective**)
social–socialize	(**adjective** to **verb**)
run–runny	(**verb** to **adjective**)

Sometimes the definition of a word in terms of its spelling actually goes against the grammatical organization of **phrases** and **sentences**. An instance is **possessive** 'words' formed by adding 'apostrophe s', *'s*, to a **phrase**. To take an example well known to linguists, the **phrase** *the Mayor of Boston's hat* contains the 'word' *Boston's*, but really, to make sense of the **phrase** you have to take the *'s* as modifying, not just *Boston*, but *the Mayor of Boston* (because the hat belongs to the Mayor of Boston, not to Boston). Another example is the **ordinal numeral** in, for example, *two hundred and seventh*. Here the **suffix** *-th* is really understood as applying to the whole longer expression *two hundred and seven*, and not just to its last word *seven*.

A word in a dictionary may sometimes be several words in a text. In a modern dictionary based on current usage,[26] there are very many entries consisting of several words in text. Many of these are idioms or stock phrases. Examples are *come out of*, *council of war*, *hard and fast*, *knock knees*,

---

26 *Collins Cobuild English Dictionary*, editor-in-chief John Sinclair (Collins, London), 1987.

methylated spirit, old-age pensioner, pen pal, quantum leap and *sharp practice*, to name only a few. All of these would have to be learnt as separate items of vocabulary by a learner of English, because their exact meanings are not simply composed out of the meanings of their parts.

When languages borrow from one another, it is normally at the level of the word. Languages don't often borrow whole **phrases** or **sentences**. Here are some words that English has borrowed from other languages:

WORD	BORROWED FROM
Kindergarten	German
canyon	Spanish
mousse	French
spaghetti	Italian
anorak	Inuit (Eskimo)
kamikaze	Japanese

Not all words have meanings, because there can be nonsense words, such as *brillig, slithy, toves, gimble* and *jabberwock*, which were invented (by Lewis Carroll) for the sole purpose of having no recognized meaning. It might be objected that these cannot really qualify as words, exactly because they have no meaning, but they do at least follow some of the rules of English word-formation.

For interest The languages of the world differ radically in how they organize words in their grammars. Let's take the definition of 'word' to be 'any sequence before and after which there could be a pause in natural speech'. By this definition, the English sentences below would be agreed to have the numbers of words indicated.

He is fed.	(three words)
He has been fed.	(four words)

In such sentences, one might, when being especially slow and deliberate, say *He* [PAUSE] *is* [PAUSE] *fed*, or *He* [PAUSE] *has* [PAUSE] *been* [PAUSE] *fed*. Now notice that several of the single words here express combinations of meanings. For example, the verbs *is* and *has* both end with *-s*, which indicates 3rd person singular present tense; and the *-en* of *been* is a regular marker of past participles. But no speaker of English would ever pause immediately before this *-s* or this *-en*. So nobody would ever say, for example, *He i-* [PAUSE] *-s fed*, or *He ha-* [PAUSE] *-s be-* [PAUSE] *-en fed*.

On the whole, English allows pauses at many places, and so it is reasonable to say that sentences typically are made up of many words, between each of which, by our definition, there can be a pause. But some other languages behave quite differently. In the West Greenlandic Eskimo language, for example, the form

* *iqalussuarniariartuqqusaagaluaqaagunnuuq*

is a single word, meaning *It is said that we have admittedly got a strict order to go out fishing sharks;*[27] clearly, this one word is also a single sentence. This language has ways of modifying verbs to indicate dimensions such as hearsay (hence the *it is said*) and admission by the speaker (hence the *admittedly*). It also has a way of incorporating the common objects of verbs into the verbs themselves, so there would be a verb meaning '*to shark-fish*'. These and other devices give rise to such long one-word sentences, in which an Eskimo speaker could not insert a pause at any point. Languages such as this are called 'agglutinating' languages by linguists.

Exercise   How many different words in a text, and how many different words in the language are there in the following passage?

- *Gaul comprises three areas, inhabited respectively by the Belgae, the Aquitani, and a people who call themselves Celts, though we call them Gauls.*

---

27 This example is from Stephen Anderson's article 'Inflectional morphology', in *Language Typology and Syntactic Description,* volume III: *Grammatical Categories and the Lexicon,* edited by Timothy Shopen (Cambridge University Press, 1985).

Answers to exercises

Abstract noun

Murder, circumstances, hours, life, hour, ceremony, afternoon, tea.

Accusative case

1 *me, them*; 2 *whom, thee*; 3 *us, him*; 4 *me, her.*

Active voice

Sentences 1, 3, 5, 6 and 8 are active.

Adjective

solemn, oval, ancient, narrow, great, grey–green, greasy, overcast, dark, rugged, cold, scanty, embarrassed, backward, lean, long, dusty, dreary, lovable.

Adverb

1 *slowly, surely, yesterday, unfortunately, here.*
2 *now, suspiciously, there.*

Affix

Two prefixes, *anti-* and *dis-*, and probably four suffixes, *-ment, -ary, -an* and *-ism*, although there could be genuine disagreement about whether *-arian* consists of *-ary* plus *-an.*

Agreement

- *Those kids at the shop were swearing at us.*

- *The shop those kids were at is on Broadway.*

- *Broadway is the street that the shop those kids were at is on.*

Apposition

The appositive phrases in the passages are underlined below.

1 *The* Nellie, <u>*a cruising yawl,*</u> *swung to her anchor without a flutter of the sails and was at rest.*
2 *Mr Baker,* <u>*chief mate of the ship* <u>Narcissus</u></u>, *stepped in one stride out of his lighted cabin into the darkness of the quarter-deck.*
3 *There, far below, is the knobbly backbone of England,* <u>*the Pennine Range.*</u>
4 *One summer afternoon Mrs Oedipa Maas came home from a Tupperware party whose hostess had put perhaps too much kirsch in the fondue to find that she,* <u>Oedipa</u>, *had been named executor, or she supposed executrix, of the estate of one Pierce Inverarity,* <u>*a California real estate mogul who had once lost two million dollars in his spare time but still had assets numerous and tangled enough to make the job of sorting it all out more than honorary.*</u>

Auxiliary verb

1 1 – *had*; 2 1 – *will*; 3 1 – *is*; 4 2 – *must* and *be*; 5 3 – *must*, *be* and *be*; 6 1 – *have*.

Cardinal numeral

1 *Four, two*; 2 *twenty, two, three*; 3 *fifty, one.*

Case

1 *She*, nominative; *him*, accusative;
2 *I*, nominative; *her*, accusative; *me*, accusative.

Clause

1 <u>*Give me a break!*</u>
2 *Where is the book* <u>*that I lent you?*</u>
3 *Wesley didn't turn up until* <u>*after the others had left.*</u>
4 *The fact* <u>*that Wesley didn't turn up on time*</u> *bothered me.*
5 *Bill told me* <u>*that Jill wanted* <u>*him to marry her.*</u></u>
6 *I tried* <u>*putting it in upside-down*</u> *but* <u>*it didn't work.*</u>
7 *I heard* <u>*Jay tell Sue* <u>*that Al wanted* <u>*me to see him*</u></u></u> <u><u><u>*before he died.*</u></u></u>

Common noun

mind, physics, century; dualism, theory, soul, body, things; arsenic, poison, quantities. (There are no common nouns in the third sentence.)

Comparative

tamer (second instance); *fitter* (first instance); *higher, lower* (second instance); *taller, stranger* (second instance), *shorter.*

Complement clause

The complement clauses are underlined below.

1 *That you lied to me disturbs me deeply.*
2 *For it to snow now would be very improbable.*
3 *The ancient Greeks knew that the earth was round.*
4 *Nobody expected Perrot to win.*
5 *The fact that he is Chinese is irrelevant.*
6 *Nobody now believes the theory that the earth is flat.*
7 *They were determined that no-one would pass them.*

Complement of a copular verb

The words or phrases acting as complements of copular verbs are underlined below.

1 *Gary is the champion and Nigel is desperate to beat him.*
2 *When he appeared to Mary, Gabriel appeared dazzling.*
3 *The weather turned cold and Seth turned the log on the fire.*
4 *When Zuleika came, his dreams came true.*
5 *Murray looked pale as he looked over the wintry scene.*

Compound sentence

The compound sentences are numbers 3, 5 and 6. The conjoined main clauses in them are given on separate lines below.

- *I had thought that I was a valued employee,*
  but
  this action made me feel I was not really wanted.
- *The man is believed to be a waiter from Radcliffe,*
  but
  police said he would not be named until his parents had been informed.
- *They have been very short of grey mares on Dartmoor this year,*
  and
  a grey gelding was the nearest to the real thing the organizing committee could produce.

Compound tense

The sentences which use compound tenses are numbers 3, 4, and 5.

Compound word

The compound words are underlined.

1 *In the village community centre, where there's a country music band on the loose, things are getting frenetic.*
2 *We cut hours off the journey time and benefit from the ideal spring weather conditions.*
3 *Joel wanted me to teach him to body-surf, but all I wanted to do was sun-bathe.*
4 *Dirk plunged into the pitch black ice-cold waters of the lake.*

255

Conditional

The conditional phrases and conditional clauses are underlined below.

1 *If you come on Monday, make it 10.00; if Tuesday, make it 11.00.*
2 *If it rains, you can stay here, if you like.*
3 *I hope to see you tomorrow, but if not, good luck!*
4 *Unless I hear to the contrary, I'll assume you want to go.*

Conjunction

1 *You may go into the fields or down the lane,*
   but don't go into Mr. McGregor's garden.
2 *Now run along and don't get into mischief.*
3 *Then old Mrs. Rabbit took a basket and her umbrella,*
   and went through the wood to the baker's.
4 *Flopsy, Mopsy, and Cotton-tail, who were good little bunnies,*
   went down the lane to gather blackberries:
   but Peter, who was very naughty,
   ran straight away to Mr. McGregor's garden, and squeezed under the gate!

Contraction

Jessica's aware that we've taken her car, but I'm afraid we didn't tell her that it's got a dent in its side.

Copula, copular verb

The copular verbs are *was* (twice), *appears, becoming* and *grow.*

Count noun

1 *city, spires, city, dreams;* 2 *winners, prizes, college;* 3 *editor, manuscripts, specialists;*
4 *design, book, designer.*

Declarative

In the first exercise sentence, one declarative clause, underlined below, is parenthetically embedded inside another declarative clause (which is not underlined below).

1 *Except for the Marabar Caves – and they are twenty miles off – the city of Chandrapore represents nothing extraordinary.*

In the other two exercise sentences, the separate declarative clauses (still underlined) are given two per line, for clarity.

2 *Ours is essentially a tragic age, so we refuse to take it tragically.*
3 *It was the best of times, it was the worst of times,*
   it was the age of wisdom, it was the age of foolishness,

it was the epoch of belief, it was the epoch of incredulity,
it was the season of Light, it was the season of Darkness,
it was the spring of hope, it was the winter of despair,
we had everything before us, we had nothing before us,
we were all going direct to Heaven, we were all going direct the other way.

Definite

The definite noun phrases are underlined below.

1 *When she was home from her boarding school I used to see her almost every day sometimes, because their house was right opposite the Town Hall Annexe.*
2 *Wilson sat on the balcony of the Bedford Hotel with his bald pink knees thrust against the ironwork.*

Demonstrative

1 *that* (second and third instances); 2 *those*; 3 *those, these.*

Dialect

Statements 3 and 4 use *dialect* appropriately.

Direct object

1 *my house*; 2 *it*; 3 *money*; 4 *such large sums of money.*

Direct speech

The underlined passages are in direct speech.

1 *'I regret exceedingly –' said M. Hercule Poirot.*
2 *'It can't hurt now,' was Mr Sherlock Holmes's comment when for the tenth time in as many years, I asked his leave to reveal the following narrative.*
3 *'Days of wine and roses,' said Wilt to himself.*
4 *'The Signora had no business to do it,' said Miss Bartlett, 'no business at all. She promised us south rooms with a view close together, instead of which here are north rooms, looking into a courtyard, and a long way apart. Oh Lucy!'*

Ellipsis

1 Ellipsis of *He reacted* and *angrily.*
2 Ellipsis of *taking the car.*
3 Ellipsis of *I hit him.*
4 Ellipsis of *Linford ran* and *race.*

Finite

had, died, occurred, was, blows, become, beat.

Future

The sentences which express future time are numbers 1, 4, 6 and 8.

Gender

Libro is masculine; *monte* masculine; *mente* feminine; *piazza* feminine; *problema* masculine; *camion* masculine; *sport* masculine. You can tell by the articles, *il* or *lo* for masculine, and *la* for feminine.

Generic

1 *high-pitched noises*; 3 *furniture, the sofa*; 4 *teeth, sugar*. (There are no generic expressions in the second sentence.)

Genitive case

my, her (first instance), *his, its, their, Halley's*.

Gerund

1 *Shooting*; 2 *Moving*; 3 *making*; 4 *worrying*.

Head

1 *meeting*; 2 *persons*; 3 *marvellous*; 4 *name*; 5 *proceeds*; 6 *go*.

Imperative

- *Look at this.*
- *Look!*
- *Look what I've found hidden away at the back of the bloody airing cupboard.*
- *Teach these boys and girls nothing but Facts.*
- *Plant nothing else.*
- *Root out everything else.*
- *Stick to Facts, sir!*

Impersonal

1 (a) *one* (first and third instances)
  (b) *they, them*
  (c) *you*
  (d) *they*
2 Sentences (b), (d) and (e) are impersonal.

Indefinite

1 *a very hot evening at the beginning of July; a young man; a house in Carpenter Lane.*
2 *a large, proud rose-colored hotel.*
3 *women; a room of one's own; one.*

258

Indicative

reached, were, paused, looked.

Indirect object

1. *Third World countries*; 2 *them*; 3 *the bank*; 4 *those poor people*; 5 *people in other lands* and *its own people.*

Indirect speech

The two passages in indirect speech are underlined below.

- *When anyone asked Frensic <u>why he took snuff</u> he replied that <u>it was because by rights he should have lived in the eighteenth century</u>.*

The corresponding sentences in direct speech would be

- *Why do you take snuff?*
- *It is because by rights I should have lived in the eighteenth century.*

Infinitive

cool, move, know.

Interjection

Aha!, Alas!, Blimey!, Coo-ee!, Oops!, Pow!

Interrogative

1 *When*; 2 *What*; 3 *why*; 4 *Which.*

Intransitive

1 *risen*; 4 *marched*; 5 *trudged, went, undressed, slept*, 6 *playing*; 7 *work*; 8 *work.*

Main clause

1 *Holmes <u>had read</u> carefully <u>a note</u> which the last post had brought him.*
2 *<u>Mr Sherlock Holmes</u>, who was usually very late in the mornings, save upon those not infrequent occasions when he was up all night, <u>was seated at the breakfast table</u>.*
3 *<u>It is a most singular thing</u> that a problem which was certainly as abstruse and unusual as any which I have faced in my long professional career should have come to me after my retirement.*
4 *<u>It was pleasant to Dr Watson to find</u> himself once more in the untidy room of the first floor in Baker Street which had been the starting point of so many remarkable adventures.*

Main verb

1 *think, opened, associate*; 2 *read, brought*; 3 *been, been, cost, cost, cost, was, judge.*

Mass noun

1 *weather, drizzle, sleet;* 2 *climate, smog;* 3 *Aluminium, steel, glass, paper.*

Modal verb

1 *might;* 2 *can;* 3 *can* (second instance); 4 *shall;* 5 *would, could.*

Modify, modification

1 *hot, spicy;* 2 *those, three;* 3 *very, very;* 4 *enough;* 5 *dangerously.*

Mood

1 Incorrect; 2 Correct; 3 Incorrect; 4 Correct.

Negative

1 *You didn't see anybody.*
2 *There wasn't anything in the box.*
3 *I have not had food or sleep since yesterday.*
4 *I cannot tolerate this in any circumstances.*

Nominative case

The words and phrases that could be said to be in the nominative case are underlined below.

1 *We secretaries were getting tired of all the new arrangements.*
2 *The new arrangements were annoying everybody.*
3 *Someone had even phoned the Glasgow Herald about it.*
4 *Through the fence, between the curling flower spaces, I could see them hitting.*
5 *An unassuming young man was travelling, in midsummer, from his native city of Hamburg to Davos-Platz in the Canton of the Grisons, on a three weeks visit.*

Noun

The nouns in the following sentences are underlined.

1 *The lean mother bear couldn't bear to lean against the tree.*
2 *When I travel, I wear my suit, in case I forget my case.*
3 *The wear and tear of travel doesn't suit me.*
4 *I was on a flight from Miami on Wednesday, and I have a meeting in Singapore next week.*
5 *I'll give up my career as an applied linguist and retire to a country retreat.*

Number

1 *woman* – singular, *books* – plural, *is* – singular, *genius* – singular.
2 *Who* – singular, *knows* – singular, *secrets* – plural, *hearts* – plural, *men* – plural.
3 *police* – plural.
4 *Sticks* – plural, *stones* – plural, *bones* – plural.

5 *Mud* – singular, *sticks* – singular.

Numeral

1 *Nine, ten*; 2 *eleventh, eleventh, eleventh*; 3 *first, six, second, ninth*; 4 *two hundred and twenty, twenty-third*.

Ordinal numeral

1 *third*; 2 *twenty-second, first*; 3 *First, Second, twentieth*; 4 *eleventy-first*.

Part of speech

The word-classes in the list are: adjective, adverb, conjunction, demonstrative, noun, numeral and verb. Of these, all but demonstrative and numeral are traditional parts of speech.

Passive voice

The passive clauses are underlined.

1 *I am being pursued by an integer.*
2 *Electromagnetism was discovered by Faraday after he had been released from tedious government research.*
3 *I can't bear to be taunted.*
4 *Coffee has been spilt over this keyboard and it has broken down.*
5 There is no passive in *Have you been to London yet?*

Past participle

The past participles are:

1 *imbedded, believed*; 2 *been, revealed, intervened*; 3 *fallen*; 4 *hit*; 5 *come* (first instance only).

Past tense

The past tense forms are:

1 *was, settled, got, lived*; 2 *was, rose*; 3 *was, was, were, had*.

Perfect

1 *have met*
2 *had been*
3 *had taken*
4 *had been*
5 *have experienced*

Person

1 *you*; 2 *they*; 3 *I*; 4 *it*; 5 *him*.

Personal pronoun

1 *He, him, He, He, them, They, He, them, he, They.*
2 *We, I, us, me.*

Phrase

The noun phrases in these sentences are as underlined below.

1 *Sherlock Holmes was in a melancholy and philosophic mood that morning.*
2 *The ideas of my friend Watson, though limited, are exceedingly pertinacious.*
3 *Somewhere in the vaults of the bank of Cox and Co., at Charing Cross,*
    there is a travel-worn and battered tin dispatch-box with my name.

Pluperfect, past perfect

1 *had come*; 2 *had been coming*; 3 *had taken*; 4 *had been taken*; 5 *had been being taken.*

Plural

1 *objects* (second instance); *travels*; 2 *ships, sails*; 3 *evenings*; 4 *beaches.*

Positive

The positive sentences are numbers 1, 3 and 5.

Possessive

1 *His* – possessive pronoun.
2 *Beethoven's, Mozart's* – both (one-word) possessive phrases.
3 *my, your* – both possessives.
4 *mine, yours* – both possessive pronouns.
5 *my brother's* – possessive phrase.

Predicate

The predicates in the sentences given are underlined below.

1 *Birds evolved from reptiles.*
2 *Sixty-four million years ago, the dinosaurs died out.*
3 *Neanderthal Man survived into the modern era.*

The kind of predicate phrases (underlined) in the sentences below are shown on the right below.

The New York subway is very unhygienic.	PREDICATE ADJECTIVE PHRASE
The Mayor is a Democrat.	PREDICATE NOUN PHRASE
Ronnie was under the influence of an astrologer.	PREDICATE PREPOSITIONAL PHRASE

Prefix

The prefixes in the given words are underlined here:

> _un_fortunate, _un_timely, _super_fluous, _super_b, _re_appear, really, _miser_, _mis_fortune, _in_kstand, _in_justice, _en_courage, enemy, _ex_plain, Exeter.

Preposition

The prepositions in the passage given, in the order in which they occur, are: _on, of, on, in, of, of, through, alongside, down, beside, of, in._

Present participle

1 _running_; 2 _blazing, bleaching_; 3 _burning_; 4 _having, keeping._

Present tense

The present tense forms in the passage given, in the order in which they occur, are: _is, live, are, have, live, carry, are._

Progressive

1 _were waiting_; 2 _were doing_; 3 _are doing_; 4 (NO PROGRESSIVE HERE, JUST A GERUND);
5 _am being_; 6 _was expounding._

Pronoun

1 _Who_ – interrogative, _you_ – personal.
2 _Which_ – interrogative, _mine_ – possessive.
3 _which_ – relative, _yours_ – possessive.
4 _It_ – personal, _itself_ – reflexive.
5 _one_ – impersonal, _it_ – personal.
6 _I_ – personal, _myself_ – reflexive.

Proper name

May, Shaston, Marlott, Blakemore, Blackmoor, Kinraddie, Cospatric de Gondeshil, William the Lyon.

Reflexive

1 _himself_; 2 _herself_; 3 _itself_; 4 _myself_; 5 _himself_; 6 _herself._

Regular, irregular

The irregular words are:
  Nouns: _foot, child, ox._
  Verbs: _come, speak, strike, make._

Relative clause

The relative clauses are underlined. In number 5, there is double underlining, because of one relative clause embedded inside another.

1 People *who live in glass houses* shouldn't throw stones.
2 We picked the apples *which the others had left*.
3 The man *who married your sister* is the brother of the girl *you married*.
4 The idea really came to me the day *I got my new false teeth*.
5 The pilots *who shot down the planes they were chasing* were given medals.

Relative pronoun

The relative pronouns (used as such) are underlined.

1 I said that that was the one *that* I wanted.
2 When can you name a time *when* you'll be able to see me?
3 Who asked who had seen the secretary *who* just started this morning?
4 Which is the witch *whose* shoes Dorothy borrowed?
5 Whose shoes did Dorothy find at the spot *where* she landed?
6 Where is there a witch *that* I can rely on when I want one?

Sentence

In the two passages, there is only one full sentence. It is at the beginning of the second passage: *I will tell you in a few words who I am:*.

Singular

The singular nouns in the passage are underlined below.

* Two *years* have gone by since I finished writing the long *story* of how I, Tiberius Claudius Drusus Nero Germanicus, the *cripple*, the *stammerer*, the *fool* of the *family*, whom none of his ambitious and bloody-minded relatives considered worth the *trouble* of executing, poisoning, forcing to *suicide*, banishing to a *desert island* or starving to *death* – which was how they one by one got rid of each other – how I survived them all, even my insane *nephew* Gaius Caligula, and was one *day* unexpectedly acclaimed *Emperor* by the corporals and sergeants of the *Palace Guard*.

Subject

1 he, she; 2 This, Peter; 3 you, they; 4 Her grandmother, her aunt; 5 I, whose mother.

Subjunctive

The verbs in the subjunctive are: *show, be, were, were,* and *use*.

Subordinate clause

The subordinate clauses are underlined.

1 The girl *I spoke to* said *it was raining in Glasgow*.

2 *I expected it to be <u>where I had left it</u>.*

3 <u>*When you come*</u>, *can you bring that book <u>that I lent you</u>.*

4 *The rules permit members <u>whose spouses have died</u> to pay half-fees.*

5 <u>*As he had brought his suitcase*</u>, *we expected <u>that he would stay</u>.*

6 *The old man <u>that Eve objected to</u> <u>because he swore</u> is actually quite nice.*

Suffix

The suffixes in the words given are separated out and underlined below.

1 *conclus <u>ion</u> <u>s</u>*; 2 *indebt <u>ed</u> <u>ness</u>*; 3 *terror <u>ize</u> <u>(e)d</u>*; 4 *unreason <u>able</u> <u>ness</u>*; 5 *neo-colon <u>(i)al</u> <u>ism</u>*.

Superlative

The superlatives are *fairest, most civilized, most fateful, most beautiful, liveliest* and *cleverest*.

Tense

will be	FUTURE
has won	PRESENT PERFECT
play	SIMPLE PRESENT
will have been dating	FUTURE PERFECT PROGRESSIVE
began	SIMPLE PAST

Transitive

1 *flunked*; 2 *hurt*; 3 *found, raiding*; 4 *told, tease*; 5 *brief, tell*; 6 *judged*.

Verb

The verbs in the passage are: *met, split, had, gotten, won't, bother, talk, had, do* and *was*.

Word

Words-in-a-text: 23.
Words-in-the-language: 21. (*The* and *call* are both repeated once.)

Index